BARRY COGSWELL

TO HAVE
BORNE WITNESS

Memories and observations regarding
human population and species loss

Let's keep hoping

Barry Cogswell

authorHOUSE®

AuthorHouse™
1663 Liberty Drive
Bloomington, IN 47403
www.authorhouse.com
Phone: 1-800-839-8640

Published by AuthorHouse 4/11/2014

ISBN: 978-1-4969-0312-9 (sc)
ISBN: 978-1-4969-0311-2 (hc)
ISBN: 978-1-4969-0310-5 (e)

Library of Congress Control Number: 2014906953

Dedicated to Jo and Colin

I wish to record my deep gratitude to my wife Kathryn, and to Al Valleau for the long hours they spent editing my manuscript and correcting my many spelling and punctuation mistakes.

Contents

List of Images

Introduction

It is believed that we humans (*Homo sapiens sapiens*) - the doubly wise, tool making, upright perambulating, bipedal human ape - have been on the earth for well over two hundred thousand years. We must have started with a few, but we have certainly multiplied.

One hundred thousand years ago we had long had control of fire as well as the ability to make stone tools. We were exploring beyond Africa. Thirty thousand years ago, when we were painting caves with images of Aurochs and wild horses, it is estimated there were probably one million of us worldwide. Ten thousand years ago, after the last ice age and during the infancy of agriculture in Asia when people began cultivating grains and figs, the human population was approaching two million. Five thousand years ago, after we had developed the plough for agriculture and the wheel for early vehicles and for making pots, and at a time when the Egyptians were building the pyramids, humans numbered about ten million. But three thousand years later, at the time of the Roman Empire, before China was unified under the first emperor Qin Shi Huang Di, and at the time when the Olmec culture in Mexico was well developed, we were approaching 200 million.

In 1750 when my paternal ancestors still lived in the English country town of Westbury and great-grandfather's great-grandfather Thomas was born, the Earth's human population was continuing its slow and gradual increase to nearly one thousand million - one billion. At that time the human effect on the Earth was negligible when compared with today.

In 1873 when my grandfather Thomas James entered the world,[1] 1.5 billion of us walked the earth.

When my father Thomas Edward was born in 1904 we were 1.7 billion and when I came on the scene in 1939 we had reached 2 billion, a three hundred million increase in 35 years. But, in the 70 years since my birth, the human population has exploded to 7 billion, a 5 billion increase.

So it took us more than 200,000 years to reach one million, 30,000 more years to increase to one billion in the year 1800, a further 140 years to go from one to two billion, then, in only seventy years, we added another five billion to reach seven billion in 2011. We now add a billion roughly every thirteen years. Five billion have been added in just my lifetime. However, at the same time we have reduced the number of wild animals on the Earth by more than 95 per cent. There are now only three thousand tigers and forty Java rhinos, but 1.4 billion cattle worldwide, and we consume 40 billion chickens a year.[2] In the years since I was born, we have also used up unimaginably huge quantities of non-renewable resources, many of which are running out, and we have radically compromised over 75 per cent of our globe's ecosystems. This is no way to run a planet.

Many people seem to believe that growth in population is, if not a good thing, certainly a necessary accompaniment to growth in the capitalist economy and human development. All of which helps prove our superiority to all other life forms; the fittest survive. But I'm with the minority who believe it is a catastrophe; a catastrophe that, as the increase continues, will have dire results for the natural world, for wild animal and plant species, for the planet on which we live and, ultimately, for the future of humanity.

The recent human population trends result from changes wrought by the 18th century Age of Enlightenment, and from the ensuing scientific and medical discoveries. Now industrialization and excessive resource extraction disregards future sustainability. They are like giant scythes that cut through and destroy all of nature. They are being forced on us by the need to provide decent lives for the burgeoning population, and by our unwillingness to adapt our economy from unsustainable to sustainable.

Once, we were fairly well united in wishing to make our society better for everyone, though we were divided in our assumptions of how to achieve that goal. Now another great division is evolving. It is a division between those who fear dire consequences for our descendants if we continue with our industrial scale exploitation of our Earth, and those who fear monetary collapse if we curtail that exploitation. It is a divide between those who believe we must find another way, and those who wish to stay the course, and by forging ahead become personally wealthier in the process.

So, which approach is desirable on an Earth that we hope will remain healthy - healthy, not just for our descendants during the next hundred years, but for the next five hundred years and beyond?

This book therefore, in focusing on wildlife depletions and extinctions, is a quest to uncover the extent of the damage that we cause. It contains reminiscences of my lifelong delight in nature. It also recounts my observations on the human stewardship of the natural world to which I have borne witness. It speaks of our failings to care for our home planet and the natural species that used to thrive on it. It regrets our shortsighted resistance to sharing the non-renewable resources with future generations, and seeks to find some solutions that might get us out of the straights in which we find ourselves. It includes some suggestions on how we might model a different way of living in order to ensure that generations to come enjoy a better life than our own. And finally, it questions our unwillingness to make hard decisions now, but instead to leave them to be faced by our children, their children, and by those as yet unborn.

I Invasive Species and Historic Extinctions

There are now believed to be between 5,000 and 180,000 Burmese Pythons *(Python molurus bivittatus)* living in the Florida Everglades. These, it is assumed, are the progeny of a few released and escaped pets. There are also multitudinous Green Anacondas, Yellow Anacondas, Asiatic Reticulated Pythons, South African Pythons and boa constrictors. Some of these grow beyond 20 feet and 200 lbs in weight.[1] They are the snakes that entwine and crush their prey, before swallowing it whole. They are all introduced species; none of them are natural to Florida.

"Oh dear," one might say, "I do hope they don't eat people."

Well, they do actually, though seldom. They eat anything they can find in the wild, including birds. Of those pythons that have been caught and examined, 80 per cent were found to have eaten birds, and that is one major problem.

The wildlife species of Florida are not genetically prepared to avoid such exotic snakes, so have few defenses against them. Herons, ibis, storks and even small wrens have been found in the snakes' digestive tracts.

It is clear that having 10,000 exotic pythons living in the Everglades is not as it should be. If Burmese Pythons were a travelling species, one that is destined to move about the Earth, they would either have wings, or spend many thousands of years accomplishing their spread. This transfusion of exotic snakes to Florida was accomplished, not by natural means, but by humans. A 2011 study released by the University of Florida states that between the first release of a non-native species in 1863 - the greenhouse frog from the West Indies - and the year 2000, there have been 137 exotic and invasive reptile and amphibian species released into the Florida wilds.

Some young couple with a love of reptiles, and a pet Burmese Python named Cedric who had grown to fifteen feet long, was surely being kind when they released him into a local body of water.

"Cedric you'll be happy here in this nice warm water. You can live out your days in peace and freedom, and we are so sorry we can't take you to New York with us, but you wouldn't be happy in a little apartment. Bye-bye Cedric and good hunting."

Well, not only did Cedric enjoy good hunting, he also enjoyed meeting saucy Cynthia, a sultry and bonny serpent, also born in Burma. She too had become far bigger than that slithery little 40-inch snake she had been when first adopted, and, like Cyril, she also had been slipped into the waterways of Florida. We can imagine, when she first realized she was no longer alone, with what ardor the sexy Cynthia fluttered her lovely eyes at poor sensitive Cyril. Cyril stood no chance. Oh the conjugal ecstasy! Oh the joinings and the squeezings! Oh such pythonic fecundity! And oh what a big family they raised! Then, once their offspring got together with the other released serpents, how the waters of the everglades boiled with ever more ritual entwinings. Those female snakes can release up to a hundred eggs at a time. So Cynthia, with Cedric as her mate, could easily have produced thousands of offspring in just her lifetime.

None of those fine nature-loving and snake-releasing human couples thought they were helping to establish dynasties of untold thousands of pythons - pythons that would work very hard to de-populate the birds and animals of Florida.

In January 2012 a US study revealed that between 2003 and 2011 many southern Florida wild animals had seen troubling decreases in their numbers. Raccoon numbers were down 99.3 per cent, opossums down 98.9 per cent, white-tailed deer 94.1 per cent, bobcats 87.5 per cent and rabbits seem to have gone completely. In that same time frame, the number of pythons caught and removed from the Everglades had risen from 50 in 2003, to about 400 in 2011.[2] It is possible that the decline in bobcats and foxes could be due, in part, to the disappearance of their prey animals, leading to starvation.

With the nest-raiding and egg-enjoying raccoons gone, the birds may be free of one predator, but they now have to learn to deal with another.

On the island of Guam, Brown Tree-snakes were accidentally introduced from New Guinea either during, or just after, the Second World War. Within forty years Guam had lost all breeding colonies of sea birds. Ten of the thirteen forest bird species had become extinct, including five endemic to that island. Also extinct were six of the ten lizard species and two of the three bat species. Amongst the forest birds lost for all time are the Guam Flycatcher, the scarlet and black/brown winged Cardinal Honeyeater, the Rufous Fantail, the White-throated Ground Dove and the Bridled White-eye. Two species still exist in captive breeding programs. They are the turquoise-grey and russet-breasted Micronesian Kingfisher and the very handsome Guam Rail.

It is believed that the Brown Tree-snakes first stowed in packing cases when the US navy was leaving New Guinea and establishing a base on Guam during or after the Second World War. They were first noted in the 1950s and became more abundant by 1960. By 1965 they had colonized the central part, or half, of the island and by 1968 had reached all parts of the island. By 1984 the Guam wildlife extinctions were complete, although there are a few other species that are managing to survive on the brink, so to speak. There are now estimated to be 13,000 snakes per square mile, which is possibly the highest density of snakes in the world. Now that the native mammals and birds have been so massively reduced we have to hope the near future will bring a mass starvation die-off of the snakes.

Since the colonization of Guam, Brown Tree-snakes have been carried by military aircraft from Guam to the Marshall Islands, Diego Garcia, Honolulu, Oahu, Okinawa, Saipan, Wake Island, Taiwan, Darwin, Australia, Spain, Corpus Christi, Texas and other places. In Corpus Christi the snake had spent 7 months in a packing case of household goods before it was found. They frequently seem to travel in the landing gear of US military planes. One snake was found in Singapore aboard a navy plane that had only stopped long enough to refuel on Guam.[3]

Among other species that have had similar impacts on the native birds and reptiles can be included rats, cats, dogs, goats, and free foraging domestic pigs. When these animals were accidentally left on islands, with few or no predators, they very quickly killed off most of the ground nesting birds, and the tree nesting ones as well.

An example of the damage that introduced insects can inflict is found with the Asian Long-horned Beetle (*Anoplophora glabripennis*). This is a large 1-1.5 inch (2.5-4 cm) black beetle with white spots and with very long horn-like antennae. Its natural home is in far eastern Asia (China, Korea and Japan) where it goes under the delightful name of the Starry Sky Beetle, or sometimes the Sky Beetle. It was first noted in 1996 in eastern USA and Canada, though it probably arrived aboard packing cases sometime in the

1980s. A study published in the Canadian Forestry Journal in August in 2011, noted that the destructive beetle shows a very real liking for maple trees, especially the sugar and red maples - those magnificent trees that supply the wonderful yellow, orange and red fall colours in Quebec and New England. They also supply the maple syrup that we humans enjoy on our pancakes. These maple forests have important economic benefits to the regions where they grow in terms of tourism, maple syrup harvesting and furniture grade hardwood. In 2011 the beetle was very well established in the maple forests surrounding Worcester, Massachusetts and was spreading.

I'm sure few people would deny a beetle a meal. After all, every country is home to many species of beetles that go about their business daily and unnoted. The trouble is that the grubs or larvae of this particular invader eat for 10 to 22 months. What they eat is the sap-rich area of trees called the phloem and cambium layers. These layers, between the bark and the new wood, are rich in sugars and are the growth mechanism of the tree. If the beetles worked horizontally, all the way around the tree, they could cut off the flow of the sap causing the tree to die. After they have munched their way up, down or around the tree they make their way into the heartwood where they pupate. After the pupa stage the adult emerges from the tree through a ½ - ¾ inch (10-15 mm) hole. These large holes open the tree to disease, and create weakness and the potential for wind damage. It also doesn't do much for the value of the furniture wood when it is found to be full of holes. Already, in Massachusetts, 29,000 trees have been removed in one area while another 20,000 have been identified as affected. The cities of New York, Boston, Chicago and Toronto have all begun measures to beat the scourge. Whether it is possible to eradicate an invader of this type is an open question. If we use pesticides they are likely to kill as many grub-eating birds as the grubs themselves. It is lucky that the beetle usually lays her eggs, all 35-90 of them, under the bark on the same tree in which she was born. It is only after the tree is overpopulated with beetles and their larvae that the Asian Long-horned Beetles leave the tree in search of a new home. Fortunately they only fly relatively short distances. A typical flight is about 400 yards/meters, and they seldom colonize a tree further than 1 mile away from the old host tree. This potentially makes control somewhat easier than with beetles or moths that fly greater distances. They usually take up to 3 years to reach the adult stage – to become beetles – but then only live for 50–60 days, during which time they mate and produce another generation of 35-90 eggs.[4 5]

We also need to consider the oceans in this context. According to the US's National Oceanic and Atmospheric Administration, the lionfish, *(Pterois miles and P. volitans)*, which hails from the Indo-Pacific Ocean, was in 2012 becoming a menace on the Atlantic Seaboards of North and South America and the Gulf of Mexico. Lionfish are multi-striped, multi-hued, and multi-appendaged strange looking things. Maybe this is what gives them their charisma. People buy them for their aquariums and then, of course, release them into the sea when they grow too large. They are well-armed carnivores with few predators in the Atlantic. They feed on crustaceans and the young of any manner of fish that we also like to eat. We have no way of removing them from the ocean, and the fear is that, in the future, they will negatively affect the commercial fishing industry. In 25 years they have spread and multiplied to such an extent that in some places there are now a thousand lionfish per acre of sea.

The above species can be described as accidental introductions; however there are plenty of planned introductions most of which turned out to have terrible consequences. In fact, we humans have done some pretty stupid things over the years. Typically, we move into a pristine environment that we decide will be a great place to introduce some useful crop. We do just that, but then find that the local wildlife thrive on this new food supply. We then bring in a second alien species to defend the first by eating the native. Then we discover that the second introduction is a bigger problem than the first. This applies to the Cane Toad *(Bufondae rhinella marina)* in Australia.

Australia was thought to be a great place to grow sugar cane - lots of Aussie sunshine, good agricultural land and great prospects for making money. But a problem arose. The grubs of the native Greyback and French's Cane Beetles thrive on sugar cane roots. They were stunting the plants and causing a loss of both sugar production and profits. What to do? What to do?

The Bureau of Sugar Experimental Stations came up with the solution: import American Cane Toads. In 1935 the Australians imported a hundred toads from Hawaii. Those original hundred quickly bred to the 3000 that were released into the cane. Now cane toads are not only poisonous to most potential Australian predators, the females also lay between 8,000 and 35,000 eggs twice a year. So in a year a single female may produce 70,000 offspring. Granted, only about 5 per cent of those will reach maturity, but that is still 3,500. A bit of quick math will show us that 3,500 young, each

5

producing 3,500 young annually, will give us a plague of toads in a very few years.

One problem is that these amphibians are not the jolly little fun lovers like Mr. Toad of Toad Hall and *Wind-in-the-Willows* renown. These are serious American troublemakers. The largest females grow to 9½ inches (24 cm) long and weigh 3 lbs (1.3 kg). Not only are they poisonous to nearly all predators that could have kept them in check, they are also very tough. They survive temperatures from 5 degrees to forty and can live in most climates although they need slow-moving or still water to breed. Anything that attacks the plump and ugly warty things usually dies. Apart from dogs and other pets, the victims include Dingo, Quoll, Freshwater Crocodile, Death Adder, Red-bellied Black Snake, Tiger Snake and Goannas. They are changing the wildlife balance in Australia.[6]

Their advance across the eastern and northern parts of the continent has been like a flood of polluted water after a tailings pond breaks its banks. At the very beginning, in 1935 and 1936, a number of scientists and others protested the releasing of cane toads into the wild. Nonetheless, they were ignored, and now none of the early supporters of the project are around to be admonished with a cry of, "We told you so."

Another successful immigrant is the Wild Boar (*Sus scrofa*). It is an animal whose home range is Asia and Europe where its natural predators were tigers, leopards and wolves. Whether in the past they ever achieved a balance in the wild I don't know. There appears little chance of a balance now though, as we have killed off most of the predators. Boars have been introduced to many countries as sport for huntsmen. The countries include Australia, New Zealand, New Guinea, Uruguay, Brazil and the USA. They have been reintroduced to the UK. In England, a few hundred range in Kent, Sussex and Dorset. Since 2005, about 100 are thought to live in the areas around Dartmoor. The numbers in the USA are reckoned to be above 4 million. They cause property damage of about $800 million per year.[7]

They are very successful animals wherever they live. The piglets reach sexual maturity at the age of twenty months, and the sows have litters of as many as ten piglets two times a year. Some other animal species, with plenty of offspring, lose a good percentage through predation. Sows, though, are very protective and vicious, so few young are killed and the numbers of animals in a group or 'sounder' can increase quite rapidly. They are opportunistic foragers and will happily consume reptiles, eggs, ground nestlings and, in Australia, lambs and young deer. A typical size of a male boar is 110 - 200 lbs (50-90 kg), though some have been recorded at over 700 lbs in Russia. A 550 lb monster was shot in a forest in France in 1999. Once established, they prove very difficult to eradicate by hunting. To introduce such animals to New Guinea, where they have no predators and will consume the ground-dwelling birds, is pure madness. It is worth remembering though, that they were made extinct in the British Isles in the 13th century, and the last boar shot in Denmark was in the early part of the 19th century.[8] So with determination they can be removed.

These few exotic introductions illustrate, in a tiny way, the damage that we cause to the planet we call Earth and home. We unintentionally enable negative changes to the ecosystems that are just about impossible to reverse. I very much regret, though, that following in this book are tales of intentional actions that are far worse and a great deal more harmful. However, I give the assurance that I'm not only concerned to list the problems, as that would be a touch negative. Toward the end of this book things do improve, and in the final chapter, which I title "The Better Life", I suggest some changes to our lifestyle that might go some way to healing our home. Those changes won't remove the exotics, but they should result in improvements in other areas.

The extinction of native species by introduced exotic species had its beginnings with the early sea borne explorations. But it became horrific during the nineteenth and twentieth centuries. For the most part it took place on islands following the release, from visiting ships, of rats, cats and other animals. Close to 200 bird species have been rendered extinct in the last three centuries on the islands that we think of as paradise. Many were rails and other ground dwelling birds, though the Hawaiian Islands among others lost such tree dwelling birds as nectar-sipping honeyeaters and honeycreepers. The West Indies lost mostly macaws and parrots. The exotic pet trade contributed to those extinctions.

Islands that are far from a landmass, such as those that rose from the sea as volcanoes millions of years ago, do not easily populate with mammals. The first flora and fauna to become established, carried by the wind or tide, are plants and seeds. Then wind-carried insects arrive. Eventually birds, lost or storm-tossed, find the small dot of land where they settle, multiply, adapt, develop, become new species and multiply again. In their fluttering and chirping ways these birds may have evolved in unexpected ways. What they usually didn't do was develop a fear of carnivorous mammals or snakes since none reached their island paradise. It was very difficult for animals to travel hundreds or thousands of miles by sea, consequently, over a long time span, a great many islands developed an ecological richness quite free of mammals. So when humans first arrived they found birds quite tame with no fight or flight instinct. Surprisingly, bats and small lizards are often found to have made their way to these distant islands.

Not only had they lost fear, in many cases the birds had also lost flight. After all, why go to the very great trouble of flying when all the food they needed was on the ground at their feet. With no predators, flight was a waste of energy. The introduction of rats, cats and snakes was devastating for the smaller land-based, placid birds. The larger ones lost their eggs to the invaders, so were not much better off. They were also easily collected by humans, first for pets or the pot and later for scientific interest.

One of the first of these human-induced extinctions that we know of started in the tenth century when the Maoris first colonized New Zealand.[9] For most of the many million years prior to their arrival, New Zealand had been a land of birds and a few bats. The dominant life forms were the huge running birds that lived on the grassland and in the forests and which the Maoris named 'Moas'. There were 15 species of these birds at the time of the landings. The largest, the *Dinornornis maximus*, was 13 ft (4 meters) high and weighed 600 lbs (275 kg). They were all large birds in relative terms with the smallest being the six species of pygmy moas, which grew to 3-4 ft in height. The Maoris hunted all fifteen species to extinction. The final giant *maximus* was killed in 1850.

Those birds showed no remnant signs of any wing bones. It must have taken a great many millions of years for them to have lost all vestigial signs of the wings that took them to the islands in the first place. When compared with the African ostrich, which weighs about 250 lbs (114 kg), the *maximus* was nearly two and a half times heavier. It is interesting that for millions of years those birds lived in peace and security on New Zealand with no threat from other animals capable of harming them. But then a new fearsome species introduced itself. It arrived by boat . . . . . and that predator was us.

One even larger bird was rendered extinct by the sixteenth century. That was the Elephant Bird of Madagascar. Skeletal remains show it was 10 ft (3 m) tall and 1,100 lbs (500 kg) in weight. It is thought to have been the mythological 'Roc' of Arabian Nights tales. The roc eggs were up to three feet in circumference.[10]

Lord Howe Island with a few surrounding smaller islands is situated about half way between the east coast of Australia and the west coast of New Zealand. It was uninhabited, and first sighted in 1788, by Lieutenant Henry Lidgate Ball, commander of the RN ship HMS Supply. He claimed it for the United Kingdom, but it wasn't settled till 1834. In pretty quick time the larger birds, pigeons, gallinules and parakeets were killed off, possibly as sport or for food. Four species of songbirds – the Lord Howe Island Flycatcher, the Fantail, the White Eye and the Vinous-tinted Blackbird survived in healthy numbers until 1918. In that year the ship Mokambo ran aground at Ned's Beach where it remained stuck for nine days. During that time, before the ship could be floated, an army of rats went on shore leave. Within ten years, four species of songbirds were extinct.[11]

Just off the southern coast of New Zealand is the 2.6 sq km Stephen Island. At the end of the nineteenth century a lighthouse was built there, and manned by a lighthouse keeper and his cat. That cat frequently arrived on the doorstep with little wren-type birds in his mouth. Eventually specimens of this bird arrived, thanks to the lighthouse keeper and others, at the Ornithologist's Club in London where it was identified as a distinct species *Xenicus lyalli*. Word of the Stephen Island wren's distinction arrived at the island at about the same time that the cat killed the last of them.[12]

The birds on islands have suffered terribly. The Hawaiian Islands have seen the extinction of at least 28 of the 68 species of land birds that thrived there at the time of European contact. The islands are considered to have had all the land bird species endemic, and 97 per cent of its plant and tree species unique and endemic to those islands.

The Hawaiian Islands are part of a volcanic chain some 1,523 miles (2,400km) long and 1860 miles from the nearest large land mass. The chain comprises eight main islands, and numerous atolls and small islands. As a result of the distances of one island from another it seems that when birds did eventually make landfall some stayed but others were blown further afield to other islands. Isolation meant that each group adapted to the different conditions and foods available in its own territory. Such adaptations as size and hue, and beak shapes and sizes are apparent. It is believed that the 68 land bird species all evolved from 15 original species that made their way to the islands over the past 3 million years. It is thought that the 9 genera, 22 species and 64 subspecies of the colourful and brilliant Hawaiian honeycreepers are all descended from one species of American honeycreeper and that the 2 genera and 5 species of the equally delightful Hawaiian honeyeaters evolved from the Australasian family *Meliphagidae*.

Of the Hawaiian birds lost, over half were brightly coloured finches, honeyeaters and honeycreepers. They were scarlet or crimson, orange or yellow and green, or in the case of the 'Ō'ōs black and yellow. To exploit every nook and cranny, or at least every flower shape, some had crazy long curved bills, and those that were LBJs, or little brown jobs, were wonderful songsters. The honey birds would feed at flowering trees and shrubs in glittering and vibrating masses of multi-coloured flocks, many birds with their heads glistening with pollen from their feeding frenzy. The recent extinctions go back nearly 200 years, and although the precise dates are not known they are recorded as follows: 1837 the Oahu 'Ō'ō , 1850 the Kiowa Honeyeater, 1898 the Mamo, 1900 the Great Amakihi, 1904 the Molokai 'Ō'ō , 1934 the Hawaiian 'Ō'ō , 1937 The Lanai Alalwahio, 1965 the Kauai Akioloa, 1970 the Molokai Alauwahio and 1985 the Kaua'I 'Ō'ō. I don't want to list them all for fear of being boring, but you get the idea. Many of the remaining endemic birds are critically endangered, so we can expect to see the extinction dates continuing into the twenty-first century. Now when one visits an island like Maui, one will see many birds but they are nearly all human-introduced species from such places as Brazil and Japan.

In about 800 CE, before the Europeans had any inkling of their existence, the Hawaiian Islands were colonized by the Polynesians. They introduced their own animals to the islands. Research shows that event was to cause an earlier extinction phase, with some 45 bird species being lost. Capt. Cook speaks of finding dogs, pigs and a type of rat already on some islands, presumably brought there by the Polynesians. With the white man, following Capt. Cook's discovery in 1778, came cattle, goats, cats, dogs, rats and mosquitoes. The grazing of cattle alone seems to have been enough to cause the decline of some species. Apparently the cattle grazed the undergrowth where many birds nested. The birds also fed in the canopies, but humans soon reduced the forests by 75 per cent, and the cats and rats had a field day in the few remaining trees.[13]

David Day, in his 1981 published *The Doomsday Book Of Animals* quotes the writings of R.C.L. Perkins who, in 1892, wrote of seeing a great many Hawaiian 'Ō'ōs: "making with hosts of scarlet Iiwi, the crimson agapane and other birds, a picture never to be forgotten." Following a repeat visit a few years later he wrote, "Although the trees were, as before, one mass of flowers, hardly a single 'Ō'ō was to be seen. The only noticeable difference was that cattle were wandering over the flow (lava) and beginning to destroy the brushwood, just as they had already reduced the formerly dense forest bordering the flow to a condition of open parkland." A little later he visited Lanai where in a ravine he found 22 dead birds "all killed by cats in the space of two days." He was able to shoot two cats that were eating the 'Ō'ōs. Other visitors to the islands noted rats swarming high in the trees during daytime. When I was in Maui, in the late 1990s, I was surprised, in one beauty spot, to find the undergrowth swarming with mongooses. On many islands the mongoose was introduced in an attempt to eradicate the rats, but instead it seems to have been a keen assistant in eradicating the native birds.

Before Europeans, the Hawaiian Islands had no mosquitoes but we introduced those as well - not only mosquitoes to a place that had been blessed with none, but ones carrying Avian Malaria. The wild life of Hawaii had no immunity to mosquito-borne disease, so the birds were soon falling to disease as well as all the other exotic life forms they had to contend with.

Birds were not the only organisms to suffer from the multiple new threats. At the time of writing, 800 plant species, subspecies and varieties are endangered with at least 270 more already extinct.[14]

So, in all the newly discovered lands, the culprits have been many: rats and cats which killed the birds, their eggs and their fledglings; grassland ploughing, logging, habitat destruction and feed-plant extinctions; agriculture, cattle and goats and the dreaded disease-carrying mosquitoes; all of which played a role in destroying the birds and their habitat. On top of all that, we can add the incredibly daft habit of humans to enthusiastically collect rare birds and animals. The more rare the species, the more enthusiastic was the collector. The consequence of this was that when species became really, really rare the collectors seemed to go to extreme lengths to shoot the last specimens they could find. There are many stories of men searching for years to find out if a species of bird or deer, for instance, was still to be found. Then when they did finally find five or six, hanging on in some very remote corner of diminished habitat, they shot the lot and carried them home to the local museum - to prove they still existed I suppose. It is very lucky that we, with our very great intelligence, are the dominant species. Just think what state the world would be in if the dominant species were stupid?

One example of the collecting frenzy was the Ivory Billed Woodpecker.

This bird was uncommon in mature forests of the South Eastern United States, where each breeding pair required very large tracts of forest. It was a large (20 inch long), tough and striking bird that had had most of its forests felled by 1900, at which time it was considered rare. Since that time, 100 birds were shot, and their skins preserved in museums, for study presumably. By 1939 there were thought to be maybe a couple of dozen still in the wild, but they are considered to have been extinct since the nineteen-sixties.

As one might expect, many islands suffered major extinctions. The more isolated the islands, the more the extinctions were limited to birds. Lord Howe Island, between Australia and New Zealand, suffered eight bird species lost for all time, while tiny St. Helena in the middle of the South Atlantic has lost two. By contrast, the three Mascarene Islands - Mauritius, Reunion and Rodriguez - have had 28 extinctions with 19 of those being birds.[15]

Wildlife must have been moving around for millennia. For instance, the majority of British birds are actually Eurasian birds as many are found across the huge stretch of land from Portugal in the west to China in the east. The gradual spread of the evolving species may have been quite glacial at times; however, the spread would have been more rapid for flying or wind carried species than for earth bound mammals. Most land-based mammals lack the ability to cross large-bodies of water. Even in some very mountainous areas, where it is difficult to make it over the mountains, winged species have developed in one valley in isolation from the species in other valleys. The height of the mountains was enough to keep them apart. Now though, with the human propensity to travel and to send trucks, ships and planes all over the world, species can be carried very easily, and unknowingly, from valley to valley or continent to continent.

There are now thousands of introduced species across the world. Probably every country has at least a few. Some are quite harmless, but many can have devastating effects in the new lands. It seems that, just like us, the adaptable and tough ones can move into almost any environment, and eventually dominate that new home. In the early days it was the rats and cats, pigs, goats and dogs that were the problems. Today it seems to be such introduced species as the pythons, tree snakes, wild boar and the cane toads. There are also a great many others not mentioned here, such as plants and mussels, some of which are even more devastating than those

I have listed. Introduced species destroy all manner of wildlife, and defeat any attempts to eradicate them from their newfound homes.

It is apparent that it is not just the great number of humans that is a problem. It is not only what we do by intent that creates difficulties. It is also what we unknowingly make possible, or enable to happen, that is upsetting the natural balance.

It is believed there are 8.7 million species of life on earth with few of the smaller ones even catalogued. Any one has the potential to become an invasive species somewhere on this little planet. If any others were sentient beings, I shudder at how many would think of we humans as invasive.

Probably the above information is known to many, possibly few really care. So, if the majority feels the health of the natural realm is so unimportant, why do I get my knickers in a twist about it? Could the reason be genetic, or could it be family nurturing? Maybe both, but I like to think that early childhood experiences were the strongest influences.

2a Reminiscences: *Purley and First Memories*

"Six on this one, five on that. Eight, no nine, over there." It is telling how well I remember that sun-drenched, but listless, scented morning and those brilliant metallic copper-green-winged Burnett moths with their scarlet spots. The scarlet hind-wings were vivid in the late morning light. They were small day-flying moths of little interest until you got up close. I was busy counting how many were taking the nectar from the mounds of purple rockery plants in my father's garden. Although I had previously noticed them amongst the flowers, never, before that morning of brilliance, had I really looked at them. It was 1945, or possibly '46. I was six or seven, and it is one of the clearest memories I have from that long ago time. One of my usual activities on those languid hot days was to poke at paint blisters on the green garage doors, but this was far more engaging. I had already counted the six red spots on their small narrow forewings and was then counting the dazzling number of moths flying from plant to plant.

Other memories are of running in the long grass chasing butterflies - a cliché of English childhood for sure, but sublime memories for me. They were usually only Chalk-hill Blues, Meadow Browns or Green Hairstreaks; very occasionally I would catch a Small Tortoiseshell. However commonplace, they held the promise of beauties as yet unseen.

I have earlier memories, but none so clear.

I don't remember traveling from Somerset and arriving at the house named Cobbles in 1942, but I do recall going into the garden for the first time on that day of arrival. I remember the door to the outside and the high stone wall that ran parallel with the house and enclosed me on the pathway, then the four or five steps, which led up to the garden, to the lawn, the trees and the flowers. Earlier memories are of the farm, of small pigs in a squealing gallop across the farmyard, and of the flanks of a vast shire horse. Someone must have been holding me up when I was two or three years old, and probably we spent most of the time near the horse's head, but I only remember the side and huge rear quarters. I also have a fleeting image of Aunt Trix in charge of a hay rake behind a heavy white shire horse named Prince. That must have been during haymaking in '42 just before we left Somerset, and the farm, for the London suburbs. However the memory of that hot day, with the Burnett Moths, is emblematic and iconic. I was getting a close-up look at creatures that I thought amongst the most beautiful and compelling I had ever seen.

From a very young age, I loved the natural world: the countryside of farms, birds and animals. As a boy, living at Cobbles in Purley, some of my happiest days were spent with my butterfly net, in The Woods, searching for Red Admirals and Peacocks. I would make for what we called The Glade, where the grass was long and the sun was warm.

I always hoped to see a Purple Emperor, a Camberwell Beauty or a Clouded Yellow, beauties that I had seen in my brother's books and imagined as larger, more beautiful and more abundant than they were in reality. Being so young, I was unaware of how unlikely I was to see those insects in the woods and gardens of the district where we lived. Purley was an outer suburb of London, on the chalk hills of North Surrey, where the town met the downs – the North Downs. Though such land was perfect for Chalk-hill Blues, Adonis Blues and Dark-green Fritillaries, the conditions were not to the liking of the butterflies that held my fancy. I never have seen many of them in the wild, but when I was young, I could always dream.

I now know that to see a Purple Emperor I would need to either ascend to the canopy of a southern England oak or beech forest or to entice the male down to the forest floor with, of all things, animal excrement. I would need even more luck to see the Camberwell Beauty - a very infrequent visitor to England - which was first recorded in 1748. Little did I realize then that 50 or 60 years into the future I would see scores of those butterflies flying above, and settling on, the high mountain roads of British Columbia, where they are known as Mourning Cloaks. Nor did I know that when seen at a glimpse, or settled with wings folded, they would appear quite dark and dowdy. However when one slowly sails close by in the brilliant sunlight the blood-red crimson and cream of the upper-wing surface is rich and beautiful. They are indeed beauties, abundant in Canada, though seldom seen in Camberwell.

All these years later I realize how fortunate I was at the time to have had so little awareness of the awful onslaught on nature that had been ongoing for centuries and was about to accelerate very rapidly. The abundance of British insects and birds that I had known would be largely gone by the time I became a man.

I could not have imagined that in the great world beyond Britain most of the world's species would soon be reduced in numbers to fewer than 3 or 4 per cent of their numbers at the time of my birth. Nor could I know that the unrelenting growth of the planet's human population would, by the year 2000, bring 30 per cent of the world's wildlife species to the brink of extinction.

In reality, when I went out with my butterfly net, the insects I saw most were dull Meadow Browns, and those I occasionally caught were small native Chalk-hill Blues. These were abundant in the few local patches of downland and woods that remained squeezed between the expensive houses built over the previous twenty or so years. Those un-developed sites were scattered in our neighborhood and were life and breath to the local children. Each had its name: The Woods, The Copse and The Fields.

They were all quite close to our house, which was on the very top of the hill. The Woods were directly across the road and were protected by a high fence on the street side and by gardens on the other three sides. Nearby lived the owners, Mr. and Mrs. Mathews, who would give us the keys to the gate anytime we wanted to play. The piece of land was probably the size of two or three building plots or about two or more acres in area, but it was so overgrown and mysterious that to us it could have been as vast as the Borneo jungle. My friends and I usually headed first for the sunny Glade in search of butterflies. It was there we always saw significant butterflies when we had no nets, but never saw any when we did.

The Copse was also close to our house, but beyond our back garden and the Cramer's house and garden. The true copse was opposite their house and across the street named Copse Hill Road. The quickest way to get there was to take a short cut through our garden and a gate into the Cramer's garden, turn right past their Victoria plum trees - without taking any - and then through another gate into another undeveloped area that we also called The Copse. It wasn't really a copse. It was, in truth, a cleared area, possibly once ploughed or bulldozed, fronting Copse Hill Road to which wild grasses had returned, and where, near the back fence, a few remnant small trees gathered. It was the best place for small blue, and occasionally green, butterflies.

Invaluable to small children as The Woods and The Copse were, the best of all were The Fields, a section of the original sloping and shrub-filled grassy downland. This was ancient habitat that may have never been under the plough - at least not in recent historic times. To the adults that six or seven acre plot may have been nothing more than undeveloped land, but to many of us children it was a jewel and a wonderland, an enchanting area of long original grasses, May blossoms on hawthorn bushes, birds and insects - a place for adventure and imagination. The Fields was a primitive strip, a true corner of old Britain in the centre of the new. It was just beyond The Copse where Woodside Road forked off of Copse Hill.

None of those playgrounds were more than two hundred yards from our house if we took the garden shortcut. All were miraculously saved when further housing development was postponed by the war.

So in itchy grey woolen shorts during the warmth of springtime and summer we would quest happily after butterflies and birds' nests. During the rare winter snows The Fields became a gathering place for boys, in the same shorts, to slide and to toboggan.

Fortunately, after brief attempts to build egg collections in the best Victorian scientific tradition, we were told by the adults that this was not a good thing. So we learned to search for and identify the eggs but not to disturb the nests. For a child to find a small neat nest containing three or four delicate blue eggs is miraculous in its natural purity. I was certainly happiest playing in these patches of remnant nature. But, never quite knowing when I was well off, I still spent plenty of time nostalgically daydreaming about being back in the real country.

As a young boy I was a champion dreamer, and I did plenty of it during those happy yet somewhat melancholy years of early childhood. Suburbia was not good enough. The Farm was where I longed to be, and nostalgia hung heavy on me at times.

In those days I never questioned where the names The Copse, The Woods and The Fields had come from, but I now realize they defined the main features of the land before the housing developments started. The first two must have been one large hilltop wood, later bisected by our streets and neighbourhood gardens. Those remnant areas simply received distinguishing names. I realize now that the street names, and location over which they were laid, give a fairly clear picture of how the countryside had been before the houses were built.

Like most residential developments, suburban Purley had a timeless aspect as if it had been as it then was for a great many years. Despite the rather young trees in the gardens, which spoke of recent plantings, it was almost impossible to imagine the area as the raw nature it had been only a few years before. The houses, gardens and streetscape were by then quite well established. However, the planning for our neighborhood had probably only started some twenty or thirty years earlier, possibly just following the First World War. Much of the building had taken place in the nineteen twenties and thirties. The development had slowed with the Depression and come to an end with the start of the Second World War. As I said, it was quite impossible to imagine that only twenty years before we moved there the land was untouched wild downland.

Our street, Manor Wood Road, straddled the top of a considerable and steep hill with parallel roads, Copse Hill and Woodside Road to the northwest, and Woodcrest and Downland Roads on the slope down to the southeast. They all led into Smitham Downs Road, which, in turn, terminated at the unlikely named Smitham Bottom Lane. A short way along that road was the old village green and 16th century oak stocks of Upper Woodcote village, now surrounded on three sides by suburban development. The stocks were where, in olden times, petty criminals sat, held by their feet. There they received the scorn heaped on them, and the rotten vegetables thrown at them, by the good, law-abiding citizens of the village. Good Christians all, with no hint of hypocrisy in the villagers of Woodcote village, we can be sure.

When looking to the natural history of the region, we have to remember that in England geological words often seem contrary to their meaning. Downs are not valleys. They are specific geological features that are actually softly rounded chalk hills or uplands. They have very shallow alkali soil that drains quickly into the solid chalk and steep-sided valleys below. Much of the soil is too shallow to support woodland, so grassland, with scattered shrubs, is widespread and this, in turn, supports many flowering plants and insects. These high grassland areas were the first to be settled by the early inhabitants of the otherwise heavily forested prehistoric Britain.

So the place we thought of as suburban London had only a few years earlier been an open area of grassy downland named Smitham Downs,

18

topped by an extensive copse and home to an old manor house. Chalk and Adonis Blue butterflies would have been plentiful, searching for the fragrant orchids and Horseshoe Vetch partly hidden by the long Quaking Grass and the shorter Sheep's Fescue, which all thrived on this chalky soil. In the recent past the valley below may have held an ancient track, known as Bottom Lane, used by carters and along which shepherds, wearing smocks and carrying big looped crooks, moved their flocks to graze when leaving the nearby village of Woodcote. Nevertheless, when we lived there, it was hard to imagine that the houses, asphalt and sidewalks had not been there for a very long time. Purley is some twelve miles from London's centre and near the very edge of Greater London at neighbouring Coulsdon. There, at Farthing Downs, the Green Belt and true country begins. Although Purley is of recent heritage, Coulsden goes back a long way. It is mentioned in the year 675 by the name of Curedesdone and in the Domesday Book as Colesdone.[1][2]

The development of raw nature and grazing land into residential land had, around London, been gathering momentum for hundreds of years, as it followed the ups and downs of the country's population.

The Norman invasion of 1066, King Harold's defeat by William the Conqueror at the Battle of Hastings, and the subsequent slaughter and passing of the Saxon way of life, may have been momentous and horrible for the inhabitants, but it started England on the path to good record keeping. As a result of William's Domesday Book we can assess the population of England in the year 1086 to be somewhere between 1.25 and 2 million. That is less than the estimated 4 million in Roman times. It then seems to have increased to 4-6 million before shrinking again in the 14th century due to plague, food production problems and starvation. In 1377, it is estimated that England held 2.2 - 3 million. We know this because hero king Edward III levied a poll tax to raise money for the Hundred Years War.[3]

Following England's unification with Scotland in 1707 the population numbers are given for Great Britain rather than England alone. In 1750 the total population was 5.74, and in 1801 it was 8.3 million. That was the year when my great-great-granddad was five and the first of the ten-yearly government censuses was held.

So: in 1801 it was 8.3 million
     In 1851 it was 17 million
     In 1901 it was 30 million

In 1951 it was 41 million

In 2001 it was 49.5 million

And, in 2011 it is approaching 60 million

In 2011 the UK's death rate was 11.30 per 1000, a little lower than the UK born birth rate of 17.1 per 1000. However when we add in the foreign immigrant birth rate of 28 per 1000, it is clear that Great Britain continues to add population fairly rapidly.[4]

We can see that prior to 1750 the population increased slowly. Then during the next 50 years, at the beginning of industrialization, it grew some fifty percent, but during the two subsequent fifty-year periods, when industry was going full blast, the population doubled each fifty years. The increases then dropped to 30 per cent and 25 per cent during the following two fifty-year periods.

A start date for the Industrial Revolution is usually given as 1760 - or 1733 if we take it from John Kay's invention of the flying shuttle loom. It required many factors coming together to make it happen. Those included the ideas on which the principals of modern democracy are founded, such the Bill of Rights of 1689 and John Lock's Treatises regarding the individual's rights to overthrow unjust government. The subsequent flowering of Britain's democratic and political institutions supported an aggressively confident, nationalistic and competitive population. With the Enlightenment came such industrial and engineering inventions as John Wilkinson's 1774 boring machine for making iron cylinders, James Watt's 1775 steam engine and his 1781 rotative beam steam engine, which could spin a shaft to power pulleys and cogs. These inventions gave industrialization a tremendous boost.[5] Other catalysts were the beginnings of a capital market, the Royal Navy's budding control of the trade routes and all the other scientific and medical discoveries of that century. Britain's rich deposits of coal, iron ore, copper, tin and clay were critical. To have accessible coal beds close to the ores and clays made production relatively easy. Another factor was Britain's long narrow shape. This enabled most goods to be carried by barge along the many rivers to the sea. The goods could then be taken along the coast and up other waterways, or straight to the ports for export. This was far more efficient then trying to transport goods overland by ox cart on non-existing roads and cart tracks. It was also a time for a great expansion of inland canals.

Although the world's first steam driven railway was the Pennydarren Ironworks tramway in 1804, the first public steam railway line was the

25 mile (40km) long Stockton and Darlington Railway, which opened in 1825.[6] The 1840s saw a massive railway-building boom. In those ten years, rail lines were built to link nearly every town and village in the country. At the same time, the electric telegraph, following its first use in 1837 between Euston station and Camden Town, was built along all the rail lines throughout the country. On top of that, most of London's major and very large terminal railway stations were built. Some of them are as grand as cathedrals - cathedrals to the god of progress and the technological future that they celebrated. Most are very large with some able to host 19 trains at a time. St. Pancras has been described as the world's most wonderful railway terminus. London Bridge Station was opened in 1836, Euston opened in 1838, Waterloo in 1848, Kings Cross in 1852, Paddington in 1854, Charing Cross in 1864, St. Pancras in 1868, Liverpool Street in 1874 and Marylebone, the final main station, in 1899. Victoria Station came together piecemeal over many years. The total length of UK rail track, at the close of the Victorian era in 1900, was 17,000 miles (27,000kms) and it carried one billion, one hundred million passengers per year.[7 8]

Throughout that time British engineers built railways on most continents of the world. It is surprising to note that in colonial India railways were first proposed in 1832, just seven years after the first Stockton and Darlington line opened in Britain. The first passenger service started in 1853, and by 1921, there were 41,000 miles of railway line in India.[9]

Before the railways everyone over the whole world had traveled as they had for millennia. They traveled mostly on foot, though some were carried by other humans. The lucky few journeyed on horse-drawn, or bullock-drawn, carts. Those who could afford to, rode horses or, as Jesus did once, donkeys. Most humans had not, of course, learned to walk on water so rivers, lakes and seas were still traversed by human-powered, or wind-powered, boats of one sort or another. The railways and the telegraphs were a huge step forward in changing our lives with the potential for movement and communication. Before they were introduced people, goods and information could be transported over 500 miles (800kms) at about 4-7 miles per hour. Typically 500 miles would take about 100-125 hours. By train, at 50 miles per hour, that journey would take about 10 hours. Information could be sent along the telegraph wires almost instantaneously. In 1802, Peter Mark Roget, of the thesaurus fame, was on a grand tour escorting and tutoring two teenage sons of a wealthy industrialist. They traveled from Paris to Geneva, a distance of 350 miles, by horse-drawn chaise and, stopping off here and there; it took them 13 days to complete the journey.[10] That was 21 years before the Stockton and Darlington Railway opened.

The Scotsman John McAdam developed the first smooth and weather resistant road surface in 1820. The material is still known as macadam in Britain and asphalt in the US. Once the rubber pneumatic tire had been invented in 1887, and patented in 1888, by another Scotsman, John Dunlop, things were ready for Mr. Benz's invention of the automobile. With these three inventions land travel was revolutionized.

Dunlop had originally invented the tire for his son's bicycle[11] and was not the actual inventor of the first pneumatic tire. That distinction goes to yet another Scotsman by the name of Robert William Thompson who patented his rubber-soaked canvas tires in 1846 at the age of 23. He demonstrated his 'Aerial Wheels' invention on horse drawn carriages in Regent's Park in 1847.[12]

It seems that, early on, the desperate conditions in the cities and high child mortality encouraged many pregnancies but few infants who lived beyond five. Then, industrialization, steady pay and improving medical care gave the people heart to have large families, but as child mortality decreased, and education and general wealth and security improved, the people decided on smaller families. This demographic shift is now evident in much of the world today. As people become more financially secure and their incomes increase, and as the women become better educated, the birth rate drops.

One result of the 19th century baby bulge of Britain was a big boom in building and infrastructure creation. It was a time when the world moved from the old to the new.

I find it surprising that the year 2012, when many of the world's cities are investigating the possibilities of building underground rapid transit systems, is the 182nd anniversary of the first underground train proposal in London. That railway line, the Metropolitan as it became known, was eventually begun in 1860 and opened in 1863. Within months, it was carrying 26,000 passengers per day. In 1890, the world's first deep-level tube line, the Northern Line, opened. The tunneling method that was developed for that line is the same system used now, all over the world, for deep tunnel digging. In the year 2010, the London underground railways carried over 1.1 billion passenger/trips over a network length of 249 miles (402kms).[13]

Positioned near the southern border of Greater London, Purley was part of the continuous development that began with the City of London and expanded, in great ripples, into the Home Counties beyond. Greater London now covers an area of 607 square miles (1572km2), though the metropolitan area is far larger but not decisively defined. In the mid-1750s, at the start of the Industrial Revolution, London covered little more than the original City's one square mile. Mayfair, now very central and part of the West End, was built on farmland between the mid-17th and mid-18th centuries. The original Buckingham Palace was a country house when George III bought it in 1762. Hyde Park was deep in the country, and Knightsbridge was a small bridge and hamlet between the villages of Chelsea and Kensington. London was the first city in the world to grow to a population of a million. The 19th century Victorians and later, Edwardians, with their industry, world-dominant commerce and empire, expanded the city into the world's largest and most powerful. In terms of population, London was the world's largest city between 1830 and 1925. Those dates more or less correspond with the period when Britannia's power was at her greatest. The population, which was 1.1 million in 1801, is now 7.75 million. London's metropolitan area holds 12 to 14 million depending on where we conclude it ends.[14]

Although the process of encroachment into nature had been ongoing for centuries, it was finally brought under some control when, following their 1945 election, the Labour Government of Clement Attlee developed greenbelts around certain cities with The Town and Country Planning Act of 1947. These greenbelts have saved southern England from becoming a vast suburban sprawl even worse than it is today.

During the 20th century we saw the same process of population growth, with huge tracts of land given over to buildings, run amok all over the world. Think of North America, of Florida and California, of South East Asia, and of Africa, anywhere that the population increases have been the greatest. Tokyo, currently the world's largest city, had a population in 2011 of 32.45 million. The natural world, and her ecosystems, has taken a terrible beating in our rush to build housing and infrastructure and to provide for our burgeoning population.

When they started to build on Smitham Downs after the First World War, it is possible that some people would have been appalled. However, it is more probable that the majority celebrated the development as a desirable sign of necessary progress. They would have swelled with pride at that manifestation of human dominance over nature. This was the tail end in Britain, at least, of a period of development - or abuse - when people seemed to view the natural world as one part of God's creation that required taming and extermination. Vast engineering projects such as continent-straddling railways and chasm-crossing bridges had been completed. To see telegraph poles marching uncounted across thousands of miles of sparsely populated land was enough to swell anyone's chest. Tall sky-scraping buildings – at first in America, then all over the world – were reflecting our brilliance and pointing the way to a future of affluence beyond most peoples' imagining. However, there were still huge tracts of undeveloped territories such as the largely unexplored jungles and forests of West Africa, South East Asia, Borneo, New Guinea and the Amazon to be exploited. The oceans were mysteries of unimagined promise. Corals were formations that ruined the bottoms of boats and tore at one's feet. I don't believe anyone, other than pearl divers, in the days before the development of snorkeling and scuba tanks, had any idea of the beauty, colours or infinite wonder that a coral reef offered.

When I was young, those under-explored territories of the world were still something to be feared. The idea of their vulnerability was neither considered nor of concern to anyone but a very few.

The wild animals that we saw in zoos were of course interesting, but my interests were closer to home. I keenly read books on the animals and wildlife of Britain, at least the species that remained. Many texts would include such notes as "now only a few pairs survive in North Wales" - when talking of the Polecat, or of the Wildcat, or "gone from most rivers in Britain" - for the Otter. That extermination in the UK and Europe had been going on for many years. Ten thousand years ago, such animals as the Cave Lion and the Saiga Antelope disappeared during one extinction phase. More recently though, a great many species have been wiped out by humans. The first animal hunted out of Britain in historic times was the 6 ft tall (180cm) ferocious Auroch, the ancestor of modern cattle. That animal went about 1000 BCE, although the species lasted in Europe until 1627, when the very last female died in Poland's Jaktorow Forest. The European Beaver *(Castor fiber)* was gone from Britain by 1525, the last Eurasian Wolf from Scotland in 1740 and the Beech Marten during the 19th Century.[15] Some of the birds that went the same way include the last Osprey from Wales by 1604, the Sea Eagle by 1810, the Great Bustard in 1840, the Great Auk in 1844 and the Great Bittern in 1861. It seems that until the post WW2 period, the great birds of Great Britain were killed with great enthusiasm. Like the wild animals, they were there to be shot for food, for sport, or as vermin.

Now though, some British people have truly changed their ways. At the beginning of the 21st Century, the people of the UK are going to considerable lengths to re-establish forests and wetlands and to reintroduce from Europe many of the animals and birds earlier extirpated from the islands. Nonetheless, since the nineteenth century, other nations all over the world have seen similar explosions of their populations, have encouraged similar great undertakings of infrastructure construction but have also witnessed far more devastating depletions to their native wildlife and plant and animal species.

It is easy to imagine a couple of old farmhands in 1925, chewing on pieces of grass, leaning on a five-bar gate on what remained of Smitham Downs and talking of change.

"Do you remember when we used to hunt badgers up by the copse? Don't see any of those about now thank the Lord."

"They were vermin, they were. Just like foxes and otters."

"Aye! You're right there Samuel. Do you remember how the old Colonel up at the Manor used to plan those Saturday hunts?"

"Yer Josh! He told me he wouldn't rest in his grave till he'd rid the whole county of badgers. An' I think he succeeded."

"Well they wouldn't be able to survive here now would they? Not with these new houses goin' up. What a turn up for the books. Progress I'm told, but it was good grazing."

"Oh aye! It's all about progress they say. At least these city folk won't have to put up with badgers and the like."*

During my time in Purley, in the late nineteen-forties, I had no idea that our endless miles of tarmac roads and hard-edged pavements or sidewalks, of set-back houses, gardens and small trees, had not been there forever. So nearly complete was the obliteration of the downland habitat and ecosystem that our suburb, and the adjoining ones, appeared almost natural and ageless. The only clues were the clumps of chalk in our family gardens, and our playgrounds, The Woods and The Fields.

---

* Similar attitudes are held by people the world over. When I was on a visit to Malaysia in 1997, I mentioned to some Malayan friends my concern for their tigers. They thought I was mad and indicated that they couldn't get rid of the last of them quickly enough.

Since those early-post-WW2 years of my childhood play, and of the UK government's enacting of the Green Belt legislation, huge areas of wild country, all over the planet, have been smothered in asphalt, concrete and buildings. In 1940, for instance, the city of Sao Paulo, Brazil had a population of 1.3 million. In 2012, the population was 19.9 million and the metropolitan area had sprawled to 3,067.125 square miles (7,943.818km2).[16] Sao Paulo is just one of an uncountable number of possible examples in every country of the world. We have to wonder how much more land will be given over to cities, industry and suburbs, to house the two or three billion more people expected by 2050.

Human power over the natural environment is now complete. Whether we build towns and suburbs on lush meadows or over primary forest, in the Florida Everglades, in the Amazon forest, or over Africa's wildlife-rich National Parks, we are able to do so and leave no sign of the wild habitat or wildlife that for thousands of years thrived and multiplied there.

In the beginning, the whole world was natural. The human footprint was really confined to just that – footprints, footprints of naked feet crossing the few areas of land on which people traveled. Now our metaphoric prints are gigantic, and the assault on the world of nature has become dreadfully focused.

How can we begin to imagine the Greater London area or New York State as it was before the arrival of humans? What calamity must befall our civilization to save the rich forests of Borneo, the Amazon Basin, or the Congo, from being totally destroyed and the land adapted to our needs. Will we ever again see forests or grasslands similar to those that covered the land for millions of years before the last century? Now wherever I am, on whatever continent, I find I view the countryside, and our urban and agriculture adaptations, through the prism of how it might once have been. As long as the human population keeps growing as fast as it seems set to do, it appears that no natural corner of our earth will be safe from human development, and no animals will be safe from having to flee and die.

The reprieve from total development of our few Purley patches of playland downs and woods was probably extended by the war in 1939. By the time our family left Purley and moved to the Isle of Wight in 1953, there was still no sign of any new housing. Our areas of childhood play and enchantment remained for a new generation of avid 6-year-old bird-nesters and dreamers.

2b Reminiscences: *Mogdangle, the Farm and War*

Colin, Mother, Barry and Jo. Mogdangle, 1939

My attacks of nostalgic dreaming at that time were for a place we called The Farm, where for the summer of 1944 I had lived and played in paradise. That was our second long stay at the place, and followed a three-year stay between September 1939 and the summer of '42. Those were both formative visits for me, and in the post-war years I had a hay-cart full of memories into which I could retreat and dream.

The first visit had begun on September 3, 1939, when, following the German attack on Poland, Britain and France found themselves at war with Germany. The long years of bored respectability followed by restless days of doubt and fear were over. Perilous deeds were the future. On that day my father drove our family, and Aunt Trix and her daughter Pam, to a Somerset farm-laborer's cottage, named Mogdangle. It was on the land of a large farm of some thousand acres. There, for safety's sake, he left us, first for nearly two years in the cottage, then for a year in a wing of the big farmhouse.

As the inevitability of that war had become evident, the fear of civilian city populations being bombed and massacred, as had happened when the Germans bombed the Spanish city of Guernica, had become intense. A friend put my father in touch with the farmer and he rented Mogdangle to us unseen. When she arrived on that day in September, my city-bred mother wept. We had left the drab of a London suburb, but the cottage was surrounded on all sides by fields, with a quarter-mile muddy track leading to the road and the two-mile distant village and store. Some of the floors were of ancient flagstones, some of earth. Water was from an outside well. There was no electricity and no bathroom, and my mother had my ten-year-old sister, my five-year-old brother and me, a pooping six-month-old baby, to deal with. She also had the fear of what might happen to my father back in London during the anticipated bombings. Yet from such beginnings I developed a love for The Farm and countryside that for many years was profound and almost spiritual.

Though only a hundred and fifty miles from London, Somerset at that time was as much removed from the capitol as was an old hay cart from our Armstrong Siddeley motorcar. The earth was chrome-orange and iron-oxide red mud. Cider was the county's main claim to fame. The local yokel speech idiom required three Zs used in every alternate word, usually consecutively. Winter was mud-soaked, summer green and lush.

My post-war affection for the mythical Mogdangle, for I had been too young to remember much of it, was such that I would spend ages poring over the photo albums showing assorted children, including my sister and brother, up trees, standing deep in mud or playing in the barn. But they were always wearing rubber boots. I appear in one photo as a toddler, with sun-speckled golden hair, wearing what look to be little bloomers and a look of both concentration and glee as I learned to walk. Maybe the delight was based on my new mobility, or possibly at being outside, and in a garden on a brilliantly sunny day. I sometimes think of that photo and wonder what my parents were feeling at the time. It is just a small photo, probably taken on one of the rare weekends when my father was able to get away from his responsibilities in London. It appears to have been taken in the spring or early summer of 1940, at a time when British people went through fears and emotions such as later generations have never experienced.

Following World War One, the British and French had adopted policies of disarmament. They believed that the war had been so horrific that another was unthinkable. Peace had to be pursued at all cost. Just one example of the awfulness of that war can be found in the experience of Harold Macmillan.

Harold Macmillan was born a member of the Macmillan Publishing family. He became a member of parliament before the Second World War, had been influential in Churchill's War Cabinet, and was Prime Minister between early 1957 and late 1963. As Prime Minister he was known as 'Supermac', but what of his early days?

Being born into a wealthy London family in 1894, he enjoyed a typical education heavy in the classical subjects. He started learning Greek and Latin at the age of six. In 1912 he entered Balliol College, Oxford, and was two years into his studies when the trumpets of war blared in August 1914 and Europe's youth went adventuring off to 'the shooting party', a shooting party that quickly became 'the war to end all wars'. England had reached its golden zenith of world power, enterprise and prideful complacency. Being British, young and of the right family, placed him amongst the gilded elite, so he no doubt spent that last idyllic summer attending lavish parties in fine country houses.

He joined the army and reached the rank of Captain in the Grenadier Guards. He served with distinction in the trenches from September 1915 till September 1916. During that time he received three wounds in three different battles, which kept him out of the trenches for much of the time. The fourth wound, at the Battle of the Somme, arrived as a bullet in the hip. He found refuge in a slit trench where, for the whole day, he lay quietly reading one of Aeschylus's plays in the original ancient Greek. This wound was so serious that it kept him in hospital for four years before healing. He was left with a limp.

The Battle of the Somme was horrific but fairly typical of the battles where men charged over open land against entrenched machine guns. On the first day of battle the British suffered 60,000 casualties and 20,000 men killed. So Harold Macmillan was lucky, at least more so than most of his friends.

The point to all this is not what happened to him but what happened to his friends. He entered Balliol College in 1912 with 28 other young men, men who could probably have been described as among the cream of British youth at the time. They were the young men who as boys had gone to Eton, or Rugby, or maybe Marlborough schools. They had received, arguably, the best and most expensive education in the world, in preparation to leading the greatest country of the age. Their spring had glowed in the warmth of early summer days. They were the Golden Ones. All 28 volunteered for the war. By the armistice in 1918 twenty-six were dead and only Macmillan and one other still lived. He had indeed been lucky as his wound had kept him out of the trenches for the last two years of the war.[1]

Harold Macmillan went on to great things, but what might the others have achieved had they not died in that bloody war? And how different might things have been for Britain and Europe had those, and the many thousands of others like them, lived on to serve the countries and society as their positions and education suggested they should. Britain – and France and Germany and others – lost more than just material wealth through that war. They lost more than the poor youths who bled as fodder to the machine guns.* Britain lost nearly a million young men, any of whom may have taken on the intellectual and leadership roles that the country would need in the future. The total international dead in that war was ten million. Nearly all were military casualties, unlike the high percentage of civilian deaths in later wars. It has now been estimated that more people died in each day of the 1916 battles, than the total deaths in all European wars between 1815 and 1915.[2]

For the people back home, those human losses were felt most strongly on a personal level: sons and husbands, brothers and cousins all gone; heirs to great families and great fortunes gone; boyfriends and fiancés dead. No wonder so many single ladies lived in Purley when I was young. Their bright dreams for a happy future of husband, home and children were shattered by the stuttering machine guns of a generation earlier. The deaths of one million of Britain's young were calamities on both a personal, and a national level. 'The war to end all wars' they called it and no one in Britain wanted another.

In 1921 an Italian general named Douhet wrote of the potential for aerial forces to cause "the disintegration of nations". Annihilation from the air was expected by any nation caught in a future air war.

One example of Britain's pursuit of peace was the near dissolution of the Royal Air Force. At the end of WW1, just fourteen years after the Wright brothers' first flight, the RAF, like the Royal Navy, was the world's largest. It was also considered the most aggressive – always taking the battle to enemy territory, while the German air corps tended to be more defensive. When the Armistice was declared in 1918, the RAF had twenty two thousand aircraft and 185 operational squadrons. By 1920 there were seven squadrons

---

* One might argue that the British people should not have complained so much about the WW1 machine guns. After all, the British had developed the first as the death-defining Maxim gun. It was initially used against such spear-waving enemy as the Matabele warriors in 1894 Zimbabwe, and the Mahdi's dervishes in the Sudan in 1898.[3] Then it had worked well at bringing colonial wars to a swift end with a minimal loss of British military lives. The warring natives had lost thousands to be sure, but that was deemed rather different than having the weapon used against one's own educated, refined and golden youth of the age. That was a little too uncivilized, even for the British.

left in Britain and a further 15 scattered about the empire, many having no ground crew or support.[4] Throughout the nineteen twenties it was touch and go as to whether the government would even keep an air force. There was great pressure to disband the whole service in the belief that old style naval supremacy would keep the peace. The admirals believed the navy would continue the role of deterrent to war making by others, as it had in the 19th century. A battle royal was fought in London between the wars. It was between the juvenile RAF and the long established Senior Service, the Royal Navy. It was for much-reduced government funds. Unfortunately for Britain in the Second World War, the RN won that particular battle, ensuring that Britain entered the next war rich in expensive and useless battleships and sorely short of good aircraft.*

That long ago dispute, between buying ships and buying planes, is not an irrelevance to the theme of this book. It speaks about politicians, and civil servants, making completely wrong decisions on really important issues. In the one case, it was British officials who considered themselves the most

---

* The RN fought to continue building very expensive battleships and battlecruisers, which were, in truth, ships of the past. Submarines and aircraft had made them vulnerable and obsolete. Such ships filled the nation with pride, as their design and construction was an early equivalent of America's Moon Mission. When it first put to sea in 1881 the Royal Navy ship, HMS Inflexible, was described as the world's most technically advanced and complex piece of engineering ever seen. They continued to be just that.[5]

Large naval battleships required far-reaching technological advances in their gun designs alone. Imagine the development from wooden ships firing cannon balls, to early 20th century ships capable of firing 1000 lb shells with enough accuracy to hit another ship at a distance of 20 miles. The old cannons had their genesis as iron shapes cast around logs. The naval guns evolved from calibers of 12 inches (30.5cm) to 16 inches and, after WW1, to the planning of 18 inch (45.7cm) caliber monsters. These individual gun barrels had a length of over 60 ft (20 meters) and weighed 350,000 lbs (160,000kg). They would have fired an eight-foot long projectile weighing 3.320 lbs (1,506kg) to an accurate range of 38 miles (61kms).[6] The designers and manufacturers had to engineer ways of building a solid steel tube of such lengths and then to accurately bore the interior of that tube to very fine tolerances. How does one bore out a tube that is 60ft long? How, for that matter, does one make a 350,000 lb, 60 ft long, but substantial, steel tube in the first place? It seems by either winding wire, or by precision shrinking steel tubes one over another.

Then, what kind machinery is needed to elevate, lower or generally direct such a monster gun barrel? And what design of rangefinder is needed to accurately fire an eighteen inch diameter shell 38 miles to hit a ship, the guns having to be fired from a moving ship in a live sea? These guns were needed apparently to penetrate 7 inch thick steel decks and 15 inch thick armour-plated hull-belts of enemy battleships.

Naval design was the most complex technology until the development of atomic power, supersonic aircraft, space rockets and satellites.

competent in the most powerful nation, deciding on government policy that nearly lost the country the war.* In the case of this book, it is about governments determining to pursue energy, mining, and development policies that will probably do irreparable harm to our planet and ensure extremely difficult times for our descendants.

On the day Britain found itself unwillingly at war, King George VI gave a radio address to the people of the Empire. In it he said, "Over and over again we have tried to find a peaceful way out of the differences between ourselves and those who are now our enemies . . . " The desire for peace at all costs was very powerful in most of Europe, but not in Hitler's heart.

The first six months of the war, or the phony war as that period was called, was a lull that bode reasonably well for the British war effort. Then, of a sudden in the spring of 1940, when I was a little over a year old, the Nazis invaded Norway on April 9th, and Britain withdrew on May 2nd. On May 10th Holland and Belgium were invaded, followed swiftly by the invasion of France. The British evacuation from Dunkirk on June 4th* was followed by the June 16th surrender of France. Following all that mayhem came the threat of a German invasion of the British Isles. Throughout the summer the German Luftwaffe tried to destroy the RAF, in preparation for an invasion, by first attacking coastal shipping and inland targets, and then by focusing all their air power on hitting Fighter Command airfields. They finally turned their attention to London and other cities, with the Blitz on September 5th.

The spring and summer of 1940 was a time when my parents must have felt their world was falling around them, and their level of worry would have

---

* One result of the procurement battles between buying ships and buying planes was the state of the Fleet Air Arm in WW2. Britain entered the war with a number of state-of-the art aircraft carriers, but no modern aircraft with which to equip them. This had dire results for such battles as the Mediterranean and Singapore. The capital ships – battleships and battlecruisers – played a very small part in the war. For the Battle of the Atlantic, small fast destroyers and corvettes were needed to defend the supply-convoys from the enemy submarines. Sending the great Prince of Wales and Repulse to defend Singapore was as good as signing their death warrants, as both mighty ships were sunk within hours of being found by the Japanese naval planes. By the time of the late 1942 Army victory at the Battle of El Alamein, the Royal Navy ships were the victors in the Mediterranean, but at a terrible cost in capital ships. The RN had dominated the Italian Navy, but was nearly annihilated by the Italian and German air forces. By battle's end all the RN's capital ships had been sunk including aircraft carriers, which still had no modern planes. The big ships were sitting targets for torpedoes and bombers.[7]

been dreadful. Father, being a very strong 6 foot 4 inch, 240 lb swimmer and boxer, may have felt less fear, and more anger and disappointment. He had good reason as, not only was he separated from his young family, he was also denied the opportunity to join the military war effort. His business was considered important and he had to remain a civilian in London.

The winter of 1939/40 was described as the coldest in living memory. Mother had to care for her young children with no husband at hand, and a very old and primitive cottage to warm and make habitable. My father remained in London, dealing with his business and attending Ministry of Supply meetings during the day, and then patrolling the streets on fire watch, as a special constable, during the night. Many evenings he never even reached his home lodgings, but instead slept in the cells at his police station. I can imagine the fears during those dark days, with daily news reports of atrocities abroad, of German advances, and the expectation of invasion at any time. They must have questioned how well they would be able to cope and whether their children would survive.

While my parents were suffering such doubts, my sister and brother were going wild with newly discovered freedoms. They had a thousand acre farm of hedgerows, woods, spinneys and farm buildings to explore. They could cycle to the seashore or the riverbank, and in those days there were neither many cars on the roads, nor bad men in the imagination. Both of them, but especially my sister who was there from age ten to thirteen, developed an abiding affection for that green rolling land. Meanwhile I, growing from babe in arms to toddler and eventually a three year old, was also developing my lifelong love for the place, though mine was more mythical whilst theirs was actual, being based on childhood adventures enjoyed through direct exploration and lived experience.

When we had arrived at Mogdangle Aunt Trix had taken my 5-year-old brother into one bedroom while mother had bedded down with 6-month-old me in the bedroom off the landing. It was decided that my 10-year-old sister Jo and 12-year-old Pam would share the third bedroom. Being senior by two years, Pam tried to boss her about but, according to Jo, without success. The toilet was a wooden board over a hole in a shed outside in the garden. There was no bath - just heated-water wash-downs in front of the fire. January and February of 1940 were both records of bitter cold. Snow and ice-hardened rutted mud surrounded the cottage. Mother or Aunt Trix collected water in a bucket from the well, which must have been an interesting endeavor during the big freeze. It was a time when body wash-downs were seldom undertaken. With the thaw the hard earth gave way to deep red boot-sucking mud. Food was scarce, though no doubt Auntie J. at the farm would have been generous with fresh milk, eggs and bacon, and wild rabbits and turnips.

Having survived the hardships of winter, the adults were then faced in the spring, which was sunny and warm, with all those military catastrophes, which fell one after another. Next came the very real threat of invasion by an enemy that the newspapers depicted as ruthless and frightful.

So what was the actual date of my first-steps photo, and how did my parents view the future on that day? The appearance seems to be of springtime. Was it the first sunny and warm day of the year? Was it April or May? Probably my father took the photo. So, was he at the cottage that weekend to reassure my mother following the debacle of Norway or during the Battle of France? Was Dunkirk behind them by then? The light has the freshness of spring so I think it was before the Battle of Britain, which began in the summer. So were the parents discussing how to make contact should the Germans invade? How confident did my mother feel that she would be able to protect her young children? Later, in the late forties as a six or eight-year-old, when I looked at that photo of myself, at 14-16 months, tottering along in the Mogdangle garden, I thought little of it. It was the least interesting to me. My brother, sister and other children up trees, wearing Wellington boots, were more evocative of the time and therefore held more of my imagination. Now, having had my own children and grandchildren, I think of that time and of the circumstances, and wonder why I had never thought to ask the really important questions while my parents were still alive.

We returned to the London suburbs in 1942, only after the Battle of Britain, the threats of a German invasion and the Blitz were well over. However, the reason for our second stay at the farm can again be attributed to Adolf. His plan to demoralize the civilian population by sending V1 flying bombs to London in June, and V2 rockets in August 1944, was working very well. During the nine months of attack, from June 1944 to March 1945, 2419 rockets exploded within the London boundary that killed 8938 and seriously wounded 25,000 civilians. The ram-jet-propelled V1 flying bombs, or 'doodlebugs' as they were soon named, carried a full ton of high explosives, which gave a blast radius of 400-600 yards.[8] They were aimed to fly from the French coast to London on a route that took them directly over Purley. If they fell short, or when they had their wings tipped by the few RAF fighters fast enough to catch them, they sometimes came crashing onto our comfortable south London suburb. The V2 rockets flew so high and fast that the first anyone knew of their arrival was when they exploded. Croydon, the borough directly to the north, and of which Purley was a part, had the highest number of hits of any of the 96 London boroughs. It suffered 145 V1 and V2 explosions. Tiny Coulsdon, a stone's throw to the south, received 54 hits.[9] Apparently Doodlebug Alley was a good name for our part of the world.

Father had bought the house Cobbles in 1942 believing the fortunes of the war had changed and we were safe to return. The outer London suburbs in Surrey appeared safe from any future bombs, and Manor Wood Road was in a desirable neighborhood. The large 4 and 5 bedroom houses with the near acre-sized gardens were good value at a time when very few people were in any position to buy houses. It seemed a good and safe place to move his family. Then, less than two years later, the Purley mothers were fearfully scrambling to keep their families safe from the new and indiscriminate threat.

To us young boys of five or six, however, the putt, putt, putt of a doodlebug on a warm drowsy summer day was very exciting. It was even more thrilling for some of us than watching burnet moths feeding on purple flowers. When you are five there seems no danger. Rather, there is a kind of excitement as we children learned of the latest technologies and war machines, even while we explored our favorite grassy areas.

However the danger was real. One morning, when, for no particular reason that I can remember, my mother and I were standing outside the front door looking over the suburban valley below, a doodlebug flew not 100 yards in front of us. It came from the south, in a shallow dive. In my memory, time slowed for a while as it glided past at a leisurely pace and at eye level. In reality, though, it was probably in sight for only two or three seconds. I had time to note the grey paint and yellow, black and red details, and it was definitely the closest I had ever been to a flying machine. It blew up a house on Woodcrest Road, just one street below us and a few houses to the north. I don't remember seeing the explosion. Probably Mother had grabbed me and hugged me to her. Of course, once again we lost our window glass, roof tiles and much else attached to the house, but we were used to that.

At the time what really, really worried my mother was that my ten-year-old brother Colin was off helping the milkman deliver milk. Helping the milkman really meant that half a dozen children sat on the milk cart and took turns holding the reins while the sleepy old horse plodded along the street and the milkman hurried along all those garden paths carrying full bottles up and empty ones back. What it also could have meant was that my brother was delivering milk to the very house that was now destroyed. My loving mother, who was definitely one of the world's best, was something of a worrier when it came to straying sons and exploding bombs. He was okay of course, but mightily miffed when he got home and realized he'd missed an up close doodlebug crash. She just didn't seem to get the idea that to us a nearby V1 landing was almost the most exciting thing that our wartime boys' brains could imagine.

Mother was also very house proud, and there were many mornings when she and we children would emerge from the garden air-raid shelter to find the house bomb-blasted again. Once it wasn't even a doodlebug, but one of our own anti-aircraft shells that had crashed through the front of the Cramer's house, destroyed eight-year-old John's bed, and exited through the back wall. It finally landed in the garden. Luckily John was in their air-raid shelter at the time. I suppose it is understandable that my mother became a little nervous, as the indiscriminate bomb blasts became very stressful for all the adults.

One night, I remember, we stood at the foot of the oak staircase on the ground floor and looked straight up through fallen ceilings and dislodged roof tiles at the stars above. We never had to move out though, as there were always enough workers to fix things till the next time. A lot of the workers were returned injured soldiers with exciting stories for us kids. One truly amazing fact is that my mother's pride and joy, the French-polished grand piano, came through the war with not one scratch. In the lounge, being a large room, the ceiling fell two or three times, and each time we would find the Bluthner piano covered by fallen plaster ceiling, usually in one piece, while the rest of the room was a chaos of dust and broken plaster. We would re-enter the house from the air raid shelter and Mother would sigh deeply, occasionally say 'bugger', look sheepish and then set to with the clean up. Nowadays people would have hissy-fits at such traumatic experiences.

That German built grand piano may have been made of Cuban mahogany, *Swietenia mahagoni*, which in Victorian times was considered the supreme wood for furniture making. It was called the Wood of Kings[10] and was preferred by such furniture makers as Thomas Chippendale and Thomas Sheraton. By mid-century, it was rare, and by the beginning of the 20th century the only trees left on Cuba were small saplings. Not only had the species been felled by loggers, it also suffered from Amrosia beetle attacks and Pyralid moth infestations. However this story of a species near extinction has something of a silver lining.

Two hundred years ago a Catholic mission was established on the Micronesian Island of Palau. For some reason the missionaries planted a grove of Cuban mahogany plants, plants that over the years flourished, spread and matured. Some Palau families planted other groves, and now the Islanders are ready to begin harvesting the wood of kings in a sustainable way.[11] Whether or not the Caribbean wood will ever again be viable for harvesting on its home island is not known.

A few years after the war was over, we discovered what might have saved the piano from scratches and bomb blast. One Christmas mid-day, after we had all traipsed from the kitchen to the dinning room laden with cooked turkey, gravy and vegetables, and as Mother closed the kitchen door, she heard a softly sighing whoosssh. After Christmas lunch was finished she went to the kitchen and I remember her gently calling out, "Tom could you come here a minute?" We found the kitchen ceiling, which had not fallen during the war, lying flat and complete on the kitchen table, but broken over chair backs and the floor. The plaster ceiling had floated slowly and gently down as a unit, with a big sigh of compressing and slowly escaping air. It must have been loosened by the wartime explosions, and been hanging there for all those years, just waiting to fall. Mother told us about hearing the sighing 'whoosssh', but of thinking little about it. The same must have happened during the war with the lounge ceiling being supported on compressing air as it gently landed on the piano like a blanket. We were all very glad it happened a few minutes after the Christmas dinner had been carried out of the room, and not before. Had that unfortunate Christmas collapse not happened, the mystery of the undamaged wartime piano would probably have been passed down in family lore as a miracle of the Good Lord's bountiful kindness to my mother, and to her adored piano.

But that was a few years into the future. Back in the spring of 1944 Mother was far more worried about our close call with a doodlebug than were her sons. We thought an eye-level, close-up view of a doodlebug in a slow-motion shallow dive was better than an ice cream in a time of rationing. One might think that five-year-old boys in grey shirts, shorts and knee socks should not be so enamored by war. I'm sure that those suffering children on continental Europe, who lived with the awful effects more closely and violently, were certainly not, but we, who saw the newsreels through the lens of childhood, and patriotically on the winning side, were thrilled. We all played the hero. Why, if a plane flew over while we were walking to school, caring ten-year-old big brother would yell 'Heinkel' or 'Focke Wolfe', push me to the ground or below a nearby hedge and lay on me. "Protection from shrapnel," I was told. It takes a long-suffering small brother, of somewhat heroic bent, to put up with that kind of treatment, as not too many bombs ever fell from our own planes. Nevertheless, such adventures did add an excitement to our morning walks, which was somewhat enjoyable.

The war was so much a part of our consciousness that, when brother and I were forced to sleep in the same bed because cousins in need of a home were staying, we would have nightly adventures. These were usually in the RAF, in tanks on the western desert or behind enemy lines.

"Rear-gunner Barry we are going to bomb Berlin tonight."

"Oh good. What time is ETA?"

"Take-off's at seven. We should be over Berlin at midnight."

"Are we airborne yet, Wing Commander?"

"Airborne, rear-gunner Barry. Over and out."

"Right-ho Winco!"

"You didn't say 'over and out."

"Oh! Sorry. Over and out."

"We are nearing the Dutch coast. Keep an eye out for fighters. The Focke Wolves are sure to be out in strength. Over and out."

"Right-ho Winco! Wizard! Over and out. . . . . . There's a fighter on our tail, Winco . . . er sorry. Over and out. . . . . . Bang. Bang. Bang. Bang-bang-bang-bang-bang-bang-bang-bang-bang."

"Did you get him rear-gunner Barry?"

"I got six Winco. . . . . but I don't want to be rear-gunner any more. I want to be a pilot."

"You can't. You're too young".

"I'm not too young. I'm five."

"Oh alright! How would you like to be the navigator?"

These adventures took place nearly every night for a month or two before we slept, and even now I'm quite impressed that my brother had the imagination, and the knowledge of war machines, to keep us both amused for so long. I continue to be grateful to him for the great number of times he was able to save my life, usually with astonishing bravery on his part and against overwhelming odds, from very dangerous situations that he and his fertile imagination had put me in the first place.

Wartime play. Cobbles garden. About 1945.

During the day, as my friends and I played, we would also try to demoralize Adolf and his henchmen by singing disdainful, and rude songs. One well-known song, sung in loud voices to the tune of Colonel Bogie, was

"Hitler has only got one ball,
Göring has two but very small,
Himmler is very similar,
But poor old Göbbels has no balls at all. Tiddily-um pom, pom."

There are some who might observe that small children shouldn't sing such lewd songs. Still, the allies won, didn't we? And Adolf shot himself. Being considered testicularly challenged by the children of his enemies couldn't have done much for his sense of self-worth.

Another darker and, from a post-war perspective, no longer amusing song was sung to the tune of 'Twinkle, Twinkle Little Star'. It was sung when the fortunes of war had shifted. The Blitz and destruction of British cities was ended, and the allies had begun to deliver Germany some of the cruel bombing that Hitler had earlier been only too happy to send our way.

It went as follows:

"Twinkle, twinkle little bomb,
How I wonder where you're from.
Up above the Earth so high,
A hundred Lancasters in the sky.
Twinkle, twinkle little bomb,
How I wonder where you're from."

One interesting fact about the war's end was the speed with which the warm wartime neighbourliness and camaraderie dissipated. It is hard to explain, but it seems that once the common enemy was defeated we all became more self-sufficient and very much less friendly.

A few years after the war was over, when my friends and I had grown sufficiently to wander further, we happened upon what was surely the bombsite of the doodlebug crash. I didn't make the connection at the time. There wasn't much more remaining of the house than the foundations, but what amazed me was the wonderful garden. It may have remained untended since that unhappy crash, or possibly a grieving husband on his return had tended it in memory of a dead family. I don't know. What we could see though, were the most exotic and radiant perennial flowers. Brilliant scarlet poppies, yellow iris, giant blue delphiniums, and others I can't name. Some were flowers we had never seen before even in our own fathers' most magnificent gardens. I never asked who had lived there, or whether they had been at home or away at the time of the hit. Maybe I was too young to care. But I do remember that the three of us crept from that garden with a feeling that it was too sacred to play in, and that we did not belong.

2c Reminiscences: *The Farm*

The farmhouse, mid 1950s.

So, with doodlebugs offering a fearsome threat, my parents agreed that my mother would take the three of us kids, by train, back to Somerset and the farm. This time we stayed in the wonderful old farmhouse as guests of the family. If the first visit, when I was a baby and toddler, created a myth in my imagination that second stay established my love for the farm and countryside as a firm reality.

Returning again and spending months in the countryside that I loved was my idea of the perfect life in a perfect world. Some children may not like the smells, but to me the fragrance of hay, molasses, stables and silage were wonderful and evocative of my kind of paradise. Even the farmhouse had its own unforgettable aromas of ancient stone floors and clotted cream. Maybe I would see a pink-breasted Bullfinch, or maybe an ochre Hawfinch. My sister had seen those birds during our earlier stay at Mogdangle, so maybe I would. Even at 5 years old such species were icons to my hopeful mind, and not seeing such wonders of nature were dreams unfulfilled. My nostalgia for the life of the farm, the buildings and the smells, haunted me for years after.

Farms were different then than now, and that farm was a perfect small boy's adventure land. It was a mixed farm. There were milking cows, a few beef cattle, sheep, pigs and chickens. The cows were black and white Friesians, brown and roan-grey Shorthorns and my favourites, the Ayrshires, which were beautiful, gentle animals of red-brown and white.

41

The one or two bulls of that breed were huge and vicious. Some fields might be sown with oats, others with wheat, and some must have grown mangolds. In later years, I spent many contented mornings delivering those vegetables by horse-drawn cart to the cows in the raw Easter fields. The loveliest were the early summer hay meadows, and the deep green, milk cow grazing, hilly summer pastures.

No matter how old the buildings, whether three hundred years or the 1920s-built milking sheds, they all had corners and activities to keep me engrossed for hours on end. In the 1940s the stables still held three or four magnificent shire horses with feathered hooves larger than a child could believe. Hanging on stable doors and walls were harnesses that possibly went back to Victorian times. The many barns of assorted ages were filled with pre-war tractors, old and new pieces of equipment or mounds of hay. The old Georgian Chapel, though short lived as a place of worship, now housed baby calves to be milk-fed by hand. And the pigsties still grunted with Gloucester Old-spots and Large White sows. Under the eaves, Barn Swallows nested, as they still do, and Yellow Wagtails could be found on the banks of the many watering ponds. Everywhere was the opportunity to work or play, or explore and learn.

Every open space and each corner of the four or five acre farmyard was perfumed and delicious. Whether open stockyards, enclosing an ever-angry bull and twenty cows, or enclosed barns stacked with feed or bedding, the air was scented with reminders of past visits. Each building had its own odor, or to me scent, of old hay or straw, of the feed for cattle or calves, or of the oils of the nineteen thirties equipment. In each building the air was lightly dust-filled and that dust was fragranced with barley or oats, with molasses or the sweet smell of cattle and fresh milk. The myriad of other evocative and unforgettable aromas were too subtle to identify. Just to stand in the centre of the yard one was blessed with that lovely and redolent air. The smells were as memorable as the sights.

There were the stables, the milking sheds and the barns, all significant structures to be sure. The walled gardens were a delight. But it was the disused workshops, and little used passageways tucked away behind walls and secret doors that were, for me, the best places of all. How they came to be, made little sense. Possibly, whoever first built the place included those rooms for a specific purpose, but soon found the initial use had been eclipsed, and simply closed the door on them. Or maybe they had held an important function for centuries until a new building was constructed and the old room was simply forgotten. Whatever their history, to me they were places of wonder and mystery. Sometimes they held cider presses and other equipment that had only gone out of use in my time. But often they were filled with old, old tools and objects that had not been used in living memory. It felt as though no adult had entered for years beyond imagining. Thinking back, I realize that the farmyard complex was so vast that when a room or piece of equipment was no longer used, the door was closed and it just waited there, who knows for how many years, till someone could find the time or the interest to clean the place out.

On a recent visit, I found that some of those lost and secret places were still unchanged and were as I remembered them from some sixty years before. The swallows were still nesting on the farmhouse walls, and the wagtails still flicked on the meadows beside the ponds.

Oh I did love being at that farm. The endless repetition of evening milking and morning milking; the horse-drawn carts and the tractors heading off to feed cattle or work a field somewhere; the smells of milk, of animals and of hay. I was always busy helping with whatever task was offered. One great delight was helping feed the new calves by putting my hand in a pail of warm milk and having the calf suck on my fingers, another was measuring and delivering the feed for the milking cows. But I also had plenty of time for play and discovery - time to visit hay-filled mangers where cats had recently birthed kittens, or to wander along the hedgerows searching for birds and wildflowers. Possibly the greatest delight was when we all gathered at the big dining room table for the daily ritual of high tea. What an excess of wonderful country food: a large bowl of thick clotted cream to be eaten with strawberry jam or fresh honeycomb on thick slices of white bread, or a plate of thin slices of buttered bread for strawberry jam without clotted cream. To be at that farm was a confirmation that all was well, that the country life had attained a perfect balance and that I was there, a part of those wonders.

Of course the balance wasn't truly perfect. I was seeing farm life partly blinkered, not with my eyes wide open. What were the pigs being fattened for? And what about market day? At first, I was too young to understand that farms are enterprises to produce food for the people and profits for the farmers. I was also unaware of the farmer's dislike of many things natural: of rabbits and foxes, of badgers or raptors, of anything in fact that could cut into the profits of the farm.

As much as I loved the farm my mystic imagination was still, and always, set in that first unremembered experience of the place before I was three. I must have been quite a trial to my mother at times during the early post-war years back in Purley. Whenever we had guests for lunch, I would always insist on stories: "Mum, tell us about Mogdangle and the times we had there," and my long-suffering mother would trot out the old tales. Tales of how she was chased by a great boar when crossing a field; of how, when passing the graveyard one moonless night, a man approached and Aunt Trix, grabbing the umbrella, threatened him while she stood behind my quaking mother. Then she would speak of my beautiful sister, ten years older than I and adored by all who knew her, who used to play jokes on Dad on his occasional visits. She would talk of the apple pie beds and tricks when he was trying to catch a Sunday afternoon nap on the hay in the barn, or of how, when my seven year old brother was learning to ride, the pony bolted and they were both missing for about half an hour. The pony finally trotted home with my brother still in the saddle and grinning happily. Then speaking again of my brother, she would tell of the time he went across the field to watch the hunt ride by, and after some time my mother saw him running home blowing his toy hunting horn for all it was worth. It turned out he needed the toilet really, really badly.

But those were family memories of Mogdangle circa 1939-41. I was too young to remember much myself, and had only one or two memories of those years. One was a Christmas Day, standing on the landing outside a bedroom as mother told my brother to keep an eye on me. In 2002 we spent a night in a luxuriously remodeled Mogdangle, and I recognized that landing quite as it was in my memory. It was the first time I had seen it since I was two or three years old and the first time I had been in the house since that time.

I was a pathetic slave to nostalgia from a very young age. For instance, I remember hearing the song *The last time I saw Paris*, when I was about 5, and it almost broke my heart listening to those words that I had heard before. Even at such a young age I was somehow affected by the conquest of a city, and the fusion of words and melody, which suggested such a profound sadness.

So, as I have said, during the post-war years in Purley I would walk to school in a melancholy state of nostalgic yearning of such intensity that I would feel quite sick. I simply longed to be back in the countryside, and my heart would ache to be at the farm. It was an early experience of homesickness I suppose. But in Purley I was at home, I was home with my family and friends so my craving was for something deeper than my loving and wonderful home life.

Now I suspect that homesickness comes out of a separation from one's spiritual base, a base that may be different and very personal to each of us. For a toddler it is probably a yearning for mother, but for a ski enthusiast it may be for Whistler's mountain snows. For the academic the yearning may be for the university halls, and for an old hippie it's probably for 1970. For me it was undoubtedly that farm and countryside of the early nineteen forties. Many individuals are strengthened by an inner resilience, but some, it seems, have to rely on external places, people or experience to feel whole.

Fortunately my parents understood my needs, and for a number of post-war Easter or summer holidays I would go back and stay as a guest of the family. In the later years, at the age of thirteen or fourteen, Uncle F., as I called the farmer, would find me real men's tasks to perform beyond just feeding calves and cleaning the cow sheds. Sometimes he would put me in charge of a tractor and harrow, and send me off to this or that field for a day. What could be better than being alone in a field, in control of a piece of farm equipment - an old Alice Chalmers tractor maybe - and with an adult job to do. I would stay rolling or harrowing till the work was done, then drive back to the farm feeling like a valued member of the farm workforce.

Uncle F. was a traditional Somerset farmer, but as business smart as it's possible to be. If he lived now in different circumstances he would probably be a multi-millionaire industrialist. Michael and Ann, his children, went to the best schools England had to offer. Michael left school with an incredible sheaf of successes in advanced exams in such subjects as Greek, Latin, math and physics, ten subjects in all I remember, most of which were passed with distinctions. He also went home with a deep love of cricket. He could have gone on to Oxford or Cambridge but chose instead to return to the farm.

One of my favourite tasks was hedging. We would walk to some distant field where Uncle would gesture toward a long hedgerow and say "Can 'ee re-lay that 'un. I'll be moving szzheep in come zzummer so mack un zztrong."

I could spend as many days as I chose remodeling overgrown hedges with a billhook. A shallow cut into the vertical growth, the bending and laying of young saplings and the resulting thigh-high horizontal weave. That weave would become a thick new hedge come summer. The new shoots grew thickly from the lain saplings. Nature knew how to make an impenetrable barrier from such a start. Ten years or more later, the process might need repeating after the light had stretched the hedge skyward.

I don't know how old those Somerset hedges were. Possibly they had been planted in the 18th century, at the time of the enclosure of communal grazing land, or maybe many centuries before. Most hedges were planted with a plant of choice to the region, hawthorn or elm for instance, and it is said that we can establish the age of a hedge by the number of different tree species that have since become established. I didn't know about any of that then so didn't check on how many different trees and shrubs grew there. Since those days, a whole lot of research has gone into every aspect of the natural world, and we now have so much more knowledge than we had then.

When I left England in 1969 there were estimated to be 600,000 miles (964,000kms) of hedges still in use even though, since 1945, over 110,000 miles had been torn up.[1] Those still growing were enough miles of hedges to go around the circumference of the earth 24 times. In the early 1960s it had been estimated that hedgerows constituted a land mass of double all the nation's nature reserves: half a million acres. Hedgerows were fundamental to the countryside of England. They not only kept animals fenced and cut the wind, which protected against soil erosion, they were also the principle means of protecting Britain's wildlife. Wildflowers and plants of all sorts grew there; insects, butterflies, birds and mammals could find sanctuary and food in a hedge, as well as nesting opportunities. They offered protected pathways for deer and other species, that were uncomfortable in open spaces, when moving from one piece of woodland, or other habitat, to another.

So, billhook in hand, experiencing a cold eastern wind or bright Easter sunshine, my days were filled with returning nature's exuberance to a farmer's need for functional order. It was perfect preparation for a future sculptor - a creator, though, of ordered steel forms not of exultant natural growth. I was truly fortunate. They were such happy days - days of so much contentment.

The downside to hedging is that it is labour intensive. That wasn't so bad before the war when large farms employed maybe a dozen workers. But after the war and the new higher wages that were introduced, economics determined hedge maintenance to be an expensive business. Now hedges are pruned by large, lawn-mower-type machines held aloft by tractors. They trim the tops and sides of the year's natural growth and leave very

46

neat looking structures instead of the tangled growth of old. Yet these new hedges become more filled with wood chips with each passing year. This hedge trimming is often done in high summer when the songbirds are nesting. The effects on the bird numbers have not been agreed, though it doesn't take a PhD in the natural sciences to imagine the results. Most hedging used to be done in late winter before the new growth had come in too heavily, and also before the birds had begun nesting. It was a tried and true country process with few flaws and many benefits to nature.

Since labour costs are the problem with using the old methods, and since so much industry has failed in the UK leaving a great many without work, I think someone should explore giving the unemployed the opportunity to earn their benefits, or dole-money with a bit of good healthy hedge-laying. They might even like it as much as I did. They would certainly get more exercise than watching TV, and would have the added benefit of gaining a new and handy skill with which to advance, smartphone in hand, into the twenty-first century.

During our second stay at the farm in 1944, my 15-year-old sister, Jo, lodged at a nearby farm and spent many days riding and caring for a fine thoroughbred mare named Vanity. There she also met James, a schoolboy from Epsom College, who was doing farm work during his school vacation. Within a year, at the age of seventeen, he had earned his lieutenant's pips and was an officer in the Indian Army. He was stationed on the North West Frontier. That frontier is now the border between Pakistan and Afghanistan. When he returned to England following India's independence in 1947, he and Jo met again as he motorcycled past the farm at just the time when she was visiting and leading Vanity along a lane. Thus began a somewhat high-powered courtship of my lovely sister, which she enthusiastically encouraged. Father told Jo she had to wait till she was twenty-one before he would give his consent. So at a large formal dinner dance they celebrated both her 21st birthday and their engagement. They married a few months later in June 1951.

My overly romantic childhood view of farming had to do with more than just the farm. I think it also pertained to the apparent timelessness of the fields, hedgerows and some of the buildings of the British countryside. Many fields and hedgerows can be traced back to Saxon times, more than a thousand years ago, and there is at least one Saxon barn still standing and in use. The natural environment has been changed over a very long expanse of time. That change started some 4000 years before the Roman occupation, which began two thousand years ago. The wild animal numbers in Britain had been gradually falling for centuries before that. In the 13th century 30 per cent of England was covered with oak forests, but the last of those were felled to build the ships of the Royal Navy in the seventeenth and eighteenth centuries. The use of pesticides was possibly the final destructive influence. This very long-term debasement from an ancient wilderness to the British landscape we now know, and call picturesque, has been accepted as the norm. In other places, Bali for instance, the shift from naturally forested hills to the beautifully terraced rice paddies, with their form-adding palm trees, was also engineered over many, many centuries. This long-term change has a different emotional effect on us, or certainly on me, than that of witnessing richly bio-diverse areas of wilderness changed to agriculture, industry or human habitation almost, it seems, overnight. Now, all over the world, huge tracts of ancient land, of million-year-old forests or of grasslands, fall to the chainsaw and plough in mere weeks or months. We are all acutely aware of the destruction, long before we are able to imagine what the resulting advantages of this mayhem might be. Today, few mourn the passing of the prehistoric British or Balinese forests, but we do lament, with outrage, the cutting and bulldozing of great expanses of the Amazon or Asian forests that were virtually untouched 60 or 40 years ago.

Changes have happened to some degree or another wherever humans settled. But some societies, the natives of Borneo or New Guinea or the First Nations people of North America, for instance, had always had an infinitesimal effect on the environment they called home. Many very fine cultures developed among people who lived for millennia on their land or in their forests usually respecting the habitat around them. Those cultures, with their primitive tools, made little change to the larger natural ecosystems. Consider the indigenous people of Sarawak who lived until 20 or 30 years ago in their riverside longhouses or as nomads in the forest. Those people were never poor, as they were rich in all they needed. They obtained all their wants from the forest or river, yet never destroyed any part of their home ecosystem save a few plots of cultivated vegetables. Their Borneo forest is reckoned to be an astounding 130 million years old. In a forest of that age, a great many new plant and animal species evolve and become established over time. Borneo now, after all those millions of years, boasts 3000 species of trees, which is 2,300 more endemic species than in all of North America.[2] Yet, starting in about 1980, the Malaysian government has cut the whole of Sarawak's forest down save a few small parks.[3]

When a forest exists for 130 million years all the accumulated fallen vegetable matter reaches incredible depths. In Borneo's case that material is now peat. The abuse on Borneo has been so appalling that that peat is now burning underground with no chance of being put out. It took 130 million years to make, but we destroy it, and cause it to burn, with barely a thought.

The first immigrants to North America, the French and British settlers of the 17th century, would have felled some forest as they relied on wood for building, heating and cooking, but it's unlikely that a few thousand Europeans with hand axes could have done more than tickle the vast eastern mixed deciduous forests at first. The giant maple, oak, sycamore and cherry trees were safe. But that changed in the 19th century when industrialized felling took hold. At the same time, the British began felling the Ganges watershed forests in India, and the forests on both continents started falling very quickly. Since then, accelerating destruction has gathered momentum all over the world. Now the escalation is horrendous in its efficiency. Land, that had been a rich tangle of uncounted plant and animal species, is, in no time, cleared and planted with agricultural crops, other mono-crops, or with exotic fast-growing trees imported from other continents entirely. The grasslands have been ploughed and planted with wheat, with sunflowers or with whatever. Wetlands and marshes have been drained or converted to rice. Heath land and other apparently non-productive land has been built over, and everywhere the wildlife has been exterminated. We have seen the engulfing of great swathes of the Florida Everglades with tarmac and air-conditioned housing, and now nearly every wild place in the world is no longer wild. How can they be when we build roads into any wilderness place we choose? With all this building and road-laying huge numbers of animals, plants and insects are destroyed – some that have never even been identified.

With this destruction continuing daily, some of us are at first overjoyed when we find an area of wilderness unchanged by plough or bulldozer. Instead we find it left in the natural state for the grazing of cattle. Pretty benign we think. The prairie and open woodland are still there, and what's more, the ranchers are fattening cattle for our consumption. Granted, the land may be so poor that only a few cattle can be run on each hundred acres, but the land is at least still natural. The cattle may be eating all the lower vegetation, and preventing new trees from becoming established, but it still looks pretty good. Then we find that the cattlemen insist that every natural predator whether cougar, wolf, bear or eagle must be exterminated to protect the cattle and calves from predation. Are those ranchers willing to share the land with the animals that have lived there for millennia in order that a balance might be retained? Not on your life. To most ranchers it seems that anything that is wild is vermin and should be shot. If you can eat it, it becomes game; in which case it should still be shot.

Predominantly though, and continually, the forests fall. They fall in Asia, Africa and South America, on the Pacific Northwest of North America and up in the Boreal zone around the Arctic Circle - in fact on every continent. The trees of the Canadian Boreal, to which so many birds migrate from tropical America, are felled to make toilet paper of all things. What an irony! Now, in the 21st century, the speed with which we can fell forests, move mountains using heavy industrial equipment, or adapt the environments to our desires, gives wild species, whether plant or animal, no chance to adapt, to flee or to survive.

As mentioned, historical time enabled us to think of farming in Europe and parts of Asia as a long-established and almost natural process. We could focus on its historical significance and on its productive advantage. It is not easy to picture some parts of our globe as they were two or three thousand years ago before humans changed so much of the natural into agricultural. But when now we witness, in other countries, huge areas of pristine natural habitat being turned to plantations or to agriculture in such a very short time it becomes easier to focus on the destruction than to feel sympathy for the new productivity coming on line. We wonder where the wildlife can go, and how we can ensure the survival of the myriad tree, plant, insect and animal species that lived on the lush land so recently. Now, much is bulldozed or put under the plough before any of the life forms living there are even known to us. And it is done with such disdain and disrespect that we should all be ashamed. We ask why we *homo sapiens sapiens*, the doubly-wise ones, can't show a little wisdom, indicate some concern for the future, plan for something other than our bank accounts, and leave at least 50 per cent of the wild places untouched and pristine for the sake of the future, of our descendants, and of our Earth. It has been calculated that 75 per cent of the Earth's ice-free surface has now been shaped, not by natural forces, but by us humans.

Now, when I think of farming, I am far more ambivalent than I was as a youngster. It is necessary to feed us I will admit, and some farmland is still better than the city, but the terrible destruction wrought in development's name cannot be denied. With the human population still increasing and potentially doubling by century's end, what will ever stop the destruction from continuing till there is nothing natural left to destroy?

3 Farming and the Natural World

Migrating Swainson's Hawks

When we hear of farmers in some foreign land ploughing up a patch of grassland, planting corn or sunflowers and thereby feeding their children, we think it relatively harmless and feel sympathetic to the family. "At least they are not chopping down the forest," we might think, "Natural grasslands or fields of sunflowers and vegetables? . . . grassland or sunflowers? . . . not too much difference really." Unfortunately, the difference can be huge and can have far reaching effects on the natural world thousands of miles away.

During the summer months north of the equator, small slim hawks named Swainson's Hawk _(Buteo swainsoni)_ may be seen flying over the North American land that used to be prairie but is now farmland. They spend a lot of time walking on the ground hunting for small mammals and large insects. They had been in decline since the early 1960s, but no one knew why. Though solitary by nature, these birds gather each fall in large flocks and fly south to some destination until recently unknown. If we look at an illustration of their now known migration, we see a large balloon representing their numbers spread over North America, flowing and narrowing down through Mexico to a thin line over Central America. It broadens just a little as they fly over the Amazon and Bolivia, eventually to settle in a fairly small area of central Argentina. That is a journey of some 7,500 miles (12,000kms).

The hawks are named after William Swainson, a well-known naturalist and classifier of wildlife who was very prominent in London's intelligentsia during the first half of the nineteenth century. He and his family were in the same circle as the aforementioned Peter Mark Roget and his family.

In 1994, the American Brian Woodbridge tracked this line of migrating hawks to discover where they spent the winter. He had attached a radio transmitter to one bird as well as a number of leg bands to others. Eventually, he and two assistants arrived a few weeks after the birds at an area of the Argentine pampas, where the hawks have wintered for millennia but which was now largely agricultural. It seems that that region is particularly rich in grasshoppers, which is the birds' main winter food. Bridget Stutchbury's excellent 2007 book, *Silence of the Songbirds*, describes at length what Brian Woodbridge and his colleagues found as they arrived by car at part of the birds' winter grounds, and it wasn't pretty. They came upon thousands of carcasses of dead Swainson's Hawks strewn across the road, fields and nearby woods. They found seven hundred bodies without even searching the sunflower fields, and estimated over three thousand dead in their area alone.[1]

The Americans learned that the deaths had occurred the day after the sunflower fields had been sprayed with monocrotophos, a highly toxic pesticide used to kill grasshoppers. It is probable that after the spraying the grasshoppers became sick and slow, making them easy prey for the hawks. The hawks gorged on the bountiful insects, were poisoned in turn and died later that day. The rancher said that many of the local farmers used the same pesticide as a defense against grasshoppers. It was pure chance that the researchers had arrived at that specific ranch at that time and discovered what was happening to the birds when they went south. The next year Brian Woodbridge returned to Argentina prepared for a dead bird count and estimated the deaths that year at over 20,000 Swainson's Hawks. The discovery of those killings led to conservation efforts and agreements by the governments of the USA, Canada and Argentina, the ranchers and the insecticide producers. This in turn led to the banning of monocrotophos in Argentina.

There are many lessons to be learned from this awful story, but one is particularly pertinent. Farmers who come across a nice piece of virgin grassland to plough, or ranchers who decide to sow a specific crop on their rangeland won't be deterred by a few too many grasshoppers. They won't stop to wonder if those grasshoppers might be part of a natural cycle on which the survival of other species depends. Instead, they will probably add the spraying of pesticides to their cost estimates and proceed as planned. The millennia old cycle of flocks of beautiful birds flying twelve thousand kilometers to and from that area, precisely because of the grasshoppers, would never be considered for one moment.

Similar stories but of different insects and birds must be common in many parts of the world. The trouble is we don't know of it. A marshland here, a patch of shrub there, a mangrove-lined coast somewhere else may on first glance seem quite unimportant habitats and perfect for development into something else. They may, however, be crucial links in some natural chain of which we are quite unaware. Who knows how often and in how many countries the residents have noted that such and such a bird is no longer seen each spring, or how few of a certain animal they now encounter? And who would realize that the disappearance results from the simple act of someone thousands of miles away ploughing the land or crop-spraying the pests?

It is also interesting to note that not only did Mother Nature make plentiful grasshoppers, she also produced a very efficient bird species in the Swainson's Hawk. That raptor evolved to arrive and to eat the grasshoppers of North and South America at precisely the time when the grasshoppers are most plentiful. Once we kill off the insects with pesticides, we are likely to starve to death the one bird capable of controlling their numbers. We thereby open up the opportunity for the insects to rebound and swarm again with nothing but our pesticides to use in defense.

Mother Nature also created another bird that was plentiful and that ate the grasshopper grubs before they matured. However that was the Eskimo Curlew, (of which more later) and we have already rendered that bird extinct.

There are some encouraging signs to this sad story. One is in the very fact that America and Canada were willing to send government officials to Argentina to discuss threats to a bird species; a second is that the Argentine government was concerned enough to enact measures to protect that species. Things in some countries do improve slowly and incrementally. If we go back 150 years though, we come upon acts that are unbelievable, horrible and unforgivable.

The Great Plains of North American

The breadbasket of the USA was, less than 130 years ago, a vast prairie grassland of 1.4 million square miles (2.8 million km2.) It stretched from southern Alberta and Saskatchewan in Canada south to northern Mexico, and from the Mississippi in the east to the Rockies in the west. That was an area close to two fifths of the total United States land mass. When Lewis and Clark traversed it in 1804-06, it took them days to ride through vast herds of bison, Pronghorn Antelope, elk and deer that stretched as far as the eye could see. They estimated some buffalo herds to be three million animals strong.[2] The animals quietly grazed as the men rode through the herds, ignoring them most of the time, but occasionally looking up without fear. The security in the vast numbers seems to have created a calm in the bison that even the wolf packs and many Grizzly Bears couldn't disturb. There were blue-grey Sandhill Cranes, turkeys, and grouse, and billions of smaller birds filling the air with song. Pure white Whooping Cranes, with their scarlet heads at the height of the packhorses' saddles, rested on those grasslands during their migrations between the Gulf States and Canada. The prairie was rich in wild flowers, brilliant butterflies, moths and grasshoppers and was abundant in an estimated 5 billion Richardson's Ground Squirrels also known as prairie dogs. These prairie dogs, which are actually rodents, lived in huge underground communities called prairie dog towns, one of which, in Texas, measured 250 by 100 miles. The prairie was a truly beautiful land - a paradise in fact. It was also the home of such First Nations people as the Sioux, the Blackfoot, the Cheyenne, the Cree and the Comanche. They had lived on the land, and at peace with the land, for thousands of years. They had a ready supply of excellent meat right there. Paradise!

It then became US Government policy to rid the prairies of: first the Native Americans and then the wildlife as a means of starving the natives off the land. So the aboriginal Americans were killed, or moved to small reservations, while the colonizing Euro-Americans were given carte blanche to destroy the ecological integrity of the land. In a few short years the prairies went from pure virgin wilderness to an exploited land.

Between 1850 and 1880 seventy-five million buffalo hides were traded through New York. It is believed that 35 million antelope were slaughtered, along with countless elk and deer. There are photos of unbelievably gigantic mounds of buffalo bones, in preparation for shipping to some rendering plant somewhere. We are talking of millions of animals. Not 75 thousand buffalo but 75 million buffalo. We are also talking of multi millions of the other animals too.[3] The 75 million skins were traded over a period of thirty years, so the calculation is that the bison herds amounted to about 65 million prior to the hunt. It is worth comparing this number with the wild herds of Africa. The famous Wildebeest migration through the Serengeti in Tanzania and south Kenya is considered one of the wildlife wonders of the world. Yet that famous herd is thought to contain only about 2 million animals. The North American bison were reckoned to be 65 million in number.

The bison skins were collected by first shooting as many animals in a day that a man could. He then secured each dead animal to the ground by a peg through the nose. Finally, by using a horse harnessed to a rope and hooks, the hides were pulled from the animals. My great-grandfather was born before this mass slaughter had begun, and my grandfather's birth was during the tail end. So it wasn't really so very long ago in generational terms.

By 1890, of the original 65 million bison, only 50 individual animals remained alive in the US, and 250 in Canada.[4] So 300 lived but 64,999,700 had been killed.

The Great Plains Lobo Wolf was rendered extinct in 1926 and by 1970 eight other North American wolf subspecies were also extinct. The social and well-organized prairie dog has been reduced to just 1 per cent of the estimated billions that once played on the grassland, and is now listed as threatened. The Heath Hen became extinct in 1932,[5] while the Prairie Chickens, Sage Grouse and many others including the great 5-foot-tall Whooping Cranes, are now all close to extinction. By 1941 the Whooping Crane, which summers north of the prairies was reduced to 11 birds worldwide. Probably flying across and stopping on their way over the US Midwest was their undoing. Still, in this new age of enlightenment, the numbers are now up to about 400 due to heroic efforts by a few concerned environmentalists. Most prairie birds, such as the Chestnut-collared Longspur, Sprague's Pipit, Baird's Sparrow and Burrowing Owl, are in a steep decline and have not been seen in many of their traditional areas for years now.[6]

Of course most of that wild prairie is now productive agricultural land that helps to give us our lives of excess and overabundance. When flying over it, one looks down on a quilt of perfect squares and irrigation circles that leave no room for any natural land. Still one has to ask, "With less than 2 per cent remaining somewhat close to its original state, would it not have been possible to have preserved 50 per cent, 30 per cent even 10 per cent of that prairie grassland? Could the carnivores amongst us not have eaten buffalo just as well as steer meat?" Buffalo meat is considered superior to steer meat. The buffalo were perfectly adapted to the prairie, and if we had saved at least a small part of the land intact we could have retained the complete prairie ecosystem of grasses, flowers, insects, butterflies, birds and mammals. Such a healthy environment would have continued on into the future and been an inspiration to us all. Now little of the natural prairie remains and nearly all grassland species whether mammals, birds, insects or plants are suffering depletion in the few numbers remaining. The North American large native animals that survive in any quantity, are found mostly in the Pacific Northwest, far northern Canada and Alaska. One problem with all this is that it sets a terrible example to the rest of the world, Africa, Amazonia, and Borneo included. One lesson is: if you want to become a wealthy nation, kill off all your wildlife and plough up all your grasslands.

Eskimo Curlew

Many factors caused a species to become a victim of extinction. A surprising one seems to have been a combination of super abundance, a lack of the fear-and-flight response and a tendency to stick together. This meant that once a species was found to be a good food supply, or to offer some other useful material, the abundance made it worth turning the small-time collecting into a large industry. To feed that large industry the workers simply used up all they could till the last bird or animal was gone. This applied, not just to the Passenger Pigeon and the Great Auk but to the Eskimo Curlew as well.

The Eskimo Curlew *(Numenius borealis)* seems to have been one of those species that became an accepted food source in North America. It is probable that the early prairie settlers needed any game food they could find for the few years it took for their land to become productive. If multi-million-strong flocks of tasty birds popped by regularly once a year, who can blame the families of malnourished farmers for bagging all they could.

They were small birds of maybe 12 inches (30cm) in length. They migrated from the Arctic Circle in Canada down the Atlantic seaboard to Argentina and Chile in the extreme south of South America. Then in the spring they flew back again, but followed a different route through the prairie states and provinces.[7] It is possible that the whole population flew in one or two gigantic flocks. They took the routes they did, to take advantage of the specific foods available on the way. Along the coasts of Nova Scotia and Newfoundland they fed on estuarine snails. On the way north they traveled inland, and it is known that they arrived in Nebraska in time to feed on the larvae of the Rocky Mountain Grasshopper, and on cutworms – the caterpillars of such moths as the Yellow Underwing. It was there that they suffered the greatest persecution from farmers and hunters, who lay in wait with wagons to be filled with dead curlews. So once the prairies were settled the birds were doomed, even though the live birds were the farmer's best friends. In 1900, one Paul Hoagland and his father came across 70 birds and shot 34. Then when he saw 8 birds in 1911 he shot 7 of them. Up until the 1960s the occasional birds were seen with 20 being shot for collections. The last was killed in Barbados in 1964.

The original many millions of birds would surely have gone a long way to keep the insect pests, the grasshoppers and cutworms, in check. Once the curlews were gone the pests were able to multiply wonderfully. Now the farmers only have the destructive insecticides and pesticides to use, which they do with enthusiasm, killing a whole host of other species in the process.

To those who see no point to concerns about wildlife extinctions, I think the Eskimo Curlew and the Swainson's Hawk offer clear pictures of what can be lost and the negative consequences that result. Cutworms, which spend time below ground eating the roots of plants - and grasshoppers and locusts, which spend their mature months on plants, eating their leaves - are well known enemies of the farmer. That being understood, one would expect farmers to be delighted to have flocks of birds come by each spring to eat the larvae, and another flock to eat the adults of their greatest enemies. The curlews and the hawks visited both the US prairies and the Argentine pampas, which were both rich in grasshoppers and cutworms. The larger the flocks of birds, the more bugs would be consumed, and the more healthy and bigger the eventual crop for the farmer to harvest. Certainly the birds would leave some bugs to feed and breed. But surely the farmers would be saved a good part of the expense of insecticides, which, after nature's predators had been exterminated, are now the lone defense against the marauding insects. It is interesting that the North American farmers exterminated the curlews through systematic persecution and ignorance, while the Argentinean farmers nearly did for the hawks through accidental mismanagement and ignorance.

It seems to me that it is a miracle that two bird species developed enough knowledge of the world to enable them to visit two good areas for food that are eight thousand miles apart. It is wondrous that they each consumed a plentiful pest, the locust, at different stages of the insect's development so they were not in competition for the same food. It is fantastic that they were able to find and learn routes - a different one in each direction - that supplied them with food for the long journey. It is awe-inspiring that they were able to fly such vast distances and not get lost or lose the will to continue. It is utterly shaming that the best we could do was kill them when they reached their destinations.

Were I not who I am, but instead a person of different beliefs, I might be inclined to believe that Mother Nature had a plan. The plan might have been that, when locusts live and multiply on grasslands 8,000 miles apart, She would introduce two bird species, one to eat the grubs and one to eat the adult insects. She would make birds that were smart enough to know where the bugs lived and strong enough to fly to those places. The birds would keep the bug numbers down and when the numbers did grow too large the birds would breed more young to help curb those pesky pests.

Assuming that we don't believe in a Mother Nature who makes plans, another reality might be that many thousands of years ago, during their peregrinations questing for food, the birds drifted south or north, ahead of the inclement weather, until they came upon the grassland insects that answered their needs. Then, as the summers ended, they headed back again following a food supply that just happened to take them over different country. It must have taken eons to find good routes, routes that each generation of young would learn from the experienced adults and, in turn, teach to their young. The routes became so well learned, and so deeply ingrained in the tiny brains of these wondrous birds, that over time they and the bugs would come to depend on each other: one to be the food, and the other to prevent the bug population from over breeding, exploding and collapsing. Perfect harmony; and then along we come. We shoot the birds and now we poison the bugs that in turn kill other hungry birds. And we turn two natural paradises into poisoned lands nearly free of nature – free that is but for the pesky and resilient bugs.

Passenger Pigeon

There were untold billions of Passenger Pigeons. Alexander Wilson studied them in 1806 and estimated that in one flock alone there were 2,230,272,000 birds. In 1813 James Audubon witnessed uncountable numbers of birds flying for 3 continuous days in such a thick mass that they turned the day into night. As flight after flight flew over at 60 miles per hour, he estimated that just one flight contained 1,015,036,000 birds. The birds flew wing tip to wing tip, in layers one above the other, in flocks one of which was estimated to be a mile wide and 320 miles long. Apparently they frequented all of forested North America from Hudson Bay in the north to the Gulf of Mexico in the south. They are considered to have been the most successful species on earth - that is until white humans with guns came along.

David Day in *The Doomsday Book Of Animals* includes some tales of those wondrous birds.

Edward Forbush, the State Ornithologist for Massachusetts, in 1917 made a record of the description by the last Pottawottomi chief of the Pokagon band of First Nations people, who spoke of a Passenger Pigeon encounter.

"About the middle of May, 1850, while in the fur trade," he said he was camping on the Manistee River in Michigan. When one morning he heard, ". . . a gurgling, rumbling sound, as though an army of horses laden with sleigh bells was advancing through the deep forest towards me." It sounded like a summer storm or a galloping herd of animals advancing toward him. But instead it was a front of millions of pigeons fluttering and calling as they approached through the forest. "They passed like a cloud through the branches of the high trees, through the underbrush and over the ground. . . They fluttered all about me, lighting on my head and shoulders; gently I caught two in my hands and concealed them under my blanket."

He was fortunate to be a witness to the birds' courting ritual before they mated. They made ". . . strange, bell-like wooing notes which I had mistaken for the ringing of bells in the distance." He watched quietly as pairs sat gently flapping, flitting and quivering on every branch in the forest.

He goes on to describe their mating, nest-building, rearing and fledging of the young. He finishes with, "It has been well established that these birds look after and take care of all orphaned young whose parents have been killed or are missing. These birds are long lived, having been known to live for 25 years caged."

The final hunt took place outside Bowling Green, Ohio in 1896, when the final 250,000 Passenger Pigeons gathered in one last nesting flock. The telegraph was used to notify the hunters and the railway was used to carry them to the site of the massacre. 200,000 bodies were shipped out as food, 100,000 newborn chicks were destroyed or left to predators and maybe 5000 birds escaped. On 24th March 1900, a young boy, again in Ohio, shot the last wild Passenger Pigeon. On September 1st 1914 the last caged pigeon died in the Cincinnati Zoo.[8]

Unfortunately the Pokagon Band of First Nations people, though fewer in number to begin with, fared no better than the pigeons and were soon all gone.

There must have been scores of billions of the birds. All humans should live in shame for what we do.

It is believed that the gross number of wild animals living in North America in 1800 was more than the numbers living in Africa at the same time, though the variety of species was far fewer. I don't know how most United States citizens view the slaughter of the prairie wildlife. Nevertheless, it can't be denied that it enabled the USA to become an agricultural powerhouse. It allowed for the settling of the Great Plains, The Great Plough Up early in the 20th century, and the subsequent massive food, corn and wheat production industries. America has grown fat on the former grasslands. Anything else is unthinkable; however, let's move the same scenario, the destruction of most wildlife to allow for agriculture, to another continent: the Borneo rain forest and the Amazon are two examples. But let's try Africa.

How would the American people now respond should the governments of sub-Saharan Africa announce that future government policy was to be the annihilation of all African wildlife in the name of food production and progress? Would the Americans not be horrified? To remove all the elephants and rhinos, the bucks and the gazelles, the giraffes and zebras is inconceivable. It would be an appalling crime against nature, the Earth and against all the people that follow us. Yet that's what happened, and is still happening, in North America, and it gives any African leader a precedent to do the same for the starving people of his own country. In fact it is a great model for Africa, or anywhere else in the world, to follow, as we will see in a later chapter.

It would help for the US to admit the grave error in wiping out the grizzlies, cougars and other animals. It would also help if the federal and state governments would protect the reintroduced wolves and other wildlife, instead of allowing the ranchers and hunting groups to always call the shots when it comes to wild animal removals. At the behest of those groups, the Wildlife Services agency of the U.S. Department of Agriculture continues to exterminate millions of wild animals each year. According to Defenders of Wildlife agents from that department slaughtered 23 wolves in just one remote area of Idaho during February 2014. Those particular shootings were part of an ongoing campaign to again get rid of wolves, and were carried out from helicopters. I know I use the word appalling rather frequently, but I can think of no other word to describe the U.S. Government's policies towards the country's predators than that. Not only are the policies appalling, but so too is the example it sets to the governments of other countries that may be looking for guidance in their own handling of wildlife.

The number of domesticated animals keeps rising as the wild ones keep falling. My guess is that, over the past ten thousand years, the decreasing wild numbers could probably be seen as a reflection of the increasing numbers of domesticated animals. Rather like the reflection of a pyramid in a lake of calm of water.

Dates when domestication may have taken place:[9]

Dog	14,000BCE plus	Undetermined
Cat	7,500BCE	Undetermined
Sheep	8.500BCE	Western Asia
Goat	8,000BCE	Western Asia
Cattle	7,000BCE	Eastern Sahara
Pig	7,000BCE	Western Asia
Chicken	6,000BCE	Thailand
Donkey	5,000BCE	Egypt
Horse	3,500BCE	Kazakhstan

These dates are according to the best archeological research often gathered from bones from burials, first references or first art depictions.

The Agricultural Revolution began ten thousand years ago when our ancestors started planting grains and legumes. It began at different locations all over the world. Even now a few remnant tribes still follow their animals as they choose fresh pastures. If the Bible is anything to go by, it would seem that the change from the roaming nomad to the plot-based permanence of the farmer evolved very quickly, but not without conflict.

In the Genesis story of Adam's sons, it seems that God favored Abel, the nomadic shepherd, over Cain, the hard working ploughman. But then, the words may not be completely accurate. A few verses earlier, Adam's wife Eve is named as the mother of all humans which is mighty odd as Cain goes off and finds a wife proving that there was at least one other mother who founded the human race somewhere. Eve's third son Seth also had a wife, so there just have to have been at least two families to begin with. Cain then joined a tribe that kept cattle. So, according to the bible, the first humans were, within one generation, intermarrying, keeping sheep, herding cattle and, to God's dismay, tilling the land. It is safe to say that farming is in our blood.*

The dates when crops are thought to have first been cultivated are all over the map, but the following timelines seem reasonably representative:

Wheat and Barley	Western Asia, Near East	10,000 years ago[10]
Pea	South East Asia	10,000 "
Rice	S. E. Asia, India, China	7,000 "
Corn	Central, South America	7,000 "
Broad bean	South West Asia	7,000 "
Kidney bean	Mexico, South America	7,000 "
Onion	Central, South West Asia	6,000 "
Potato	Lake Titicaca, Peru	6,000 years ago
Millet and sorghum	Africa	6,000 "
Oats	Europe	3,000 "
Quinoa	Andean Mountains	3,000 "
Lettuce	used in Roman times	2,000 "

As we found animals, grains and vegetables to cultivate and protect, it seems we focused our attention on controlling those life forms that were intent on harming our food supplies. Those animals would have not only included the predators of our stock, but also the herbivores that ate our crops.

---

* It seems clear that Adam was the founder of the Jewish tribe and faith, not of humanity. When he and Eve had their family there were obviously lots of people of other tribes around. It is also clear that agriculture and herding were well established by that time.

However, that is all history. What is now happening in the name of farming is a move from the natural that is very alarming.

The farm I knew in Somerset was what was known as a mixed farm. Chickens clucked and scratched around the yard, great shire horses stomped and whinnied in the stables, and cows came morning and evening to be milked. There were two fierce bulls as well as many calves, pigs and sheep. All sorts of crops were grown and harvested in the fields, and the farmer made a very good living. But that was then. Now few of those farms remain although the Somerset one is still lovely even as only a dairy farm that grows its own oats and other feed crops. Now most farms are nothing more than factories. Large enclosures surrounded by countryside, which is used for growing crops, and on which no animals, whether domestic or wild, are welcome.

This form of intensive animal farming is widespread in the developed world. 68 per cent of eggs, 50 per cent of pork and 48 per cent of beef is produced by this method.[11] In many countries it is a very controversial method of producing meat as the animals live their whole lives housed in massive concrete-floored buildings. They never graze in a field, and never enjoy the taste of fresh grass. It is industrialized farming, and already billions of farm animals suffer this fate. Barn-housed and antibiotic-stuffed cattle that, become increasingly unhealthy, are replacing the healthy cattle that used to chew their way across green fields. Apparently 50 per cent of the globe's antibiotic production is now being used on farm animals.

Massive cattle barns have been the norm in the US for some time, but in the UK the gross sized units had been resisted. Then in 2010, plans were afoot for an 8,000-cow mega-dairy. Other similar plans have been proposed.

These industrialized mega food-production factories, be they for battery-reared chickens, pigs, milk-cows, or beef cattle are becoming the preferred methods for feeding the billions of humans who now populate this planet. The trouble is, productive as they might be, they cause untold suffering for the poor animals, they create hot beds of disease, they feed cereals, fish and animal by-products to herbivore animals instead of grass, they produce mounds of manure that is laced with chemicals, and they fill rivers and lakes with foul animal effluent. Effluent that, when it reaches the sea, creates extensive marine dead zones.

In the 1980s in the UK an average dairy cow produced 5,000 litres of milk a year and lived for 15 years. Now the cows are being reared to produce

7-10,000 litres, but with the disadvantage that the animals are worn out and ready for the slaughterhouse after only five years.[12]

It is all done because we, the selfish ones, want to eat meat and drink milk and are unwilling to enjoy a healthy vegetable based diet. There is an ongoing debate about how much less efficient it is to get our food from animals as against plants. We have to compute the acreage of land; the amount of water, energy, fertilizer, transportation, medications and goodness knows what else that goes into getting the food to the table. Then we have to compare the differing qualities of food value. It seems to me that the results of research into the matter are very variable, but one thing is certain. Meat does not feed us with anything like the efficiently of plants. That being a recognized fact it seems remarkably counter intuitive for us to allow the farmer/industrialists to foist the awful cruelties on so many poor suffering animals.

So now, when I think of farming, of that healthy and traditional lifestyle that was so enormously appealing to me as a young boy, I mostly think of it in terms of the destruction it has wrought. Yes! We need to farm because we need to eat and if the seven billion of us were still hunter-gatherers shooting wildlife for our dinner, there would be no wildlife at all by now. But I do regret the blind foolishness of farmers and ranchers who show no respect for their domesticated animals, and even less for the wild animals. Too many farmers are unwilling to share. They see nearly all forms of wildlife as the enemy to be exterminated by any means possible.

I understand that a piece of grassland that is ploughed, then harrowed and raked, and then sown and later harvested by a huge machine with ground hugging cutters can no longer be a nesting site for birds or small animals. The birds' ancestors may have lived on that piece of land for a hundred thousand or more years, but fauna are not given papers that prove ownership, so they can't complain: . . . they just have to go off and die. If they won't, the farmer has plenty of potions in his barns to poison huge numbers of animals, birds, insects and soil microbes.

But if we were truly wise, as our Latin name 'doubly wise' suggests, would we not set aside 50 or 40 or 30 per cent of the land as habitat for the first comers? And then, when set aside, should we not take care to protect that habitat to ensure that the dwellers upon it, or within it, are safe into the future? Of course we should.

4 The Avon and Other Rivers

Hurn Court School, 1953

The farm wasn't the only beautiful place I was fortunate to know as a youngster. I was also lucky enough to be sent to boarding school, an experience I cherished for the first year or two. I had just turned 13 when I finally attended Hurn Court School. My sister was married at 21, and my brother started his National Service with the RAF at the ripe old age of 17, so I was left at home as a lone child. It couldn't have been much fun for my parents either, with a house full of maturing young people one minute and one mooning younger son the next. For a couple of years I had been asking to go to boarding school as a result of reading an excess of English boys' adventure stories. My parents finally agreed and sought, and found, Hurn Court. It was a new school about to open for the summer term of 1952.

Mr. Tyler, the headmaster, was a progressive educator who offered subjects that went beyond just the academic. The curriculum included the normal subjects but, instead of Latin and Greek, we had agricultural science, technical drawing, welding and such. The boys also provided the manpower to work the home farm. Academic subjects were held from 8:30 am till noon and then from 5 pm till 6:30 each day. The period of 1pm till 4 pm six days a week was given to sports and the practical subjects. Private prep was held from 7 pm till 8:30. Oh, I forgot to mention that we also had to run a couple of miles each morning before breakfast. We did work hard, but we had the time of our lives.

For the first year or two, a large class would be anything more than fifteen students. As a school it was paradise, and I thrived.

The house, which had been built in 1804 on the site of an Elizabethan manor, was a grand, four-story, multi-gabled palace of a place in large grounds set deep in the country. It had been the home of the Earls of Malmesbury until a year or two before we moved in. One can well imagine the dilemma he was in. The new post-war socialist government, as well as upping the death duties, had levied very high taxes on the rich - a super-tax of 95 per cent above a base amount, if you can believe it. This put many, trying to get by on old money, in the position of having to sell up to cover the tax bill.

The then earl may have been an aristocrat with inherited debts, but he may also have been a thoroughly decent man. So I can't help sympathizing with him and the many others like him. Following the introduction of wheat from America, the landed gentry had been very hard hit by the depression in agricultural prices. Value of home agricultural produce was halved. Farming became no longer profitable as many tenant farmers quit the land and the landowners' incomes sank to rock bottom. The landowners lost their tenants, and then much of their land, but they still had those huge houses to run and to staff. On top of that, death duties kept increasing till by the late 1940s those, such as the earl, had some seriously hard choices to make. They knew they were in the sights of the taxman, and the struggle to save at least some of the inheritance and their family heritage must have been very bitter.

"Do I sell the home and gardens that have been in the family for 150 years but which cost so much to maintain? Or do I sell the last farm and land that has the potential for income? Hmmmmmm? Family-seat or farmland? Home or land?" Of course he made the sober decision, but it must have been a very sad time for him and his family - sad, even for an earl. Few could afford to buy or to live in such places as his old home. Mr. Tyler bought it in 1951 for the give-away price of £6000, about double the value of our house, Cobbles.

From child to mature man, the earl had grown up in a place of magnificent loveliness. And now, thanks to pure luck, we young schoolboys were going to enjoy the place as he had.

The house, or Court as it was known, was on the acid soil of the New Forest. From the northern main gates the North Drive swept half a mile below mature sweet chestnuts to the mansion in which we lived and studied. The West Drive passed through mature woodland for a rather greater distance, while the drive to the south traveled even further, first beside the gardens and lake and finally past open farmland. A retreat more separate from the world outside would be hard to find. The gardens had been designed as open parkland that sloped down to the artificial lake and island. It contained exotic trees and mature rhododendrons of significant age and size. The Giant Sequoia tree, a native to California, was probably planted shortly after 1853 when the first seeds of that species were carried to England.

Just to the east of the house, the gardens were separated from the adjacent farmlands by a half-mile long ha-ha. It was probably dug at the time of house building and was typical of that 18th century innovation. For those not in the know, which probably includes most of us, a ha-ha is a deep and wide ditch with a fence running along the lowest part. They were designed as barriers to keep cattle and other undesirables out, while not introducing a visible interruption to the view. Much of the Hurn Court ha-ha was pretty well full of stinging nettles when we were there, so it had the added benefit of being attractive to a great many Peacock, Red Admiral and Tortoiseshell butterflies, which lay their eggs on the nettles. A ha-ha, which becomes filled in time with nettles, brambles or other thorny shrubs, makes an incredibly effective, though hidden, barrier.

I can't say how large the grounds to the house were, but I guess about 20 to 30 acres.

The interior of the house was for the most part unchanged from the earl's days; just the furniture had been removed. Some of us studied English in the breakfast room, some in the formal dining room, others did math in the withdrawing room. His library was our library though with a different collection of books, and his splendour was our splendour but without the chintz. Though many of us slept three or four to a room in what had once been the servants' quarters, others slept in large dormitories that had been family bedrooms. A few slept in the earl's bedroom. In that large room, where ten or eleven young lads had their beds, the walls were still papered with black and gold striped flocked wallpaper. That room had a private loo, mahogany paneled and quite long. When in need of a visit, one strode down that aristocratic little room to the far end where one mounted the three room-wide steps to the mahogany-encased throne-like porcelain toilet. There, we boys would avoid math or chemistry whilst we sat, went about our business. . . and contemplated greatness.

Endless glass cases of stuffed birds, shot by the earl's forebears, lined the walls. It was whilst admiring those that I saw, for the first time, examples of such North American birds - though stuffed - as Rosy Finches and quail (both California and Mountain) with their curled and somewhat exotic head plumes. The house was very large but also magnificent in a post-war rundown sort of way.

As a boys' school, it had the advantage of little central heating, with the consequence that heroic measures to toughen us up were deemed unnecessary.

Being on the edge of the New Forest to the east and old heathland to the west the neighbourhood was rich in British fauna. The most common of the birds that I remember seeing were Curlews and Lapwings - or Peewits.

Beyond the lake to the south was the River Stour a few miles from where it joined the Hampshire Avon near Christchurch. It was in the Stour that I saw my first salmon. A couple of us had wandered down the south drive to take a look at the river, and, while leaning over the balustrade of the bridge, we saw three very large fish lazily making their way up river. I believe Atlantic Salmon were quite rare on southern rivers at that time, so we were very lucky.

I had a slight knowledge of the Hampshire Avon as my father had inherited the leased fishing rights for three miles of that river a short distance from the Tudor village of Breamore. Three miles actually meant one mile of each of the left and right banks and a mile of the river's centre. Our rights started maybe a mile below the weir and old watermill, flowed south-eastward through ancient water meadows and then passed into a large section of steeply sloping forest known as Godshill.

The Avon is a gentle river. It begins in Wiltshire from two sources, one of which drains the Vale of Pewsey near Devizes. Since the Vale is the divide between Salisbury Plain and the Marlborough Downs, two more areas of high chalk downland, the water is somewhat alkaline and very rich in fish species.

Our boathouse, where we moored a shallow, flat-bottomed fishing boat, was reached by crossing open farmland along a narrow footpath. On summer days we would pass brown and white cows, some grazing quietly on the meadow grasses and some standing up to their knees in the shallows of the river. All was so peaceful - a scene from a John Constable painting. Dad would row to some chosen fishing spot, throw out the anchor, and there we would sit, munching on sandwiches and occasionally catching small Pike or Chub, Roach or Dace, or other inedible fish. In they went to the boat's central flow-through fish chamber where they would stay till we freed them back to the river at the end of the day. For me, the best time was when father rowed to and moored in the sheltered and forested stretch. There the views were more restricted and less sun shone, but the steep wooded hills on each bank spoke of mystery and adventure. I realize now that we never once stepped onto either bank to explore that forest. Probably the banks were so overgrown that they were unapproachable from the water.

In my grandfather's time, he had caught quite large fish including a 29 lb Pike, which was stuffed and hung on the wall in my brother's bedroom. There were also glass cases of other stuffed large fish in the offices of the family business. My father told me of Atlantic Salmon being caught on our stretch in earlier times. We would usually visit and fish for two or three weekends a year. We always stayed at the Bat and Ball pub.

I remember a trip when I was about ten, when Mum hooked a very large pike. We watched the line rushing through the water, a large tail beating the surface, but then the line went slack. So we knew there was still at least one very large fish in the river before 1950. Sadly, I also remember Sunday lunches, four or five years later, when Dad and his friends would wonder where all the fish had gone and what had caused their disappearance. Whatever it was, the river seemed to be sick in some way.

It certainly couldn't have been over-fishing; the effects of two weekends a year by a family of amateur fishermen catching a few fish would have been negligible. We had no knowledge of stealthy moonlight poachers stripping the river. Besides, what would they have done with ten-inch-long inedible fish? Maybe they had looked into the future and started a production line of canned cat food, but that was very unlikely. What was the cause? Was it too much weed? Or was it too much weed clearing? Was it something that was happening up river in one of the cities? The Avon is only 60 miles long (96km), so it is not a large river. From its source near Devizes it travels through the village of Upavon, then goes through Amesbury, Salisbury and Ringwood till it enters the sea at Christchurch. So the river drifted through farmland, woodland and small country towns all the way. It was hardly an industrial part of the world, but there was probably some light industry. Could that have produced enough pollution to affect the river? I doubt it. Nonetheless, even now, when we have more knowledge of the damage toxic waste can do to the environment, mindless idiots still discharge tanks of waste into waterways, usually by night. So maybe in the early fifties some unknowing twit regularly emptied his biannual supply of nasty by-product into the river. After all, what else was he going to do with it in those days?

Some hundreds of years ago, more of the river was probably forested. Now most riverside forest has gone, and is replaced by farmland along the majority of its route. Although, sixty years ago, very few people thought of farming as a threat to rivers, some were aware that the new insecticides seemed to be affecting more than the problem insects against which they were directed. So possibly the culprit could have been the runoff of such insecticides as DDT or Dieldrin. DDT had been applied since the 1940s and Dieldrin since the 1950s,[1] so if those were the problems, they started affecting the rivers very quickly.

Since the early part of the 19th Century, Pyrethrum, a natural insecticide made from the flowers of chrysanthemum, had been used in Britain. It was deadly to fish, but, as it was very expensive, it is unlikely it was used excessively, if at all, by most farmers. Possibly a couple of rich landowners used it, but they would have had to be very profligate with such an expensive pesticide to have poisoned a whole river. Synthetic versions of that poison using the name Pyrethrum were introduced late in the 1960s. They were lethal to insects and, although also poisonous to fish, they broken down easily in water. They were also very expensive.

Rainfall and runoff will carry much of what is applied to the land into the rivers, whether it is natural animal manure or chemicals. It seems that the chemicals we pour on the land nowadays can very easily kill the local aquatic insects and then be carried all over the world by rivers, by seas and by infected wildlife. Because of this, a river such as the Avon would be the first stage of the long journey the toxic chemicals take. Fish of course have to eat, and they eat a myriad of small water-borne insects such as the aquatic larvae of alderflies and caddis flies and the aquatic nymphs of dragonflies and damselflies. Killing the insects in the river could easily explain the depletion of the Avon fish.

It seems highly probable that when we destroy the insects, of which there are more than 20,000 species in Britain alone, and which we have done en masse all over the globe, we both poison the fish that eat the dead insects and also starve the fish by cutting off a major food supply. We have the same effect on many bird species when we starve them by killing the insects.

In my memory, the 1950s were the years when chemicals were first being used widely on the land. Though I realize it was all a part of the agricultural Green Revolution of the time, I think it was a mistake for farmers to turn away from the traditional organic crop rotation methods that had been the norm for so many years. We now know that the chemicals, herbicides, insecticides and fungicides are ingested by insects and small birds, and on up the food chain to the largest animal and bird predators.

I came upon a study entitled *Fish Populations on the River Avon, Hampshire, Downstream of Salisbury, in 1987* by R.H.K. Mann, W.R.C. Beaumont and J.A. Blackburn. The research had been carried out in response to observations that the fish were less plentiful than they had been before 1970. So the diminished fish numbers my father had mourned were by then, twenty years later, considered the norm. But from that norm, the numbers had again diminished. The authors noted that they could find no previous data with which to compare their findings, so they found no conclusive evidence that fish numbers were down - or up for that matter. They listed some circumstances that could possibly affect the numbers, such as farming practices; industrial, domestic or agricultural waste; predation by pike, trout or herons; loss of nursery areas; and weed-cutting and changes to the old water meadows. But there was no finger pointing to any specific culprit.

Some might question whether these reports of diminishing fish numbers and sizes are not the result of fishermen's melancholy. After all, fishers of rivers are perennially disappointed that the fish they catch are never as large, or as many, as they had hoped. Could there have been no reduction in the number and size of the fish in the river? Is it possible that each generation of fishermen looks back on the earlier years of fishing as being better than the most recent just because so many days for fishermen end in disappointment? The Avon runs through pretty idyllic country, so it is not easy to point at recent developments or new factories and say, "Look what they have done."

But if fishermen from different generations and dates thirty years apart all believe there has been a diminishment of fish in their times, I think that probable it is so. I also have the advantage of first-hand knowledge of my grandfather Thomas James's stuffed and mounted fish, which were plentiful and huge compared with the insignificant ones we caught. They were all taken in the 1920s and 30s. He died of a heart attack on the day of a German attack in 1942, when his business received a direct hit from an enemy bomb. Bombs aside, his fish collection convinces me that the pre-war fish were far larger and more plentiful than they were when I used to fish beside my dad in the late 1940s.

It seems very possible that there is an overall and long-term decline in the productivity of the river. Could the very fact of our human presence - of our distant industries, our scientific developments, our new chemicals, our air pollution and the acid rain that we cause - affect the waters of even the most pristine rivers in ways that we can't even imagine? I am convinced that our use of pesticides, herbicides and insecticides penetrates to, and infects, every part of the natural world. Every medicine, chemical and hormone we ingest is eventually excreted from our bodies into the sewer system and eventually into nature's water. Why, even the fish and mammals of the high Arctic contain chemical pollutants, though there is very little industry up there.

I am sure similar questions to those of my father in the 1950s were being asked along quite a few of the world's rivers at that time. Now such questions are being asked all over the world, even of rivers that one would expect to be quite pristine. Reports of sick rivers are now commonplace with 60 per cent of the world's rivers considered under stress.

Before Britain industrialized, the traditional old water wheels were an adequate way to power the few looms, sawmills or other examples of early enterprise. However, it was the invention of powerful steam engines fired by coal that gave industrialization the tremendous boost and old-world-shattering thrust into the world we know today. And it was coal that polluted and changed the environment of Britain in ways never seen before. Coal was dug and burned to power everything, from household hearths to industrial factories, at a time when no thought was given to environmental concerns. It was a time to make money, to get out of poverty, to get on in the world and to introduce new ideas and new inventions. It makes sense that, with its high density of population and lack of foresight, Great Britain should be among the first to encounter the ecological and environmental problems that resulted from that headlong rush into industrialization and the modern world. In the process, the buildings and countryside were changed. The industrial West Midlands of England was known as 'The Black Country' for a reason. Black coal was on the surface of the land, black coal was used to power the engines, black coal heated the houses, black coal dust filled the air and every man-made building and piece of machinery was black with coal dust. Even some moth and butterfly species changed colour to match the environment in a process known as species adaptation.

When I was a child, most buildings in London were black from soot. There were no beautifully rich, warm stone-coloured Houses of Parliament then. They were black like most other buildings. In London, deadly smogs, when a person couldn't see beyond arm's length, were frequent and normal. I remember, when traveling by train as a child, being told to keep my hands off the horizontal surfaces and sills of the carriage windows. They were covered with soot. The black coal dust we could see and measure, but what about all the other pollutants now in the air that we don't see? Those pollutants, when they fall as acid rain, land on the watersheds, then make their way to the rivers and out to sea affecting every living thing that makes contact.

Few other animal species are as adaptable as we humans. We live and survive under almost any conditions; whether the coldest arctic winter or the hottest desert heat, whether the most awful dust-filled air in a mine deep underground or the most degrading and fearful First World War trench warfare, we adapt and we survive. Unless we are physically killed or denied air or water, we survive almost any conditions no matter how horrible. But what of those other life forms that can't adapt? What if many other animal species are more willing to quit and give up the struggle when things become just marginally less agreeable than their preferred environmental conditions? Many of them do just that.

Few wildlife species can adapt the way humans can. When thinking of birds we find that most species have a very particular ecological niche in which they survive and flourish. They live in oak woods, or pine forests, in marshland or heath-land. They live up to one thousand feet above sea level, or above five thousand feet in the cloud forest. Some feed in the forest canopy, whilst others seldom leave the forest floor. Most have very small niches that they find acceptable. There are, of course, the survivors of the avian world, the adaptable ones: the sparrows, the starlings, the crows and the grackles, but those species are few, though the numbers of each are large.

In the mammal world the most successful species and the most like us in terms of adaptability is probably the rat – an animal that we hate. An animal that we admire for its power and speed, the cheetah, is apparently one of the least adaptable and the first to stop breeding when the going gets tough. So maybe the fish in the Hampshire Avon find it hard to adapt. Maybe what we think of as minimal changes to the chemical makeup of the water, or to the insect numbers, can mean breeding failures or death to the fish. If that can be the case for the Avon fish, it can probably be the case for fish anywhere.

It seems that through history we humans have used rivers as both a source for drinking water and a convenient place to dump our waste. It doesn't sound too smart, but I suppose it can be justified if the waste goes in down-river from where the drinking water is drawn out. However that doesn't do much for the people downstream who also need to get their water from the river. Still, in the old days, everything that went in would at least have been natural – animal, vegetable or mineral – and presumably relatively harmless in the long term, a few cholera outbreaks aside. Nowadays a good percentage of the waste is toxic.

I suppose by now we have all heard of London's 'Great Stink'. That was when, during an uncommonly hot summer in 1858, the smell of human waste in the London stretch of the River Thames became even more overpoweringly foul than usual. It was so foul that parliament even considered moving upriver to Hampton Court or even Oxford.[2]

Historically, London had collected human waste from the population in over 200,000 cesspits, most of which were in peoples' basements. Those cesspits were emptied by night-soil men - lucky chaps - for a fee of one shilling.[3] In those days, a shilling was a sum that few residents could easily afford. Carts of night soil were taken out of the city to farms, where it was used as manure on the land. I do wonder how often these night-soil collectors washed and had baths. Though I realize that is very much an aside, it may have been of some consequence to their wives. That system of disposal started to break down as London expanded from the original square mile, and as the distance to farms became too great to allow the poor old plodding night-soil men any profit. They also had the developing problem of competition from the new industry of guano mining and importation. Who would have thought that the discovery of coastlines and islands tens of thousands of miles away, loaded to great depths with bird manure, would reduce the number of carts being trundled about the British cities and countryside laden with human feces? One result of all this was that in 1815, out of desperation, it was made legal to direct human waste into the Thames where it was expected to be taken out to sea by the flow of the river.[4]

Unfortunately the river's current only took the waste part way to the sea, but then each rising tide brought it right on back again. The consequence of this regular inflow, with no outflow, was as might be expected: a foul and smelly river sloshing about in the very centre of the nation's greatest city, and the largest city in the world at that time.

It is worth noting that in 1815, the year human waste was officially allowed into the river, the river was still one of the city's major sources of fresh water. That situation continued for seven years until new fresh water sources were made available. Aside from a lack of sewers, it strikes me as mighty strange that those sophisticated fops of the Restoration and Georgian eras couldn't get it together enough to build decent water closets. They had houses lined and furnished with gorgeous silk brocades and velvets but had no sensible toilets. Did they not notice? Or was human crap as commonplace to them as dog poop on the pavement when I was kid? Now I cringe when I see the occasional dog poop in oh-so-clean Vancouver, with its stringent 'poop, stoop and scoop' laws. Is it possible that our revulsion against excrement in the living room is a recent foible? I simply fail to understand why toilet rooms in houses were regarded as afterthoughts in those days 200 or so years ago.

The result of the 1858 Big Stink was another big stink in Parliament, and the eventual designing and building of a sewage system that took the waste to a point beyond the influence of the returning tide. In the early 20th century, that system was improved so that now, instead of sending the effluent out to the sea, it is sent to inland sewage treatment plants. Now many modern cities have a thoroughly efficient modern sewage infrastructure included as part of the city's planning. However, not all, and with 60 per cent of the world's rivers under stress, we can be sure that much of the world still uses their rivers as convenient dumps for anything that is unwanted.

The Ganges

The Hampshire Avon of my youth is somewhat dissimilar to the great Ganges of India. It is true that they are both rivers. But, while the Avon is 69 miles long, and appears from nowhere more interesting than the fields and spinneys of rural southern England, the Ganges is 1,560 miles (2,510kms), and starts with five tumbling and vigorous glacier streams close to Tibet, in the high Himalayas of India.[5] The Avon is soft and enjoyed with affection, but the Ganges is heroic, awe-inspiring and religiously iconic.

The true source of the Ganges is thought to be at a place called Gaumukh, though a more interesting secondary source is from a nearby cave of glacial meltwater and great religious significance. The cave, named Gangotri, is at 10,000 feet (3000 meters) and is the source of the river Bhagirathi. The religious attraction, to make a pilgrimage to a cave at 10,000 ft in the Himalayas, must be very powerful to the worthy adherents. The Gaumukh, the Bhagirathi, the Alaknanda and two other rivers soon join together to form the young Ganges or Ganga. Ganga is the Hindu Goddess of Creation and Abundance. It was on the banks of the river that the animist and nature worshiping Hindu religion developed.[6]

After gathering its swelling waters from the source streams, the river flows at a more leisurely pace, some say sluggishly, on an east-southeasterly course across northern India to the great Ganges Delta in the Bay of Bengal. At first it flows through lands of grasses high enough to hide the wild elephant and one-horned rhino that still survive there. Then it used to flow through the great northern forest, but it now flows through cleared agricultural land of great richness, with topsoil kilometers deep in some places. Along its route it picks up more water, and more rich silt, from the many tributary rivers cascading down from the Himalayas to the north. The lower system seems to be rather variable with many routes having changed up to as much as 40 miles over the last hundred years. Once the Ganga reaches Bangladesh it is joined by the mighty Brahmaputra and Meghna rivers. Eventually it feeds the many distributary rivers at the great Ganges delta.

It is estimated that the Ganges drains more than 25 per cent of the landmass of India and that the Ganges-Brahmaputra system, at the delta, discharges 1,086,500 cubic feet (30,000 cu meters) of water per second. That great flow of water carries with it 1.84 billion tons of sediment per year.[7]

150 years ago, the prime virgin forests, through which the Ganges flowed, covered nearly all of northern India and were inhabited by elephants, tigers, leopards, guar, rhinos, and a huge number of other species. Now that rich and productive environment of a million species is all gone. The British, who needed the wood to build the Indian railways, felled it in the late 19th century. They also hunted to extinction, or near extinction, the

Indian lions, cheetahs, rhino and others that they labeled vermin. It was a crime to match the North American prairie destruction of the same era.

The Ganges also passed many small cities with relatively few people. Now the river passes many large cities including Delhi, Agra, Meerut, Allahabad, Lucknow, and Varanasi and myriad villages with a population of about 400 million. The basin is now one of the most densely populated in the world. It is also one of the most fertile and productive agriculturally. To achieve that distinction though, the forests became victims, and are all gone. So too is the wildlife, save a few smaller deer, jackals and boars. In 1900 the total human population of India was less than 200 million. In 2012 it was 1.22 billion.

All those cities, and the hundreds of millions of people are thought to discharge billions of litres of sewage contaminated water into the sanctified waters of the river each day. One can only hope that that noxious discharge, along with the many partly-burned remains of the religiously cremated bodies carried by the river, add good fertilizer to the delta flood plains and agricultural lands at the end of the river's journey. Unfortunately, the dead human and animal bodies are accompanied by untold quantities of plastic and other waste. Another discharge is a large quantity of Chromium, used in the many leather-processing factories, along the river's garbage-rank banks.[8]

One positive note: at the very terminus of the river system at the seaward edge of the delta can be found Bengal Tigers, Marsh Deer and crocodiles. They live in the large 3,861 square mile (10,000km2) mangrove forest known as the Sundarbans. That wildlife-rich area, which is a UNESCO World Heritage Site, has the most biodiversity of any mangrove forest anywhere. Protection of the Sundarbans is shared by both India and Bangladesh.[9]

A notable tributary of the Ganges is the Yamuna, or Jamuna, River that originates at the Yumanotri Glacier near the former British hill station of Mussoorie, in the Himalayas. It travels 855 miles (1376 kms) past New Delhi and then past the Taj Mahal at Agra before joining the Ganges.

A beautiful river of pure Himalayan water flowing past the Taj is the image one might expect. Well actually, no! Pure and blue for a short while, yes! But then it passes by the 21 million people of New Delhi where it picks up 2 or 3 billion litres of contaminated water each day. This it carries as a sort of homage to the Taj Mahal.[10] New Delhi was built by the British in the beginning of the 20th century and, like most of their colonial engineering and development projects, was well designed and solidly built. However

Edwin Lutyens, the architect, either didn't know of London's Big Stink, or didn't expect India's population to grow so much, and instead of directing the human waste away from the river, he sent it into the river.

In 2011 the politicians in the capital introduced The Yamuna Action Plan.[11] The plan calls for the sewage to be directed elsewhere, the river to be cleaned up, and its banks transformed into a park. We can hope that sometime in the future visitors will have both the Taj Mahal and a clean river, hosting bounteous wildlife, to admire and wonder at.[12]

I have found it hard to obtain accurate and believable figures for the amount of raw sewage going into the rivers. However the total amount of garbage of one sort or another, especially plastic, is huge, though uncounted.

One other related problem concerns the groundwater, which has dropped an average of one meter throughout India. In some states the drop is so great that the users are now bringing up polluted water to drink.[13]

Rivers haven't been used as convenient dumps for only human excrement. I suppose it is understandable that once, a long time ago, they would have been used for that purpose with little obvious effect. If a few dozen people lived by a river centuries ago, or even if they do so now, a fast- flowing river seems a natural way to see off the stuff they don't want lying about in the hut. Off it goes. They never see it again nor do they think of it. Even as the settlement grew to a village, and then a town, and finally a city, the sewage was quickly out of sight and only a problem for those drawing fresh drinking water from the river downstream. Even discounting the potential for disease or sickness, at least what was entering the water was all natural. Overtime, of course, the good citizens started disposing of other unwanted clutter: the bug-infested straw from a mattress here, broken kitchen chairs there, a painting of the mother-in-law or the odd murder victim. The like of those items didn't have much effect being, again, all natural.

For centuries, such establishments as abattoirs had purposefully been constructed beside rivers for the simple convenience of disposal. I remember one summer in about 1962 when I was hitchhiking through France on my way to Spain. In those days, I used to sleep in fields or pieces of wasteland in a light sleeping bag. One morning I arose at about 5 am and toddled down to the river where I cleaned my teeth. I remember thinking, "How lovely! A beautiful river, a lightly warming day . . . this is the life." Then, as I admired the sun-dappled water hurrying by, I noticed bunches of strange, pale-purple-pink-bobbing things floating with the current.

"Lo!" I thought, "What drifts yonder?" Then "yuck!" I thought, "They're the insides of animals. Urgh"

Indeed they were. They were intestines, stomachs and other body parts. There must have been a slaughterhouse and meat processing plant just upriver from where I was. I wasn't sure just how clean my teeth were after that. Rivers have always been great for disposing of any waste that resulted from almost any human endeavor or industry.

The trouble was that, as the industrial processes moved away from such natural earth-derived materials as wood, cotton, wool, leather and animal parts, more and more toxic materials were introduced to the rivers. With the advent of hydrocarbons, and the petroleum and plastic industries that developed from the oil industry, some pretty noxious substances were released into the rivers. When we got, not just one factory here or there, but conglomerates of huge enterprises, established one beside the other along the riverbanks, the nature of the effects became terrible. A few animal parts were one thing, but thousands or millions of gallons of oil waste or chemicals pouring into the river was another. Add to that the billions of plastic bottles, bags, and other objects used by populations with no recycling laws or systems, other than the river, and we have a terrible, terrible problem. Oils and some chemicals float on water, and while they do they emit fumes that, in many cases, are flammable.

The Cuyahoga

Rivers in the US have been catching fire since the middle of the 19th century. So, for that matter, has the odd harbour. We are not talking about the riverbank catching fire. We are talking about what one would think of as water catching fire. Rivers have burned in New York, Pennsylvania, Ohio, Maryland and Michigan, but the one that got people's attention was a fire along the Cuyahoga River in Cleveland, Ohio during a hot June in 1969. The flames leapt to heights of 50 ft (16 meters). Still, Fire Chief W. E. Barry described it as ". . . strictly a run of the mill fire." The first fire on the Cuyahoga was in 1868, but the biggest was in 1952. That one burned an office building and boats to the tune of a million dollars' worth of damage.[14]

The river is not large; it is just 100 miles (160kms) long and was possibly, at one time, quite beautiful. It is a meandering river formed at the time when the glaciers retreated at the end of the last ice age. The Cuyahoga may have been rather like the River Avon at the time that Cleveland was first founded in 1796. That was the year my great-great-grandfather Joseph was born and the population of the US was a little over 3 million – three times the size of London at the time. I find it amazing that it only took seventy-two years between founding a city, on the very edge of what was then the American wilderness, and polluting the river so much that it would burn – and then burn time and time again for the next hundred years.

Before the 1969 fire, the river was described in a research report as having heavy black oil several inches thick on the surface. The water temperature was said to increase to 15 degrees above its normal temperature, due to discharge into it of industrial cooling water. It was found that nothing at all lived in the water, not even leeches. After the fire, Time magazine reported that "Falling in the river, a man does not drown - he decays."[15]

I believe such a burning river to be a terrible indictment of our industrial world. The Americans stand as the ultimate example of human power and authority on our globe. Yet, from its first official exploration in 1796, they turned a river, that was unknown and pristine wilderness, into a dead, chemical-soaked, industrial hellhole within a human's lifetime. It first burned in 1868. The fact that it then burned a dozen more times, pales in comparison to its primary change from pure, sparkling, wilderness to inferno in those few short years. That says all we need to know about our misapplied industrial might.

One good thing to come from that particular fire, though, is that, along with other environmental horror stories of the time, it helped provoke the establishment of environmentalism. It also resulted in the US government passing the Clean Water Act in 1972. Cleveland sits at the mouth of the river where it flows into Lake Erie. At the time, that great lake was considered dead. By 2011 however, thanks to the Clean Water Act and the Great Lakes Water Quality Agreement between the US and Canada, Erie supported a $600 million fishing industry.[16]

Those polluted waters of the Cuyahoga are a terrible indictment of what can happen when the sole concern of industry is economic, and when industrialists and governments look no further than the increase in monetary wealth and the tax base. What happened on that river can be applied, to one extent or another, to rivers all over the world on which industrial cities have been established. The Tyne and Clyde, during the industrialization of the UK, were little better, and now there are plenty of Chinese and Brazilian rivers that are heading toward the same horrors. Probably the terrible river pollution that resulted from Cleveland's industrial might is happening to rivers, to one degree or another, in newly developing economies all over the world. Some city and state governments will have been wise enough to learn from Cleveland's experience, but we know that many have not.

It is also worth remembering that the cleanup of that iconic river, and America's Clean Water Act, would not have happened without the leadership and intervention of the environmental movement, a movement, not of concerned industry, but of concerned citizens. Without those people the river would probably still be burning. Yet they are the very people and organizations that many governments consider as bad as enemies of the state.

The Pearl River, USA

On the 9th of August 2011, the Louisiana Paper Mill, owned by Temple-Inland Inc., discharged a waste liquid material that they call 'Black Liquor' into the Pearl River at the city of Bogalusa, USA. The Black Liquor immediately sucked the oxygen right out of the river and killed every aquatic animal for some 60 miles. It killed everything from Gulf Sturgeon, to Ringed Sawback Turtles and on down to the Heelsplitter Mussels. Downriver the surface was solid with dead fish.[17][18] Now, this is recorded as having happened in the United States of America, whose citizens, we can be sure, are onto any environmental catastrophe in pretty quick time and in high dudgeon too. Consider how often such a thing must happen in those poorer countries that are working with energy to become members of the industrialized world. A mere river kill is just one of the prices to pay for jobs paying 15 cents an hour. Anyone foolish enough to mention a toxic spill may well be told to look for another job. In any case, in those parts of the world, no one would notice a toxic spill that kills fish, as there are probably few fish left to die and float to the surface, so who's to know?

The Mississippi

An American river that, for a short while, defined a frontier, was the Mississippi. As the American colonial expansion spread west into the lands of the native people, it did so in steps, which often stopped for a while at the next natural barrier. Before 1783, the western frontier had been, more or less, the Appalachian Mountains. Before 1820, the Mississippi had been the frontier. After another twenty years, the frontier was somewhere round the 100 degree longitude mark near the centre of the Great Plains. By 1890, there was no frontier. Below present-day Canada and above Mexico, all the land was the USA. Between 1846 and 1890, America had fought 54 battles to wrest the land from the natives and the Mexican state. The great American ideals of liberty, democracy, prosperity and good health worked fine for the white Americans who settled on the land, but for the indigenous tribes the antonyms became more applicable: confinement, tyranny, poverty and death by disease and the gun became the lot of the native peoples. Not many other colonial powers showed such appalling contempt for their conquered people as did the Americans.

The Mississippi was a natural barrier to the west in those early days, but it is now the watershed for what is unquestionable the world's greatest farming breadbasket. It is one of the largest rivers in the world at 2,530 miles (4,070 kms), and it drains 1,245,000 square miles (3,222,000 km2) of land, which is nearly 40 per cent of the landmass of the USA. It actually drains all or parts of 31 states and parts of two Canadian provinces. The true source of the Mississippi is Lake Itasca, Minnesota, but the Missouri tributary gives greater length to the river as it is thought to rise at 8,800 ft (2,700 m) in the Rockies at Brower's Spring, Montana. The Missouri drains three major western rivers, while the Ohio River is the main tributary from the east.

Draining such an enormous part of the USA, and considering that the surrounding land is possibly the most fertile agricultural land in the world, it is hardly any surprise that the main pollution the water carries is agricultural.

The Mississippi is probably the most engineered major river in the world. On the upper river, before it even reaches St. Louis, Missouri, it hosts 43 dams, the lower 23 of which contain locks to ease navigation. It is the 5th largest river in the world when taking into account the outflow. Depending on the time of year and the snow pack in the mountains, it discharges somewhere between 200,000 and 700,000 cubic feet of water per second (6,000-20,000 cubic meters). Of course this amount of fresh water doesn't immediately mingle with the salt water of the Gulf of Mexico. Instead it flows as a giant plume carrying with it all the sediment and pollutants. As the main pollutants are from farms, we can be sure the river carries an abundant amount of residue from insecticides, pesticides, herbicides, animal waste, and fertilizer in the form of nitrogen and phosphorous.

Other pollutants are the residue of antibiotics, bacteria, pathogens and other chemicals.[19]

The couple of hundred milking cows on the farm in Somerset are a different order of things from the thousands of cattle kept in huge pens on the livestock farms of the USA. The UK milk cows are contented and happy beasts that experience just one bad day at the slaughterhouse. That bad day follows a lifetime of blissful hours, filled by grazing on the green fields of old England. Many of the US cattle, on the other hand, spend most of their lives in fenced yards with seldom a sight of grass and no place to roam. They are fed feed containing excess cadmium, chromium, lead, zinc and arsenic. These animals excrete large quantities of those metals as well as such salts as magnesium, chloride, nitrate, potassium and others as well as antibiotics and growth hormones. This chemical-filled manure is stored in huge million-gallon manure and urine lagoons. It is believed that cattle excrete between 75 per cent and 90 per cent of all antibiotics administered to them. This waste, being far more toxic than human waste, requires time to become non-burning fertilizer when it can be spread on the land. Unfortunately more is produced than can be used, and much finishes up in the rivers and streams that feed the Mississippi. The same applies to the disease-causing pathogens and ammonia concentrates in the manure, which, when in water, can cause serious illness in humans.

All this eventually makes its way to the big river or into the ground water. Many farms get their water from wells sourcing water from the ground. It is quite amazing that, with the ground water, the insecticides and the herbicides, so many US farmers seem intent on poisoning not just themselves but their families also.

When this toxic brew reaches the Gulf of Mexico, it causes a dead zone that is some 8,500 square miles on the surface. I don't know how deep it goes. It is called a dead zone because the high concentrations of fertilizer absorb all the oxygen from the water making it uninhabitable for any fish or mammal.

Another interesting fact is that, according to the US Environmental Agency, 40 per cent of US lakes, rivers and coastal waters are unsuitable for humans to drink, to fish or to swim in, due to the high levels of contamination. On top of that, according to a 2011 report entitled *The good, the bad and the ugly: implementation of the Great Lakes Compact*, by Sara Gosman for the National Wildlife Federation, algae blooms are clogging the Great Lakes shorelines. These blooms are fed by agricultural run-off containing excessive amounts of fertilizer. The bloom in Lake Erie, which was up to 2 feet thick in places and extended to nearly the central area of the lake, contained toxins that were measured at one thousand times more toxic than the drinking water guidelines suggested by the World Health Organization. The bloom is said to be worse than those in the 1960s when the lake was declared dead.[20]

Some Great Lakes are suffering from invasions of exotic mussels. According to an April 2011 study by three scientists from the University of Michigan and authored by Mary Anne Evans, lakes Michigan and Huron are being destroyed by exotic Zebra and Quagga Mussels. The Zebras, which originated in south-east Russia, and the Quaggas, which come from the Ukraine, are destroying the algae and food chain in deeper lake waters. The algae feed small shrimps that in turn feed larger fish. With the algae all but gone from the depths the shrimp have declined by 94 per cent over 10 years. This has resulted in a 95 per cent reduction in prey fish numbers. The report speaks of "massive ecosystem-wide changes" in lakes Huron and Michigan. Maybe the mussels will now migrate to the shoreline and eat the algae there. It seems that the Great Lakes, which contain one fifth of the world's fresh water, are again close to ecosystem collapse.

The Potomac

The Potomac is a river of some importance to Americans. It runs through Washington, the capital city of that great nation. Most of us would expect that the river flowing through the most important capital of the most powerful nation of the world would be an example to us all of how perfect a river can be. It must surely be sparkling in its purity and clarity. Why, even the fish must be proud to swim there! It seems that once again we have it wrong.

The Potomac is a river 400 miles (650kms) in length. It rises in West Virginia and flows into Chesapeake Bay on the Atlantic coast. At the time of contact with Europeans, the upper reaches of the river were known for the great many swans and geese that nested there. The river has a watershed of 147,000 sq. miles (380,000 km2) that attracted many settlements and agricultural and mining enterprises. By the early eighteen hundreds the river was beginning to suffer from sewage and harmful run-offs from those activities. Its pollution became so foul that apparently Abe Lincoln would flee the capital in the summers to escape the stench. A repeat, it seems, of the Big Stink of Thames fame. The same problem for the same generation!

By the nineteen sixties the algal blooms and other pollutants had become so bad that Lyndon Johnson started a clean-up, saying the river was a national disgrace. In 1972, the Clean Water Act was introduced. Sewage treatment plants were constructed or expanded, detergents and phosphorus fertilizers were restricted, and, by the new millennium, the water quality was greatly improved. It is still nowhere close to what one might describe as a pristine river. Despite many views of the river that are hilly, forested and beautiful, the watershed is still home to five million people, a lot of agriculture and a fair bit of industry. As a consequence, many toxic metals and chemicals find their way into the river as a result of normal storm water flow. In 2007, the Potomac Conservancy, made up of involved environmentalists, gave the river a grade of D-plus. Apart from all the pesticides, phosphates, heavy metals and sewage in the river, it seems there are also chemicals in human waste that effectively create inter-sex fish. Some male bass fish now carry female bass eggs. People have been warned not to eat the fish they catch, nor to swim in the river. Of course all this pollution carries on down the river to Chesapeake Bay where it pollutes the crabs and other shellfish. Despite earlier improvements to the sewage system, it still seems that nasty pollutants, all 9.4 billion litres of them, are getting into the river and lakes. 60 per cent is carried by water run-off from the surface of the land, parking lots and road asphalt. The rest comes from the 19th century sewage system when it overflows.

In response to this situation the president of Potomac Conservancy, Hedrick Belin, asked, "If we can't figure out how to clean up, and be able to swim in a river and eat the fish you catch, if you can't do that in the nation's capital, what hope do we have?" Well a plan has been worked out. This plan involves building 26 kilometers of large tunnels to divert the runoff from the river and lakes and to hold it till it can be processed. The cost of this project will be $2.4 billion.

So the Americans are now starting to spend nearly two and a half billion dollars to clean up a mess that, it might be argued, should never have developed in the first place. However, I suppose we can't really blame the ancestors. As noted, 500 years ago dumping stuff in rivers was general practice. Then, there was no problem. The rivers naturally washed away the excess rainfall, fallen trees, drowned large animals and other waste from the watershed, so who can blame us for also using them for that purpose? It made a lot of sense when we were few and had no toxic chemicals. However now, with so many of us and the nature of our chemicals, we have to find other ways.[21]

Animal manure was good for the soil so if a little ran into the rivers it probably didn't do much harm. But that was before the age of chemistry, the oil industry, and the chemicals developed by those industries. In 1976 there were 60,000 different chemicals being used in the USA. In 2013 there were 84,000 in use. Of these, the US Environmental Agency monitors 1 in 400.[22] Now the Potomac not only carries the likes of asbestos and chromium VI, nitrogen and phosphorous, but polychlorinated biphenyls and endocrine disrupters, which are found in pharmaceuticals, cosmetics and pesticides. Apparently there is more involved, when deciding to take the birth control pill, than just a personal decision. When a young lady on the pill goes to the toilet, she passes the chemicals in her urine. These then proceed through the sewage processing plants and are carried by the treated water into nature's wild water flows. From the rivers, lakes and oceans they are taken into the fish and other animals swimming or drinking there. The same applies to our medications, and chemical soaps, cosmetics and other personal care products.[23]

Could this great expense of cleaning the Potomac have been avoided by not fouling it in the first place? Probably not! It had been such a smooth and unremarkable development from getting rid of a little personal waste, to a lot of personal waste, to a factory's worth of toxic waste and on to a nation's worth of chemical beauty products. If there are future generations to care, they will have a horrendous clean-up bill to pay when they try to deal with our generation's mess. In fact, it is possible the toxicity cannot now be removed.

The Mekong

In China 70 per cent of lakes, rivers and reservoirs are badly polluted. Many are very badly polluted. The Mekong River has its source on the primal Tibetan plateau. From there it enters China's Yunnan province and continues in a general south-southeasterly direction, as it flows through Myanmar (Burma), Laos, Thailand, Cambodia and Vietnam, where it joins the South China Sea through the Mekong Delta. For a little less than half its journey, the upper river loses 14,500 ft (4,500 metres) in altitude as it tumbles from Tibet to Myanmar. For about 62 miles (100kms), it is the Myanmar and Laos border, but then it becomes a long border between Laos and Thailand, save for a distance when it flows within Laos. After reaching the Golden Triangle, it levels off into a generally more leisurely flow to the sea through

Cambodia and Vietnam. In all, the Mekong is reckoned to travel 3,050 miles (4909km) and to drain 307,000 square miles (795,000km2) of land along its length. It is the seventh longest river in Asia. In Vietnam it flows into nine distributary channels before emptying into the South China Sea.[24]

The Tibetan Plateau is hard, sparingly vegetated land. But as the river descends through the stunning gorges of Yunnan and northern Laos, it becomes more forested till arriving in the thick forest of the lower reaches. A good part of the length is mountainous and very beautiful. Until recently, the land of the lower reaches was heavily forested. Since the middle of the last century, though, much of the forest has been cleared. Northeast Thailand for instance, although 42 per cent forested in 1961, had that reduced to just 13 per cent by 1993. To the northeast in Laos, which is more mountainous, the land for many years has been cultivated by the slash and burn method of shifting agriculture. This has meant that at any one time 27 per cent of the land was being farmed. Unfortunately, although the soil only takes about 20 years to recover and be suitable for replanting, it takes very much longer for the land to re-vegetate naturally. In the highlands of Vietnam the forests have been reduced to less than 50 per cent, whilst in the delta area less than 10 per cent remains. Cambodia is the most heavily forested area with over 50 per cent still intact.[25] These lower reaches of the river were once an exceedingly rich forest. Now nearly all is gone. Some forest patches remain, but they are continually dwindling. With all that deforestation ongoing, on this once virgin watershed, one current problem is now the high level of soil erosion. No wonder really, as the lower Mekong is home to a great many poor, and mostly agrarian, humans.

This erosion is pretty well shared evenly between the upper and the lower rivers. The upper river only supplies about 20 per cent of the final total water flow. Of that, 30 per cent comes from the snowmelt of the Tibetan Plateau. So it is clear that the tributaries and rainfall of the lower altitudes make up 80 per cent of the river's eventual flow.

The Mekong River supports a huge freshwater fishing industry, which at 6 billion dollars a year is the largest in the world. It provides 80 per cent of the protein consumed by Cambodia's people. In the river's delta, Vietnam grows rice and obtains two or three harvests a year, which is fundamental to their economy and food supply. The river feeds over a 100 million people in total. All these rely on the Mekong agriculture and the fish, which are migratory and travel up and down the river, some as far as the river's source on the Tibetan Plateau.[26]

The populations of those countries seem to vary according to the source, but using the figures in *www.nationsonline.org/Oneworld*, the 2010 figures were as follows: Cambodia 15.1 million, Laos 6.4, Myanmar 53.5, Thailand 68.1, and Vietnam 89 million. That gives a grand total of 232.1 million people living on the lower 50 per cent of the river's length. One hundred years ago there were probably about 20 per cent of that number in that part of the world.

During the decade leading to 2012 the amount of cargo transported on the river has grown from 500 tons to 200,000 tons. That is a factor of 400.[27]

As so many rely on the Mekong economically and for a substantial part of their diet, it would seem a good idea to protect the integrity and water quality of the river. Rivers have annual flow cycles that are determined by seasons of rainfall and the snowmelt in the mountains, which in this case are the Himalayas. These flow cycles determine the migration times and patterns of the fish. Change the water flow, alter the amount of sediment in that flow, and those changes will disturb the fish migration patterns.

However, the Mekong is also seen as having the potential to produce enough hydroelectric power to provide electric energy for all of those nations in that region of South East Asia. The following figures mostly come from Jonathan Manthorpe, the esteemed international affairs columnist who has written extensively on the subject. The upper river is believed capable of providing 29,000 megawatts of power, while the lower river is thought to have a potential of 30,000 MW. Since the turn of the millennium enough dams have been brought online to provide China with 3,200 MW of electricity.[28]

Already China has built four dams on the upper river. They did this with no consultation with their neighbours on the lower reaches. In 2011 there were two dams under construction with another 134 projects being planned for the river of which at least eleven will be dams. Myanmar, Cambodia, Laos, Thailand and Vietnam are all considering new dams, but it seems the consultation between countries is not all it could be.

Of the two dams under construction in China, the Nuozhada Dam will be the largest and the world's third tallest. It will be 858 ft (260 m) high, produce 5,850 MW and flood 27,500 sq miles (71,224 km2), at an altitude of 2,664 ft (812 m).

In Cambodia the Lower Se San 2 Dam is planned jointly with Vietnam. It will only be 246 ft (75m) tall and will flood 137 sq miles (355km2). Nearly a hundred villages will be flooded and 38,000 people, including many indigenous inhabitants, will be displaced. The people express great dismay regarding what this dam will do to the migrating fish. Also in Cambodia, the Prek Liang 1 Dam is under study for the Virachey National Park. This park is one of the most important conservation areas in Cambodia and is one of only two ASEAN Heritage Park sites. There should be no way the government would consider it for flooding.

By 2011, with interstate conflicts and disagreements escalating and pressure from her downstream neighbours, Laos first stopped and then resumed construction of a $3.5 billion Xayaburi hydroelectric dam. The dam is designed to generate 1,280 megawatts, 95 per cent of which the Vientiane government is intending to export to Thailand as a way of generating income for Laos. The Xayaburi Dam is intended to be only the first of about 55 to be built on the lower Mekong and its tributaries. The Laos government first agreed to hold off on further dam construction till environmental studies were carried out. In November 2012 Laos began construction in earnest.

I understand that the Laotians are poverty-stricken, and need all the income they can get. I also realize the government has few opportunities for economic relief, but I still believe such irresponsible dam building is terrible. China is being particularly irresponsible. It clears rocks and sandbars, blasts rapids and gorges, floods some sections and dams others. Water levels have dropped on many reaches and now ferries get stuck. River crossings from the Thai city of Chaing Rai to Luang Prabang now take 2 days instead of the old 8 hours. Apparently fish can't swim upstream due to low water, and it's not reported what happens when they reach the dams. Did any of the planners ask the North America fisheries authorities about our experiences with dammed salmon rivers? Now fish catches are half of what they were before the Chinese dams were built. On top of these irritations, agricultural organophosphates runoff is causing algal bloom, and pesticide and heavy industry runoffs are turning the waters toxic. Water hyacinth growth is becoming another problem.[29]

However, who can blame the people of these developing nations from following the lead of the rich governments in the developed world? Dams and hydro energy have helped make the USA and Canada wealthy, and neither of those countries will hold off on new developments to save their environments. Why not pursue similar development projects? Because we now know of the terrible harm such dams cause to the environment.

The Mekong was second only to the Amazon for biodiversity. The greater Mekong sub-region had 430 mammal species, 1,200 bird species,

800 reptiles and amphibians, 20,000 plant species and an estimated 850 fish species. The Mekong region boasts 200 eco-regions, the greatest concentration on mainland Asia. It has the most large fish species of any river in the world. Those that grow to over 9 ft (3 meters) in length and 660 lbs (300 kgs) include the Mekong Giant Catfish, the Siamese Giant Carp and the Giant Pangasius. The Mekong Freshwater Stingray has a wingspan of up to 14 ft (4.3 meters). As might be expected, due to engineering projects and over-fishing, all are now in serious decline and close to extinction. The once common freshwater Irrawaddy Dolphin is now exceedingly rare, though not as rare as the Saltwater Crocodile, which is now extinct on the river. That crocodile used to be found along the full length of the lower river as did the Siamese Crocodile, which is now only surviving on a very few isolated pockets on the Laotian and Cambodian sections. Now the Mekong Dolphin and Mekong Dugong are endangered, with about as much chance of surviving as most of the other Mekong creatures. And again, once they are gone, they will be gone for good.[30]

Sixty years ago the lowland areas would have been well populated with a great many impressive mammal species, such as elephant, Javan Rhinos, Sumatran Rhinos and tigers. Now the rhinos have certainly gone with the poaching of the last Vietnamese Javan Rhino sometime after 2008. The tigers have been reduced, from a population of 1200 in 1998, to a few over 300 in 2011 – a 75 per cent decrease in 13 years. The last tiger seen in China was killed in 2009. In the same time frame a few scattered herds of wild Asian Elephants still hang on in those forested areas large enough to accommodate them.

Despite being one of the most varied landscapes anywhere, with enormous biodiversity, the Mekong is now one of the most threatened areas in the world. It holds five types of forest: deciduous, evergreen, diptocarp, mangrove and swamp forests. It has fertile lowlands, grasslands, floodplains and the delta ecosystem, as well as massifs, plateaus and limestone karsts. In the upper river, rapids roar over ravines and mountain streams sparkle in the high meadows. It is a place of wonder for sure, but at the hands of the massively increasing number of local humans, it suffers. It suffers logging, both legal and illegal, agricultural development, both industrial and slash and burn, rapids-blasting, dam-building, mining, road-building, over-fishing and poaching for the wildlife trade. And of course it has to handle all the expanding amount of human waste, and the agricultural, industrial, and chemical pollution. It is also a place that is likely to be especially hard hit by global climate change. All of Laos' biggest cities are on the Mekong as are many in the other countries. They are all becoming vulnerable to low water flow and pollution.[31]

It seems that, due to the high sea levels that inundated the South China Sea coastline up to about 9000 years ago, the Mekong Delta has only held its current geographic position for about 6000 years. That isn't very long in the grand scheme of things, but 6000 years seems a veritable eternity when compared with the 50 to 60 years it has taken us to nearly complete the destruction of the biological richness of that river.

How can we blame the people for putting so much pressure on the river and for wanting dams for power? We can't really, unless we acknowledge that having so many babies and allowing their populations to grow so large is the root cause of the problems. The Mekong is suffering terribly from human poverty, economic success, development and industry. But these problems are not confined to just this river. Really the Mekong should be considered just another example of the many rivers worldwide that suffer in similar ways.

In the Americas one of the largest lakes outside of the Great Lakes system is Lake Cocibolca, which is also the tenth largest lake in the world. In contrast to the great scale of the mighty Ganges many of the rivers that sometimes flow into that lake are tiny. Two of these run through Granada, Nicaragua. Not only are they tiny, they are infinitesimal. The names of both are prefixed by 'arroyo', which in Spanish means stream, as against 'rio', which signifies river. When they flow, they do so west to east on either side of the city centre and empty into Lake Cocibolca. Granada is a small colonial town of some 110,000 people on the Pacific side of the country. It is in an ecosystem known as Pacific dry forest. The countryside has intermittent rain from May till November, so most of the year the arroyos are dry.

When we stayed in Granada early in 2010, we rented a house that backed onto Arroyo Aduana. That suited me as there was still a stand of old riparian (riverside) forest at that point and the trees were usually full of birds. Two species of North American birds I saw every morning and evening were brilliant orange and black Baltimore Orioles and dark-red and black Orchard Orioles. Others I saw escaping the cold northern winters were more familiar to a British Columbia resident. Then there were some quite new to me such as a flock of Scissor-tailed Flycatchers, pairs of Crimson-fronted Parakeets and assorted parrots.

That small remnant of arroyo-hugging forest sounds rather delightful and a good place to spend some time birding. Unfortunately, it was known as an unsafe place to go, and even if one did venture to the stream's bank all one found was a solid bed of plastic waste. It is hard to say how deep the garbage was, but it appeared that, where the stream was fifteen feet wide, the plastic was three feet, or a meter, deep from one bank to the other. It was typical plastic: plastic bottles, plastic bags and plastic wrap of all sorts. And why shouldn't it be there? There was no other place for people to put it. I don't know whether there is enough flow of water in the rainy season to flush all the plastic into the lake, but judging by the appearance much of it looked to have been there for years. Lake Cocibolca is very large, but there is little hope for its future purity and integrity as long as it is used as a dump for all the local plastic waste.

Bali in Indonesia is another wonderful place to visit. However I discovered it's not good to swim off the northwest beaches when the tide is flowing out from the Javan southeast coast. I did and found myself swimming in a sea of plastic waste. Underwater, I guesstimated each cubic meter of water held four pieces of floating plastic. I naturally didn't venture too far in my quest for plastic statistics as I was on holiday, for goodness sake. Still I did see enough to assume that that stretch of sea was loaded with non-natural waste. I was told that it happens each time the tide changes and sweeps the outflow from Java's rivers past the Strait of Bali to the Java Sea beyond.

In the North-central Bali village of Munduk, one can find a local tourist attraction. It is called the Plastic Pyramid. This architectural wonder was produced on the initiative of the local headman. He encouraged the local school kids to collect all the plastic they could find along the roadside and other places. Seems fair, as they had probably dropped it there in the first place. Then, using traditional brick-making methods, the village molded the plastic into bricks and produced the pyramid which, when we were there, if I remember correctly, was some 15 ft high. With luck, the lessons of non-littering have now been learned, and the pyramid will grow no more. The basic problem is manifest all over the non-developed world.

I first noticed the problem of plastic litter in 1974 on my second trip to Peninsular Malaya and my first to Bali. In towns throughout the peninsula, the street vendors were selling food and drink in plastic bags.

The multi-coloured drinks were displayed in large flagons of clear plastic. From those, sweet drinks were dispensed in small clear plastic bags with a protruding plastic straw. One could choose a pink drink, a red drink, a yellow drink, a green drink, a blue drink, an indigo drink, and probably even a violet drink. There were drinks of every colour of the rainbow, but the plastic bags were always colourless. When finished with, they were dropped on the ground no matter where the person happened to be. At that time in Bali, however, we could still buy street vendor food wrapped in banana leaves. I don't remember seeing any of the multi-hued drinks vendors then on the island. Probably the sweet soft drinks had not reached the streets of Bali at that time. The point is that all over the undeveloped world people had wrapped their take-out food in such natural materials as banana leaves. When dropped on the ground, they quickly composted back to earth. The change to plastic had not been accompanied by a change in habits nor in an expansion of the municipal garbage collection system.

It is the typical problem; entrepreneurs come up with ideas of how to make a buck, which is what Free Enterprise Capitalism is all about. Societies eagerly adopt consumerism, but there is no thought to the disposal of the waste. Nor is there any money to clean up the resulting mess. Somehow one can forgive those people in the newly industrial nations when they first taste the fruits of the consumer society. It is not so easy to forgive the people in the rich nations of the world.

In 2008 the USA consumed an estimated 33.6 million tons of plastic. Of that, 2.2 million tons were recycled and 2.6 million tons were converted to energy by burning. That leaves 28.9 million tons that finished up in the landfill or in the sea - a rate of nearly 86 per cent. Now, in many respects, the USA is the world's most advanced country, so one would expect it to be the one country to lead the rest in waste management. Therefore one might conclude that, if the US can only remove 14 per cent of the plastics from the landfill, the statistics for most other countries must be even worse.

In 2009, the USA consumed 50 billion bottles of water each year, or 1500 every second. Of those, 80 per cent were thrown away, and 17 million barrels of oil were used to produce them.[32] Globally 100 million plastic water bottles were purchased every day, and the world spent over $100 billion per year on bottled water. Whatever the precise figures, a huge number of plastic bottles are produced each year. Yet if the US can't recycle its bottles, what chance for recycling in the less advanced countries?

I don't know how much plastic was strewn along Granada's Arroyo

Aduana, probably only a few score tons, but nothing to the millions of tons of plastic thrown out elsewhere. During the first years of the 21st century, Europe was using about 800,000 tons of plastic bags each year. In 2010, the Los Angeles River in California carried 410 tons of plastic trash out to sea. That's 840,000 lbs, or a heck of a lot of plastic bags (we know how heavy a plastic bag is). Of course, being in LA, the river outlet to the sea is rather less a beautiful estuary of grassy banks and willow trees than a continuous dry bed of concrete with outlets that flow with water only on rare occasions. The city of Los Angeles has now, in 2011, decided to use stainless steel screens to catch the garbage before it enters the sea.

The few river examples given above are, unfortunately, more typical of current rivers than remarkable. There are untouched rivers in the less developed areas of our earth - Alaska, Northern Canada and Siberia - but they are becoming fewer as forestry, agriculture and particularly resource extraction, move into those areas. 60 per cent of the Earth's rivers are said to be in trouble, but that number is rising fast.

The troubles rivers are facing may be any one, or any combination, of the following:

- Natural pollution
- Agricultural pollution
- Chemical and industrial pollution
- Damming for major power projects
- Excessive and ill-considered building of 'run of river power projects'
- Concreting of river banks
- Building of dykes to prevent the natural cycle of flooding
- Excess water being drawn off for agricultural purposes
- Gravel extraction
- Blasting of rapids
- Dehydration caused by forestry
- Watershed erosion
- Over fishing
- The melting of the source glaciers due to global warming

Unfortunately rivers flow into lakes and seas, so that whatever affects the rivers also influences the receiving bodies of water.

If a relatively clean river like the Hampshire Avon, which runs through clean countryside and small towns with little industry, can suffer noticeable declines in the fish stocks, what of other rivers? Surely it is reasonable to conclude that rivers in developing countries, such as the Mekong with its plans for so many dams and lots of new industry along much of its length, will suffer massive devastation to all of their natural systems. This, unfortunately, is already true of too many rivers.

Early in September 2013, the UK's Guardian newspaper reported on the Fuhe River in Central China. Apparently a local chemical plant, accidentally or on purpose, dumped ammonia into the river. The result was an estimated 100 tons of dead fish, which, according to Wang Sanqing, the Huanghualao village Communist Party Secretary, covered the river's entire surface and "looked like snowflakes." Rivers with great areas of the surface covered in dead fish now seem to be an oft-repeated occurrence. If it can happen to the Fuhe River in central China and to the Pearl River in the USA it can happen anywhere. And if it can happen anywhere, it can happen everywhere. It can happen everywhere that industrial plants are situated beside life-giving rivers.

Hydroelectric dams, which can provide multi-megawatts of power more cleanly than hydrocarbon burning power stations, have many advantages. To emerging nations, with burgeoning human populations, dams can be the answer to their electrical needs. However, building a dam along a river where fish and mammal species have always traveled from estuary to headwaters presents a terrible dilemma. We can all understand that it is wrong to do so, but that still isn't enough to stop the dams. As a consequence the ecosystems are destroyed. By 2003 there were 48,000 large dams over 15 meters high worldwide, with another 1600 being constructed. Most were in the basins of the Mekong, Yangtze, Indus, Ganges, Tigris-Euphrates, Amazon and La Plata River in South America, though dams are also being constructed in Malaysia, Ethiopia and just about any developing country with a river. In 2003, the Yangtze basin was the most at risk with 46 dams planned or under construction.

According to WWF Global and The International Commission on Large Dams *Position Paper on Dams and the Environment,* one result, which has been exacerbated by these dams, is that freshwater species populations fell by 50 per cent between 1970 and 2000. Many of the future dams are planned for rivers that, until recently, had been almost pristine.

It is also reasonable to assume that in developing countries, all over the globe, there are, even now, new Cuyahoga Rivers being polluted with so much industrial effluent that they also will catch fire one day.

There are now river estuaries that were once rich with distributary streams, wildlife-attracting mudflats, mangroves and marshes covering many thousands of acres, but that have seen no water for years. Some are now dried up deserts. All the water has been diverted, or otherwise used up, before it reaches the lake or the sea. Apparently a full 50 per cent of Chinese rivers have disappeared over the recent past. Presumably they have been diverted for agriculture or industry, or simply built over by cities and other infrastructure.

There are good news stories though. In a report in the 14 July 2009, *Evening Standard* newspaper, London's Thames, which in 1957 was declared biologically dead, is now reasonably clean and described as teeming with fish. It is thought to be the cleanest it has been for two hundred years, which possibly means four hundred years, as it was certainly pretty filthy in 1809. 125 wildlife species have been counted on the river and all the fish now attract such predators as seals, porpoise, and dolphin and, in 2006, a Northern Bottlenose Whale. In the upper reaches of the river are such typical British freshwater fish as bream and chub. Around the city centre fly fishermen have caught trout, while salmon have been seen swimming upriver. In the estuary, 200 commercial fishermen now catch plaice and sole, cod and bass, haddock and herring and a bunch of other species. Even colonies of Short-snouted Seahorses are now to be found in the Thames.

Even the Cuyahoga River, of Cleveland fire fame, is now very much more healthy thanks to the Clean Water Act. Counts indicate that the river is now home to nearly sixty species of fish, including Steelhead and Largemouth Bass, which in turn attract ospreys, eagles and herons. However when, if ever, the fish will be fit for human consumption is questionable due to the high levels of mercury and other metal contaminates still in the river.

I think this illustrates an interesting point. London was the world's largest port, financial center, and a place of corporate head-offices, but the factories were elsewhere. London's Thames didn't suffer as much industrial and chemical pollution as many other cities, even though it had been receiving human waste for at least 2,000 years, but that was more or less all it was polluted with. But it took less than two hundred years of industrial waste to make the pristine Cuyahoga chemically polluted for a very long time.

Rivers can be brought back from some awful abuse. But as we return a few to health, we start and accelerate the abuses of so many more as new countries industrialize. It is as if we learn nothing. We, the multitudinous ones, insist on fouling and damming the rivers and their waters even though clean water is one element on which we are absolutely dependent. As we try to provide for our huge new populations we are laying our rivers, and their bio-systems, to waste.

It is believed we have lost 30 per cent of the freshwater biodiversity - both flora and fauna - since industrialization began, but most since the middle of the 20th century. A report, by the Organization for Economic Cooperation and Development, on water to 2050, projects a 130 per cent increase in demand for domestic water, a 140 per cent increase for power generation and a 55 per cent increased water demand for manufacturing.

5 Malaysia, Borneo

In his 1911 book *In Malay Forests,* George Maxwell writes of the vast virgin forest that covered the land from coast to coast. At the time the, jungle had barely been penetrated and nearly all the small population of some hundreds of thousand Malays and Chinese lived for the most part along the banks of the many rivers that flowed down from the interior highlands. He describes the forest at length; how nearly all the coast was mangrove; how the clouds, rushing in from the sea, behaved when they reached the mountains; and how timeless the forest was. He writes, "Neither the season, nor the flight of time, leaves a mark upon the forest; virgin in the days of which we cannot guess the morn, virgin in our days, virgin it will remain in the days of generations yet unborn." It is now believed that the forests of peninsular Malaya are a hundred million years old. Europeans first entered them only about 200 years ago. The land he wrote about, Peninsular Malaya, covered the area from the border with Thailand (then Siam) in the north to Singapore in the south. The country we now call Malaysia is a federation of the peninsula with Saba and Sarawak in Borneo.

His book is a wonderful document recording the customs, practices and beliefs of the Malays, as well as the lore of the wildlife he encountered, at the turn of the 19th and 20th centuries. It is possibly my most beloved book. Maxwell was one of the more decent Britons of the time: well educated, adventurous, interested in the sciences and philosophy, and supportive of, and comfortable with, the native peoples among whom he lived. He also indulged in what we would call trophy hunting; however, most of the hunting that he recorded was to help the local villagers by shooting trouble wildlife – man-eating tigers and rogue-elephants – that were killing the people and destroying their crops.

Personally I dislike hunters with a vengeance unless they are true subsistence hunters who have to kill for survival, but I can forgive him. He was from the tail end of the age discovery, of exploration, of science and, regrettably, of a destructive approach to nature. Like Darwin, Alfred Wallace and Audubon, he sought knowledge of the natural world, of the newly discovered, and was a conservationist at heart. He was, unfortunately, also part of that age and ethic which determined that to study and learn about a creature, you had to kill it first. It is what we children were attempting to do in 1945 with our egg and butterfly collections. So when Maxwell went deep into the forest in quest of a Sumatran Rhinoceros or Malayan Tapir it is possible that he was one of very few Europeans ever to have seen such elusive creatures. To me the most impressive thing about his book is the portrayal of this huge unknown and unconquerable ancient forest, a forest full of mystery and of wonderful insects, reptiles, birds and animals, of unknown plants, orchids and other things seldom seen unless one reached the canopy - a place where few humans ventured and where industrial humans didn't belong.

We now know that the number of tree and plant species endemic to a forest as old as that of the peninsula is huge. It has several times the biodiversity of North America. Most of North America and Northern Europe had been under ice until 18-10,000 years ago, meaning that the land has only had that amount of time to welcome plant species. The tropics never saw that ice so have had millions of years to attract and evolve new species of both plants and animals. Consequently, the equatorial areas are extremely rich in diversity while the glaciated ones, such as Canada, are relatively poor.

Maxwell writes about a kramat Javan Rhino in the state of Perak that had killed at least three men on different occasions. A kramat animal might have been described as one bewitched. It was often credited with supernatural powers, and, in time, such a beast came to be considered the reincarnation of a well-known local inhabitant. Some kramat animals were thought of as benevolent, such as a local tiger that never attacked people, even children. This rhino, though, was malevolent and fierce, and, for more than 25 years, would attack anyone it met on the jungle paths. It had been a threat since well before the British started governing Perak in 1874. The local people had done everything in their power to kill the animal as it was preventing them from entering the jungle for any purpose. One hunting party of Malays believed they had fired 50 shots into the animal without effect. It was definitely kramat. It was also described as having a blue horn. In those days Malays believed the Java Rhinoceros were of four categories based on the horn colour: the wax-coloured horn, the flame-coloured horn the blue horn and the black horn. Maxwell notes that at that time the Javan Rhino was considered 'somewhat rare' on peninsular Malaya when compared to the Sumatran Rhino. The hunt, and final killing of the animal, makes interesting reading: it took three days of skirmishes and at least six times the animal charged him and his trackers – but always to a point some distance behind and to the side of them.[1]

That rhino was a Javan *(Rhinoceros sondaicus)*. Those animals used to frequent the forests of South East Asia from Burma in the north east, through Thailand, Laos, Cambodia, Vietnam and Malaya and across to the islands of Sumatra and Java. That is an area of some 2.800,000 km2. There are certainly no Javan Rhinos on Peninsula Malaya, and poachers shot the last surviving Vietnam rhino in May 2010. The forty remaining Javan Rhinos are now confined to the Ujung Kulon National Park, a small 1206 km2 peninsula of forest on the western tip of Java. So in about one hundred years we have caused that animal to go from 'somewhat rare' over an area of about 2.8 million square kilometers to virtually extinct in an area of 1200 km2. Using the curennt density of the final 40 animals suggests that, historically, there may have been some 94,000 of those rhinos living in their forests.[2]

The range of the smaller, and hairy, Sumatran Rhinoceros *(Dicerorhinus sumatrensis)* covered some of the same territory though it also included the very large island of Borneo. Now, with their ancient and magnificent forests of South East Asia nearly all gone only about 100 Sumatran Rhinos survive worldwide. 12-15 of the Rhinos may still survive in Sabah, Borneo, while the rest of the 100 live in three national parks in Sumatra. The few that still survived on Peninsula Malaya into the 1980s are believed to be no more.[3] The maps below indicate the declines.

Historic Distribution of Sumatran Rhino

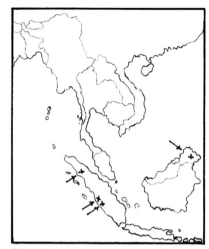

2012 Distribution of Sumatran Rhino

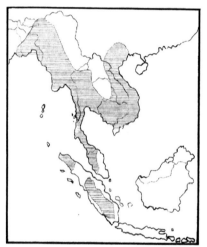

Historic Distribution of Javan Rhino

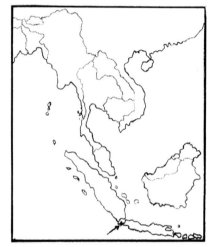

2012 Distribution of Javan Rhino

The above diagrams show with alarming clarity the loss, from forest destruction and from hunting, of habitable land for just two species. Unfortunately, similar maps would describe the pitiable state of most of our planet's mammal species. All the parks where the rhinos still exist have to be patrolled continually to counteract poachers. The rhinos are just two of the South East Asian species to be near extinction. Many other animals, such as the wild elephants, Borneo Pygmy Elephants, tapirs, tigers, Clouded Leopards, Guar Bison and scores of others are similarly depleted and, where they do survive, do so in scattered remnants of forest with no connection one to the other for breeding purposes. Tigers, for instance, are thought to have numbered about 100,000 in the 1930s but they are now reduced to about 3,000 worldwide. We all know of tigers, as they are icon species, but the percentage that they are reduced – well over 99 per cent from historic levels – can probably be applied to most of the other animals with which they share any specific habitat.

We note the tiger numbers, but are unaware of the millions of other species. We are unaware of the reptiles and amphibians, the small mammals and the insects. And what of the myriad plant species? It is estimated the up to 75 per cent of all the world's plant species grow in tropical rain forests, and that 50 per cent grow in the canopy alone.[4] It is reasonable to assume that when we fell the forests and reduce the numbers of an iconic species like tigers, we do the same to the plants that grow in the tropical forest canopy and on the forest floor. In reality, when one goes, they all go.

In 1957, about fifty years after Robert Maxwell published his wonderfully interesting, though near-forgotten, book, I was fortunate to be posted to Malaya. Like many of my British contemporaries, I was doing my National Service in the army. In those days, one was likely to be sent to any number of places across the globe, some interesting, some dreaded and some, like Malaya, an active service war zone where we fought communist terrorists.

It was a wonderful country; very hot and humid but with an exotic odor that is indescribable, entirely memorable and wonderfully evocative. Butterflies of every colour flew lazily by, and our very basic atap (palm leaf) thatch-roofed huts, or bashas, daily entertained enormous insects the like of which we would never see in England.

Our camp was a small place on a hill, surrounded by baluka or secondary jungle. The bashas were built of forest saplings and such, with atap roofs and concrete slab floors. They were open to every breeze, as the chest-high wooden walls met neither the floor nor the ceiling but allowed large gaps to the outside. The open floors allowed, not just the cooling air, but any passing wildlife to cruise right on through. The atap roofs made comfortable homes for insects of all sorts, including a nesting Praying Mantis that later revealed herself to me when the nest, mother and a few dozen baby mantises landed on my face while I was enjoying an afternoon snooze.

At this point it might be worth recounting our first night in camp.

We were intrepid young National Service men, fresh off the boat, who had completed a truck journey some way up country for which we were fully armed against the possibility of ambush. At that point, the nearest any of us had been to a jungle had been the daffodils and primroses in our suburban gardens back home. So we imagined what the jungle would be like and how we would face a confrontation with the deadly terrorists. Some of us even fantasized on what great deeds we would perform for queen and country. Then, when a dozen of us settled down to our first jungle sleep in a large basha, we tried to be brave, although the screeches, croaks, and scary noises from animals in the forest, created a certain doubt. Suddenly the tension was rent by a fearful scream that came from Pete's bed. Almost as one, we sat bolt upright in the darkness, fear in every eye and our British noses straining against the mosquito nets. The less foolhardy amongst us had their heads buried under their pillows. Had an animal attacked? Had Pete been knifed by a terrorist? Had a poisonous snake bitten him in his bed? What monster was abroad?

It turns out that Pete had been lying on his back, admiring the inside of his mosquito net, when a huge fang and claw invested animal leapt from the low wall and spread-eagled itself onto the net directly above his head. What kind of jungle monster could it be? . . In truth it was our camp cat, tortoiseshell-furred and friendly as could be. She was just making a visit to the new lads from England. Unfortunately she hadn't told Pete to expect her.

After a short acclimatization we moved to the top bashas, which each slept four of us for our 20-month tour and, although the camp was a little more extensive than I have described, (it had a brick guard-room), it was, in reality, something close to a primitive vacation eco-resort. We were a tribe of young men of eighteen or nineteen years. It seems we were sent all that way to follow dogs through the forest, which was very interesting and somewhat scary at times. When not working with the dogs or on patrol, we spent a good part of our days lazing about the holiday camp wearing nothing more than flip-flops and shorts, or an army towel around our waists. The towels were coloured forest green. The dogs tended to be more formally dressed.

Trusty the tracker dog, 1958

Malayan tigers frequented our camp at that time, attracted to the few dozen military dogs that we trained for patrol and tracking work. Apparently, dogs to tigers are as roast beef and Yorkshire pudding to Englishmen. Earlier, in the comfort of a western cinema watching Hollywood films, I had gained the fearful impression that entering a jungle was an invitation to attack by wildlife of all sorts. Tigers would be stalking each human, and deadly snakes would hang from branches just waiting to fall onto anyone passing below. The teddy bear picnic theme song 'If you go into the woods today you're sure of a big surprise' seemed to be a deadly warning. But not in Malaya, it turned out. In that jungle, wildlife was seldom seen. In fact, one great disappointment was how little, apart from leeches, one did see. Patrolling in the jungle was really a matter of traveling as silently as possible, drenched in sweat, but almost blindly. The undergrowth was so dense one could see little more than a few yards in any direction, hence the patrol dogs. They were trained to identify any ambush that might be ahead. The other dogs were used for tracking following contact with a terrorist group.

Our camp was in a relatively safe area so off-duty we were very relaxed. However, our friendly camp tiger alarmed plenty of towel and flip-flop-equipped young soldiers when he, or she, suddenly appeared in a lonely spot. But the threat seems to have been imagined because none of us were actually eaten.

A fine account of the truth of animal threats of the South East Asian forest can be found in Colonel Spencer Chapman's book *The Jungle is Neutral*. It is an account of his three and a half years spent behind Japanese lines in the Malayan jungle. He was performing small terrorist raids against the Japanese, and organizing resistance groups of the communists, who were enthusiastic to fight. During most of those years, from January 1942 till August 1945, he had minimal communication with British regular forces and must have traveled alone and on foot in the jungle many hundreds, if not thousands, of miles. He wrote that during all that time he glimpsed only one tiger crossing his path more than hundred yards ahead. He didn't see much else either although he often became dreadfully sick and weakened by disease.[5] So it turns out that the animals weren't the threat to us that we had, in our naivety, expected. However, the history of the past couple of centuries proves what a terrible threat we were to those animals.

Our own local tigers - I never knew if there was more than one - were occasionally glimpsed in late evening. The most scary contacts, though, were when they were seen looking into the open guard room door at three in the morning, or padding past a lone guard patrolling in the dead of night near the totally open and unfenced camp perimeter. The tigers were protected and not to be harmed, which was very unnerving to me at eighteen when doing lone patrolling guard duty. The moonless nights were most frightening. In the full moon one could almost read a book and certainly see some hundreds of yards, but moonless nights were totally black. I quaked at the thought of how many unseen tigers, or how many terrorists for that matter, had a very good idea of where I was . . . thought me easy meat . . . and were making plans for my painful demise.

I had no idea that three subspecies of tiger were either going, or had gone, extinct in recent years, and that I would soon be worrying, not about my survival, but about theirs. Our fear of wild animals seems to have been greatly overblown. Our terrible threat to them was seldom acknowledged.

It was the tail end of what was called The Emergency: a time when a small army of 4,000 Chinese communists had returned to their camps hidden deep in the jungle. They had decided to wage a guerilla war on the colonial government, through murder of plantation managers and the local population in general. It was an attempt to force a communist government on the country. When, following the Japanese invasion, the British army officers, Col. Chapman among them, had remained behind in the jungle to assist and arm a resistance force, they had developed a friendly working relationship with the enthusiastic communist participants. This was done with the promise that Malaya could expect independence shortly after the war was over. However being unwilling to wait, and following the lead of Ho Chi Min in proclaiming North Vietnam an independent republic in 1945, and Mao Zedong's continued victories in China, the Malay communists decided, in 1948, to start their own revolution. India had been granted independence the year before, in 1947. Burma was to get independence that year. A communist government had been proclaimed in North Korea. The communists were winning in French Indochina, and the Javanese were on the brink of winning their demand for independence from the Dutch. All this created a fear in the West that much of Eastern Asia would become a vast communist monolith of non-democratic nations dominated by China. As the overwhelming majority of Malayans, whether Malay, Chinese, Tamil or Orang Asli (inhabitants of the deep jungle and the true first people of the peninsula), were not communist, the government resisted and the ensuing Emergency lasted until the late 1950s. Some hard core CTs (communist terrorists) remained in the jungle till the 1980s but were quite ineffective by then.

European colonialism has a bad name now, but it is worth noting a couple of things. In September 1872, there was so much lawlessness, chaos and warfare between different groups in the Malay States that Chung Keng Quee, and 44 other Chinese leaders on the peninsula, signed a petition requesting the British become involved. They wanted the British to protect the population and to bring peace.[6] Then in 1874, when the British were first getting involved, Queen Victoria gave the following instructions to Prime Minister Disraeli, "We must . . . bring the peoples of these countries to the stage where they can govern themselves." This was accomplished some seventy years later with Merdeka (Independence) in 1957.

Off the west coast of the Malay Peninsula is the old trading island of Penang. Lim Kean Siew was a member of a prosperous Penang family. He was educated in England, became a lawyer in Malaya, a member of parliament of significance and, later, a senator. He explains in his family memoirs, *The Eye Over Golden Sands*, why the Chinese flooded into the British-ruled States - in this case Penang - during the height of colonialism. He says "many Chinese were lured to its shores because the British had brought *Pax Brittanica* there and life was peaceful with plenty of opportunities." Everyone could live by the rule of law instead of the whim of some despot, as was the case in China and many non-colonial states. His grandfather was "a typical immigrant fleeing from poverty and the rampaging, rapacious feudal warlords at the height of Manchu corruption ..." Under British rule he prospered and became very wealthy.[7]

For the Chinese in particular, that peace and prosperity was destroyed when the Japanese invaded and conquered Malaya in 1942. That occupation ended in 1945 with the Japanese surrender following the atom bombings of Hiroshima and Nagasaki.

In the book *Tales from the South China Seas. Images of the British in South-East Asia in the Twentieth Century* Richard Broom states:

> I wish that critics of colonialism could have been present when the British returned to Malaya after the Japanese surrender. Their reception was totally rapturous from all sections of the population. Three weeks after the surrender it was still going on; as I drove up-country people were coming out of their houses by the roadside and waving and cheering. The obvious relief on their faces was something terrific to see.[8]

I believe I am correct in saying that during British rule the people of Malaya were, for the most part, happy, prosperous and free to enjoy fulfilling lives. It certainly seemed a happy place when I was there. As white off-duty soldiers, we could go anywhere at any time, unarmed and with no fear at all of the local population. The people and different religions seemed to co-exist in harmony, and there was absolutely no sign of the fundamentalist Islamic restrictions that now pervade the country.

One outcome of the Chinese communist emergency was that it nurtured the suspicion with the British authorities that the Chinese in Malaya were primarily loyal to communist China. Even though thousands of Chinese were fleeing the new communist state and flooding into Hong Kong, the British government seems to have equated a person of Chinese descent with a communist and more or less excluded the Chinese from the Malayan Independence discussions. This was despite the fact that the first wave of Chinese settlers came only a few years after the first wave of the Javanese immigrants who became the Malays. So, during the self-rule discussions, the Chinese community, which at the time was 40 per cent of the population with a majority decidedly non-communist, and more pro-British than the Malays, was largely excluded. One result was that the Malays who, at the time, were only 50 per cent of the population would dominate the future government.

But the politics of sixty years ago are probably irrelevant to the wildlife crisis in the country that has since developed. Under British rule, wildlife suffered badly, and under Malaysian rule it has fared even worse.

Although I suspect the numbers are filled out a bit, the Malay government says there are between 600 and 800 of the endangered subspecies Malayan tigers *(Panthera tigris jacksoni)* living on the peninsula in two separate enclaves. The majority live in the Malayan parks of Taman Negara, in the peninsula's center, and Belum Temenggor Reserve, on the border with Thailand. This subspecies of tiger is amongst the smallest, with the males having a maximum length of 93 inches and weighing only 260 lbs (120 kg). A typical Siberian tiger, in contrast, weighs 389 lbs (176 kg) with large ones weighing 490 lbs.[9] I must say, had I known that the Malayan tigers were so small I might, when doing guard duty, have demonstrated a little more backbone at the thought of an encounter. But in those days, a tiger was a tiger, and a fear-producing animal at that.

I had been to Taman Negara, the national forest park, in 1958 when four of us were given a seven-day leave to visit. In those days it was still called the King George V Game Reserve, as it had been established in 1938 by the colonial British government to conserve Malayan wildlife. To reach the park, we traveled by train and a small boat, and had to be armed at all times. The highlight of the rail journey was a branch line through thick forest, along which the driver would stop whenever a sarong-clad native indicated he needed a ride. We never saw a single village, just dense forest, a rare pathway, and the occasional native getting on or off. After being dropped at a village the only way to complete our journey to the park guesthouse was by a four-hour boat ride. This was along the Tembeling River, another memorable part of the trip. Along the riverbanks I saw my first spectacular Paradise Flycatcher and a great number of assorted kingfishers.

When we arrived, we found a small Malay kampong beside the river and a lone middle-aged Englishman who was the warden. On the first evening of our arrival, he called us to his bungalow to view a herd of Saladang or Guar Bison that had moved out of the jungle and were grazing in an adjacent clearing. He told us how fortunate we were to see such shy and fierce animals, but I was too callow to understand or appreciate the rarity of our good luck. Now it would be a near miracle to see such animals in Taman Negara, or in the Endau Rompin Forest in Johor to the south. The only remaining herd of note is in Belum Temenggor Park, to the north. Those three parks preserve a total forested area of 6,318 square kilometers or just over 5 per cent of the land mass. So although close to 95 per cent of the primary forest has been felled, it does seem that a few of the larger Malaysian species are holding out in the three parks. They include elephant, Saladang, Tapir, Sun Bear, Serow, Samba Deer, and Bearded Pig. It is encouraging that some forest remains, as the forest destruction in most of Malaysia has been so ruthless and complete, but with no connecting corridors It is doubtful that the inbred animals will remain healthy in such small areas.

The warden also told us that the terrorists had killed his brother. I now wish I had spoken with him more. I am sure he was quite lonely for British conversation.

When our period of National Service ended in December 1958, a group of us flew back to England in an old Avro York, a prop plane developed from the wartime Lancaster bomber. We sat in backward-facing seats. The flight was slow and low, and, on the peninsula, we could see endless jungle. There were some rubber plantations, which could be identified from the orderly trees planted in grid fashion, but most of what I saw was forest. I didn't think too much of it as it looked as one might expect a forested land to look. Little did I know how quickly a hundred million year old forest could be destroyed.

Less than 20 years later, in 1975, when I flew for a second time from Peninsular Malaya I saw little forest, just regimented plantations of palm oil and rubber formed up one against another as far as the eye could see. The few remnant forested areas were in hilly country too steep for agriculture. Now the only other forest is reserved as parks. These constitute a tiny part of that of a hundred years ago. George Maxwell's thought that the forest would "remain virgin for generations yet unborn" was good for about two generations, and his human population of "some hundreds of thousands" was now, one hundred years later in 2010, 23 million strong.[10][11]

Another thing I think noteworthy is that sixty years ago, under British rule, religion seemed a non-issue. There were temples, mosques and churches of one sort or another, but no outward sign of any tensions. The Muslim Malay women, so beautiful in their bright sarongs and white blouses, with their glossy black hair visible for all to see, were far freer than they are today. They lived more freely than they now do under the present strictures, which insist that all Malay women at least wear headscarves. Many are fully covered. In 1998 when I lived in a suburb of the capital, Kuala Lumpur, for 6 months, I noticed quite a few Saudi Arabian imams who were attached to the village mosques. Presumably they were a later version of Christian missionaries. I guess they were in the country to encourage the people to toe the line. One of the Malay employees in the office of the college where I was teaching arrived one morning very upset. Her husband had been instructed by the local imam to insist that she cover her head. Neither her husband nor she wanted that.

That was my last trip to Malaysia, and was at a time when the nearby island of Borneo was suffering massive devastation and huge fires. They were mostly set by national companies intent on reaping the 26 per cent annual profits they could make by planting and owning palm oil plantations. The fires were also being set by landless Javan immigrants, immigrants who are still being encouraged to leave their over-populated island for the promise of land in under-populated Borneo. Many of those Javanese were clearing land in the hope of growing crops at something better than subsistence levels, but most of the once-forested land has proved unsuitable for agriculture. At the time, about 48 per cent of the forests had been cleared. By 2011, about 57 per cent had been destroyed although that figure is on the low side and unconfirmed.[12] The fires continue to produce smoke haze over large areas of Southeast Asia. The fires also don't do much to help the hundreds of thousands of rare insect species that are being incinerated. The Borneo forest is an estimated 130 million years old, though I could find no source for that estimate, so the depth of fallen vegetable matter – leaves and dead trees – which has become peat, is very deep. Now, because of the fires, the abundant peat burns underground with no likelihood of ever being put out. Not only is the invaluable and priceless forest being wantonly destroyed but, also, so is 130 million years of peat.

By 2013 at least 80 per cent of Malaysian Borneo Forest had been logged.[13] With Sabah having 8 per cent of its forest intact and Sarawak having just 3 per cent of its forest unlogged.[14]

A forest of such an age may not sound very exciting. After all, what's a few million years here or there? Such an age is surely not too significant. Is it? It turns out that, when put in context, such a forest is of great significance. By comparison, the island of Hawaii, the youngest of those paradise islands was, a million years ago, a group of five undersea volcanoes. Those volcanoes pushed above the ocean and became an island only 500 thousand years ago. The first Hawaiian island, Kauai, rose from the sea about 4-6 million years ago.[15] Some 100 million years before Kauai existed, Borneo's forest was already 24 million years old. About 40 million years ago, the landmass we now call India was still pushing against, and sub-ducting below, southern Asia, causing the land to elevate, buckle and form the Himalayas. The Himalayas are given an age of about 35 million years.[16] Before the mountains were formed, much of that rock was seabed. So, long before the world's highest mountains had risen out of the sea, Borneo's forest was in the early stages of its long growth. Only the Daintree Rain Forest, in northeast Australia, is believed to be older.

The plateau that we now know as Mexico's Yucatan only lifted from the seabed 2 million years ago.

One hundred and thirty million years is a period that has seen an awful lot of interesting happenings. The dinosaurs were wiped out 65 million years ago, so whatever the catastrophe that killed them off must surely have affected the forests of Borneo. Another great challenge would have been the super-volcano eruption of Lake Toba on nearby Sumatra. That ejection sent billions of tons of sulphur-laden ash and rock exploding out of the volcano. Over time, the massive volcanic event created sulfuric acid rain, blotted out the sun and caused the world's sea temperature to decrease by 5 degrees. The explosion left a hole in Northern Sumatra that was 100 km long, 30 km wide and half a km deep. The hole filled with rain and is now Lake Toba. That happened only 75 thousand years ago.[17] With a history of surviving all that, such a forest, and all the tropical forests, should be considered sacrosanct, and natural wonders of the world. Felling them is a terrible crime, but even now the last stands are being sought and felled.

The tropical forests include those of Central and South America, including the Amazon, West Africa, including the Congo, Southeast Asia and the area of New Guinea and northern Australia. That of India is nearly all gone, as are those of Asia.

The coniferous forests of British Columbia and the oak woods of old England can be no older than the end of the last ice age when the glaciers melted from the land. That is a period of some ten thousand years. In that case, we can assume that, when destroyed, these forests could rejuvenate if given another few thousand years.[18]

Around the Equator, however, there was no ice age and forested jungles thrived for eons. Jungle trees live and jungle trees die and, whether they are a hundred years old or a thousand, once they fall they decay to become humus or peat. Presumably, it is from the depth and age of the peat that the age of a forest, such as Borneo's, can be ascertained. Others are thought older and some younger. Whatever the age, we are talking about enough time for species within the ecosystem to evolve, flourish, multiply and die out. They evolved from the primitive beginnings of millions of years ago to the current diverse species that they are today. When these tropical forests are destroyed, we have to assume they will take more millions of years to rebuild to anything comparable to the mature biological complexities that they were when uncut.

Borneo is the earth's third largest island, and the only one divided among three different nations – Indonesia, Malaysia and Brunei. It is rather like Britain except that Britain is presently united as one kingdom. We know that, when it comes to environmental degradation, there are many governments with totally appalling records. Those of Malaysia and Indonesia are currently amongst the very worst, and Borneo is reaping the catastrophe of those countries' development plans.

However, when I was born, Borneo was, like most of Southeast Asia and the islands of what is now known as Indonesia, a paradise of unexplored primary jungle. It is said to have had the richest biodiversity on earth. In a recent WWF survey, it was found that one 6.5-hectare block of Borneo lowland forest contained more plant species than are indigenous to all of the US and Canada combined. The US and Canada have 750 species of trees.[19] Borneo's forest is known to contain at least 3,000, including countless fruit-bearing trees, 15,000 species of flowering plants, a host of unique mammals and birds, and untold numbers of insects. The terrestrial mammal species alone number 222, and the resident birds over 420.[20] Since 1996, 361 new animal and plant species have been discovered on the island. I think it correct to say that such ancient forests are true wonderlands of biological riches, the majority of which have not been investigated in any depth at all. Who knows how many medical cures or useful plant materials, such as rubber, may be found there. Surely, of 15,000 flowering plants, some may hold ingredients that could be valuable or beneficial to us. Such an awesome part of the world should be considered inviolable, and untouchable.

So Borneo, with 4 per cent the landmass of the US and Canada, holds five times the number of tree species. It contains ten times England's 35 indigenous trees. If there are 700 tree species in only 6.5 hectares of Borneo forest, consider how many insects, reptiles, amphibians and plants live there.

As already mentioned, tropical rain forests are believed to contain 75 per cent of all plant species. In the canopy of one tree may be thousands of epiphytic and parasitic plants, a number of vines, or even shrubs. All of these plant forms may be home to a wonderful array of animal species. Each vine may host the caterpillars of brilliant butterflies and large moths. Every water-filled hollow may be home to a small amphibian, and each cupped flower to a minute frog. The flowers of the canopy and draping vines will feed nectar-sipping birds and multitudinous insects. Every crack and crevice may be home to a small animal, and each branch, fork and hollow may become an overnight resting place for a primate or other large animal. The jungle canopy will be many times richer in wildlife than the already rich floor below.

Whether flowering plants or fruiting trees, fearsome carnivores or small furry animals, whether miniature insects or large horned beetles, brilliant birds or multi-hued amphibians, over vast expanses of time, whatever lived there evolved to become new subspecies, or, eventually, unique species. Who knows what life forms lived there at the end of the Cretaceous period when the dinosaurs died out. Since that time, though, we can imagine how the biodiversity developed. Think of a specific species surviving over eons. Geological forces might then create a mountain range that separated a single bird species into two groups. The mountains might have had plentiful rainfall on one side and dry conditions on the other. In the valleys on either side, flowering and fruiting plants would have had to evolve to the changing conditions. In turn, the animals that were separated from each other would also evolve. If the conditions were different enough, one bird species would quite quickly become two. All over a large landmass, weather patterns and geological features would cause habitats, and the species within them, to change, to evolve or to die out.

One result would be that some species become isolated in pockets. Individual species don't always cover the land like a delicate veil or thick blanket. A few do, but most are distributed like ponds on a prairie. One species of bird may inhabit only a thousand acre area of dry habitat in the north, while another thrives only in a swamp to the east. These ancient forests are now recognized as the richest ecosystems on earth for the numbers of species they contained.

So now, with so many animal and plant species having evolved to fill specific ecological niches, when thousands of hectares of forest are logged, we can be sure that millions of plants and small creatures are lost. Large mammals and birds can flee, but not the insects and smaller animals. By clearing the trees from huge expanses of the rainforest, incredible numbers of isolated species are simply destroyed along with their forest home. Huge numbers of unique species have nowhere to go – they simply disappear from the Earth. Our planet is despoiled and made less rich. The best thing we can think to do with these wonderful repositories of unique natural forms is fell the trees and then burn nearly everything. By any measure, this must now be the most abhorrent crime that we humans have perpetrated on our home planet.

Some of Borneo's trees should surely be considered of great value. The Borneo Ironwood *(Eusideroxylon zwargeri)*, for instance, grows extremely slowly, some years adding only about ½ mm to the radius of the trunk. At that rate, after one hundred years of life, it may have a diameter of only 10 centimeters. A thousand year old tree could have a trunk of only 3 ft (100cm) across.[21] As a consequence, a block of that wood is heavier than water and is incredibly rot resistant. Still, such trees grew to be thousands of years old.

Yet the Malaysian and Indonesian governments can think of nothing better to do with those forests than burn them, or cut them down to sell as pulp for papermaking or as lumber for cheap furniture. They then cover the land with palm oil plantations or other monoculture tree species, such as Acacia. This completely destroys the ecological integrity of the land and provides no home for all but a very few animal species. The reason for these irresponsible government policies, is the profits the politicians and their wealthy friends make from the plantations.*

The Orangutans, the great apes of the Borneo forest, range over large

---

* It is worth noting that palm oil is one of the least healthy of all the food oils. I also wish to mention that I tend to think of the legal logging companies as the great despoilers and the illegal loggers as a side irritant. However, in the *Economist* of September 22, 2012, it was noted that illegal logging is a $30 billion a year industry - hardly a mere irritant. When the wood appears for sale in our local lumber store in whatever country on whatever continent, we have no idea whether it has been legally or illegally harvested.

areas feeding from trees as they come into fruit. They travel here and they travel there, knowing where and when they can get a meal. When a section of the forest is felled and palm oil seedlings planted, the apes still arrive expecting the tasty fruit they have always enjoyed from that part of the forest. The trouble is, on their arrival they find everything changed. The forest is gone. The primates are traumatized. Some descend from the canopied forest edge, where they find quite tasty palm oil seedlings. The apes taste this new plant, and the plantation owners become angry. It was revealed in December 2011 that the plantation workers are being paid by the management to kill the Orangutans.

Furthermore, not only do Orangutans become a problem. Any herbivores that used to range over vast areas in search of food or mates, when confined to shrinking pieces of habitat surrounded by plantations or agricultural land, become problem animals when they travel beyond the forest. As an example, elephants, which once roamed over many thousands of square miles of forest, don't understand that they are now supposed to be content with the area set aside for them. Of the eight parks in the Kalimantan (Indonesian) part of Borneo, four are smaller than 800 sq miles (2000km2), and only one is bigger than 3,100 sq miles (8,000km2). When the elephants raid the new agricultural land and plantations, they become the despoilers. The recent immigrants, who chopped down the trees just five years earlier, are viewed as the innocent victims.

The Malaysian Company, IOI, began operations in 1969 as Industrial Oxygen Incorporated Sdn. Bhd. Then, in 1982, it went into property development, and in 1985 into palm oil plantations. In 2010 Palm oil produced 48 per cent of the company's $4 billion profits. As of 2009, the group operated 152,000 hectares of palm oil in Malaysia and 83,000 hectares in Indonesia. According to the United Nations Environment program, the palm oil industry is the third largest emitter of carbon worldwide, and is the principal cause of deforestation. According to the NGO, Friends of the Earth, IOI continues to cut forests illegally and against Indonesian government legislation. It develops new plantations, without approved environmental impact assessments, and continues to burn peat and forests illegally. It is a corporation of total irresponsibility. Nestlé, Unilever and Neste Oil all deal with IOI, though in 2012 Nestlé temporarily stopped buying from the company.

In June 2012, the Malaysian company FELDA Global Ventures Holding, the worlds biggest palm oil trader, floated stocks on the Malaysian stock market by which they are hoping to raise 3 billion dollars to enable the company to buy more land in Indonesia and Africa to fell and plant with palm oil. Even the German Deutsche Bank is supporting FELDA in floating this stock option. What hope is there for forests, when those intent on their destruction can raise billions of dollars through international banks, and when people, and their pension funds, will invest money in the enterprise? It is desperately alarming that huge corporations, and banks, with no responsibility to anything beyond making money, can just forge ahead with raising money to destroy the Earth. And they can do so despite the outcries of citizens worldwide. How many of us, I wonder, while concerned for our pension, are actually invested in forest destruction without knowing it?

As stated, Borneo is shared between Brunei, Malaysia and Indonesia. The two federated Malaysian states of Sarawak and Sabah constitute about 26 per cent of the landmass. The tiny independent state of Brunei is 1 per cent, and Indonesian Kalimantan has the tiger's share of about 73 per cent. It is worth mentioning that the people of Borneo have no historic ties to either the Javanese of Indonesia or the Malays of Peninsular Malaya. The people of Borneo were, until very recently, tribal people known as Dayaks. This ethnic group consists of over 40 tribes such as the hunter-gatherer Penan, the Iban and the Bayau sea-people. Along the coast lived the Melanaus, the Land Dayaks and the Ibans and Bayau or Sea Dayaks. In the interior and in the highlands that formed the border with Kalimantan, lived such tribes at the Kelabits, Kayans and Kenyahs. These people all lived along the rivers, with the majority in traditional longhouses. 91 per cent of Dayaks converted to Christianity during the colonial period. Others still hold animist beliefs.[22]

The Javan Indonesians took over Kalimantan as well as Sumatra and Celebes when they won independence from the Dutch in 1949. It was a sort of Asian colonization to match the Dutch. They claimed all the other Dutch possessions as well, which included a whole string of islands stretching to New Guinea. They invaded the Irian Jaya half of New Guinea in 1961. In 1969 the United Nations held a vote in which the Papuan leaders voted to join Indonesia, though many of the people rebelled. The Indonesian possession is now known as West Papua.

In the British colonies of Sabah and Sarawak, and the Brunei protectorate, there was first an attempt to form the Federated States of North Borneo, but that fell through because of troubles in Brunei. The

British then encouraged Sabah and Sarawak to join with Peninsular Malaya in a federation, though there had been no previous ties. This concept won out in the end, helped along by the aggressive stance of the Indonesians who wanted control of Borneo in totality. That neo-colonial take-over bid caused the Confrontation (or the Undeclared War) from 1962 to 1966. Britain, Australia, New Zealand and Malaysia fought off the Indonesians and, following a vote, two of the three British parts of Borneo were ceded to Malaysia in July 1963 and became East Malaysia. The old Malaya, or Peninsular Malaya, became known as West Malaysia. Brunei remained a colony for a few more years till it became rich from oil and was granted independence.

I visited Sarawak once, and Sabah twice in the 1990s and heard quite a number of disgruntled complaints along the lines of "in the old days we could get along on merit" and "they take our resources and spend our money on mosques." That was before the logging started in earnest so it would be interesting to hear what people say now. An ex Malaysian Air Force helicopter pilot told me that the reason he left the service was that he would have to convert to Islam to be promoted. There now appear to be two classes in Malaysia: the Muslim Malays and the rest (Chinese, Indian, and Borneo tribal people).

I find it disheartening that, in many ways, the people of Sarawak were better off being ruled by the White Rajahs of the Brooke family than they now are as a part of Malaysia. The first White Rajah was James Brooke who was made governor of Sarawak in 1841 by the Sultan of Brunei. That was in reward for ridding the Sultan of the pirates and other malcontents who had thrown his Sultanate in chaos. At that time, the Sultans controlled the coastal ports but had few dealings with the unexplored interior country, which was in the hands of numerous tribal groups living along the riverbanks. War and headhunting among the various tribes was apparently business as usual in those days. In 1842 the Sultan appointed James Brooke 'Rajah.' Brooke then explored the interior, set a rough boundary along the interior mountain range, and proceeded to begin the process of banning headhunting.

In the meantime, the island of Labuan had been a British trading post since 1846 and a British crown colony since 1848. The land that is now Sabah was leased, by the Sultan of Sulu, to an Austrian titled Baron von Overbeck and a Briton named Alfred Dent. This, in time, became the British North Borneo Company. In 1888 both Sarawak and Sabah became protectorates of the Crown, though not colonies. The British North Borneo Company was a trading business that felt no compunction in felling forests and planting rubber plantations, but in Sarawak it was different.

James Brooke was Rajah from 1842 till his death in 1868, and his son Charles ruled till 1917. Then the title of Rajah passed to Charles Vining Brooke who ceded Sarawak to the crown in 1946. Sarawak, it seems, was a paradise of paternal, low impact government. Some Chinese and Malays had settled in Kuching, the main town, but the White Rajahs were anxious to protect the ways of living, and the cultures, of the indigenous tribes, and also to protect the forests on which they depended. Despite their history of headhunting, the people of these tribes were admired and regarded with great affection by the young Englishmen who were employed by the Rajahs as District Officers. They are described as very attractive and "hardworking, very courteous and very charming."[23]

Again quoting from *Tales from the South China Seas*, Anthony Richards, one of those young District Officers (DOs) describes the Ibans thus:

Because of their poise and their immense natural dignity one was never conscious that they were in any way naked. The men wore their hair long, with a fringe at the front and knotted up into a sort of teapot handle at the back. They had copper-coloured skins with dark blue tattooing in the form of rosettes just inside their shoulder on the front and on their arms and legs and they wore long scarlet loin cloths which hung down at the back and front with long tasseled ends. They also wore black and silver arm and calf bracelets so that the general effect was of copper, black and red.

The women were just as striking in appearance and character as the men. Many were very attractive and in general they were anything but reserved in their behaviour; one tends to think of women as second-class citizens in these communities but nothing would be more remote from the truth. They really had a say and a big say, too. They would sit round with everybody else and often played a very forceful part in the discussions. They were monogamous and their moral code was very rigorous indeed – but the young people could have lots of fun before they married.

The young DOs were often hired straight out of school, mostly from the better public schools, at the age of eighteen. They had to have pretty strong characters, as they would be expected to remain in each district for at least three years. Spending three years, deep in the forest, beside a river, with the nearest other white man some miles away must have been truly daunting. They were expected to protect the interests of the people under their care. In the early days, the 1850s, just two of them were sent to a huge district where they not only had to protect the people but also had to build forts and fight off other headhunting Dayaks.[24]

The second Rajah, Charles Brooke, 1868-1917, was so intent that the European officers should become a comfortable part of each Dayak community that he discouraged the officers from marrying white women. He considered the conditions rather too rough for them. Instead, he encouraged each young DO to adopt an attractive local mistress, housekeeper, and language teacher. Apparently this practice became quite widespread and was considered "eminently sensible," as the officers learned not just the language but the local dialect as well. The women became known as "sleeping dictionaries." Apparently one downside to this policy was that, as Dayak women had a different way of expressing themselves to that of the men, the district officers were likely to learn to speak like women.[25]

The Brookes wanted their officers to learn and respect the culture, taboos, and omens of the locals so that they could respond appropriately.

If the members of the longhouse believed that seeing a certain bird meant you had to stop a journey and turn back, then the DO would turn back out of respect for the locals, no matter how inconvenient.

But to know and respect these and other omens was one way of maintaining the easy relations between Tuans and natives that was characteristic of Brooke rule, for it was the custom that if you just wanted a chat with the DO or a gossip, you went along to his house in the evening. The door was always open and there he was, surrounded by people from up and down the river. So you went in and you chatted and talked late into the night. It was the same with the Resident. He wasn't a sacrosanct, remote figure as was the case in other places.[26]

No roads were built into the jungle, so all travel was by boat along the rivers. Right into the 1940s, when an officer needed to visit the longhouses in his care, he would simply get into a village boat and, with a boatman, paddle up river till his first destination was reached. He would usually spend a night or two in the longhouse then continue his journey to the next place. The Rajah and Ranee, his wife, took regular trips along the rivers when they would visit and sleep in the longhouses and listen to the observations and concerns of the people. The people loved them profoundly.[27]

The British insisted that in 1946 both Sarawak and Sabah be ceded to the Crown as colonies. This was in preparation for granting independence regardless of the wishes of the people. They both became federated states within Malaysia in July 1963. I think it is an understatement to say that the end of colonialism was of little benefit to either place.

Sabah and Sarawak together have a larger landmass than Peninsular Malaya but they only have 20 per cent of the Malaysian population. Being relatively undeveloped the Malaysian government treats both states as repositories of resources to be harvested. Consequently, the government began felling the forests of Sarawak in the 1960s soon after federation. This of course was very beneficial to the logging companies and politicians involved as they all became very wealthy from it. The people who lost out and continue to lose are the indigenous peoples of Sarawak. All the indigenous tribes have seen their traditional ways destroyed and many continue the fight to protect their dwindling forests, among them the Penan or Orang Ulu. The Malay words, Orang (people) and Ulu (river), gives their name the meaning 'Up-river people.' They are nomadic hunter-gatherers who now number about 16,000, with 200 still living the traditional hunter-gatherer life. Following the Second World War, missionaries convinced many to settle in longhouses in the Ulu-Baram and Limbang districts. So their way of life had been under threat for some time before federation.[28]

Under the Brooke rule, and in colonial times, government treaties were signed confirming the tribal ownership of the forests, but since federation with Malaya, the new government has chosen to ignore those treaties, and the land has been logged. When the tribes found their legal approach falling on deaf ears, they took to building roadblocks on the logging roads.[29] These led to major confrontations with the loggers, and with the army and police sent to support the companies. In 1987, the Malaysian government passed Forest Ordinance Amendment S90B,[30] which made it a major offence to block a logging road. Since then there have been deaths and many arrests of the indigenous resisters, and the whole country has been logged save a few small parks.

During the time that all this was going on in Sarawak, across the border in Kalimantan, the Indonesian government set aside millions of acres for plantations. To assist in the forest clearance, Indonesia settled thousands of unemployed Javans on Kalimantan. This of course resulted in violent clashes and near war between the indigenous people and the slash-and-burn Javans. The consequence has been hundreds of deaths and thousands now living in refugee camps.

One can imagine what all this does for forest tribes such as the Penan, who lived by the tradition of 'Molong'- the ethic of never taking more than is necessary.[31] Logging has meant the destruction of every part of their culture and way of life. With logging, they no longer have access to rattan and their other building materials, to the game animals, the fruiting and other food trees, and plants such as the Sago Palm, their main supply of carbohydrates. With the forest gone, their medicinal plants and those invested with spiritual or sacred significance have also gone. The rivers have become clogged with sedimentary runoff from the cleared watersheds, which, in turn, affects their drinking, bathing and fishing. In fact, all aspects of the river/forest peoples' and of the hunter-gatherers' millennium-old ways of life and culture have been destroyed.

There is a difference between a tough life and a poverty-stricken life. It is that disconnect between having everything you need in the life of the hunter-gatherer, and being poor in a city of wealthy individuals. In reality, having all those many square miles of forest made the indigenous people very wealthy. The natives, who may have lived on their land for ten thousand years, had no papers, other than European colonial ones, to prove ownership. The trouble was, the new Malaysian and Indonesian colonial governments chose not to recognize that ownership and deemed the natives poor.

With the destruction of the native cultures and the traditional ways of life, the destruction of the natural world is ensured. It means the destruction of the Borneo Pygmy-elephants, the Sumatran Rhinos, the Banteng Oxen, Sunda Clouded-leopards, the Sun Bears and the Moon Rats, the Bearded

Pigs and the Proboscis Monkeys, the Orangutans, and the many species of gibbon, langur, macaque, tarsier and loris, and so many more. On Borneo alone, there are five species of cats: Clouded Leopard, Bay Cat, Leopard Cat, Flat-headed Cat and Marble Cat. With the logging the question is how many of the 3,000 tree species, and 15,000 other flowering and fruiting plants, or the fungi, birds, butterflies and insects will be brought to extinction. The Malaysian government is clearing their forests at a faster rate than anywhere else in the world. While a typical Asian rate of forest clearance, per annum, is 0.32 per cent of the landmass, the Malaysian rate since the year 2000 has been 0.65 per cent.[32][33]

In 2011 the Penan were still trying to defend their way of life. They had been moved from their original home territory, which was to be flooded to make way for the Muran Dam, to a new piece of forest. However, the logging company Shin Long was already logging their new home in preparation for planting palm oil and acacia tree plantations. True to form, the government doesn't really care, as its position is that these people must be moved out of poverty and encouraged to become part of mainstream civilization. This is a similar position to that the Canadian government took a hundred years ago, when it forcibly tried to Europeanize its First Nations people and to "take the Indian out of the Indian." It is a bit of a moot point whether people who live well outside the mainstream capitalist society, who live entirely off their environment and who have no need for money or automobiles are in fact poor. The Penan do lack the medical interventions that have been introduced from the West. Their average life expectancy is 53 years, and they do have a high infant mortality, but if they choose to live without western economics should they not be allowed that right? If they consider themselves rich, as they have everything they wish for, who are we to say they are poor? As already suggested, the real poor are the destitute souls in the cities who live with little income but are surrounded by people of wealth.

In 1961 the population of East Malaysia was 900,000 in Sarawak, and 600,000 in Sabah, for a total population of 1.5 million. The total population in 2010 was 5.6 million. East Malaysia covers 76,510 sq miles (198,161km2). West Malaysia – the peninsula – is 50,800 sq miles (131,600km2).

During The Emergency in colonial Malaya, the army used Dayak and Penan trackers from Borneo. When contact was made with a group of CTs (communist terrorists) they would be pursued by Commonwealth troops following either tracking dogs or a Dayak tracker from Borneo. I met a few. They were small people with many tattoos and broad grins. They were able, when tracking, to estimate how many were in the group they were following, their physical condition, and even what weapons they carried. One way they did this was by noting the marks on trees left when weapons were leaned against the tree during rest stops. Just as some people can operate the TV remote while I view it as totally alien, a Dayak could read dozens of messages in the forest floor while all I saw was mud and leeches. The forest was their home, and they could read it as clearly as we read neon ads for beer or cosmetics.

Peninsular Malaya had its own hunter-gatherers: the 18 tribes of the Orang Asli. Orang means people, Asli means original or indigenous. The name of the great ape, the Orangutan, means people of the forest (utan). In my army days we knew almost nothing of the Orang Asli. In 1950 the colonial government had established a Department of Aborigines, but to most people they were more myth than a definite population. Apparently they were well known to a few military personnel as they played a substantial role in the fight against the CTs. They were certainly not then well known, and the government was happy to protect them and allow them to live safely with their forest, their culture and beliefs intact. Before the colonial government's arrival, they had apparently been taken as slaves by the Malays who thought of them as 'non-human' and as 'forest beasts.' The colonial government banned Malayan slavery in 1884, shortly after getting involved in the country.[34]

Since independence the Orang Asli people have become truly impoverished as the Malaysian government has forced them from their traditional lands and lifestyle. When in 1998 I paid my second visit to Taman Negara, the park reserve that I had visited as the King George V Game Reserve in 1958, I came upon a camp of Orang Asli beside the main park facilities. They had been moved from their original forest home and told to build their leaf structures in this new place. They looked a sad little group. There are said to be 148,000 of them. The Statistics Department of Malaysia considers their poverty rate to be 76.9 per cent with 35.2 per cent being called "hardcore poor."[35] Again, the question of whether they were more, or less, poverty-stricken when living their traditional lives in the forest and far from the mainstream, has to be answered. It is clear that the government pressure to move them from their land had to do with the desire to clear the forest and make money, free of the embarrassment of the needs of the forest people. I doubt very much that the Malaysian government feels any true concern for the welfare of those indigenous peoples.

One aspect of the Orang Asli really fascinates me. They, like the aborigines of Borneo, look just like the Bushmen of Africa, I like to fantasize about happenings of long ago and to make connections. The settling of the earth by humans is mighty interesting. In that regard I have long wondered whether the Orang Asli could be among the most direct descendants of those first "out of Africa" people. Those were people who must have either hugged the southern coasts of Asia, or made it through the un-forested land of Asia. If they traveled along the coast, they would probably have become quite comfortable making the odd rafts to get around headlands or across river estuaries and, in time, to islands and such. Those people could have made the ultimate trip to Borneo, New Guinea and Australia. The ones following the inland route though, may well have roamed all the way to the Malay jungle and then decided to stay when they found the sea blocking further progress. Maybe they found the jungle offered them all they needed including sanctuary and complete independence from the coastal-traveling peoples.

Now the Malaysian government considers them, and the Orang Ulu of Borneo, destitute and in need of education. However I think it true that they are very highly developed in ways that we don't recognize. Untold thousands of years of living happily in the forest, in isolation from other branches of *Homo sapiens sapiens,* has enabled them to develop all sorts of traits and accomplishments that are quite different from those of other peoples. I place them light years ahead of the rest of us at forest living. To consider such people impoverished may be, not only wrong, but also criminal. Unfortunately, no matter how long they have been thriving in the forests, whether ten thousand years or sixty thousand years, the Malaysian and Indonesian governments are not now going to allow them to continue. This is another loss to the world, thanks to our exploding population that is increasingly allowing no deviation from the norm of the majority.

Most people now disparage European imperialism, as some very bad things were done under its name. Conquering highly civilized peoples can't now be condoned, even if it was 500 years ago. In the earliest years, when the Portuguese and Spaniards sailed off into the unknown, the cultures they came upon were often as advanced as their own, and, in some cases, more advanced. When the Portuguese first arrived in India about the only advantage they had over the peace-loving Hindu and Jain Indians was their penchant for violence. Pizarro and his conquistador colleagues were awestruck by the magnificent Inca city of Cuzco. It was there they defeated the Inca and began the Peruvian conquest. That city was said to be better planned and more beautiful than any city in Spain.

But it might be argued that destroying the Aztec civilization and the priests' ritual ceremonies had its merits. After all, who could support a culture that ripped the still-beating hearts from the chests of a believed 50,000 sacrificial human victims a year.

Really there were a number of streams of imperialism. One might be the unjust conquest of highly sophisticated cultures that were the equals of the conquerors. Another might be the discovery of vast lands populated by a few people who had progressed no further than the development of stone-age tools. A third was to defeat and re-educate cannibals, headhunters, slave-trading kingdoms and the like. A fourth was simply the need for an island or port for the navy and to secure trading routes for shipping. And a final one, of the many possible, was the quest by European groups who wanted a better place to live, such as the Pilgrim Fathers, or, as in the case of the Conquistadors, who were looking to pillage lands that they considered rich.

I suspect, that, overall, benign colonialism has brought the peoples of many cultures to good government, universal education, good health care and technologically advancing economies more quickly than had there been no colonialism. On the other hand, I also believe that the natural world has suffered more radically than if the less-advanced peoples had been left untouched by European technologies. I think it can be argued that some of the tribal peoples of Malaysia and Indonesia were better off under European colonialism than they are under the neo-colonialism of their new masters.

That being said, I think we should mourn the impoverishment of the cultural richness that adorned our globe one hundred, or even just sixty years ago. As the diversity of wildlife is diminishing, so is the diversity of cultures being lost. Soon, the ways of life of the Orang Asli, of the Penan, and of all those other tribes from all continents, will be but memories in old folks' minds. Alternate ways of life to our own will be as surely gone as the natural world that sustained them.

6 Art & Extinctions

I have said that as a small boy I had little knowledge of the threats to my much-loved world of nature - as it should be for children I've no doubt. Youngsters should enjoy naivety. We learn by observation and have no knowledge of the historical context in which to view things. There were cities and houses, and there were fields and woods and the seashore. The fields were of long grass, buzzing insects and sunshine, or of short-cropped grass, cowpats, and often, some fear of cantering horses or hidden bulls. The woods were usually dark places in which nothing much was to be seen but trees, either large with big open spaces beneath, or small and spindly and too crowded to allow much play. In nature we were always watching for birds or butterflies, but it required extraordinary luck to glimpse any kind of wild animal either large or small. Above all, nature was the natural world as we assumed it had always been and always would be.

But by my teens this naivety was slipping, and it was clear that something was up. I remember standing with my brother, somewhere on the Isle of Wight. We were leaning on a five-bar gate, as all good English country folk do, and I was probably chewing on a long stem of grass. We were bemoaning our observations that we seldom saw butterflies any more, that when I tried attracting moths to a lit sheet after dusk none came, and that the river and fish at Breamore seemed to be in some sort of difficulty. This would have been maybe ten years after English farmers had begun using insecticides and pesticides. Still, all this was becoming of diminished importance to us by then. Colin had just left the RAF, and I was a teenager passing through an unpleasant puberty - a puberty that set my mind off in directions altogether different from the farm, and made my focus very much less singular. Conscription into National Service was also fast approaching for me, so we both had to decide what kind of direction our lives would take. The world of nature was slipping to a remote interest.

The idea of being a farmer, to which I had staunchly held until I was 16, had lost its attraction and nothing seemed to replace it.

Now in 2012 a young person, with the interests I then had, would go to university for environmental studies of some kind, but in those days in the UK few people went to university and very few of those would have studied biology or related subjects. 'The environment' was not a known expression in those days. In my youth, in England, work with wildlife was confined to such jobs as forester or gamekeeper. The suggestion of forester came up once, but I unthinkingly put it aside. As my two years of army service drew to an end, I developed daydreams of possible careers. I considered boat building for a while. I tossed that around with the idea of having a chicken farm. In each case, there was no thought of anything to do with the business side of things. Rather, my plans all centered round the design of the buildings I would need to house the boats or chickens. It was a repeat of my childhood fantasies of my own farm. Then it was where the dairy should go in relation to the milking sheds and farmhouse. Now it was how the boat slip would project into the harbour, or whether the chicken houses would surround a courtyard entered through an archway or along a border of perennial flowers and shrubs. It was many, many years before I twigged I should have studied architecture or possibly even landscape design.

In my first school report, at the age of five, written in April 1944 my kind head teacher wrote, "A very good little worker. . . . Is still rather confused about writing his letters and needs plenty of practice." Then a couple of terms later he wrote, "Although struggling with writing, spelling and arithmetic, he does well with nature studies and art." He certainly had my number. So some sixteen years later, and after a couple of years of employment missteps, I finally went to art school. I say finally as that route had been suggested yearly from the age of seventeen, but I had resisted. Drawing and painting and making things, at which I was very good, had always been wonderful ways to spend long hours of contentment. They had never seemed to be any way to work for a living.

When I finally decided to go to art school, which was less a decision than the desperate act of a lost soul, it was life changing. The two years spent working in London after the army had been a difficult time. It had been like struggling through a bitter February; a thoroughly depressing spell of cold and dismal days. Going to art school was the miraculous dawning of a bright spring morning. The days glowed, as on one of those rare sunny spells that we so value in Britain; I stepped out from the gloom, and the sun was shining, the sky was blue, the air was scented, flowers were blooming and the days ahead were to be magic. Art school was unquestionable right for me. I was twenty-one and emerging from my chrysalis. Being a depressed and introverted caterpillar, on an unappetizing shrub named 'unrewarding work', had been rough; metamorphosing into an art student showed great promise.

The first thing I noticed on that day in September 1960 was that we were two cohorts of first year students. The other group had a healthy mix of males and females, but in my group I was one of only two callow youths in a class with twenty-two girls. And what girls! And what a way to introduce a young chap to the hardships of study. It might have been a bit tough on the girls though.

Not actually the second item of note, though close and certainly up there in my memory, was when walking along Lime Grove with two lovely leggy fellow students named Celia and Catherine, hearing Catherine say "Look at his lovely thin legs. I love skinny men." She was speaking of a young man walking along ahead of us. Well! That was the first time I had ever considered the option that beautiful ladies might find skinny men in any way desirable. What a revelation. I had had a few girlfriends by then, but had always seen myself as an improbable fill-in till a Charles Atlas look-alike happened by. But Catherine's words gave me the opportunity to imagine I was no longer 'He who cast no shadow', but was now 'The princely ideal of narrow elegance,' or, on a good day, maybe even 'slim elegance.' And all this, as a result of four little words, "I love skinny men".

Daily enjoying something I was good at - art making - and then discovering that at least some beautiful girls were attracted to slim men was almost more than this chap could take.

Another realization that gave me something of a boost was that I seemed to be amongst the most talented of the group. Drawing, sculpture and any of the subjects where creativity and technical skill showed to an advantage were my subjects. Even the lettering classes fulfilled me. But it was pottery and sculpture at which I excelled. I had never in my life thought of pottery as something I would want to do, but once I was on the wheel there was little else. While many students were still having difficulties with the basics of centering the clay and pulling cylinders, I was off making my own teapots with bellies, feet and lips, and with rims, lids and flanges, and knobs, spouts and handles and all the other complexities found in such functional pieces. The first teapots were not masterpieces, maybe weird even, but I soon became the king of any pots that required a design sense, technical expertise and attention to detail. I had the ability to plan the complete pot, to understand every unique detail, and to figure out how to make and glaze it before I had even wedged the clay. I soon discovered that I was first and foremost a very skilled creative designer. My studies became focused 20 per cent on sculpture and 80 per cent on ceramics, and almost every day that the college buildings were open, my friend Jim and I would spend 12 hours potting followed by an hour in the pub. Surprisingly, once I graduated and opened my own studio I went into industrial ceramics. The only potting I did after art school was when teaching the craft. This became a pattern. I would study an art or skill for four or five years until I felt I knew it, and then move onto something else.

Later, after thirty years of working quite successfully as an artist, I began a series of paintings dealing with the environment. This was in the early 1990s, and by that time my belief and interest in the values of the academic art establishment had diminished somewhat. My interest in the natural world had returned as a deep concern for some years. The realities of the human population explosion, and the resulting issues of species extinctions were causing me distress and angry frustration. Nearly everything else can be revisited or put right over time. Human suffering and death is unbelievably tragic, particularly on the personal level, but there are lots of us. Once another species has gone, it is lost to the Earth forever.

I was at a place of personal contentment. I had had some success as a sculptor. I was married to an accomplished and beautiful wife, our two children were bright and on track for university. We lived in a pleasant house surrounded by remnant pieces of secondary forest in the country outside of Vancouver, where there were plenty of birds, deer and other wildlife. Our life was just fine. The problem was that I believed humanity was destroying the Earth and the human population explosion was, in a nutshell, a catastrophe.

During the eighteen years we lived in that house the human population grew by 25 per cent, from 4.5 billion to over 6 billion. It was clear that all those billions were wreaking untold damage on the environment and that the world could not support the nine and more billion projected for the near future without further harm. If we truly believe in social justice and equality, and if we believe that our North American way of life is good and should be the goal to which all should aspire, then we have to believe that the untold more billions soon to populate the earth should live as we do in the developed West. That means that all 9 billion people alive in 2050 should own two gas-guzzling cars, 3000 sq ft houses, huge fridges, and buy new suites of furniture every 15 years. We should produce tons of waste during each lifetime, consume unsustainable amounts of seafood, rip every resource possible out of the earth, and continue to deplete the groundwater at an unsustainable rate. We must also believe in capitalism and unlimited business growth, and, in general, behave as selfishly as we in North America assumed is our right to behave. To do that we will need half a dozen planets just like this one. But we only have one.

So are we actually fostering a future of billions more people living secure and contented lives, as we in the developed West live? Or are we creating a world that will eventually cause many more to live lives of stress and revolution, of bombings and starvation. Starvation in the time after our generation had selfishly destroyed the greater part of the natural world?

I do not, believe that humanity is on the correct course. A sustainable course would try to ensure that our descendants, not just our grandchildren but also our great-grandchildren's great-grandchildren and the people two or three hundred years beyond, will have the opportunity to live in a world of social justice, comfort, security and peace. It should also be a world rich in the natural beauty that the fortunate ones among us knew as children and young adults. Our descendants should have the natural riches that we enjoyed. Not just an intact and healthy natural world, but also a world bountiful with the mineral wealth that made us rich. Our grandparents' generation developed the means to exploit that newly discovered wealth - a mineral wealth that we seem too keen to over exploit, and to squander as quickly as possible, leaving nothing behind for those who come after us.

We can live well with less if we choose. But if we are not willing to accept a sustainable lifestyle now, why should we expect our descendants to bear the burden of a reduced life style in their lifetimes?

I like reading history, and to me the time of my great-great-grandfather's father Joseph, who was born in 1774, seems only a very short while ago. He died in 1814, but his tenth child, my father's grandfather, died in 1885, which was only 19 years before my father's birth in 1904. Tales could have been told to my grandfather about the time of Napoleon, of the pride felt following the victory at Trafalgar, or of the horrors poor children suffered in industrial London during early Victorian times. Those stories might potentially have been recounted directly to me from my grandfather or father. I could have passed them on to my grandchildren born in the early 21st century. They have the potential to live into the 22nd century. Time - two or three hundred years - is not a massive gulf but a slow-moving stream. Generational time is only as yesterday or tomorrow might be.

I don't believe we should assume that two hundred years hence is too far away to think of. We should not take the chance that we might leave our descendants an Earth bereft of clean air or fresh water, of wild places and nature to wonder at, or of any useful minerals with which to build or power their industry. Every mineral that we need now we should ensure will still be plentifully in the ground for the use of our descendants. I don't want them to grow up at a time when they curse our generation for our blind stupidity and intolerable selfishness. At the moment, that seems the most likely way they will view us.

So, in 1994, when I went back to painting, which I hadn't done since my second year at art school, it was with a very different attitude than my approach had been before. My later sculptures were built on the underlying themes of minimalism and the human search for spiritual wisdom, but that was somewhat abstract. The distressing facts about what we are doing to the planet are concrete and very real.

To start painting pictures about species extinction may seem a futile exercise in the context of my beliefs. It was a thought that worried me when I started the work. Surely I could do something more direct: stand in front of earth-moving machines, stand with the Ibans of Borneo to protect their forest, get a soap box, give lectures, make a movie, become a Member of Parliament. There are any numbers of ways to make statements and to make a difference. If we don't try to improve society and the world, what is the point of our lives? The trouble is I know myself too well, and I know what I'm not. I'm not a politician or great orator. I hate office work, and although I can lick stamps, I need something more fulfilling. I'm still basically very shy and not good at networking or being out in society. In conversation in a large group the shyness turns my brain to peanut butter and words fail me. I would make good cannon fodder but didn't fancy that too much. So I chose the optimistic path of making paintings. It was one thing I knew I could do. I could address the issues, and, through sales, I hoped to raise money for environmental organizations.

Finding believable imagery was at first difficult. Then one day I painted a very large expressively rendered butterfly, just for fun, and I realized how very close to my heart such a subject was. Not quite the stuff of modern art to be sure, but the very core of my inner soul. Butterflies had fascinated me when I was young and, though I had thought little about them as an adult, I still believed that the world would be desperately poorer if they were no more. If art truly is about the individual expressing his or her innermost and most essentially dithyrambic soul, I knew I had to find the courage to paint them. They fitted perfectly with my extinction concerns.

I knew enough about the context of art in the modern world. I had been teaching it at the post-secondary level for nearly forty years. I had exhibited sculpture in prestigious contemporary art galleries including two one-person exhibitions in the Vancouver Art Gallery. I had also received one of the largest Canadian federal government sculpture commissions to that date. I understood the importance of defining oneself as an artist through the quality of one's work. I was also aware of how easily the intent can be misjudged based on the choice of subject matter, so I knew how unlikely it was that the academic art establishment would accept the type of art I was contemplating. It would consider such a subject below contempt, superficial and stupid and would despise me for it. But, although I cared about the opinions of my peers, I knew this work was going to be right for me. I also believed it to be important. This was at a time when butterflies seemed not to exist, at least in the popular imagination. They were out there somewhere of course, but were seldom, if ever, mentioned in the popular media.

There were books that illustrated examples of butterfly species for the keen entomologist. Also, attention had been drawn to the American favourite, the monarch, since the wintering site of the eastern subspecies had been discovered in a pine forest in the mountains of Mexico. But few people seemed to care, and if every last one in agricultural areas was destroyed by pesticides, so what? Most would believe it a small price to pay for our abundant, and inexpensive, food. This was before butterflies were even used in advertising, as they were early in the new millennium. At the time, they seemed a forgotten life form. All that aside, my problem was how to use them. I wanted the quality of experience, in both producing the work and viewing it, to be both profound and demanding.

I didn't want some gentle images of butterflies flitting over flowers on a sentimental afternoon. I wasn't into butterflies lite. I determined to use them as a symbol of all the vanishing species that were daily being erased from the planet, oftentimes even before their existence was known. After many trials, I chose an approach and technique, and a way to use the butterfly image as an emblematic figure. I would render the butterfly as accurately as I could on a raised, separate panel and display it as it might be seen in a museum collection. The majority of the painting would be of the leaves of the forest canopy as if one were looking horizontally at the very top leaves of a tree. I used one or two leaf images that I had photographed but mostly I invented the leaf patterns based on my understanding of tropical plant growth. For the ground on which to paint I built somewhat sculptural panels of $^1/_8$ inch plywood on frames, typically of four or five feet in width or height, though I also produced series both smaller and larger.

In short, the leaves were symbols of the flora that had to be protected in order that the wildlife, represented by the insect, could survive. I hoped that the use of fine $^1/_8$ inch plywood, instead of cotton canvas, would address another question. That question is, "What is the appropriate use of the materials that are available to us and what is the least environmentally damaging surface on which to paint?" It is not an easily answered question.

Assuming the forest is cut, the question is whether it is then better to plant fields of cotton to make canvas or to plant, and fell, trees for veneer and plywood? Which type of crop uses the least or no pesticides? Which will best offer a home to insects, birds and animals in the period before it is harvested? So, since the forests are being cut down regardless of how suicidal I might feel about it, what is the lumber being used for? Are the trees being cut to give us beautiful hardwoods, with which to build fine furniture, or are they being squandered for pulp to make newsprint? Is the intention to simply clear the land to graze cattle or is it to plant crops? Assuming the death of the forest, the question might be whether the land is used for palm oil, for agriculture, or for plantations of productive trees. Most desirable would be to replant the area with original species and let it regenerate to natural forest.

Every action we take and each material we use has some effect on nature. I believe we should always be questioning our smallest acts in terms of our responsibilities to the Earth. So should I use cotton canvas or birch plywood? Finally plywood won out, though it finally came down to an aesthetic question about the surface and forms that I wanted.

After painting a number of butterfly types, I settled on the eleven species of the Ornithoptera Birdwings of the New Guinea area. This genus contains some of the largest and most brilliant butterflies in the world. Many large males measure 6 or 7 inches wingtip to wingtip, while female Queen Alexandra's Birdwings have been found at up to 11½ inches (28 cm). They were perfect insects for me to render life-size.

I recalled seeing Birdwing butterflies as a child in the collection drawers at South Kensington's Natural History Museum in London, and knew that they were significant. My good old mother would take me there when I was eight or nine, and I was fascinated by those endless rows of drawers of butterflies. The last time I went to that museum, the collection was hidden away in the basement and I had to get special permission to see it. In the old days they were almost the first things we came upon after passing the giant dinosaur in the entrance hall. The collections are, for the most part, of the butterflies collected from all over the world by such intrepid Victorian explorers as Alfred Wallace and A.S. Meek. It was there I first saw the famous Queen Victoria Birdwing (*Aetheoptera victoriae*) that was shot in 1885 by the naturalist John McGillivray while he accompanied a Royal Navy expedition. The story is that they didn't know what the large gliding things, 150 feet above their heads, were, so a shotgun became the last resort. With pellet holes in the wings, it seems rather a dowdy specimen now, after 135 years. But that specimen is old and worn; a live male of the species can be an incredible iridescent beauty.

The eleven species of the genus Ornithoptera used to all be known by that scientific name. Now they are being classified into four different genera; however, I will still refer to them collectively as Ornothoptera. The females are usually brown with a lighter patterning on the wings and are considerably larger than the males. The males are all brightly coloured with a typical wing pattern that is usually black with one or two diagonal stripes of iridescent emerald-to-yellow scales on the forewings. The hindwing is often yellow with a black border and detailing. Different species have variations in the wing shape; the patterning is also variable. Some subspecies tend more toward blues of different intensities such as the dark purple/silver blue of the Solomon Islands based *Ornithoptera priamus urvillianus*. The *Ornithoptera croesus* from the Moluccas Islands is overall a dark orange, which from some angles reflects green. When Alfred Russell Wallace saw his first example of this butterfly in 1859, he considered it very rare as it took him three months to finally capture one. As with most of these butterfly species, the Creosus's forests are due to be logged soon, which may well mean the end of this singular butterfly and natural delight.

My personal favourite Birdwing is the *Ornothoptera chimaera*. These fly above the 3,000 ft (1,000 metres) level in the mountains of New Guinea and have iridescent apple green/yellow and black forewings with yellow and black hindwings. The largest males grow to 6 inches (150cm) and the females to 7 inches (180cms) wing tip to wing tip.

In any gathering of birdwing the males usually outnumber the females by a large number, hence the male's need to be the most beautiful of all his brothers and cousins. How else will he attract those big plump females?

The Queen Victoria and Queen Alexandria *(O. alexandrae)* have similar wing shapes, which might be described as oval spatulas. They are very different in shape and design to most of the other Birdwings. In the Queen Alexandra's case, the patches of iridescent colour are mostly silvery blue, turquoise and apple green. The Queen Alex survives on a total of less than 90 square kilometers of scattered habitat in Papua New Guinea, but that habitat is under constant threat from forest destruction and ever-expanding palm oil plantations.

When we look at a map of a country or a forest, it is easy to assume that any species of wildlife living there will be quite evenly distributed over the whole area. With some species that is true. However many species, the Queen Alexandra is one, are unreasonably picky. Nearly all examples of a species may be confined to just one piece of habitat or feed on an uncommonly rare vine. Even when first seen by the European naturalists during the 19th and 20th centuries, many butterfly and insect species were incredibly rare. Some had evolved over millennia in one isolated valley, or on a rare species of tree.

When I was doing my National Service in Malaya I used to spend most of my off duty hours exploring the surrounding jungle. I would see butterflies of course, but I clearly remember coming upon one tree that was enveloped with a type of butterfly that I saw nowhere else–ever. That butterfly species seemed to have evolved to like just that one tree. I have no idea how widespread that tree was or whether or not there were others within a hundred square miles.

It is very easy for a logging company, or an unsuspecting native, to move into an area and fell every one of the trees on which a species depends. Those loggers would never know what they had done.

This raises an interesting question. The Queen Alexandra is very large, incredibly beautiful, rare, though plentiful in its small home range, and commands thousand dollar prices from collectors. It is internationally protected by CITES from collection and transportation out of Papua New Guinea. The question is this: since the butterflies' home rainforest is considered less valuable than the palm oil that could be planted when the forest was removed, would it not be better to encourage the local natives to collect and sell a few examples of the butterflies each year thus increasing the value of the intact rainforest? If the locals could make a good living by farming and selling butterflies, of any species, there would surely be less incentive for habitat destruction. Some of the subspecies of Birdwing butterflies are being farmed on certain islands and, although the value drops when the insects can be purchased legally, it does seem one good way to protect the forests.

This question of placing a value on the wildlife living within an intact habitat to preserve that habitat is used in many discussions regarding forest destruction and species survival. It becomes very heated when the suggestion turns to, for instance, preserving the forest in order that wealthy hunters might pay large sums of money to hunt tigers or other large animals. Similar arguments, pro and con, can be used regarding the collection of insects and butterflies. Whether tigers or insects, they both finish up dead when collected. However, while the few tigers might live long lives in the jungle and reproduce slowly, the many butterflies only have a life expectancy of a few weeks and reproduce rapidly. I must say, overall I am strongly against trophy shooting of large animals, but I would not be against the local people taking a few butterflies each year if the money they earn helps protect and preserve the forest.

So, as if mounted above areas of tropical leaves, I rendered the butterflies life size and as accurately as possible. After having painted some 120 or so of them, I feel I know them quite well. I value their right to exist even more than had our acquaintance been only fleeting. The fact that some logging company, from somewhere over the seas and with the government's permission, can just take over their islands, fell the trees and destroy the habitat and food plants on which they rely, and then move on with a pocketful of cash but leaving a number of extinct species in their wake is, to me, atrocious. The fact that few people even care makes it worse. So I hope it is clear that, though the paintings are of butterflies and leaves, they are not about butterflies. The insects were used only as symbols of all the natural world that is daily under threat of annihilation.

Once I was on my way with the project, I became as passionate and totally immersed as I had been during my pottery and sculpture phases, but I believed that this work was far more important. With all the previous work I believe I had been as intellectually, as perceptively, as spiritually and as technically rigorous and stringent as I was capable, but now I was working on an issue of very great relevance. It may all sound quite naïve but when I considered which of my previous sculptures had received serious critiques and national recognition, I knew that none of them had the relevance to important issues that this painting had. What is more important than the sustainability of the earth?

The earlier sculpture had all been serious research. I was making "art about art", which was in accord with the progressive art of the time. But I believed that this painting was far more worthy. I know that many of my artist friends looked askance at my work and tut-tutted or threw their hands up in disgust. They probably thought 'Art isn't about political agendas, and certainly not about rendered wildlife in any form. And what about all the years of academic art scholarship that have gone before?' I, of course, knew that most of the history of art is about marching in step, while the radical changes came from those few who tottered along out of step. The advances came from the square pegs and round holes. I knew of the numerous examples of reactionary academic establishments discounting the new and the different. Think of the scornful academics of the 19th century condemning the Impressionists. I knew that the current art academics at the end of the twentieth century were, and continue to be, just as reactionary, while believing that only they know the truth - a truth that was taught in academia, and that they were passing on to the next generation. It is true that art is, in part, about the freedom to express oneself, but not if one crosses the line drawn by those people. Taboos still pervade the art establishment.

Still I knew that the work I intended to do would be the most valuable I had ever done. Others might not agree, but I believed it was right for me and more close to my true soul than any of my earlier art. For many artists, a lifetime of art is really about getting to the very essence of self. It is the quest to uncover, reveal and release his/her central character, which is at the foundation of the soul. This core can be revealed through the person's ultimate art form. I continued the work full time for about ten years, had some exhibitions, sold some work and raised a few thousands dollars for such environmental foundations as the World Wildlife Fund and David Suzuki Foundation. Unfortunately though, I failed to raise the amount of money for which I had been aiming and which would have given the work a value beyond that of my own satisfaction.

Where my work was a success throughout those ten years of painting was in encouraging me to get more serious in my search for information on the subject of species decline and loss. Just as the more one makes art and studies and knows about art, the more one understands the academic establishment, so with species loss, the more one knows, the more one is likely to become totally dismayed and angry at what we, the self-proclaimed elite species, thinks it's our right to do.

The few individuals who do care, apply years of their lives and huge amounts of money to protecting the habitats of the ever-diminishing species. It is apparently easy and often very profitable to destroy a species but very, very expensive to protect that same species or to bring it back from the brink. Sometimes there is good news, and we hear that a tract of forest somewhere is to be protected; then those who care praise the powers that be for their wisdom and we feel we can relax as the battle is won. But avert our focus, give them a few years, and some developer, some miner, some logging company or some poor dirt farmer, just trying to feed his wife and six children, will be back in there stripping the land of all life before we even realize it is an issue again.

Canadian mining companies, and international oil companies have an appalling record of abuse in third world countries. As often as not, the site for their new mines or oil wells will be tracts of protected virgin forest in a poor country's designated parkland. I am sure they get the politicians onside with promises of wealth just as they do some villagers with promises of jobs or health-care centres. Then they move in, move the indigenous people out, destroy the forests, pollute the rivers, render some unknown animals extinct, and after thirty or forty years move on, leaving not only huge areas of desolation and native despair, but tailing ponds of incredible toxicity, which overflow year after year polluting the environment for decades into the future. The mining companies leave greatly enriched. The country and its people remain behind desperately impoverished.

The tales that come out of the forests of South America and South East Asia are terrible indeed. However it is not always companies that are the problem. Sometimes the selfishness comes from dumb individuals.

I had earlier followed with disbelief the 1970's extinction in the wild of the magnificent Arabian Oryx by jeep-driving and machine-gun-toting Saudi princes. They knew what they were doing, yet seemed to view as a worthy goal and sign of brave manhood the killing of the last remaining Oryx in the wild. What utter stupid idiots. I often wonder which species it is that should be shot. The Princely *(Arabianus princus stupidiius)* seemed, at the time, to be one most deserving of that fate. So, in the early 1990s, I found myself looking more deeply into the history of this extinction phase in which we find ourselves. I began to know more of the species and the causes of the recent, and the ongoing, annihilations of so much of our wildlife.

We may already know that there were once buffalo on the American prairies until there were not, or that there are few wolves or grizzlies south of the US/Canada border. We all know about the logging of forests and the plight of the tigers, elephants and rhinos. Giant Pandas have been the pin-ups of extinction-bound species for decades. That's the kind of information we all carry with us on a sort of superficial, yet subconscious, level at this time in history. When I looked into the issue of species extinctions more deeply, the facts of the matter shocked me profoundly and supplied a foundation to my developing realization that our value systems, and the economy that is based on them, are both terribly flawed.

Two species involved in ongoing extinction battles are the Spix's Macaw in Brazil and the Bali Mynah in Indonesia. The last wild Spix's Macaw finally disappeared in 2000. To think of that lonely last male blue bird partnering with a similar, but smaller green/blue Illiger's Macaw in the last remnant of his home forest is very sad.

Spix's Macaw

It was the German naturalist, Johann Baptist von Spix who, while traveling through the Bahia state in Northeastern Brazil in 1817, first identified and named his macaw *(Cyanopsitta spixii)*. The bird's other name is the Little Blue Macaw. It is only 22 inches (57 cm) in length, is pale blue with a grey head and black under wing and tail feathers. The bird has long been collected for the pet trade. In the wild it lived in caraiba gallery woodland where it nested in tree cavities. Over the years, its woodland habitat was completely destroyed by browsing cattle, which killed all the new shoots and saplings of the trees the birds favoured. To top it off, the birds were attacked by introduced Africanized bees. The bees took over the tree holes favored by the nesting macaw couples and killed the adult birds. Following his lonely pairing with another macaw of the wrong species, the last male went missing in the year 2000. The Spix's Macaw is now believed extinct in the wild.[1 2]

Great efforts are now being given to breeding Spix's Macaws in captivity. There are known to be 85 in collections across the world, but only 73 are part of the official breeding program. What is now a coordinated program, began as independent programs in Germany, in Tenerife, Spain, in Qatar and in Brazil. A number of zoos or private collectors gave their birds to the larger centres to help in this effort. Now a branch of the National Heritage Department of the Brazilian government is overseeing the program with particular success coming out of the Qatar organization. The Al Wabra Wildlife Preservation Center in Qatar is the biggest with 56 birds. In the six years before 2012, a total of 33 young macaws have been raised, 5 in Tenerife and 27 in Al Wabra. The plan is that, once a large enough area of the caraiba woodland has been reestablished, birds will be released into the wild. It is moving to think that birds, who for two or more generations have only known cages, may one day fly free where their ancestors once flourished.[3]

The Illiger's or Blue-winged Macaw *(Primolino maracana)* of the type that our lone and lonely Spix's Macaw befriended during his final years is still quite widespread. This is despite habitat degradation and the pet trade. It does suffer, though, in Argentina where the farmers kill them as pests. If it's not one threat it's another!

Other than habitat destruction, the biggest threat to macaws and other parrot species is collection for the pet trade. This is no surprise as so many macaws are incredibly colourful. It seems that there are 15 species extant in the world and anywhere from six to eleven extinct over the past 300 years. All the remaining macaw species are threatened to some degree or other. The Glaucous Macaw *(Anodorhynchus glaucus)* is critically endangered and may be gone while the Blue-throated Macaw *(Ara glaucogularis)* of Northwest Bolivia has only 50 wild breeding pairs left. Spix's is the only one known to be recently extinct in the wild.

The Indigo, or Lear's Macaw *(Anodorhynchus leari)*, named after the poet and artist Edward Lear, is metallic blue with a green diffusion and is larger, at 30 inches (75 cm) in length, than the Spix. Although the forest and food trees are different for both species, the larger macaw has also suffered from the pet trade and habitat loss where its Licuri Palms have been reduced to 1.6 per cent of the original land coverage. The birds nest in sandstone cliffs, which may have saved them from the Africanized bees. Who would think that the decision to make holes in cliffs instead of trees might be the difference between survival and extinction? Both macaws lived only in Bahia state. In 1994 there were only 140 Lear's Macaws surviving in the wild, but following efforts by the Brazilian government, the numbers had increased to 751 by 2007 and to about 1000 by 2009.[4]

Bali Mynah

The Bali Mynah is another bird that has suffered both habitat destruction and the pet trade to the point that very few still fly wild. Bali is a small island with a very large human population. The people are industrious and, in efforts to survive, have carved large areas of the island's surface into rice paddy terraces. Now only a tiny remnant of original mynah habitat survives, and to that shrubby land of long grass and trees, the local Bali Mynah, or Bali Starling, *(Leucopsar rothschildi)* clung for survival. This bird is beautiful, stocky, sleek and snow white with a white crest, cerulean blue eye patch and black tips to the wings and tail. It is 9 inches (24 cm) long and highly desirable for the pet trade. In 1978 there were about 550 in the wild northeastern part of the island. In 2001, there were 6.[5] By that time, some efforts had gone into breeding programs, and the program was very successful. So successful that on 20th November, just before a release back into their diminished corner of their island home, a group of armed men broke into the facilities and stole 39 cage-bred birds that were ready for release At that time a live Bali mynah was selling for $2000.[6]

The fortunes of this bird are now looking up though. They have been introduced to a small island named Nusa Penida, 14 kms off the coast of the main island. Before the release, a local avian veterinarian, Dr I. G. N. Bayu Wirayudha, convinced the island villages to add bird protection to their Awig Awig, or traditional regulations. With the acceptance of this new rule, the villagers are obligated, both spiritually and socially, to protect the birds on their island. As a result, the predation by poachers has been controlled and the Bali Mynah is now thriving on Nusa Penida. Numbers fluctuate, but it seems there may only be two left in their West Bali National Park homeland on Bali itself.[7] Apparently for every bird in the wild there are thought to be 200 in cages.

On 25th March 2013 a report, co-authored by Tim Blackburn of the Zoological Society of London and released by the journal Proceedings of the National Academy of Science, gave information on research undertaken on fossils from 41 Pacific islands. That report concludes that the arrival of humans to those islands, which include such places as Tahiti, Hawaii and New Zealand, resulted in the extinction of over 1,000 bird species. Intrepid people first reached those places within the past four thousand years. The hunt for food caused most of those extinctions, but probably the accompanying animals also played a role.[8]

Unknown numbers of species died off before we humans noted such events. It is calculated that without human influence about one species would have become extinct every thousand years, however we do know that during the 300 years up to 1980, nearly 300 species and subspecies of animals were rendered extinct. Of those known, 148 were birds, most of which lived on islands. From the plant world at least 120 are known to be extinct, but with so many species out there, and so few scientifically identified, one wonders how anyone would really know the true total. It is on small islands, far from land, that most species have been lost. One reason for this is that the birds that flew there have often had millions of years to adapt, become complacent, lose the instinct of fear, and lose the ability to fly. Secondly, their safe island may have become a trap from which they couldn't escape when predators did finally make it ashore. And those predators usually made it ashore with the help of humans.

For the following tales of extinctions after the 16th century, and prior to 1980, I have relied on David Day's 1981 book *The Doomsday Book of Animals; A Natural History of Vanished Species.*

The Mascarenes are a group of three islands in the Indian Ocean to the east of Madagascar. Mauritius is the main island, with Reunion 100 miles (160kms) to the west, and Rodriguez 300 miles (480kms) to the east. They are far enough apart that the species that did find their way there tended to develop independently of each other.

On Mauritius, the extinctions include probably the most famous of the last few hundred years: the Dodo. That bird was an overgrown, flightless dove, with a gentle and trusting manner and, like most island birds of the time, an inability to recognize new threats when they presented themselves. Or as some have said, "They were stupid." An early visitor to Mauritius, in 1627, Sir Thomas Herbert, described the bird thus: "First here and here only . . . . is generated the Dodo, her body is round and fat, few weigh less than fifty pound, are reputed of more for wonder than for food. Greasie stomackes may seeke after them, but to the delicate, they are offensive and of no nourishment . . . . . her appetite strong and greedy."

Quite a good number of the sailors who visited the island must have had 'greasie stomackes', for the bird was extinct some fifty years later, in 1680. The Dodo's wings were tiny and no longer suited for flying. So, like so many birds on islands situated a long distance from a large land mass, the lack of fear of any sort of predator had, over eons, rendered the Dodo completely fearless with absolutely no fight or flight instincts remaining. Even if they didn't kill them for the pot, it seems the seventeenth century human visitors simply took delight in killing them for sport, which they could do with a stick. It is interesting that in Britain, farmers, egg producers and anyone who keeps groups of birds, dislike foxes with a vengeance. The hatred stems from their habit, when they get into a chicken coop, of killing every bird in the enclosure regardless of how few they can actually eat. It seems to me that too many of us humans are more like the despised foxes than we willingly admit.

The Dodo of Mauritius was just one of four species of overgrown, ground-dwelling doves on the Mascarenes. Reunion had two: the Reunion solitaires, which were all gone by 1700, and the Reunion White Dodos, which were all killed by 1770. Rodriguez was home to the Rodriguez Solitaire. All four seem to have been as large or larger than turkeys.

The story of the Rodriguez Solitaire *(Pozohaps solitarius)* is a sad tale indeed. Those who reported on it describe it with great tenderness and affection. One writer was François Leguat, one of the first humans to settle on the island, which he did for two years when exiled from France in the 17th century. He describes the females as "Wonderfully beautiful, some fair, some brown . . ." He uses the word fair in the context of European fair hair. So were they blond or flaxen? He goes on to talk about how well-maintained and sleek they were, with plump thighs covered with rounded feathers, and of their lighter coloured craws ". . . which lively represents the fine bosom of a beautiful woman. They walk with so much stateliness and good grace, that one cannot help admiring and loving them." It does seem possible that 2 years without a woman on the island was rather too much for Monsieur Leguat. However, for all their stateliness and feminine qualities, the Rodriguez Solitaire could be quite aggressive in defending its single chick.

An outstanding part of his description is of the weddings they performed. He tells how, a few days after the chicks left the nest, a group of two or three dozen other birds would visit, ushering another young bird along with them. Then, with the original parents and fledged chick, they would all walk off to another place. There, the two young would remain after the adults had strolled away in couples or in groups. Apparently they remained faithful for life and also had interesting mating displays. He wrote that he and his friends "frequently" followed the marriage groups, so he isn't just enlarging on one isolated example of endearing and illuminating behavior.

A later visitor to Rodriguez wrote of how, when the birds were captured, they would shed tears while making no sound. One might be forgiven for thinking, after hearing of these tales, that Rodriguez was rich in magic mushrooms. However those writers also went to some length to describe the physical characteristics of the birds, which were all proven correct when skeletons were unearthed 110 years after they went extinct. The last we hear of those wonderful birds is that some still lived in 1761. No mounted specimens were produced. It is worth noting that the Dodo was always described in such disparaging terms as "stupid," "melancholy," and "greedy," while the Rodriguez Solitaire was considered "beautiful," "intelligent" and "delightfully edible."

I can't help wondering at the amount of time needed for birds on islands to develop the singular traits of the dodos and solitaires. I can understand that finches on different islands can develop different-sized beaks or that macaws can evolve glamorous colour combinations. But it has to take a very long time for doves to transform flying wings into tiny wings. The Mascarene Islands are volcanic. They rose from the sea some 8 to 10 million years ago. They were, before the European discovery, densely forested with a variety of unique species of trees and vines. I assume the birds flew to the islands in the first place. So, one wonders how much time was needed for them to grow huge and for their wings to become tiny. I wonder if a million years would cover it? Or did it take 8 million years? The giant moas of New Zealand had no wing vestiges remaining at all, so how long did it take for that adaptation to evolve? François Leguat settled on Rodriguez in the 1690s, and eighty years later the solitaires were all gone. So, it took one to eight million years to perfect the bird, but eighty years to destroy it. That just about says it all.

Another Mauritius dove that was rendered extinct quite early on, in 1826, was the Mauritius Blue Pigeon, or Pigeon Hollandaise (*Alectroenas nitidissima*). It was a very striking bird as it was dark blue in colour with a grey head and crest, and an orange-rufous eye, tail and under-wing. It was good to eat so suffered a great amount of persecution until another introduced species finished it off. Those introduced animals were not one of the usual culprits but pet monkeys. There had been no monkeys on Mauritius, or any other mammal than bats, so the birds had nested quite safely in the island forest since the time of their first arrival. Then, once the monkeys escaped, or were released into the forest, they consumed the pigeon eggs in such numbers that few young fledged from the nests. In a short time, the last hopeful egg-laying adults either died of old age or were shot leaving no plump progeny to coo happily in the treetops and supply dinner for hungry white men.

One wonders why the humans didn't think to domesticate or farm them. The pigeons were very tasty, so could be described as offering a ready food supply. They could have been domesticated into an ongoing benefit. Instead, in 1775, the government started offering a bounty for all "vermin" shot. That category seems to have meant all the local wildlife. Yet the same government did nothing to eradicate the introduced rats, cats, monkeys and who knows what other animals the Europeans had introduced. In the past, we seem to have viewed any wildlife as undesirable threats to our own safety and food supply, and called them vermin.

Other Mascarene extinctions include five species of giant tortoise. Like the Mascarenes, the Hawaiian Islands also lost 28, but all birds.

It is interesting to compare the destruction on these islands to that of the Seychelles group of islands. While the Masccarenes is an east/west string of distant islands situated in the Indian Ocean to the east of Madagascar, the Seychelles is a cluster to the northeast of that large island. Both groups shared many species, though somewhat removed due to geography, and the time needed for evolution and species adaptation. One might expect the species on both to share similar fates, yet the Mascarenes lost at least 28 between 1680 and 1980, while the Seychelles suffered only two extinctions: the Seychelles Parakeet and the Marion's Giant Tortoise. The Seychelles Islands also had an infestation of rats and cats, but it is probable that the large number of small islands, close by but not easily reached by the new exotics, gave safe havens to the birds capable of flying to them. The Seychelles Parakeet was shot, as it was thought to represent a threat to the maize crop that had been planted as food for the workers in the new coconut plantations. The parakeets were 16 inches (41 cm) in length, and green with pale blue tails. The last was shot in 1881.

Some extinctions are really well known and others hardly at all. Why, I wonder, do most of us know of the Great Auk, but very few of the Sea Cow?

Great Auk

Probably, next to the Dodo, the Great Auk is the most well known early extinction. It was one of those birds that were collected for food, though its extinction was brought about by the feather trade. It was a large bird, up to 33 inches (85cm) tall, and was the speediest of the water birds. Few predators were capable of catching it under water. For as long as the auks had existed, they didn't have to fear predators on land either, since they only lived on the most secure islands in the North Atlantic, which only such avian predators as the White-tailed Sea Eagle could reach. So on land they were imperturbable as they guarded their eggs, and simply waited to be caught by the human hunters who sailed to their islands. They nested on islands from Massachusetts Bay to Newfoundland and across to Iceland and the Outer Hebrides. There were scores of millions of them.

The European populations had been wiped out by the 16th century, save a few hanging on here and there. They had been used as food since Viking times, and there are records of sailors setting off on long voyages with few provisions, but in the certain knowledge that they could stock up at the nearest auk island. Jacques Cartier tells of his ships each salting down six barrels of salted auk after spending half an hour collecting the birds. Quite a large industry developed around collecting their eggs for food, but what clinched the auk's fate was the demand for feathers. The super warm eider down had been collected till the 1760 depletion and near extinction of the Eider Ducks and other ducks with suitable feathers. When I was a child our warm bed covers were always called eiderdowns regardless of what filled them, even if it was chicken feathers. To keep Europeans and North Americans warm at night, auk feathers became the standard replacement for eider down. In pursuit of those feathers, a disgusting, cruel and horrendous process was used.

It was simple. A crew of men would land on an island of Great Auks, set up huge cauldrons of water, the fire for which would be fed by the fat bodies of auks. While the water was heating, the collectors would round up the birds into huge pens. The men would then club the birds, throw them, unconscious or not, into the pots, rake the feathers into sacks and dispose of the naked bodies either on the fire or on the shore for the tide to wash away. They could clear a complete island of birds as the trusting creatures stayed put by their eggs and just waited to be collected. It says something about the lengths to which men would go, when we consider the conditions in which they worked. The islands were usually barren of any vegetation and covered with thousands of years' accumulation of bird droppings. The stink was overpowering, the smoke black and foul-smelling, and the work degradingly cruel. The men became as black and foul as the smoke or as the backs of the birds, and there were no baths on board even had they wanted to use one. The last of the islands of horror was Funk Island off the Newfoundland coast. It was given that name on account of the smell. Funk became the sole source of Great Auks from 1810 till 1840, when the birds were no more to be seen. A final sighting of the species took place in 1844, when three Icelandic fishermen came upon a pair of breeding birds with an egg. It might have seemed a great opportunity for one man to stay and protect the birds while the other two sailed to the city to spread the good news. Well no! Two clubbed the birds to death while the third stomped on the egg. The names of the three fishermen are on record as Jon Brandsson, Sigourer Isleffson and Ketil Ketilsson, the egg stomper.

This story, and so many others, says something about how far some of us have come in the last 150 years through education and a heightened awareness of our responsibilities to our fellows, our communities and to the earth on which we live. Very few of us now wish to own slaves, to condone corporal punishment or see public hangings, which were all enjoyed just a few centuries ago. I believe that now very, very few would wish to be party to the killing of the last two of a species of wildlife whether bird, animal or even insect. However, even now, there are evil men with no conscience who would do precisely that, given the opportunity. We only have to think of the ivory poachers, the rhino horn poachers and the shark-finners, all of whom do their dirty work for money. It is those people we have to spend vast amounts of wealth to guard against.

Sea Cow

One final tale of an extinction, which took place earlier than the Great Auk, probably in the time of my great-grandfather's great-grandfather, or the 1760s, was also dreadfully cruel. Steller's Sea Cows *(Hydrodamalis gigas)* were giant sea mammals related to the Manatee and Dugong. They measured 30 ft in length and weighed up to 14,000 lbs (6,400 kg), making them the next in line to elephants by weight. Tenderly gentle, having few known predators, they had the unfortunate habit of going to the aid of their own species when one was in difficulties. They inhabited the coasts of Copper Island and Bering Island in the Bering Sea. When Russian explorers discovered them in 1741, thousands could be seen lying in great rafts in the shallows, their backs above the salt water, feeding quietly on seaweed. Each would occasionally lift a head to breath, but the general impression was of great quiet and perfect peaceful co-existence in the world of ice and cold. They seem to have been the Arctic marine version of cows grazing in the green fields of a summer's day. They were very solicitous of the young, keeping them always protected and surrounded by mature animals when traveling.

Those animals suffered a number of serious disadvantages when they came into contact with humans. Not only were they peaceful and gentle and unafraid, they also tasted delicious. A mature animal had a one-inch (2.5cm) thick skin, 4-inch (10cm) thick layer of fat and very red meat. The fat was described as being like "May butter" infused with the sweet flavour of almond oil. The meat was described as superior to beef, while the young animal's meat was like veal.

The first sighting of Sea Cows was by men of Vitus Bering's last expedition who had become shipwrecked on Bering Island. That island is a 90 km long strip of desolate land and foul weather off the Kamchatka Peninsula in the Bering Sea. Though, for many, the discovery of the island and of the Sea Cows ended with their own and many animals' deaths, it was fortunate that the naturalist George Wilhelm Steller was attached to the expedition and was interested enough to record extensive observations regarding the Sea Cow's physical and behavioral characteristics. Were it not for a couple of skeletons and his writings, we would now know nothing of the animal. The types of men who followed Steller, and effected the total destruction of those huge sirenians, seem not to have been the types to either record their thoughts or observations nor to suffer conscious guilt for their actions.

Steller wrote of the animals at length. His observations and descriptions are such that we possibly know more of those contented giants than we do of many animals still surviving in the wild. We know that before mating the female would coquettishly play hard-to-get with her mate, until she would suddenly lie on her back and welcome him to her face-to-face embrace, as a lady might her human husband. The young and adolescent animals were cared for very diligently and assistance was given to other members of the herd.

For a description of the killing of the animals we can best read Steller's own words.

> Their capture was effected by a large iron hook, the point
> of which somewhat resembled the fluke of an anchor, the
> other end being fastened . . . to a very long and stout rope,

held by thirty men on shore. A strong sailor took this hook and with four or five other men stepped into the boat, ... , they quietly hurried towards the herd. The harpooner stood in the bow of the boat with the hook in his hand and struck as soon as he was near enough to do so, whereupon the men on shore, grasping the other end of the rope, pulled the desperately resisting animal toward them. Those in the boat, however, made the animal fast by means of another rope and wore it out with continual blows, until tired and completely motionless, it was attacked with bayonets, knives and other weapons and pulled up on land. Immense slices were cut from the still living animal, but all it did was shake its tail furiously and make such resistance with its forelimbs that big strips of the cuticle were torn off. In addition it breathed heavily, as if sighing. From the wound in the back the blood spurted upward like a fountain. As long as the head was under water no blood flowed, but as soon as it raised the head up to breath the blood gushed forth anew . . . . The old and very large animals were much more easily captured than the calves, because the latter moved about much more vigorously, and were likely to escape, even if the hook remained unbroken, by tearing through the skin, which happened more than once.

He goes on to say,

When an animal, caught with the hook, began to move about somewhat violently, those nearest in the herd began to stir and feel the urge to bring succor. To this end some of them tried to upset the boat with their backs, while others pressed down the rope and endeavored to break it, or strove to remove the hook from the wound in the back by the blows with their tail, in which they actually succeeded several times. It is most remarkable proof of their conjugal affection that the male, after having tried with all his might, although in vain, to free the female caught by the hook, and in spite of the beating we gave him, nevertheless followed her to shore, and that several times, even after she was dead, he shot unexpectedly up to her like a speeding arrow. Early next morning when we came to cut up the meat and bring it to the dugout, we found the male again standing by the female, and the same I observed once more on the third day when I went there by myself for the sole purpose of examining the intestines.

If the habit of always protecting the young by ushering them away from where danger may lurk, if coming to the assistance of distressed other animals by trying to dislodge the hooks in their resisting bodies, if returning to the body of a female mate for three nights after capture, and if trying to protect others in danger indicates some sort of sensitivity, then those Sea Cows displayed concern, empathy, caring and possibly even affection. To have butchered them alive, before killing them to end their suffering, says something terrible about the cruelty of humans.

The year spent, stranded on the snow-covered island, with no wood for fires or shelter other than that from their wrecked exploration vessel the Svyatoy Pyotr (St. Peter), must have been very harsh. Vitus Bering and 28 of his men died on that uninhabited island. Witnessing the deaths of friends and their leader, in the time it took before they were able to construct a get-away boat, must have been terrible. It was indeed fortunate for the men that the Sea Cows offered a near-at-hand food supply. Possibly, like Steller, some of the men felt compassion for the animals they killed. However, the sea otter hunters who followed them and who used the Sea Cows as ready food, seemed to have had no charitable thoughts. They managed to kill every last Sea Cow within 27 years of their discovery.

George Willhelm Steller gave his name to more than just the Sea Cows. He gave his name to six animals in total. The Steller's Spectacled Cormorant was rendered extinct by 1850. Of the four remaining, the Steller's Sea Eagle, the Steller's Eider, and the Steller's Sea Lion, are all in severe decline or are endangered. Soon only that blue and black rascally Steller's Jay, so well known in the Pacific Northwest, may perpetuate the great man's name.

The belief is that, under normal circumstances and natural selection, the number of extinctions would be about one species every thousand years. The rapid seaborne spread of Europeans to every continent and island of the globe was not historically normal, and the wildlife losses accelerated to three hundred in three centuries, or nearly one a year. However, though humans were sometimes the direct cause of exterminations, their actions often resulted in unintentional eradications. The introduction of rats and cats caused mayhem to the smaller species on islands where no predators had existed before.

At 54 extinctions, the West Indies lost the greatest number of species by 1980. Most were such small animals as rodents, reptiles and amphibians. Birds weren't affected as badly, apart from the desirable collectibles for the pet trade – amongst them the brightly coloured macaws and parrots. The birds that were eradicated because of the pet trade include the Jamaican Yellow-headed Macaw, ext. 1765; the green, red and yellow-breasted Dominican Macaw, ext. 1800; the Jamaican Green and Yellow Macaw ext. 1842; the red, orange and blue Cuban Red Macaw ext. 1864. To the list can be added the Culebra Island Amazon ext. 1899.

The second greatest number of extinctions took place on the North America continent, which lost 46 identified species. The great majority of extinctions occurred in the USA, which lost 14 subspecies of large mammals amongst others. These include 8 wolves, 2 bison, 2 elk, 1 jaguar, 1 bighorn sheep. It also lost grizzly bear subspecies galore. Mexico lost a total of four species including the Mexican Silver Grizzly Bear and 3 fish, 2 of which were tiny minnows. Compared with the American number, Europe and Asia together, from Portugal to the Siberian Kamchatka peninsula and Bali in the south, lost a total of 21 species and subspecies. Of those, 11 were large mammals, many of which had been under serious decline for thousands of years. Included in this group are the Tarpen, Auroch, Caucasian Wisent and Syrian Onager.[9]

From 1980 till 2011, another 600 species, including at least 21 birds, are known to have become extinct. So the numbers have increased from one every thousand years, to one a year before 1980, to the current twenty a year. These are sure signs that extinction rates are accelerating. In 2011 another 190 species were classified as "Critically endangered." Critically endangered means that a species' numbers have, or will, decrease by 80 per cent in 3 generations and that that species is facing an extremely high risk of extinction in the wild. Many have reached this sorry state due to their habitat having been reduced to extremely small pockets.

The percentages of assessed species currently threatened with extinction, though not conclusive, are as follows:

Mammals	25 per cent
Birds	13 per cent
Amphibians	41 per cent
Reptiles	28 per cent
Invertebrates	36 per cent
Reef building corals	33 per cent
Freshwater fish	37 per cent
Plants	20 per cent

Of course local extinctions will be very much higher than the above. "Local extinctions" mean national or regional ones. For instance, species that traditionally inhabited Eurasia from Spain to China may well be extirpated from Europe but still exist in central Asia somewhere. Or a species that once thrived across all of equatorial Africa may become confined to a small piece of mountain forest in only one of the original dozen countries that hosted it.

Endangered Species International, one of the many NGOs dedicated to the protection of species has assessed 44,835 species and found 16,928 are threatened with extinction. They found that, by 2006, 784 species had been made extinct and that by 2011 that number had risen to 905. In the most recent two years, 121 species had disappeared from our Earth and the numbers are rising fast.

Anyone wanting to know more about species extinctions, prior to this terrible time that Prince Charles calls *The Sixth Great Extinction*, may like to read David Day's Book. It deals with the 305 species that were made extinct between 1680 and 1980.

Here is a selection of recent news from the sixth great extinction.

In November 2011, two rhino subspecies were declared extinct. These were the Western Black Rhino *(Diceros bicornis lingpies)* and the Vietnamese Javan Rhino *(Rhinoceros sondaicus annamiticus)*.

According to the International Union for the Conservation of Nature, the Northern White Rhino *(ceratotherium simum cottoni)* is possibly extinct.

Also in 2011, the US Fish and Wildlife Service declared the American Eastern Cougar *(Puma concolor couguar)* extinct.

The Japanese Ministry of the Environment declared the Japanese River

Otter *(Lutra lutra whiteneyi)* officially extinct, after the animal had not been seen for 30 years.

In Taiwan, the Clouded Leopard was declared locally extinct in April 2013. The last of its kind was seen in the island's remnant forest patch in 1983.[10]

And finally, the last of the Pinta Island Galapagos Tortoises *(Chelonoidis nigra abingdoni)* died in 2012. That giant tortoise had been given the name Lonesome George. He died on 24th June, at an age believed to be over 100 years. He was first discovered in 1971, after most of the other tortoises had either been killed by hunting, or had starved following the introduction of vegetation-destroying goats to Pinta Island. George was removed to the island of Santa Cruz, where he spent the next forty years with two tantalizing females of another tortoise subspecies. Unfortunately, none of the resulting eggs proved to be viable. George's species is now extinct.[11]

However, amongst all this gloom, there are occasional pieces of good news. One such is that, on the Indian sub-continent, the number of Asian Lions in the Gir Forest had increased to 411 by 2010. This is an encouraging improvement. There were 13 still alive in 1907 when they were given protection, and 234 were counted in a 1936 census.[12] In 2012, though, due to losses from overcrowding, and fears of epidemics, natural disasters and human factors, it was decided necessary to establish another population of Asiatic Lions in the Kuno Wildlife Sanctuary in the Indian state of Madhya Pradesh. It seems we have saved the lions, but in an area that is too small for a population of more than a hundred or two.[13] The Gir Forest is a tiny remnant that is surrounded on all sides by human development.

7 Of Wheatears and Other Birds

The Venerable Bede described Britain as abundant in wildlife, but that was twelve hundred years ago and the island was a very different place then. We don't know how plentiful nature once was. Each generation assumes that the way they live is the norm, and the young, when told by an older generation that things were once better, don't really believe it. I suppose it is our vaunted adaptability that enables us to live with huge changes to the world around us with nary a squeak of complaint. I often used to wonder, when looking at books of British birds, why I had never seen birds described as common – and still haven't.

When looking through books of British birds, whether as a kid of seven or as an adult, the Northern Wheatear *(Oenanthe oenanthe)* often held my fancy. It is described as a reasonably common bird of wide distribution and nearly 3 million individuals worldwide. The historic number was possibly many more millions but those days are long gone. The bird is there in all the books with a buff-white breast, bluish-grey back and black wings and eye-mask. The males are attractive and look kind of perky. The name has nothing to do with wheat, but rather has to do with the white rump, which is most visible as it flies away from the viewer.

In Anglo Saxon *hwit* meant white and *ears* meant arse. So the name was actually *hwitears* or 'white arse'. In Middle English it became *whiterres*, but wheatear in the vocabulary of the more genteel Victorians.

They are small birds about the size of a sparrow and weigh less than 1 ounce or 25 grams. Yet, like so many others, they are mighty migrators. During the summer, many millions of Northern Wheatears encircle the Arctic across northern Europe, Asia, Alaska and Canada, but they spend the winter in sub-Saharan Africa. The birds, from such East African countries as Kenya, fly northeast into Asia, arctic Siberia and on to Alaska. The West African birds,[1] from countries such as Mauritania, head northwest to Iceland, Greenland and Canada. Some fly via Britain, and a small group stop off in Britain and fly no further.

Scientists from Germany's Institute of Avian Research, Canada's University of Guelph, and the Ontario Ministry of Natural Resources, have come up with some amazing statistics. The Royal Society published the study in 2012, in the journal *Biology Letters*, describing some wheatear migrations.[2]

46 wheatears, from both Alaska and Baffin Island, had been tagged with 1.2-gram geo-locators. It is these electronic wonders that enabled the scientists to come up with their amazing findings. I consider it a miracle that 25-gram birds were able to fly large distances with 1.2 gram pieces of luggage attached.

The Alaskan birds were tracked flying across the full width of Asia to Arabia. From there they continued on to the East African countries. That is a distance of 9,000 miles (15,000 km) each way. Those birds flew at an average of 180 miles (290 km) a day, covering the distance in 91 days in one direction and 55 days in the other. They, of course, could stop off along the way to fill up with insects.

The birds that left Baffin Island and Canada's high Arctic flew as two distinct groups. The first flew a fairly direct flight to West Africa via Labrador, and a trans-Atlantic flight to the Iberian Peninsula. That was a distance of 2500 km of ocean flying.

The second group, from Baffin Island to Mauritania, made a stop-over in Britain and flew a total of 4,660 miles (7,500 km) in 26 days at an average of 288 miles a day. Of the 46 birds that began the study, only 4 were found at the end, to provide the flight information.

On the northern migration from Africa, some flocks drop in on Britain, Iceland and Greenland on the way. Still others spend the summer in Britain where they nest, raise young and go no further. The birds that breed in Britain are somewhat smaller and less vivid than those that pass through on the way to the Arctic.

A great many questions come to mind. How can a tiny bird weighing less than an ounce, first store, and then produce, enough energy to fly across the Atlantic from Labrador to Spain? Apparently, before they leave, they double their weight, to close to 50 grams by feeding on insects and spiders. Okay! But then how can such a bird undertake a journey of 9000 miles between Alaska and Africa over the full length of Asia? Being insectivores how do they know where to stop off for food? How can they consume enough food at each stop to enable them to continue? Why don't we humans stand in total awe of such fantastic little birds? More to the point; what are the results when we plough the grasslands or spray insecticides and herbicides that destroy the food they are counting on along the way?

Although the Northern Wheatear are abundant, and the two most northern groups migrate to lands that so far suffer no pesticides, the lengthy migration across Asia leaves that group open to any disruption to their feed-stops. Insecticides or herbicides applied, in all innocence, to a patch of land in central Asia could mean starvation to the birds when they drop in for their annual food top-up. Hopefully, one day we humans will learn to treat such remarkable little birds with reverence and wonderment. They are miracles of life and we, instead of going around the world adapting everywhere to meet our needs, should make protecting the needs of such mighty little travelers one of our priorities.

Most migrating seed eaters suffer just as badly. On grasslands, over millennia, the grasses and flowering plants will have evolved to great abundance. Each flower head and stem of grass will produce a great many seeds. The seeds fall to the ground where they remain as a food supply for a year or more. Over large areas these seeds will amount to a cornucopia of bountiful food for migrating and resident seed-eating birds. For millennia the birds will have been confident of copious food on those grasslands.

Then, when we plough up those lands and plant crops, we deny the hungry birds their food. The more land we plough, the less chance there is for the hungry and exhausted migrants to find good areas of food to sustain them. We have ploughed 99 per cent of the North American tall grass prairie. According to Richard Westward, Professor of Environmental Science at the University of Winnipeg only 1 per cent of that original habitat remains. This means that, of that once vast area of grassland, 99 per cent is now off limits to the mammals, birds, butterflies, moths, insects, and bugs that once lived there. It is also off limits to migrating birds.

Many migratory birds, and such migrating butterflies as Monarchs and Painted Ladies, have a really tough time nowadays. Over the past multi-millennia they had found routes that enabled them to rest and stock up with food along the long flights. They had found pieces of land that suited their needs, whether boundless grasslands, dry heath, or marshland, and the timing meant their arrival coincided with the flourishing of local insects or the maturing of seeding plants. Birds are great at keeping the insects that we consider undesirable - mosquitoes or grasshoppers for instance - in check, so we should show a little appreciation for all they do for us.

When birds and butterflies wing their tiring trips to destinations some thousands of miles away they need to be reasonably sure that, when they stop along the way, the land will be as it has always been – rich with fat grubs, grasshoppers, seeding grasses, milkweed, or whatever else is required. Recent, human-built, changes in the northern tundra have probably been negligible. Possibly central Asia has the least changed grassland of anywhere. The changes in Europe, and west and east Asia, have been taking place gradually for thousands of years, but in other parts of the world, where other long distant migrants fly, the recent changes to the land have been fast, radical, and wide-ranging. It is in the Americas, Africa, and Southeast Asia where the most drastic and far reaching changes have recently taken place. The 19th and 20th centuries saw massive land developments that have been devastating for birds.

Consider the birds of the North America continent. The prairie grasslands are now ninety-five percent agricultural land, and the birds' winter homes in Central America and beyond have been massively deforested. The Canadian boreal forest is a huge area that has the potential to house billions of birds during the northern summer, yet those birds now have to fly south over a changed landscape to equally compromised destinations. How do the once abundant migrating birds now survive the journeys south? And then, how do they survive once they arrive? Presumably they don't. Presumably a great many of those birds from the north simply starve and die. The survivors then have to fly north again over the ravaged prairie.

With that in mind, what chance do wee birds have? It was bad enough when European grasslands were turned to field agriculture, as at least a few old meadows, hedgerows or road-margins remained. Now though, for many migrating birds, when they arrive exhausted at the next food stop they find the last ancient meadow gone, and a sterile golf course, or parking lot for a mega-mall, in its place. Either that or they find we have sprayed the very life out of the local plants and insects. The birds have to fly off and search elsewhere for sustenance and rest. We work really, really, hard to kill off the weeds, grasshoppers and insects wherever they are. In so doing, we do untold harm to the migrating birds' food supply.

The same difficulties can be applied to Monarch butterflies. When they leave their Mexican or Californian wintering forests and head north they do so in the expectation of finding milkweed plants to lay their eggs on. Instead most of the milkweeds have been poisoned by agricultural concerns. As evidence of their decline, the Guardian Newspaper reported, on 29th January 2014, on the diminishing sizes of the overwintering Monarch colonies. In 1997 the largest of the colonies, that in the Mexican mountains, covered 44.5 acres (18 hectares). In 2014 the area was 1.65acres (o.67 hectares). This was not a one off bad year, but was the result of a long series of declining years.

We can liken the plight of migrating birds, and migrating butterflies, to long distance truck drivers delivering fruits and vegetables between central Mexico and eastern Canada, or between Spain and Scandinavia. The truckers know where to stop for gas and a meal. They have done it for years. The gas stops are strategically placed; the motels and cafes are plentiful. But imagine the chaos if one day they traveled the route and found the gas stops closed and all the eating-places either boarded up or offering poisoned food. Those routine journeys could no longer be undertaken and transportation by road would be impossible. It would never cross our minds to close all the gas stations on the highway; it would be a really dumb thing to do. Yet we close down Mother Nature's filling stations, by ploughing grasslands, felling forests or spraying pesticides on locations rich with insects. We do these things without even knowing what the effect can be on the overall health of the environment.

If the earth is to survive with nine or ten billion of us enjoying the benefits of the place, I believe it vital that we become more circumspect in all our ventures into development and changes to the habitat. Many countries now have environmental reviews that precede large national development projects. Reviews are carried out for dams and pipelines, but they should also be held before any piece of land is ploughed up for agriculture, sprayed with herbicides or insecticides, or turned into a mine or housing development. The developer or farmer needs to know how the piece of land is used every day of the year. If it supports a number of widespread and common species for some months of the year, then that is one thing. If, on the other hand, flocks of unusual birds drop in over a few days once or twice a year it probably means the land is a crucial food stop for that migrating species.

When the first American and Canadian settlers arrived on the prairies, they were welcomed by the heavens full of song - bright, cheering, wonderful song. No, it wasn't the angels on high welcoming the good Christians to a new Promised Land. It was millions of grassland birds, attracting mates, and possibly just celebrating the rich life they knew in those days. Many of these were not the colourful tanagers, buntings and orioles of the tropics, but rather what the British call LBJs or 'little brown jobs'. They are thus known on account of their somewhat dowdy and indistinguishable plumage. Many of them were species of sparrows, longspurs, and skylarks, and being so dowdy, they had to sing to be noticed by potential mates. And sing they did.

It is probable that most of the early farmers and ranchers took scant interest in identifying the little brownish birds that made the air melodious in those early days. They were too busy with survival and gaining something to eat. But, before the settlers traveled to this new land, there had been one or two earlier explorers and surveyors who took an interest in the wildlife through which they passed. It is thanks to those people, from the early 19th century, that we have, if not a record, at least their observations of the bird species, and numbers to be found in the parts of the country that they visited. With that information on hand we can now see that many prairie birds are in deep trouble. Trevor Herriot writes about these birds in his 2009 book *Grass, Sky, Song. Promise and Peril in the Land of Grassland Birds*. His book makes fascinating reading in the detailed depth with which he covers the declines of the birds and some of the causes.

Of course not all prairie birds are LBJs, but many can be described thus. The grassland used to throb to the sound of the bird life, but then it also used to thunder to the hooves of the buffalo. However, although the great American Prairie was brought under the plough, with no room for buffalo, there were always edges and margins left untouched where birds could find sanctuary. Early settlers tended not to plough surfaces that were too rough, too steep, too marshy, or too dry. A margin was usually left along a fence and along the side of the road. Then of course some land was not ploughed at all but left as rangeland for cattle or horses or as open treed land. In the early days, there was no thought of poisoning all the insect pests that some of the birds liked to feed on. So, although the area of grassland was greatly reduced, and the bird numbers were too, there were always some patches where birds could feed, nest and continue the age-old migrations. In recent years though, many of those patches have gone or have been sprayed with bird-killing insecticides. Consequently the numbers of many species have been falling fast.

Trevor Herriot gives some telling numbers. For many years he surveyed a string of sites close to Regina in Saskatchewan. With these surveys it is always necessary to be consistent with the time and approximate day of the year. Over twelve years from 1990 to 2002 he recorded declining numbers on nearly every species he saw. The first and the last counts give the following numbers:

". . . Western Meadowlark, from 39 to 20; Chestnut-collared Longspur, from 15 to 0: Burrowing Owl, from 3 to 0; Savannah Sparrow, from 29 to 11: Horned Lark, from 174 to 8."

Since 1965, the US Fish and Wildlife Service and Canada's Wildlife Service have been carrying out an annual survey of bird numbers, named the Breeding Bird Survey, or BBS. The system employed is quite straightforward. A few thousand survey-routes had been determined and each year on the same date amateur ornithologists follow the lines stopping at certain intervals to identify and count any birds they see or hear. Now after about thirty-five years a lot of data is available. The birds that are shown to be in the most serious decline are the prairie grassland birds. The survey reveals that the average percentage annual declines over North America went as follows. Between 1966 and 2008 the decline of Swainson's Sparrow: 1 per cent per year, Horned Lark: 2.4 per cent, Sprague's Pipit: 2.6 per cent, Baird's Sparrow: 2.7 per cent, Chestnut-collared Longspur: 4.3 per cent, McCown's Longspur: 5.1 per cent.

A 3 per cent annual decline from 1,000 birds doesn't sound like much. However it results in 650 birds lost over 35 years with only 350 remaining. A 4 per cent annual decline reduces 1,000 birds to 250 for a loss of 750. If we continue those rates of decline for another 35 years we come up with 62 birds. So a 4 per cent decline over 70 years reduces 1000 birds to 62. A count in another area of Canada's prairie showed longspur numbers pretty steady at 250 birds for many years till 1987. Then in ten years the numbers declined precipitously till in 1998 they numbered six.

In the chapter titled 'The Poisoned Land', Trevor Herriot describes many of the agricultural changes that may influence these prairie bird declines. He writes of the farmers quitting summer fallow in favour of continuously planting crops on the land. He speaks of the increased use of pesticides, and the resulting increased incidence of breast cancer among the farmer's wives. He also writes of the farmers and politicians in Saskatchewan, Manitoba and Alberta, insisting that the land be sprayed with pesticides to kill off the grasshoppers. It wasn't just the crop-bearing land that had to be sprayed, but the road allowances, railway rights of way and every piece of land where grasshoppers might lurk. That land was also the last refuge for the birds. One of the poisons being used was Carbofuran, which is a neurotoxin capable of killing a man if he ingests as much as a quarter of a teaspoon. Well! If it will kill a 150 lb human and will kill a tiny grasshopper, I can see no reason whatever why it shouldn't kill off hungry prairie birds, weighing one or two ounces. Trevor Herriot reports that Canada's Pesticide Management Regulatory Agency was finally encouraged to research the number of birds dying from the spray. Although that agency would not release the figures, a wildlife toxicologist from another agency said the number of birds killed per year was anywhere from one hundred thousand to a million.

Anyone interested in the sparrows of North America will find at least thirty species as well as another four longspurs and three buntings. They are all classified, along with juncos and towhees, under the family name: *Emberizine*. All of these LBJs are identifiable either by subtle plumage variations, their songs or their habitat of choice. A Sage Sparrow naturally tends to inhabit different habitat from a Swamp Sparrow. All of them are declining to one extent or another.

These noted reductions in North American grassland bird numbers can probably be applied to birds anywhere in the world. In Europe, Asia and the Americas, observant people are noticing diminishing numbers of birds.

The threats to birds come from many unexpected places. I bet few people think of their pet cat as a bird menace of the first degree. After all, the occasional bird that our pets catch can't possibly hurt bird numbers. Certainly one cat isn't a serious threat, but a huge group of cats most definitely is. According to MapsoftheWorld.com, the US has 76 million pet cats; China has 53 million and the UK 7.7 million. The top ten cat countries have 204 million pet cats among them. The trouble is, not all cat owners are responsible with their little dears. Some even let them outside, and others even set them free when the people have to move, or otherwise can no longer look after them. There are now believed to be 60 million feral cats in the US, which is a little less than the number of pet cats. So if that relationship of pet to feral cats is similar in other countries it suggests that those top ten countries have a total of about 350 million cats. The 200 million pet cats are presumably well fed but what about the feral cats? What do all those cats eat? Most survive on wildlife. A 2010 report entitled *Feral Cats and their Management* from the University of Nebraska School of Natural Resources estimates that the US cats don't just eat mice and rats, they also eat 480 million birds each year. This is a death toll that costs the US $17 billion if we are to believe the figures worked out by the good folk at the U of N.

This sounds like a lot of cat-killed birds, but I can believe it. I had cats once many years ago. One was a ginger neutered tom who was affectionate, liked cantaloupe melon, and was too soft to catch anything. But his sister was a little black and white holy terror. I was walking one evening along a wooded lane and she had decided to follow me along the margin. Of a sudden, a man walking his dog came round a corner and that little cat, with a howl of anger, leapt from the bushes and fastened herself onto the poor dog's head. I finally got her off and naturally apologized to the man, and to his quaking dog. I must say, she was the only patrolling-guard cat I have ever known, and before that evening I had no idea such an animal existed. I mention this anecdote as an indication of just how fierce that otherwise gentle little cat could be. While she lived with me I would often go downstairs in the morning to find animal parts strewn up and down the stairs. I was on the phone once when she strolled by with a snake writhing from each side of her mouth and I would guess she probably killed something most days of her life. The point to all this is that, though she was a very well fed cat, the killer instinct hadn't left her. She lived to hunt. Her brother, the ginger tom, also enjoyed a hunt, but he was unwise in the ways of stealth, and invariably gave himself away before he got within a couple of yards of his target.

Most of the cats I have known, whether at the farm in Somerset, at my parent's home, or in my own home, have been killers. One barn-cat on the farm used to kill full-grown rabbits to feed her litter of kittens. That is one reason I haven't had one for thirty years. I think we can assume that most of the other cats are also hunters.

Let's assume that each cat kills only one bird a week, but only during twenty warm weeks of the year. With those numbers, we finish up with 20 killings times 350 million cats which is 7 billion birds a year. If the cats kill only one bird a month for six months of the year, it is still 2.1 billion birds per year. Or at two birds a week for forty weeks a year we arrive at 28 billion killed birds. However, I fear that my high number may be the most accurate. A New Zealand study of 37 cats, found that they each killed 82 birds and 296 other animals per year.[3] That number works out at 28.7 billion, so my lower figures could be serious underestimations. What is even more scary is that we are only counting the cats in the top ten countries. There must be at least double the number scattered all over the world, so the total number of killings for all the cats worldwide could even be double the 28.7 billion. Such numbers appear outrageous, and I sincerely hope they are wildly inflated. We can only hope that many cats have few chances to hunt. Pet cats are in actual fact an invasive species in the majority of countries where they live. Worldwide they are known to have been responsible for the extinction of at least 33 species of birds.

In 2010 and 2011, Karl Evans of the UK's University of Sheffield led a study of the effects that the mere presence of cats has on nesting birds. His research found that when cats appear, the nesting birds respond with alarm calls and nest-defense activities that alert third party predators. The predators, be they squirrels or corvine birds, then know where to look for eggs or young chicks. Not only do the cats assist others in finding the young birds, but also the very disturbance caused by the cats reduces future nesting successes of the parent birds.[4]

The American Humane Society estimates that a pair of cats can produce up to five litters a year ranging in size from two to ten kittens. If all survive and go on to breed that adds up to a total of 400,000 offspring over a period of seven years.[5] The way things are going, the feral cats could soon wipe out a whole lot more wildlife than they have done already.

Birds suffer terribly. Despoiled land and disturbed migration routes all take their toll, but another hazard now presents itself. On April 25, 2012 a report on research carried out by certain United States Agencies and Universities, and by Environment Canada, states that communication towers north of the Mexican border kill 6.8 million birds per year. The lead writer for the report, entitled *An Estimate of Avian Mortality at Communication Towers in the United States and Canada*, was Travis Longcore from the University of Southern California. Apparently there are now 84,000 communications towers erected over North America. Some are more than 500 meters high surrounded by a great number of supporting guy wires, and topped by red, and other brightly-coloured, lights.

These bright lights attract migrating birds. This is especially bad on nights of dense cloud, when the moon and stars are obscured. The birds fly toward and encircle the lights. Travis Longcore suggests they fall under "the spell of the lights".[6] We all know how hard it is to see in the dark when we have a bright light shining in our eyes. The same happens to birds. They collide with the wires, bump into each other and many of the survivors finally collapse out of exhaustion. These are not just the LBJ prairie birds mentioned earlier. They include all those birds that summer as far north as the boreal forest and winter as far south as South and Central America. Those brilliant orange and black orioles that over-wintered with me in Granada, Nicaragua may well have met their deaths on one of those communication towers. So might the Yellow Warblers that built their nests in the vine in Lilly's garden.

The towers are used to send TV and radio signals, some of which are important communications on which we rely, while some are just our favorite TV shows, or the trite nonsense that pervades our popular culture. The lights that crown the towers are in place as warnings for aviation. It is anticipated that as both the US and Canada continue the transition from analogue to digital broadcasting, even more very tall towers will be constructed.

By 2012, a few years after the introduction and great success of the smartphone, telecommunication providers were anticipating a huge expansion of communication services to mobile phones. Apparently, across the world in that year, more humans had mobile devices than had running water or electricity. Also a smartphone on average consumes 30 times as much airtime as does a cell phone. This suggests that a formidable increase in the provision of wireless radio waves, on which the smartphone signals travel, needs to be provided all over the planet. I assume this means building a great many more communication towers with their guy wires and bird-attracting lights. We can soon expect bird numbers to plummet.

Till now we have been talking about the problems of the North American continent with a population of 315 million. However we have to remember the population in Africa is expected to double to 2 billion by 2050. I assume we all hope those Africans will be able to live as we do with a smartphone each. So! We can expect Africans to need a far greater density of communication towers than North Americans have. It is clear that if there are going to be any birds left to delight us on this blue and green globe, we had better come up with some bird-friendly communication towers in a hurry.

In our contemporary world, it is hard to argue against communication towers and against warning lights, but it is also difficult to support a system that kills 6-7 million birds a year in North America. It is especially difficult when we know they are also suffering from so many other threats. It is really tough for migrating birds in the Americas. They have to fly over cities, suburbs, villages and homesteads bright with millions of lights that mess up their navigating abilities. Lights high on towers attract them. Their rest stops are oftentimes now ploughed-over land, polluted or poisoned with pesticides. And on top of all this, these little bundles of energy have to fly thousands of miles to reach their second home. The Bobolink is another widespread bird that flies long distances, in this case 6,200 miles. It is mostly black with feathered markings of white and cream and weighs 1.5 oz. It has to fly that distance to reach its austral summer home on the Argentinean pampas. Then a few months later it has to fly the same distance back again to North America. Instead of getting help from us, the wise ones, on such a daunting undertaking, those little birds find we have, often as not, turned their route into an unending obstacle course, and their ultimate destinations death traps laced with poisons.

Small birds have many things to contend with as I have witnessed myself. It must have been about 1975. I was sitting at my kitchen window overlooking the stream, enjoying an afternoon cup of tea and the sight of the many birds feeding at the bird table when, wham! An explosion which, when the feathers cleared, revealed a Cooper Hawk with a House Finch in her talons. After moments, during which the finch struggled desperately, the hawk jumped into the stream shallows, held its prey under for a minute or two till it was drowned, and then flew to a stump where it enjoyed the meal. On another occasion, on Bali, I was watching a family of fledgling kingfishers beside a reservoir, when a raptor took one of the young and flew off, hassled by the parent kingfisher. Raptor strikes are typical problems birds have evolved to deal with, and birdlife is a battleground for survival.

So now, after untold thousands of years of trying to survive all the threats directed at them from the natural world, we throw a heap of new ones their way. Now the birds have to put up with their forests, grasslands and migration-food-stops destroyed and turned to agricultural monoculture. The flyways are now littered with killer communication towers. Their nest sites are now doused with herbicides to kill the food plants we call weeds, and their feed insects are doused with insecticides because we don't like them. On top of all this they have to try to avoid cats.

We read a lot about the threats to wildlife all over the world, and I personally find it thoroughly depressing. Every day we read of the last patch of habitat, and the few remnant pairs of some dependent species under threat of ranchers, loggers or developers. Frequently those interests have much to gain by going ahead with whatever project they have underway, and they don't appreciate some bleeding-heart getting in the way of their plans, especially when it's just to save a couple of birds. This is depressing as I say, but the good news, I think, is in the very fact that we do read about it. It is reported. This indicates that people out there are concerned enough to get the word out. And they often do so at considerable risk to their personal safety. The stories reported are often depressing, but at least they are reported. That in a way is encouraging. However, for every one we read about we can be sure there are thousands unreported.

Here follow a couple of tales about birds from a short period of the news.

During three months of the 2011 fall migration of songbirds from Europe to Africa, more than a million were killed on the island of Cyprus.[7] This was to feed the local delicacy, named Ambelopoulia. The birds were mostly caught by lime on twigs or with drift nets. This was termed an ecological disaster. When people in Northern Europe wonder where the songbirds have gone, who would guess the people of certain southern European nations ate them?

When I was in Milan, northern Italy in 1968 I was horrified to see hundreds of tiny songbird carcasses displayed for consumption in the cafes. Whether they were barbecued, fried or roasted I can't say. They seemed to be very popular fare though. That was more than forty years ago and I believe it is now illegal to hunt songbirds for food. However, there is an unhealthy illegal trade between Malta, Italy and the Balkans, where the birds are still thought of as good eating and a way to make money.[8]

Hunting small birds is a strong tradition with some people in Italy. One thing that is truly amazing is that the only people a landowner cannot legally ban from his land are hunters.

The big problem is that most bird migrations are north/south, and birds prefer to over-fly land than wide stretches of water. As a consequence northern European birds fly to Africa through either; Spain to Morocco, down the length of Italy to Tunis via Malta, or across the Balkans, Cyprus or Levant routes. Now songbirds are being shot in the millions as they pass through the country of Albania, where people can earn good money by exporting them as a delicacy.[9]

Over on the island of Malta, during the same fall 2011 migration, the police had their time cut out trying to catch a group of hunters who knowingly delighted in shooting such protected species as storks and ibis when they rested on those islands. In 2012, hunters in a high-speed boat, coordinating with hunters on the cliffs, shot the last Peregrine Falcon on the islands.[10] The Peregrine is also known as the Maltese Falcon. Why would anyone want to do such a thing? I simply don't understand.

In Central America, where many of the most rare and the most beautiful northern American birds head for the winter, the forests continue to fall. The birds include such colourful glories as the Painted Bunting, Rose-breasted Grosbeak and Baltimore Orioles. Further south in the Amazon the Motto Grosso – declared protected in 1990 – is now called 'destruction Crescent' thanks to illegal logging and illegal ranching.

So now, one question might be: just what are we willing to give up to ensure that songbirds, and all other birds for that matter, continue to survive into the next generations? Will we all agree to turn the farmland back to natural meadows in order that the birds and bees might flourish again. Most of us, in North America and northern Europe, will probably agree that those who enjoy the delicacy known as ambelopoulia should be willing to give up eating songbirds. Others will say that the hunters, who delight in shooting small birds in the name of sport, should willingly stop hunting. But then, will those of us in the most developed countries quit using our cell phones because the towers are causing the deaths of millions of birds on their migrations? And hands up all those who believe cats are the biggest problem. In fact, who is willing to get rid of their pet cats because they are an invasive species that should be removed from the towns and countryside?

I am sure that nearly all of us will mourn the songbirds when they are no more. But what are willing to do to save them?

8 Oceans

We humans have a strong attachment to the sea. We dream of living or, at the very least, holidaying beside it. In the tropics the water may be a sparkling pale-turquoise blue, in the north a cold steel grey or, in Greek litreature, the "wine dark sea." Whatever our ambivalent and romantic perception, that calm or storm-tossed surface hides beneath it a salty realm that is in deep trouble. Like the terrestrial animals and plants, the fish and all the sea creatures are also seriously threatened. The causes of these threats are many, but all human induced.

They include, in no particular order, overfishing, the destruction of the foundation fish, drift nets, vacuum fishing, shark finning, specific species fisheries destroying more by-catch than the numbers they bring to market, and overfishing at the oceans' fish-gathering place. On top of that are water temperature changes due to global warming, ocean dead areas caused by agricultural fertilizer run-off, disease caused by fish farming, pollution from oil spills and marine discharge, acidification of the oceans, noise pollution and plastic trash floating in the oceans. It is an alarming stew of problems.

I recall reading a newspaper article sometime during the 1950s. The gist of the article was that the oceans were too vast for our puny human activities to have any negative effects in the long term. The headline was something like: "Oceans can't be hurt by human activity, scientists say."

Yeah, right! As the expression goes. Now, 50 years later, every form of sea life is under threat. Once again our human experts have been proved so very wrong. Actually, the scientists quoted were probably not at all impartial, but were rather in the pay of the fishing and resource extraction interests that felt under threat and in need of an early defense of their industry.

Over-fishing is one of the biggest problems facing the oceans. Consider the North Atlantic cod fishery. In the northern ocean, there are two true cod species: the Atlantic Cod *(Gadus morhua)* and the Greenland Cod *(Gadus ogac)*. Europeans have fished them for over a thousand years since the Vikings began in the 9th century.[1] It amuses me to think of the Vikings fishing for the Greenland Cod, as Gadus Ogac sounds rather like the name a Norseman might have gone by.

Imagine a shipload of Vikings somewhere in the far North Atlantic:

"Hey! Gadus! What's that white lump yonder on the horizon?"
"That, Morhua, you smelly minion, is Greenland."
"Greenland? Doesn't look very green to me. What idiot named it that?"
"I did. And you'll feel like the idiot when you have to swim to it."

Ogac, not wishing to miss out on all the jolly repartee, pipes up from the back of the boat, "Are you sure there will be fish where we are going, Gadus?"

"Of course, Ogac, more than a dimwit like you can ever imagine. Why do you ask?"

"I'm getting cold, and I can tell you I am beginning to doubt the wisdom of this cruise idea of yours."

"Now, now, Ogac. We'll entertain no complaints from you. We've only been at sea for four months, and, come March, it may stop snowing. When we get to my new found land you'll see more big fish than you ever imagined. So pipe down and just keep rowing."

And they were big fish too. Apparently the *G. morhua* have been known to reach 220 lbs (100 kg) in weight and 2 meters in length, though currently a typical fish has been in the 10-30 lbs (4-13 kg) range. Again I like to imagine Vikings pulling aboard fish the same weight as themselves. That, and terrorizing Britons, was what Vikings did best. When John Cabot reached Newfoundland in 1497, he was totally amazed to come upon those fish that were so dense in the sea that they impeded his ship's forward momentum. There must have been billions upon billions at the time.[2]

I think we can imagine the oceans then, before humans had had any significant effect. They must have been immensely rich with fish and mammal numbers. From sardines to swordfish and from walruses to whales, the sea would have been teeming. And what about all the sea birds? There would have been many times the numbers that are seen today. Maybe we haven't totally destroyed the oceans yet, but we have brought them to a tiny fraction of the rich and vibrant ecosystems that they were two hundred years ago.

Once the Europeans and North Americans got really organized with their fishing, the Grand Banks, to the south east of Newfoundland (or the Rock, as that island is known), became the fishing grounds of choice. Another area was the sea between Newfoundland and Labrador where, for a hundred years until the 1950s, the annual catch would be around 250,000 tons. Really, the only reason people settled on Newfoundland was for the fish. Fishing was the basis of the Rock's economy. No one settled on that island for the balmy climate. After the mid-50s, factory fishing came into use. For this, the ships would use huge nets weighed down with steel plates, chains and rollers, which they would haul across the ocean floor. Not only would those massive nets capture whole schools of fish, they would also scour the sea floor of all living things, of the crustaceans, corals and sea grass. The fish were then processed aboard the factory ship and packed in deep freezers. The take of fish increased till it reached 800,000 tons in 1968. This take included all the fish in the sea: the haddock, the hake, the flat fish, the long fish, the short fish – the lot.[3]

By the 1970s, scientists and environmentalists were warning of sustainability issues and the potential for ecosystem collapse if the fishery was not curtailed. In 1976, Canada extended its national waters to 200 nautical miles from the shore and banned all foreign fleets from fishing within those waters. With that, the annual catch declined to 139,000 tons.

Still, the Canadian catch alone increased again to 250,000 tons and, despite all the warnings, the government did nothing. "It's the economy you know. The economy and jobs must take precedence." How many times do we hear that cry from governments all over the world that are destroying their, or someone else's, environment?[4]

In 1992, the fishery collapsed. There were no more fish to fish. 40,000 people lost their jobs. The economy of Newfoundland went into a tailspin and now the men of Newfoundland are working on their province's, and Alberta's, oil patches. This is causing another looming catastrophe. Not that we can blame them because that's what Canada's economy is set up to do.

One might be forgiven for assuming that the governments of fishing nations all over the world would take note of what happened on the Grand Banks. Once again, it seems not. Over-exploitation continues all over the world, and as fish stocks deplete in one area, the fleets move to the final few areas of ocean that do have a few fish remaining. The basic trouble is that human populations keep increasing at such an incredible rate, and those mouths just must be fed.

Tuna are warm-blooded fish that can travel at 90 miles per hour when in a hurry.

There are eight species of true tuna. One, the Atlantic Bluefin Tuna *(Thunnus thynnus)*, has two distinct populations; those born in the Gulf of Mexico being the Western Tuna, while the Eastern Tuna breed in the Mediterranean. They are considered the prime sport fish with healthy adults weighing 1,500 lbs (684 kg). Since the introduction of longline fishing in the 1960s, the Gulf of Mexico fish have been brought to 1.5 per cent to 3 per cent of the earlier numbers. The Mediterranean Tuna is also greatly reduced to some 20 per cent of those before 1960. At the present rate of catch, the numbers, within a few years of 2012, will be down to 5 or 6 per cent of the earlier numbers. The fishery is supposed to be overseen by ICCAT (the International Commission for the Conservation of Atlantic Tunas), which has jurisdiction over marlin, swordfish and others as well as tuna.[5]

Not content with nearly extirpating all the large adult fish, the US National Marine Fisheries Service (NMFS) encouraged the fishing fleets to trawl through the nursery areas to catch the juveniles for cat food. The Western North Atlantic Tuna are as good as all gone; though, with protection, the remaining large adults could possibly breed sufficiently to bring the species back. The fish take twelve years to reach maturity at an average weight of a little above 600 lbs. The Eastern, or Mediterranean, fish mature at ages 4 to 5 years and at weights of 85 to 135 lbs. Those figures make clear the necessity to protect the young for many years to allow them time to mature, to mate and to spawn. Without fresh spawn, young juveniles can't hatch, and without juveniles, there will be no new generations of fish to grow and mature.

Both types of fish could be saved. Not so the Southern Bluefin Tuna. Those fish used to breed off the north east coast of Brazil but the Japanese longliners and the American purse-seiners went to work in that part of the South Atlantic. None of those fish have been seen for forty years. They are assumed extinct.[6]

Tuna are fished in nearly every ocean, with the Pacific having the most abundant numbers. By the mid 1960s, the annual world catch had reached 1,000,000 tons. By 2000, the catch had risen to 4,000,000 tons. The Japanese love the tuna for sushi, so much so that they will pay enormous prices for the fish. In 2011 a tuna weighing 754 lbs sold in Tokyo's Tsukiji fish market for 32,490,000 yen or US$350,000. In 2006, the Australian government alleged that the Japanese fleet often took between double and three times their quota of 6,000 tons. That would be worth some US$3 billion to the industry. Again, money and greed override all other considerations.

With all this uncontrolled fishing going on, it is hardly surprising that many tuna species, including the Eastern Atlantic Bluefin Tuna, are now in mortal danger.

One way to find tuna used to be by locating pods of dolphin, with which the tuna associate for protection from sharks. The fishing method then used killed many dolphins, so a new technique for finding them has now been developed. This entails using a FAD or Fish Aggregation Device. Apparently, a FAD is a group of tethered buoys that for various reasons attract more than 300 species of fish and other sea animals. The trouble is that these devices now cause the incidental catching of turtles, rays, small whales and, again, dolphins. Another tuna device, which was first used in Australia, and is now being tried in other areas including the Med, are large net corrals to which whole schools of netted immature fish are taken and kept for fattening up. They are fed such fish as anchovies and mackerel. The trouble is it takes 25 lbs of those fish for a tuna to put on one lb. Of course these small 'foundation' fish are now also in trouble.

A few other interesting facts about the Mediterranean fishery include the following:

- Every Mediterranean nation fishes for tuna.
- The International Convention for the Conservation of Atlantic Tuna (ICCAT) always sets higher quotas than the scientists advise.
- In 2010 the total allowable catch quota for the Mediterranean Tuna was 13,500 tons. The different fishing nations reported a total catch below that number, yet the international trade in the fish that year was for 35,000 tons, which is three times the catch reported.
- The fishermen regularly catch 4 times the allowed quota.
- The longline fishing technique, on average, catches one ton of sharks for every tuna caught.
- Few fishermen make money.
- The European fishery is supported by 2 billion Euros in subsidies, which includes money for new boats, which is another attempt to keep the economy going.[7]

I am just speaking here of two species of fish but the horror stories continue for nearly every species of edible fish and in nearly every area of sea water on our lovely, but very wet planet. The places where the fish like to gather, for instance where two currents rich in sustenance meet, are the very places that the fishing fleets gather in their most predatory denseness.

Apparently, when flying at night over the South China Sea, one is likely to believe one is still flying over a city, such a density of lights are there below. However, it is not a concrete city; it is, instead, an aquatic one. It is the Chinese fishing fleet. China has a total of 300,000 fishing boats and eight million fishermen. The distant water fleet alone has 2,000 vessels that range the oceans searching for fish. In 2005 the wild fish catch was 17,000,000 tons. The nearest competitor was the US at 4,900,000 tons. The South China Sea is now heavily depleted, and I wonder just how long the earth can sustain such reckless overfishing. China's aquaculture production – fish farms and the like - totals 60 per cent of the world's output. China is into fish in a big way.[8]

Some fish types are known as keystone species. They are the small silvery fish that travel in huge numbers. On the TV shows, they are shown to swim close-packed, presumably on the assumption that there is safety in numbers, and in the hope the other guy will get eaten. As a mass, they dart about with incredible rapidity and split-second timing. A school of a hundred thousand fish can appear to be one organism, a silver bubble darting through the ocean.

The Pacific Herring *(Clupea pallasii)* are small silver fish that are found from Japan, up through the Bering Sea, past Alaska and BC and along the West Coast of North America as far south as California. A typical adult is about 13 inches (33 cm) long although some can be half as long again. When spawning, the female fish can lay 20,000 eggs, which would mean enormous numbers of adults if all eggs survived to maturity. However, few do survive, and, in reality, the replacement rate is thought to be just 2 adults resulting from each spawning female. I find this hard to believe, as the fish, being so heavily predated, would not survive long at such a low replacement rate. There must have been millions of tons of those fish once as the catches by the British Columbia fleet were in the region of 200,000 tons a year in the early 1960s. Those numbers soon declined toward collapse till the fishery was closed in 1967. By 1974, the spawning biomass had climbed back from about 7,000 tons in 1965 to close to 80,000 tons in 1974. In 1972, the Department of Fisheries opened the herring roe fishery, which averages 35,000 tons per year. The Pacific herring again collapsed in 1993. Since 1983, the Canadian Department of Fisheries and Oceans (DFO), has tried to keep the permitted fish catch to only 20 per cent of the estimated spawning biomass. In December 2011, the DFO opened the Pacific herring to a 6,000 ton-a-year winter food and bait fishery, which is small compared to previous years, and indicates the reduced number of fish in the wild.

I have read of herring described as a cornerstone species, a keystone species and as a foundation species. Whatever they are, they seem to be important. So when we fish them from the sea what do all the other predators down in the deep ocean do for food when the herring are no more? Research coordinated by Caroline Fox of the University of Victoria suggests that herring account for 62 per cent of the diet of Chinook Salmon, 58 per cent of Coho Salmon, 71 per cent of Lingcod and 32 per cent of Harbour Seals. Caroline Fox's report also states that the great mass of eggs deposited by spawning herring, "often attract tremendous numbers of predators and scavengers. . . In some areas millions of marine birds, hundreds of sea lions, seals and dozens of humpback and grey whales actively forage for several weeks." So the eggs are important to more than just the survival of the herring themselves. The eggs are an important part of the sustenance of a great many other species up the food chain. The name "cornerstone" or "keystone" seems to suggest that, just as the keystone in a building supports the integrity of the whole building, a keystone species supports the complete ecological system of which it is just a small part.

Herring roe sells for up to $150 per kilo in Japan and in 1993 BC fishermen sold $180 millions worth. The roe fishery then employed up to six thousand people for the five months till the beginning of July.[9]

European immigrants have been fishing for Pacific herring in British Columbia since 1877. In that 135 years, the government departments responsible for fisheries have had plenty of time to research the fishery, draw conclusions, make recommendations, make mistakes and come up with new conclusions and recommendations. We can hope that the fishery is regulated as well as frail humans can. These fish are in the waters of Japan, Russia, Canada and the USA. However, what of the fish in the waters of countries with no fisheries officials, and with neither research nor guidelines? And what happens in countries where the controls are based on corruption and payoffs? We will never know as, I assume, no records are ever kept.

The East Coast herring are in an even worse state. The Atlantic Herring *(Clupea harengus)* frequent both sides of the Atlantic, and used to school in 40-mile-long pods along their range from Northern Labrador to North Carolina. Like their Pacific cousins they are migratory fish in that they travel from their winter range to the spring coastal spawning grounds and then on to the summer feeding grounds. At the feeding grounds, they play the role of the herbivores on dry land. They feed on zooplankton, vegetable matter and such microorganisms as fish eggs. They are called 'forage' species, as it is they, the prey fish, who convert base foods to protein. They, in turn, are predated by the larger fish: by tuna, cod, bass, seabirds and marine mammals. As with the other cornerstone species such as sardines and capelin, the 21st century stocks are a small fraction of historic levels.

The American fishing fleet uses huge cone-shaped nets to capture complete schools of fish. The nets also fill with such bycatch species as bass and haddock, dolphins and turtles, and even whales. They also catch another type of herring known as river herring. These unintended fish are thrown back into the sea, usually dead.[10][11]

If these cycles of overexploitation - collapse and, if luck holds, eventual recovery - are taking place now in coastal North America, we can be sure they have been happening around the European shores for far longer. The population collapses of the Icelandic summer-spawning herring, the Norwegian spring-spawning, the Georges Bank and North Sea herring all happened very quickly. However, the recoveries all took over a decade.

Herring are harvested for farm feed, Omega 3 fatty acid pills, bait and sushi. Overall, the numbers have been reduced by 85 per cent in the past 25 years, which is putting the whole ecosystem in jeopardy.

Government catch targets have been exceeded every year since 1960 with no penalties. One problem with managing any fisheries and making accurate assumptions regarding the actual abundance of fish spawning on any particular coast in any specific year, is the unexpected changes in fish numbers that can't be accounted for. According to Fisheries Resource Conservation Council in August 2009, one example of successful projections is that of the Norwegians in the latter part of the first decade of 2000. The Norwegians were able to safely harvest one million tons of fish from an estimated biomass of ten million tons. Had there been a surprise return of fewer than two million tons, for example, that million-ton harvest would have seriously jeopardized the stocks.

The river herring mentioned earlier as a bycatch of the Atlantic Herring fishery are, like salmon, seagoing fish that return to their home river to mate and spawn. In historic times these runs of fish were huge, giving the rivers the appearance of being totally full of fish, and they were important food sources for the Native Americans and early settlers alike. The numbers are now about 98 per cent reduced from the numbers in the 1960s. A small matter perhaps but indicative of how broad the sweep of this seaborne scythe has been over the century.

In the many coves, small harbours and marinas on the coastal areas of British Columbia, a visitor will notice some of the thousand upon thousand white fiberglass pleasure boats that so many people on the West Coast delight in owning. Among them, one will usually see a few fishing boats. They are easy to pick out, being scruffier, much more heavily built and usually stacked high with rods and fishing gear. I think of them as being the progeny of the old style traditional fishing boat. By that I mean a boat that a couple of hardy folk could handle and which took from the sea sustainable numbers of fish.

I would like to think of the local boats as cottage fishing boats that use nets to catch and haul aboard a couple of hundred fish at a time. Or that use rods to entice fish a few at a time. I choose to think of them not as boats that destroy the ocean, but as boats that take a little of the rich bounty and leave lots for spawning and repopulating. I know I am being naïve and possibly wrong but I'm not too keen to know just how wrong. At least, I assume they are not the ugly factory ships or destroyer trawlers that gouge and scrape everything out of the sea that they can get near to. I suppose my thoughts regarding fishing run parallel to my views on farming. I can think of few occupations better than organically growing and harvesting crops on a small farm in the countryside, or of sailing out to sea and bringing ashore a few dozen fish with which to feed one's village neighbours. Of course those small population days are long gone, and such activities will never feed the current seven billion people who need feeding.

Husbanding the land as a large-scale farming businessman becomes rather an ugly occupation when it involves saturating thousands of acres of natural land with tons of pesticides, insecticides and herbicides. So it is with the commercial factory fleet vessels that haul tons of fish and unwanted birds and animals aboard. They diminish the standing of the fishermen and remake their chosen careers into something destructive and wholly undesirable.

I remember something unforgettable that I saw from the troopship heading to Malaya in 1957. One day I saw a small native sailing craft with one man aboard sailing alone in the vast tropical sea. I think we were midway between Mauritius and Ceylon (Sri Lanka), and I could not understand what that vulnerable little man in that little open boat was doing so far from land on that huge sea. I don't remember how long it took us port to port, but we were probably two or three days out of Mauritius with a similar number of days to go before we docked in Colombo. I now realize he was probably from the Chagos Archipelego which may have been just out of sight somewhere over the horizon.

Nevertheless, I assume he was fishing and not lost, as he seemed to show no interest in our great ship sailing by. I have occasionally thought of him since. Alone and brown and unbelievably courageous under that hot sun, he surely had some way of knowing where he was and which way to go to reach home. He was a link in that chain of fisher-folk going back to the time when humans first launched themselves onto the sea many thousands of years ago. They were a part of the natural world, and the fishing they did never had any chance of affecting the fish numbers and the natural order of things.

We have progressed a long way since that lone fisherman was overtaken by our troopship. We now have factory ships with attendant fleets of fishing boats taking from the sea everything that swims below the surface and killing much that flies above it as well. Is this progress? The factory ship owners would unequivocally say, 'Yes! We are feeding the billions though we profit too.' However, I know that lone fisherman and the thousands like him must be totally appalled. There would have to be many hundreds of thousands like him to bring home a catch equal to the one the factory ships can bring ashore. The unemployment problems of many coastal states would be solved if groups of cottage fishers did the work of the factory ships. But, how fresh would the fish be by the time they reached the consumer? Not very, unfortunately,

Most of the fish caught by the modern fleets are captured in a few types of nets. There are many other forms employed by individuals or small groups who cast from the shore or fish the local rivers and open seas from small boats. Over time, such individuals have little effect on the local numbers of fish. The nets that really do the damage and impinge on the numbers and survival prospects of marine creatures are those used by the commercial fishermen. Following years of using biodegradable hemp fibers for the netting, manufacturers began, in the 1950s, to produce nets of such synthetic materials as nylon. Not only are these materials transparent and almost invisible to the sea creatures, but also they only biodegrade over very long periods if at all, so it is important that the nets don't become lost at sea.

Trawl Nets

The most basic net is the trawl net. These nets are dragged behind the fishing boat or trawler and are typically conical in shape with a large mouth at the forward end. Floats on the top edge, weights on the lower edge and doors on the vertical sides keep the mouth open. The doors are designed to hydroplane through the water in the required outward direction.

A mid-water trawl net does little damage to the marine environment other than its lack of selectivity. It is usually used to catch pelagic fish, and the net can be very large, especially when towed by two really powerful trawlers. In any one pass, it may catch as many undesirable fish, or protected fish, as the intended species. When fishermen head out to sea with a license to catch only one or two species of fish and they use a huge net to do so, they have no way of being selective. The net may also capture dolphin, sharks, sea turtles and who knows what else. Most of this bycatch dies in the crush as it is hauled aboard and so is usually thrown back to the sea dead. A friend of mine, while boating in the islands north of Vancouver, came across an ejected load of by-catch. Washed against one side of an island were dead fish in a dense mass a hundred yards across, just floating quietly as the tide rose and fell. They constituted tons and tons of dead fish that the fishermen didn't want, or weren't allowed to sell onshore. When fishermen catch protected or out-of-season fish, they don't report the fact. They just throw them back and carry on. Huge quantities of fish are killed and wasted this way.

Probably the most destructive of all nets are the bottom-trawl nets, or dredgers. These are heavily weighted on the bottom edge and are intended for catching such bottom fish as plaice, sole, and shrimp as well as such semi-pelagic species as cod, halibut and squid. These monsters scour the seabed. Since the fishing is done hundreds of feet below the surface, the fishermen have no idea what the sea floor is like as they pass over it. The nets may be scraping up sand, or corals, or rocks, or seaweed and grasses, or who knows what. They certainly disturb the mud and sand causing it to intermix with the water. The nets then create the potential for those sediment particles to settle on living corals and such sessile animals as oysters and barnacles. The doors themselves, which weigh many tons, scour deep into the sediment and lift settled pollutants and undesirable particulates back into the water and food chain. It is rather like running earth-moving bulldozers through woodland, parkland, shrubbery and beds of flowers, a very efficient way of destroying absolutely everything. The turbidity produced in other than the deepest waters by this destruction of the ocean floor can be seen on satellite imagery. The damage to the seabed and the life on it can be terrible, though the passing fishermen never know.[12]

Bottom trawling is known to be incredibly injurious wherever it is used, and a few countries have brought in legislation to protect parts of their national waters. Only the tiny nation of Palau has banned all bottom trawling in its national waters. The president of Palau, Tommy Remengesau, tried to have legislation passed at the United Nations that would have banned unregulated bottom trawling in international waters, but by 2012 had still been unsuccessful. Since then Tuvalu, the Marshall Islands and the Federated States of Micronesia joined Palau in seeking a ban at the United Nations but, of course, more powerful nations blocked such legislation. This inability to stop or control a harvesting system that everyone knows is destructive in the extreme, says a great deal about the future prospects for the Earth and her ecosystems. It is clearly wrong. It is clearly destructive and threatens the long-term viability of the oceans. But it is profitable so the industry carries on regardless.[13][14]

It is interesting that the problems with this destructive form of fishing were recognized in Britain in the 14th century when Edward III was on the throne. In those days, the bottom trawl was named a 'wondyrchoum.' It had an 18-foot long wooden beam and 10 foot wide net. It took so many fish that a petition was sent to Parliament in 1376 asking for its prohibition. In part, the petition read, "The fishermen aforesaid take so great abundance of small fish . . . that they know not what to do with them, but feed and fatten the pigs with them, to the great damage of the whole commons of the kingdom, and the destruction of the fisheries."[15] So six hundred years ago, wise heads recognized the ill-advised nature of bottom trawling. Yet now, all these centuries later, not only do we continue with the practice but have taken advantage of the time to develop it to be even more destructive.

Seine Fishing

Probably the second most basic net type is the seine net. It is a long rectangle of netting with buoys on one of the long sides and weights on the other. With the buoys and the weights, the net hangs like a very long shroud in the water. Two men in a shallow bay might hold a small seine net. One would take up a position while the other walks away from him letting out the net till it is fully extended. Both men would then walk through the water dragging the net and moving toward each other till they meet and the buoys form a circle behind them. They then pull the net in till all the trapped fish are gathered in the small encircling space. The same basic principle applies with fishing boats except that one common practice would involve a large buoy supporting one end, while the other is dragged in a large circle by the fishing boat. This system is usually used to harvest such pelagic schooling fish as herring, mackerel, sardines and anchovies. It also works against salmon when they gather in huge quantities in river mouths to begin the journey to the inland spawning grounds.

There are two main types of seine net. The purse seiner has a rope threaded through rings along the bottom edge of the net which, when pulled, gathers in the bottom of the net to prevent the fish from escaping. With Danish seiners the net is shaped to include a bag section near the centre where the captured fish gather.[16]

Gill nets

A third type of net is the gill net. These nets are a type of seiner. They allow the fish to penetrate part way into the mesh and then be held either by the gills or by other protuberances from the body. This seems to be an ancient technique and is perhaps the least controversial net, being the easiest to design for catching specific species of a certain size. This method is the easiest to limit the bycatch numbers. The nets form panels that are hung in the water either as a wall or in a circle surrounding the fish. These encircling nets can be used by large ships, or by groups of local fishermen in open boats. In the case of fishermen, once the nets are set they typically paddle, or row, to the centre where they splash and disturb the water thus panicking the fish out toward the net. When the fishermen pull up the nets, they are able to release any unwanted bycatch alive back into the sea. The nets have floats along the top line and weights on the lower edge that can be increased to lower the level at which the net hangs. When touching the sea bottom, the netting along the lower section is usually a mesh designed to catch bottom-feeding fish.[17]

Drift nets

In 1992, the United Nations General Assembly banned the practice of drift net fishing, which had been ongoing for a great many years. These enlarged gill nets again have floats along the top edge and weights along the bottom, but while gill nets are actively handled by the fishermen, the drift nets are released into the sea and left to drift. They can be 30 miles (50 km) long and over 100-feet (30 meters) deep. Imagine a wall that size floating in the oceans entangling nearly any wild fish, mammal or bird that comes into contact with it, and then imagine thousands of these things deployed at any one time and we arrive at a possible one hundred thousand mile barrier to ocean-crossing fish migration.

Naturally our old friends the sea birds, turtles, dolphins, whales, sword fish and sharks were dying by the millions and the accidental bycatch - that which was discarded - was estimated at 27 million tons a year. This estimation was not made by some loathsome environmental NGO intent upon putting the poor, misunderstood and quite innocent, fishing industry out of business. The United Nations Food and Agricultural Organization made the estimate in 1994. It was estimated that 30,000 tons of sharks and skate were taken as bycatch. Many nets were lost and never retrieved meaning they float for close to an eternity killing most animals that come into contact with them.[18]

Drift-net fishing has been banned since 1992, but with the diminishing fish stocks more and more people are now fishing illegally. And since the fishing is illegal anyway, why not use the easiest method out there? So drift nets continue to be deployed and, because enforcement is so difficult and expensive, few fishermen are ever caught, or charged, or convicted and punished. The mass slaughter continues uncontrolled and largely unreported.

Long-lines

Not all fishers use nets. Another equally irresponsible method of fishing is by long-line. These lines can be 60 miles (100km) long with baited hooks attached at intervals by side lines. They are dragged behind the fishing vessel. It is estimated that something in the region of 2 billion hooks are used each year. They can be used at various depths of down to 1,800 fathoms (3,300 m). The lines near the surface are the ones that attract the sea birds of course. A great many other sea creatures are also killed by these lines, including: sea turtles, dolphins, porpoise, sharks and many species on the verge of extinction. The estimated annual unintended kill includes 40,000 turtles, 300,000 sea birds, untold thousands of such sea mammals as whales, dolphins and porpoises, and millions of sharks.[19] The sharks are hauled aboard, their fins are sliced off and then the still-living creatures are dumped overboard to sink and die in the ocean's depths. Shark bycatch is likely with almost any of the fishing methods. The estimate, is 38 million sharks killed for their fins each year between 1996 and 2000. That has increased to one hundred million killed each year. Yes! The oceans really are vast when we can take 100,000,000 sharks a year.[20] For how long can the numbers of the ocean's top predator last with such a horrendous death toll?

When a species is critically endangered, and therefore not to be fished, what happens when they are caught? Well they become bycatch and are dumped back in the sea. Untold numbers of bycatch fish are returned to the sea - usually dead. No reports are made and no questions are asked.

There are 70 Hawaii-based long-line vessels that mostly fish for swordfish. This fishery was closed in the year 2000, then reopened in 2004, then closed again in 2006, then reopened in 2010 only to be closed again. The reasons for these closures were the great numbers of loggerhead and leatherback turtles being taken and the failures of the remedial fishing methods put into place. So the American fishing industry, with lots of promptings from environmental foundations, do have ways of controlling the fishing activities of the commercial boats registered in that country. That can't be said for many other fishing nations. Hawaii's 70 long-line boats are overseen, but what of the 1,500–1,700 Asian commercial long-line fishing vessels? Those vessels work under little jurisdiction, few controls and even fewer requirements for reporting. We will never know the turtle, bird, and sea mammal losses caused by their fishing practices.[21]

Long-line fishing is considered the single greatest threat to seabirds across our earth's oceans. The very way of life of most seabirds is to glide over the oceans searching for fish or other food near the surface. With 2 billion hooks baited with the likes of herring running along the ocean's surface to tempt them, one can imagine how many birds take the bait and subsequently drown. Albatrosses, and many other species of seabirds, are considered extinction-bound unless long-line fishing is discontinued.

However, not only birds suffer. When Portuguese long-line fishermen go after swordfish, they catch 3 tons of sharks for every ton of swordfish.

In June 1999, the United Nations Food and Agricultural Organization (FAO) Council endorsed three plans that had been first adopted by the FAO Committee on Fisheries in February 1999. These plans were the "International Plan of Action for Reducing Incidental Catch of Seabirds in Long-line Fisheries," the "International Plan of Action for the Conservation and Management of Sharks," and the "International Plan of Action for the Management of Fishing Capacity." All three agreements are entirely voluntary. Only 17 countries have signed up to honour the agreement.

Whatever international agreements are eventually agreed upon and signed there will always be the pirate fishing boats continuing the slaughter of birds, turtles and mammals.

The oceans and the fleets

The above methods of fishing sound very bad to anyone more interested in the health of the oceans than in the abundance of his fish dinners. They become even worse though, when we consider the numbers of fishermen on the oceans, inlets, straits, gulfs, lagoons, points, harbours and any other stretch of water in which fish survive. As already noted, China has 300,000 fishing boats and 8 million fishermen - a very great many. But then consider how many more there must be on the coasts of Bangladesh, Myanmar, Thailand, Malaysia, Indonesia, the Philippines, Cambodia, Vietnam, Korea and Japan. And that is only looking at one little corner of our earth from the Bay of Bengal to the Sea of Japan. Every continent except Antarctica fishes and considers fish an important part of the economies and diets of the people.

Meanwhile in the Eastern Pacific off the coast of South America over-fishing continues apace. A 2012 report by ICIJ (International Consortium of Investigative Journalists) says that fishing fleets from much of the world convene on that coast "to decimate fish stocks across the Southern Pacific." The home governments of these fleets continue to subsidize their fishing industries while ignoring threats of over-fishing. One cornerstone species, the Jack Mackerel, has been reduced by over 90 per cent in just the past 20 years. It has gone from "an estimated 30 million metric tons to less than 3 million metric tons." The oceanographer Jack Pauly from the University of British Columbia believes that such a decline of Jack Mackerel could signal a general worldwide fisheries collapse. "When they are gone everything will be gone," he said.[22]

The Humboldt Current off the coasts of Chile and Peru is known as one of the world's most productive fishing areas. It is a northward-flowing current that develops from the eastward movement of water around Antarctica. When that broad mass of cold water runs into the Chilean coast, the greatest mass is forced north while a smaller portion is squeezed south of Cape Horn. The northbound water is compressed along the coast near the border with Chile and Peru, but it then spreads out as it passes Peru and turns west to flow south of the Equator. The Humboldt Current supports the world's largest fisheries, is considered the world's most productive fishery, and produces about 18-20 per cent of the world's caught fish. All along the coasts of those two countries, thousands upon thousands of local cottage, or small family fishermen, keep their boats and provide for their families from the sea's bounty.

The current is forced west when it meets the southwest bound El Niño Current bringing warm water down from Mexico, Central America and Colombia. This warm water intermixing with the nutrient and krill-rich cold water attracts huge numbers of small keystone fish. These great schools of fish naturally attract larger pelagic fish. How fish from thousands of miles away know where to go to get a good meal is beyond me, but gather there they do. The softly rounded coastal protuberance of northern Peru and Ecuador is the richest place in the world to find fish of all sorts. Every species, from shrimp to anchovies, through herring and mackerel to tuna, swordfish, sailfish and marlin, all gather in those waters to feed and be fed upon. The area is a sport-fishing Mecca where fishermen from around the world gather to enter contests for marlin and sailfish. It is also where factory fishing vessels gather to scoop up as much of everything as they can possibly get away with.[23][24]

This gathering place is a large fish's sublime fish restaurant. It collects fish and nutrients from all around the Pacific, and, attracting huge numbers of fishing vessels, has now become the ultimate execution site for the creatures of the sea. How long the area will remain productive is hard to know. That the Pacific will in time become nearly bereft of fish seems inevitable. The wails of complaint and regret that will be ascending from the sport and industrial-fishing communities can surely be predicted.

The only way to save the fish in these waters off South America's west coast is for all nations to decide on, and abide by, a strictly-adhered-to conservation plan. Otherwise, we can be sure it will soon go the way of the other wondrously rich fishing grounds that are now depleted and almost void.

One can't help but wonder what is going on down there in those huge, deep oceans. When the top predator sharks are being finned and killed at an estimated one hundred million a year, the cornerstone species very near the bottom of the food chain are being reduced to less than 10 per cent of recent numbers and many tuna species to 5 per cent or less, what kind of balance is remaining down there? Is the web of sea life collapsing? Or are we taking so many herring, haddock, bass, tuna, marline, swordfish, sharks, and just about every other species of marine creature that some kind of balance remains, albeit a balance that is 10 per cent, 5 per cent or 2 per cent of the mass that it was when I was born?

In January 2012, a Maui's Dolphin (*Cephalorhynchus hectori maui*) was killed in a net off the coast of New Zealand. Not very noteworthy news really as it was just another of the thousands of dolphin killed as bycatch. However, this was a subspecies of dolphin with only twenty-five females, of 100 individuals known living in the world. This is not very important in the wider scheme of things, but it seems very possible that a great many other species of sea creatures are also suffering similar diminishments to their numbers. These are reductions that are tipping them over the edge to extinction.[25]

The fishing industry seems to be one industry that is very difficult to control or to monitor. Once a fishery is established, governments seem powerless to restrict its activities. Nations can put in protections in their own waters, but if more powerful nations don't like them, the protectors may be out of luck. In 1958, Iceland, out of concern for their diminishing fish stocks, extended its national waters from 4 to 12 miles. Then again in 1972, Iceland extended the limits to 50 miles from shore. On both occasions, other fishing nations responded with great hostility. The most hostile was Britain. Her fishing fleet had been fishing for Icelandic cod for hundreds of years, and, since she had depleted her own fish stocks, she had no intention of losing the Icelandic fish. The result of Iceland's attempts to protect her fish, was that the UK sent in the Royal Navy to keep the waters open for Britain's fishing fleets.

Then in 1974, following the United Nation's support on the question of 200 mile national coastal zones, Iceland declared a 200 mile economic zone. They needed to protect their own fish as that was one of the few economies that small country had. Britain once again sent in the navy. In this cod war, each time the fishing fleet approached Iceland's waters it was accompanied by nine frigates of the Royal Navy. These were there to protect the trawlers against Iceland's four Coast Guard patrol vessels. Again, a compromise was reached in June 1976 when it was agreed that four conservation areas would be closed to fishing and that Britain's fleet within the 200 mile zone would be limited to 24 vessels.[26][27]

A similar situation arose in the early 1990s, when Canada's navy had to try to keep the Spanish fishing fleet off Newfoundland's fishing banks. This was shortly before a fishing moratorium was imposed in 1994, which followed the total cod fishery collapse.

Over-fishing and fish stock reductions had been noted well before the 20th century. In the late 1800s, Denmark had tried to limit Britain's right to over-fish the Icelandic waters. So the 1970's concerns were not new, and neither are the present concerns. We have been warned for long enough that restraint and wise quotas must be set in place - and abided by.

It seems to be up to each country to try to protect its own fishery; however, when one jurisdiction puts a stop to the fishing of an endangered fish species in national waters, the fleet of some other nation – nowadays often from East Asia – simply moves in and grabs as much as it can. Maritime nations' navies then find themselves spending most of their time chasing high-powered foreign fishing vessels that not only have good speed but also modern radar capable of identifying approaching naval ships from many miles distant.

On January 25, 2012 in Manila, Philippines the United Nations released a report on the worldwide fishing industry. The report stated, "The potential economic gain from reducing fishing capacity to an optimal level and restoring fishing stocks is in the order of US$50 billion per annum." In other words, if we would lay off for a while and give the fish a chance to mature, breed and multiply, we could have a healthier marine ecosystem and make more money too. Amina Mohammed, the deputy executive director of the UN Environmental Program, went on to note that, "Many ocean industries and businesses stand to benefit directly from cleaner, more ecologically robust marine ecosystems."[28]

The report noted the usual problems and culprits that we have known for so long yet seem unable to do anything about. These include: overfishing; mangrove, coral reef and fish nursery destruction; pollution and excess fertilizer run-off into the sea. The algae blooms that occur in the dead areas created by this agricultural run-off absorb the oxygen from the water effectively drowning the fish.

Personally, I don't believe any major fishing country will commit to reducing their take by any meaningful amount. Things have to be far worse than they are now before the major fishing countries will agree. What I see happening, will be large fishing concerns suggesting that the small individual peasant fishermen should be discouraged from fishing. After all, those darned little peasant fishermen take some of the fish that the factory fleets need to fill their quotas. And who is paying the business taxes and therefore deserve government protection? The factory fleets of course.

A New Economics Foundation report published on 10 February 2012 stated that if fish stocks were given the chance to recover, the European fishing fleets would enjoy future catches of 3.5 million tons more than at the time of the report. The short-term fishing policies of the fishing nations keep the fish numbers, the industry and the fish economy in crisis. The report gave the economic benefit of restoring fish stocks at £2.7 billion a year, and the employment opportunities within the European fishing industry at 100,000 new jobs. More than three-quarters of Europe's fish stocks are considered to be over-fished.

Co-author of the report, Robert Crilly, believes that "Restoring fish stocks is within politicians' power," however, the fishing industry seems hell-bent on continuing its unsustainable practices. No one wants to fish within quotas or allow nursery areas to be established where no fishing can take place. The fishermen want to continue hauling aboard huge quantities of edible fish. They then don't mind discarding half of them back into the sea as dead bycatch. This incredibly wasteful practice is carried out only in order to bring the most valuable and expensive fish back to port and the market. It seems amazing that while such practices continue, the European fishing industry receives subsidies of 2 billion Euros a year.

Trash in the oceans

Albatross are birds with very long and very slender wings that they use for gliding over vast distances and long months at a time. There are 21 species with 4 genera. The species with the greatest wingspan is the Wandering Albatross *(Diomedea Exulans)*. Typically, the wingspan of this bird is about 10 ft, though the largest recorded had a span of 12 ft (3.66m). That is a very large wingspan indeed. The known oldest bird was still alive in 2013 at the age of 62. She was 'Wisdom" who was first banded 54 years earlier in 1956. Albatross mate for life, and the only time they land is to lay eggs and feed the one chick. On the 3rd February 1913 Wisdom successfully hatched another chick, which was possibly her thirty-fifth. It is believed her mate was her third.[29]

For the most part, albatross glide over the southern oceans close to Antarctica and over the North Pacific. Nineteen of the species are threatened with extinction. Two of the biggest threats are pretty obvious. The first is our old enemy the introduced rat along with other introduced species that destroy the eggs or young on the nesting beaches. The second is human overfishing, which greatly reduces the fish that make up a good part of the birds' diet. The third threat we know about is accidental bycatch. The estimate is that up to 100,000 albatross are drowned each year when they go for the bait attached to long-line fishing gear. One hundred thousand albatross killed in this way are far more than the numbers of chicks the birds are capable of rearing each year.[30]

The fourth of the current threats to albatross is the great amount of plastic waste now floating on the surface of all the oceans. One might assume that albatross are relatively safe from pollution, but not so. People are discovering a large number of dead chicks on the nesting beaches used by the birds. What kills them? Well, as their bodies rot away, the stomachs of the birds reveal piles of plastic bottle caps, cigarette lighters and other plastic waste. When I say, 'piles' I mean big piles. Enough to quarter-fill a football. It seems that as the adult birds glide over the surface they are attracted to pieces of plastic that they assume to be food. These they feed to the young who in turn die of hunger – while possibly feeling quite full. Plastic is also proving deadly to other sea creatures. Sea turtles have been known to consume plastic bags, which they mistake for jellyfish. The dead young albatross are the victims we know of. They have not flown yet. They hatch on the beach. They live on the beach, they die on the beach, and they rot on the beach for all to see. But what of the millions of other creatures, the turtles, the mammals and the fish that ingest the plastic, die and drop out of sight? We have no record of them, so they create no statistics to cause us concern.

It is quite amazing to me that albatross can spend a year gliding over the southern oceans and then arrive at some obscure nesting island within a few days of the mate's arrival. How do they find the island? There are no landmarks, just endless expanses of water. How does an albatross decide that it is time to head back along the three thousand mile trip to the nesting island in order to meet his mate there, a mate who may at that time be 6,000 miles away? And then, miracle of miracles, they both arrive at the nesting site within a day or two of each other. It is just another of Mother Nature's miracles.

Seventy years ago when humans sailed the Seven Seas, they crossed huge expanses of ocean that were as pure as they had been for thousands of years. Anything that was not wildlife or was out of the ordinary was referred to as 'flotsam and jetsam'. The first would have floated off a sinking boat or out to sea down a river, and the second would have been thrown overboard. Either way, there would have been precious little of it, and what there was, was natural materials. Sailors in the 1970s began to notice quite large amounts of trash floating on the sea far from land. Now the oceans are home to huge amounts of mostly plastic waste, gathered into trash dumps far larger than the British Isles. According to Professor Iain Stewart we unload 26 million tons of plastic into the oceans each year.[31]

Actually, I tell a lie. The Atlantic wasn't quite as pure 70 years ago as I make out. The Second World War had seen the sinking of thousands of ships, many of which were oil tankers, but all of which carried engine oil of one sort or another. Those sunken ships discharged a considerable amount of oil into the water. Some of that oil appeared on England's west coast beaches as pellets of black tar that we often stepped on during our late 1940s summer holidays. Still compared with the state of the oceans now, it was then very pure indeed. Also those oil tankers so explosively sunk in the early forties were cockleshells beside the huge tankers that now ply the Seven Seas.

The recent concentrations of trash are the result of ocean vortices or 'gyres' and consist of the plastic conveniences that a good part of 7 billion people throw away every day. It is the stuff that is dropped onto the footpath or roadway, is carried by the wind, the rain, or the garbage collectors to the rivers and from the river is handed on to the sea. Little of it sinks, and it stays afloat for years. Some does get ground down through wave and sand action which is why when you take the sand from many beaches and look at it under a magnifying glass you will find it interspersed with brightly coloured grains of plastic. Beach sand used to be ground up rocks, shells and coral. Now it is those and plastics too.

The oceans' currents on the Equator generally flow easterly in what is called the Equatorial Countercurrent. However, ocean currents immediately above and below the Equator tend to flow in a westerly direction. When the currents encounter land, those above the Equator turn north and those in the southern hemisphere turn south. In the North Atlantic, for instance, the current that flows west from Africa continues up the east coast of South America, past the Caribbean and southern USA, and across to western Europe. It then turns south past the west coast of Africa till, near the Equator, it joins the westerly flow once more. This cycle continues endlessly. The same basic circular system applies to all the oceans. Any matter floating on the surface will be carried along those routes while at the same time slowly drifting toward the ocean's centre. There it eventually becomes becalmed and just sits. The process is somewhat similar to a hurricane, the eye of which is calm and quiet while the winds around the edges are howling.

So, in the North Atlantic, the plastic waste that is dumped in the sea or makes its way down the rivers to the sea from the east coast of North America, or from Western Europe or West Africa, gets carried in a long, long journey. Eventually, it reaches the vortex, or gyre, in the middle of the North Atlantic, where it remains as a huge garbage dump. The five major gyres are in the North Atlantic, South Atlantic, Indian Ocean, North Pacific and South Pacific. There are many other locations to which the junk is carried and where it eventually accumulates. The North Brazilian Current flowing close to the North Brazilian and Venezuelan coasts is too far inshore to flow north toward the Arctic. Instead, it gets caught by the West Indies and the Island of Hispaniola and is thereby channeled due west toward the Central American coasts and eventually the Yucatán Peninsula. On the peninsula a little north of Belize, but a couple of hundred kilometers south of the Cancún resort beaches, much of the current's trash comes to rest. It was once a pristine area of white sand beaches and wild coastal habitat with few humans living there. Now it is a dropping off place for the ocean's trash.[32] There are other places around the world where the oceans' currents slow, become trapped and where the sea unburdens its unwanted harvest on the beach or in a bay.

These gyre garbage dumps are indicative of our population whose desire for an easy life goes far beyond our intelligence. Our plastic waste clearly takes us beyond our ability to care for the home on which we live.

When thinking of a garbage patch, one is likely to imagine a huge pile of trash floating on the water. This is true in a few places, as images of miles and miles of floating junk attest. However, most of the trash is floating below the surface. Much of it has already broken down, the oldest to microscopic particles, some to flake sized particles an inch or a centimeter across, but much, of course, is still full size. The densities in the water vary from fewer than 3000 particles per square mile to 200,000 pieces per square mile. In the North Atlantic the lower density surrounds the outer edges of that ocean's gyre from Brazil in the south to Newfoundland in the north. East to west it stretches from the Caribbean to beyond the eastern tip of Brazil. Further east in the Atlantic, there has been little research and little is known, though the extent in the western North Atlantic is probably repeated in the east. The heaviest concentrations are found to the north of Cuba and to the south of New York. It is believed some concentrated patches near the ocean's centre could be the size of England. One 22-year-old ongoing study by the Sea Education Association of the USA, has found little increase in the amount of floating plastic despite a huge increase in the amount of plastic produced. This may indicate that the plastic has an ocean life of a determinate number of years and is either breaking down to microscopic sizes, or falling to the ocean floor. This suggests that if we could just stop releasing the stuff into the ocean the garbage patches would disappear over time.

The Great Pacific Garbage Patch has been estimated at up to 5,800,000 sq miles (15,000,000 k sq) in extent. Since it has no defined beginning and end perimeter, but, rather, consists of small amounts of plastic increasing to large amounts near the centre. I suppose it is true to say that the garbage patch is the size of the Pacific.

Most of the plastic has already broken down to flakes that float below the surface, but the depth to which it goes has not been ascertained. In August 2009 the American Scripps Institute of Oceanography took a 1,700 mile voyage through the centre of the patch. Along the way, they took one hundred netted samples at different depths and found plastic garbage in every one. As the plastic flakes break down to microscopic sizes, it is assumed that they are ingested by small organisms, thus entering the food chain. The plastics are not benign as they degrade since they release, amongst other chemicals, PCBs, polymers, polystyrene chemicals and bisphenol A into the food chain. One estimate gives the weight of plastic in the Great Pacific Garbage Patch at one hundred million tons.

Noise pollution

Another matter of which most of us are possibly unaware, and which seems fairy innocuous at first, is aquatic noise pollution. The kinds of sounds of concern are those created by such activities as construction, naval sonar, military bombing exercises, oil exploration, geological surveys, blasting, scare noise, and our shipping. Many marine mammals and fish move by echolocation, especially in the deep waters beyond the range of light, which is below about 100 meters.

The natural sounds of the depths are thought to have increased by a factor of 10, or 1000 per cent from what they were prior to industrialization.[33] The sounds then would have been all natural; the gentle roar of waves breaking on the beach, the wind disturbing the surface either with an equatorial gentleness or the frantic howl and shriek of an Antarctic storm. There were the random and isolated sounds of some land-forming geological upheaval. The Hawaiian Islands must have made quite a din when they lifted above the waves some six million years ago. But those cataclysmic noises would have been relatively few and far between in relation to the generally mellow and hushed sounds of the sea. What the animals would have been listening for, and recognized, would have been the squeaks, chirps, clicks and songs of everything from shrimps to dolphins and whales. By hearing the sounds reflected back to them or communicated to them from afar the animals would know where they were and where their friends or enemies were.[34]

A few years back, had anyone asked me how far and fast I thought sound traveled under water, I would have probably answered, "slowly and not far." I would have thought of water as a great soggy blanket stopping sound pretty well in its tracks. It turns out I couldn't have been more wrong. Sound actually travels very fast and very efficiently under water. It has to do with the water molecules being more densely packed than those in the air. In the air, sound travels, in aircraft parlance, at Mach 1 or about 760 miles an hour depending on altitude. That is 372 yards per second (340 meters/sec.) through the air. Through water, sound travels at 1,345 yards per second (1,230 m/sec.), or about four times as fast as through the air.[35] Sound travels further under water and at very loud energy levels. When humans blast under water to build a structure or prospect for oil, that sound can be heard more than a thousand miles away.

All the sounds we make, from motorboats to cruise ships and oil tankers crisscrossing the oceans, affect the sea's soundscape, but some of our newer sounds are particularly damaging. A recently developed US Naval Sonar, known as Low-frequency Active Sonar, works near the same low frequency sound, of around 1000 Hertz, that whales use.[36] During tests of this system, as reported in an August 23 press release in the San Juan Islander 2003, it was found that cetacean mammals became disorientated, acted erratically, beached themselves, and sustained "injuries consistent with acoustic trauma." Other research published in the 'Proceedings of the Royal Society B' has shown that whales and dolphins in the North Atlantic near major shipping routes are living with increased levels of Glucocorticoids. These hormone-related chemicals are normally released in highly stressful fight-or-flight situations and are intended to help the animal cope with frightful moments. They are not intended for release over the long term, as they cause growth and reproductive problems. The fact that they are present in such high levels for long periods indicates unusual stress. These high stress levels dropped only once in recent years. That was during the 9/11 emergency when maritime traffic on the Atlantic coast of North America was near a standstill.

One piece of research suggests that a whale's range of communication has been diminished to less than 5 per cent of the range before the recent, 60 - 100 year old, introduction of modern sound pollution. Now whales find it difficult communicating between pods and between each other and their calves. Finding food and avoiding predators is becoming more difficult. Man-made sound can disturb the hearing of the creatures and can drown out their own sounds, so they cannot locate beyond a very short range. We really don't know what's going on down there in the depths and some might say that a bit of inconvenience, or hearing damage, to whales and dolphins is a small price to pay for progress. On the other hand, if these new sounds we are introducing are actually causing the sea creatures great distress and acoustic trauma, our activities indicate this is another strand of our planet's web of life that we are destroying.[37]

In May 2012, the results of US Navy research into marine mammal behaviour found that each year the Navy's use of sonar and explosives probably results in 1,600 experiences of hearing loss and other injuries to marine mammals. The projection was that 200 of them would be killed a year as a result of training and explosives testing. The good news on this issue is that the Navy is very conscious of the problems it causes and is working hard to find ways to reduce the damage to the mammals and other wildlife of the oceans.[38]

The Arctic Ocean is one ocean that one thinks of as relatively unaffected by human activity and industry. However, since global warming has been melting the summer ice, we won't be able to count on the purity of that patch of water for long. Already by early 2012, President Obama had given initial approval for Shell Gulf of Mexico Inc. to start drilling exploratory wells during the following summer. This will be in the Arctic's Beaufort Sea, and the Chukchi Sea off Alaska's northwest coast. The Chukchi is an area rich in Bowhead Whales, Walrus and Polar Bears. Drilling creates a great amount of noise pollution, so we can expect the mammals in those waters to be subject to industrial noise for probably the first time. How the pollution associated with underwater drilling, up to 70 miles from the coast, will affect all the marine mammals no one can say. Nevertheless, the decision portends the end of the innocent purity of those relatively pristine waters.

Although Shell, and the other arctic oil exploratory companies, will deny it, the potential for accidents, environmental damage, and oil spills will always be there. The Chukchi and Beaufort seas are up to 1000 miles from any Coast Guard bases, so a clean-up would be very difficult. Still, Shell has six oil-spill ships always on standby in case of an accident. If BP had difficulty cleaning up the Gulf spill in 2010, imagine how much more difficult it will be to stop a spill in the Arctic. The Gulf of Mexico is surrounded by warm land, some in rather poor countries but much of it the coastline of the most technically advanced nation in the world. There are ports and major highways, maritime infrastructure, and engineering companies galore. When a spill occurs in the Gulf, anything needed can be brought there in a jiffy. None of that applies in the Arctic. There are no ports and no highways. Anything not on site that would be needed to stop, or clean up, a leak would have to be brought in by sea or by air from the south. A leak under ice will offer a host of new problems.[39]

Still, thanks to global warming, we may not have to consider ice coverage for much longer. In 2011, one half of the Ellesmere Island coastal ice shelves melted. This is ice that has been in situ for thousands of years. It is estimated that in 2010 one hundred billion tons of ice melted from Greenland.

In Antarctica, in 2002, 60 per cent or (3,250 km2) of the Larsen B Ice Shelf broke away and floated out to sea. The shelf may have been 12,000 years old and 720 feet (222m) thick at the time. That southern ocean, which has waters encircling the landmass in a perpetual eastward movement, is absorbing 40 per cent of the Earth's CO_2. The world's longest ice core, taken by the British Antarctic Survey, extends for two miles (3 km) and records 800,000 years worth of environmental information. That core reveals that atmospheric carbon dioxide and methane gas are now increasing at a faster rate than at any time on record. It is believed that the Antarctic seawater is becoming so acid that it will, by 2030, corrode the shells of crustaceans as quickly as they can manufacture their shells.

One way that we are collecting data regarding the amount of CO_2 being produced is through an institution known as the Global Carbon Project. Those scientists estimate that in the year 2010 our CO_2 emissions increased by 5.9 per cent, which is the largest increase on record. This increase, and the resulting global warming, is having a huge effect on the oceans. Another study in 2010, by Nature Geoscience, together with the GCP, indicated that the oceans absorb 2.3 billion tons of carbon dioxide per year.

The Antarctic's Ross Sea is one of the globe's last pristine marine wilderness areas. It was discovered in 1841 and is a large part of the planet that few have seen. Humans have had little effect so far. Having been discovered by the UK, it was that country that first claimed it. However, seeing no particular use for it, Britain ceded it to New Zealand. A good area to be protected and preserved one might think. Well, so did Evan Bloom, Director of the Office of Ocean and Polar Affairs of the US State Department.

By the fall of 2012, the United States, under Evan Bloom's leadership, and New Zealand had spent two years discussing turning the Ross Sea into a marine sanctuary, a sanctuary where penguins and marine mammals would live safe from human predators, where science would prevail and where fishing would be banned. Well, although an agreement between the two countries had been reached, the New Zealand government ultimately rejected it. It seems that the New Zealand Seafood Industry Council will have no part in having their fishing rights curtailed, even though the fishing they do in the Ross Sea accounts for just $16 million of their $1 billion industry. The total international catch of Ross Sea fish amounts to $60 million.[40]

I have friends who have visited Antarctica. They described that white land as utterly beautiful, awesome and a part of the world that, absolutely must be protected. One would think that a nation such as New Zealand, that is considered one of the environmental good guys, would be willing to give up such a small catch for the sake of maritime good health. It seems the fishermen who fish the world's oceans will give up nothing for the greater good.

It has to be incredibly difficult to calculate the numbers of fish in the sea. A calculation of the numbers, or biomass weight, in say 1800 or 1900 or 1950 can be little better than a guesstimate. Still, scientists do make these calculations, and although they may not be super accurate, they must surely reflect trends of which all but the most blinkered of us are aware.

At the annual meeting of the American Association for the Advancement of Science, which was held in Vancouver during February 2012, it was announced that the total biomass of commercially fished species has declined 55 per cent in the forty years since 1972. Villy Christensen of the Fisheries Centre at UBC said, "There's been a drastic composition change. This is global, this is for everywhere."[41]

We have to remember that the date 1972 followed at least a century of sustained fishing, so that 55 per cent was of an already reduced amount, which we can only guess at. Unless we radically change our fishing ways, by the end of the next 40 years, there will be another 55 per cent reduction of the approximately 40 per cent remaining. That will, by 2050, take the fish numbers to about 17 per cent of the 1950 numbers. By that time, the human population is projected to have increased to nine billion.

Is this over-fishing another case of we *Homo sapiens sapiens* showing ourselves at our most wise? Or do we show ourselves at our most rapacious, greedy and stupid? We have known since the 1940s and 50s that the human population was going to go through this massive increase. So during the sixty or seventy years since that time, we have reduced one of our most healthy and reliable food supplies to a fraction of what it had been. During the next forty years, will we continue the depletion at the same rate? That is one very big question. In 1950, the human population was 2.5 billion. By 1970, it was 3.7 billion, a 50 per cent increase in twenty years. Since then we have grown to 7 billion: a 100 per cent increase in forty years. So while the human population doubles every 40 years, our marine food reserve is being reduced by more than half over the same 40-year period. One doesn't have to be a marine scientist, or a mathematics wizard, to see where these two progressions are heading. Are we capable of reducing the fish harvest when the demand for fish is so strong? My guess is that we are not capable of making any of the right moves. I also believe that we will continue fishing till the oceans are all but barren. Even if we cut our current fish harvest by 50 per cent and stayed at that figure for the next 40 years, I don't believe it will be enough to allow the fish biomass to return to numbers close to those of 40 years ago. I see nothing to suggest that enough of us are capable of reining in an out of control situation. We can expect fish to become an even more expensive luxury food in the future.

I have mentioned my remembered news item, of the late 1950s or early 60s, that reported the opinions of scientists who believed we humans could have little effect on our oceans, as they were so vast. Well I bet the people making those statements never guessed that our activities would, in fifty years, be causing pathogens found in our livestock to be transferred to the mammals of the sea. The fact that diseases associated with goats and cattle would start showing up in Harbour Seals, sea lions, porpoises and whales was probably beyond even Hollywood's imaginings at the time. It is assumed that such pathogens can either be swept from agricultural land into streams, then rivers and finally to the sea, or can be carried from tropical regions on air currents till they fall in rain and are washed into the sea.

Among these toxins can be listed *Toxoplasma gondii, Sarcocystis neuroma, Crypococcus gatti, Enscherichia coli* and *Coxielle burnetti*, and that is just a few of them.

Toxoplasma gondii was usually found in wild cats and domestic dogs, but is now found in British Columbian Harbour Seals and sea lions as well as sea otters in California.

Opossums normally carry the parasite *Sarcocystis neuroma* but it has now been found to be the cause of a large number of marine animal deaths, including Harbour Seals.

The fungus *Cryptococccus gatti* can be fatal to humans. It was first found in Habour Porpoises in the 1990s, but the great fear is that it could soon transfer to transient Killer Whales.

Enscherichia coli, as well as *Enterococcus*, have both been found in the intestines of Harbour Seals in the vicinity of Vancouver and Victoria, BC. Both have been found to be resistant to eight antibiotics used to treat livestock.

Coxielle burnetti can cause abortions and sickly young in dairy cattle and goats. It is now found in Harbour Porpoises, Harbour Seals, sea lions, and Northern Fur Seals. The route from farm animals to marine animals is not yet understood.[42]

As yet we have no idea how much of this pathogen transference can be directly attributed to human agricultural practices and how much is entirely natural. I believe it is very possible though, that our practices facilitate the transference of these diseases from terrestrial animals to marine mammals. It is obvious that all the drugs, toxins, pesticides, chemicals and poisons that we produce by the millions of gallons each year don't just evaporate and disappear after we have used them. I believe they are long-lived and, though excreted or washed away, diluted in sewers, rainwater run-off and the oceans, they swirl around, building in parts per million and in total toxicity as we produce more. They gradually change the chemical make up of the air and water on which all life depends. I fear that our science-based economy, for all its short-term advantages and good intentions, is ultimately poisoning the whole world little by little and in the most tender, yet malicious, of ways.

I would like to tell one final anecdote regarding the oceans and fishing. Early in 2012, some Philippine Navy vessels caught Chinese fishing boats fishing on the disputed Scarborough Shoal after they had fished the waters of the Philippine island of Luzon. Regardless of the validity of Chinese claims that they own more or less the whole of the South China Sea, and ignoring that the shoal is within the Philippine 200 nautical mile zone, it is what was aboard the fishing vessels that was alarming. The large vessels had on board specially constructed compartments that were full of such illegally taken items as giant clams, corals and live sharks.[43]

The photos I saw showed thousands of giant clams, which can be 4 feet (1.2 meters) or more across and are highly endangered. That was in one hold in one ship. There were eight ships with goodness knows how many giant holds. Those images made me sick to my stomach. They also gave me cause to remember the snorkeling I had done from a small island off the south east coast of the Malay Peninsula.

I was with my wife and two young kids and it was our first snorkeling experience. We were on the island at the invitation of an old friend who was keen on diving. Lee Leng belonged to a Singapore diving club that owned a cabin on that nearly uninhabited island. The club members seemed to spend most of their time flying about the world on diving trips, so I think they knew about good reefs. And the reef off that island was possibly the most incredible sight I have been fortunate to see. Commonplace words, the likes of red, green and blue won't do when describing such saturated colours of fish and corals. We saw no ebonies and ivories there, evocative as those words may sound. The colours we saw were: aquamarine, azure, and cerulean; carmine, chartreuse, and crimson; magenta, sepia, sienna and aureoline-yellow. They were ultramarine, viridian, vermilion, and violet. No artist could ever devise such heart-stopping combinations of hues, nor such fragile and delicate fish and structures. We saw a great clam, which, if my memory is accurate, had rich purple lips and aquamarine rims. No wonder snorkelers and divers are requested to look but do no damage. The many-millennia-old coral ecosystem could be injured at a mere touch.

The miracle, I think, is not that such pristine wonders exist, but that, with all the fishing vessels out there, some continue to thrive. A couple of passes with a trawl net and the destruction would be total.

So with what delicacy did the eight Chinese fishing boats collect their bounty of deeply coral-embedded giant clams from the sea? Not having been there at the time, I don't actually know. However, I assume they sailed back and forth across the reef dragging nets weighed down with metal plates to scour all the thousands of clams off the structure along with the epoch-consuming and laboriously built top layers of coral.

What more can be said, when thinking of the unutterably selfish and stupid actions of men with powerful machines at their fingertips? To use such machines against corals, among the most delicate constructs of nature, is utterly inexcusable. However! That was just one case where the fishermen were caught, but what of all the other hundreds of thousand of unforgivably destructive acts that take place yearly? Whether poor fisher-folk or ruthless businessmen, there are too many who continue to destroy the natural ecosystems of the world. They do so while most of us continue our busy lives assuming everything out there is just fine, thank you very much.

"If it isn't fine," we think, "well there is nothing much I can do about it anyway." Whether the coral reef that my family and I visited is still pristine I cannot say. I hope so, but if it is still untouched I think it will be a miracle.

For any one out there with an inclination to fret or to succumb to attitudes of negativity I apologize, but I feel it is worth mentioning that there are other problems facing the oceans that I haven't covered. These include ocean acidification, diseases caused by fish farming, the prawn fisheries, oysters and such more easily remedied issues as mangrove loss. However, not wanting to flog a dead seahorse, I think I will leave the matter of the oceans at that. The oceans may be huge in size and depth; they may be where life on earth originated and be fundamental to the operation of earth's weather and bio-systems, the oceans are mighty, but Man, the human ape, is mightier still. We can screw-up the oceans just as we can screw-up everything else.

9 Population

The year 1942 was noteworthy for more than just our family's move to Purley. Although the British didn't recognize it at the time, '42 was the year when the United Kingdom was surpassed as the globe's leading nation. Following the Japanese attack on Pearl Harbor in December 1941, when the United States of America entered the Second World War, the US slipped into the top spot without most of the British people realizing what had happened.

It makes perfect sense now, seventy years after the event, when we see how truly powerful the USA is, look at the comparative size and wealth of the two countries, and see how many more regions are now industrialized.

Britain's world dominance began in 1815 following the Battles of Trafalgar and Waterloo. In that year, Britain had a population of 10.3 million[1], while America's 13 states was 5.5 million[2]. By 1914, when the British Empire was at its greatest, but when the technological innovations of the steel industries of both Germany and the USA were surpassing Britain's, the UK's population was 46 million. Meanwhile, the US population had doubled to 92 million, and the nation straddled the continent coast to coast.

The Great Depression brought down all industrial nations, but especially the USA. However, Max Hastings, in his book *Finest Years*, suggests that during the early years of WW2, when Britain alone stood against tyranny, America was able to kick start its economy by selling to the UK the war supplies required to defend democracy. By war's end, the British treasury had been stripped of its gold reserves, its industries located in the USA, some of its overseas bases, and most of its wealth.[3] With the coming of peace, very few in Britain understood how much had been lost, how impoverished the country then was, nor how massively enriched the war had made the USA.

By 1950, when the USA was undoubtedly in charge, the US had a population of 151 million while Britain's was only 50.2 million. The US land base is 3,794,083sq miles (9,826,630km2) of resource-rich land, much of which, in 1950, still waited to be exploited. The United Kingdom had just 2.5 per cent of that much land, whose resources had been pretty well used up over the previous few millennia. So, with the US covering a land mass over 40 times the size of the UK, it is clear that size does matter, or at least it helps quite a bit. It certainly matters in relation to the proportion of population to resource base. When Britain was strongest it had that huge empire covering a quarter of the globe from which to import resources for its industries. The colonies well compensated for its small homeland base. Nevertheless Britain was still powerful then; though by 2012 it had slipped to the sixth strongest country economically.

From the day they entered the war, the Americans never questioned their supremacy. Why should they? However, in my memory, during the early post- war years the average Briton still wistfully thought the UK was the tops, and they resented the Americans having so much wealth and authority. We took great pride in being British. We then felt the kind of national confidence enjoyed recently by the Americans and Russians, and, maybe, by the Chinese in 2013. The British people had accomplished, and still were accomplishing, great things. Individually most of us may have accomplished absolutely nothing, but we all took pride in the glory reflected off our great statesmen and heroes. All very foolish I know, and probably just another aspect of human stupidity, but it was a fact at that time. We can now see that Britain's greatness was exhausted by 1918, but, for the next twenty to thirty years the country, like the tottering patriarch of a great family, had been unwilling to cede authority to the younger and stronger nephew by the name of America.

One strange area for national competition in the late 1940s, as presented by at least one of the London newspapers, was whether London was still the largest city in the world, or did New York then hold that title? It seems crazy now, but it did catch my interest then. My mother read the Daily Express, which was one of Canadian Lord Beaverbrook's newspapers. Beaverbrook was ardently pro-British which was reflected in his papers' editorial content. The *Express* was also easy to read, so as a young boy I found it interesting. For a while one of the main focuses of the *Express* seemed to be which city was the biggest.

London had been the world's largest during the Victorian age and early in the twentieth century, but post WW2 the question that vexed Londoners was whether New York had recently bypassed London, and which city truly had a population of over ten million. The answer seemed to hinge on how much of the urban sprawl, and contiguous suburbia, could be counted in that calculation. It seemed that both populations could be counted at ten million if the books were cooked a little.

Now, more than sixty years later, such a question is even more laughable than it should have been in 1948. No longer only London and New York have populations of ten million or more. There are now a host of cities of that size. However, even now there are different ways of assessing the sizes of cities, and a number of lists with different totals can be found. It seems to come down to which parts of the city are included. On the one hand, some take into account only the metropolitan area, while others include all the suburbs from which labour can be drawn. One list shows that there are twenty cities with over 12 million and thirty-seven at over 6 million. In this assessment, Tokyo is the largest at 32.5 million, Seoul is second largest at 20.5 million, Mexico City is third at just under 20.5 and New York is fourth with 19.74. London is number 18 at 12.87 million.[4] It is calculated that there are 27 cities with populations of 10 million. The growth in cities has been enormous over the past sixty years, but then so has growth in the total population.

The 2 billion humans at my birth are now, 72 years later, 7 billion and rising. Numbers such as 2 billion or 7 billion are hard to comprehend and don't really tell the story in an understandable way. The graph below does.

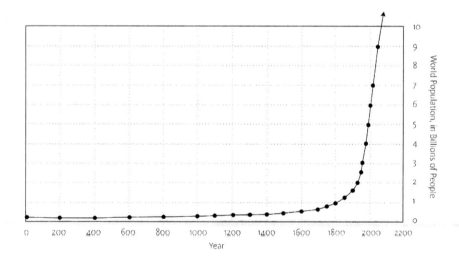

One can see that 2 thousand years ago the globe's human population was about 250 million. That slowly increased to one billion over eighteen centuries. The number then doubled to 2 billion in the next 150 years and continued doubling over shorter and shorter periods till today.

It is that huge growth in the twentieth century that some of us consider a catastrophe. However we have no one to blame but ourselves. Or rather no one to blame but all those who came before and had, and those who continue to have, more than two children.

It seems that in early Victorian England, it was fairly normal to have families of eight or ten children, many of whom died. A number of famous Londoners had every one of their children die before the age of ten. One of my father's ancestors, Thomas, was born to Robert and Unity, in 1775. He was one of seven siblings: two of whom had died in infancy. So Thomas and his wife Sarah were having babies around the turn of the nineteenth century. That was a little before the River Thames was designated a full-time sewer as well as the water supply. London, at that time, was a truly unhealthy place to live – and heartbreaking too. Sarah gave birth to eight babies but five died in infancy. In the next generation my great-great-grandmother Sarah Jane had ten babies with seven surviving, which was an improvement.[5] However, after London's water supply was cleaned up and health prospects improved, and as their financial security also improved, Londoners had fewer babies.

My grandfather on my father's side, Thomas James, was one of six children, four of whom survived. My father was one of four siblings while my mother was one of five. They all survived infancy. My father and his brothers and sister each intended to have two children. It seems my parents only had three because I was a mistake, arriving five years after my brother. Two of my mother's siblings had no children, the others had two or three. Nearly all of my parents' friends had only one or two children. So we can see that as expectations progressed at the beginning of the 20th century, most UK citizens were choosing to have fewer children. The UK birthrate in 2011 was 1.84 births per UK-born woman and 2.18 for immigrant women born outside the UK.[6] A rate of 2.1 is suggested as the normal replacement rate.

To my mind, a low birthrate is obviously more desirable than a high birthrate. If it is too low, though, it creates all sorts of financial problems such as too few breadwinners, fewer taxpayers and lower real estate values. Still, the UK population is heading for 62 million, the largest it has ever been. One factor in these upward-trending numbers is immigration. A second has to be the relative birth and death statistics. In England, the 2011 rates were: births 10.71 per 1000, and deaths 10.13 per 1000.[7]

Increasing longevity is part of these figures, but no one lives forever, and eventually the large number of retired people will pass away. Then the country's population figures will decrease rapidly. This will work well for the long term and for the Earth, but in the short term, there are fears of the economic results of diminishing numbers of productive wage earners.

In many parts of the world, the birthrate during the last half of the twentieth century was very high; in some countries it was at 6 or 8 babies per female. The fertility rate in Asia for much of the 20th century was around 6, though it has now fallen. Africa is presently at 5.5 per female, although some countries are still at 7 to 8 births per female. It should be remembered that health care is now enormously improved over what it was in Victorian England. Then, a far higher percentage of children died than die now.

The different future results from couples having 2 children and those having 6 children are remarkable. These differences are easy to illustrate when we compare three hypothetical islands. On one, two children are produced per couple. On another, 6, and on the third, 4 children are born per couple.

Imagine fictional idyllic islands set in the South Pacific. A few generations ago a couple of dozen seafarers made landings on each. Now, after much hard work, they have turned the flat land into small farms of ten acres, and there just happen to be 1000 farms on each island. Each farm is worked by one happily married couple. This gives each island a population of two thousand people. A large part of each island still remains wondrous virgin forest. On the sun-filled edges of the woodland, brilliant birds fly busily amongst blossoming trees flashing their gaudy feathers to excite their more dowdy mates. Glorious butterflies of iridescent hue flit and flutter from flower to flower. Big caterpillars munch happily away on the forest leaves, but that's no problem as some of the birds have developed a taste for fat caterpillars and so keep their numbers in check. All is harmony. The people are happy, as they have lots of land to grow food and the sea provides plentiful fish. In the evenings, the grandfathers tell stories of the good old days, the children never cry, and it's all a bit like our rose-coloured image of Hawaii or Tahiti before the white man barged in.

We will give these fictional islands the evocative names of Island A, Island B, and Island C.

On Island A, at the moment when each couple has ten acres of arable land from which to produce food, a very wise leader pops up. He does a bit of math and suggests that they must all agree to have no more than two children each for generations into the future. On Island B, no wise leader appears. Their leaders are all a bit middling really, are very religious and believe strongly in the freedom of the individual. The people are told, "Go out and multiply." The comparison of what happens on each island is quite instructive.

For the sake of clarity I am assuming that in any family of marriageable aged adults, when they mate, one will bring a spouse from the other family, and one will leave and go to the spouse's family.

On Island A, each couple has two children resulting in a second-generation family group of four people. When the two children become adults, they find mates; one brings his mate into the family and one of the two goes to the property of his/her mate. When the young couple has their own two children, there will now be six people in three generations living off of each ten-acre farm. We can assume that, as the old grandparents die off and the young people produce two children per couple, the family will remain on average at six people. If the great-grandparents achieve great ages, all four generations will live together, at eight per ten-acre farm. This means that the total population of Island A will always remain at about six to eight thousand people, give or take a few.

On Island B, however, where the people are not wise, are profligate, and put personal choice and freedom before community well being, they average six children per couple, each of whom mates. Three of the mated children go off to their partner's land, and three spouses come in to the family resulting in second generation family groups of eight people: two parents and three young couples. When the three young couples have six children each, they produce a total of 18 young resulting, by the third generation, in a family group of 26 people per ten acres (two grandparents, six parents and 18 children).

When those 18 young people take partners, 9 couples will remain at home and produce 9 x 6 children or 54 children. So, by the fourth generation, assuming the original great-grandparents have died, there will be 6 grandparents, 18 parents, and 54 children for a total of 78 people struggling to live off the same ten acres. This multiplication can continue on generation by generation.

The fifth generation will be 234.

The sixth generation will be more of a tribe than a family at 702.

The seventh generation will be 2,106 per ten acres.

The eighth will be 6,318.

The ninth will be 21,546.

And the tenth generation will be 55,862 per ten acres of land. There are still one thousand ten-acre farms. The ratio increase from the original two is half the generational total.

So by the tenth generation the population on Island B will be fifty-five million, eight hundred and sixty two thousand (55,862,000).

On Island A meanwhile, the tenth generation's population is still the same as it was for the fourth, or sixth, or the eighth generations, at a total of six to eight thousand (8,000). On this island, there are still only 6 or eight people to each farm. The forest is still rosy and ripe with flowering and fruiting shrubs. Brightly coloured birds continue to flutter, and brilliant butterflies, of glorious hue, still flitter. A positive paradise is Island A.

On poor Island B, of course – well you can imagine the devastation – the forests are long gone, no birds fly, and the last butterfly was seen in grandfather's grandfather's time. Everyone has become incredibly competitive and aggressive, as they fight to fend off their neighbors, and to feed off the two fish remaining in the sea. Murder, mayhem and melancholy have become the order of the days. It is not a happy place, our Island B.

Of course, we know that things would not have worked out as suggested on either island. On Island A, some nutcase would have appeared who would have said, "I don't like this. I want more women, I want more children to fight for my rights, I want my neighbours' farms and the rest of you do-gooders can pipe down." And on Island B some hardy souls would have long since set sail, discovered Island A, made a landing, killed or enslaved the wise people, and then set about overpopulating that place too.

If we take a look at a third island, Island C, where they all have 4 children, the total population of the tenth generation will be 1,908,000 including grandparents.

The numbers on any of these three islands do not of course reflect real life. They are simplified illustrations of the different outcomes of 2, or 6, or 4 theoretical children, over a period of ten generations. They don't take account of the B Island adults who come to their senses and reduce their fertility rate, nor of the A islanders who rebel. They take no account of infant mortality, childhood diseases, or youthful accidents. Nor do they take account of the typical number of adults who die before they reach 55 years. Actually, the adults don't matter too much in the population increase; it's the number of young people who have children that matters most. If all the grandparents are removed from the tenth generation of Island B, the overall population of 55.8 million will only lose 6.3 million and still be left with 49.5 million. If all post-child-bearing adults are removed, the island will still have a population of 34.3 million children, children who will no doubt go on to have 6 children per female, and multiply magnificently.

Island A requires the young people to use a very rigid birth control program - but why not? We now have the pharmaceutical knowledge for the whole world to use birth control pills, and maybe those bright and educated people, on Island A might even be able to start a coop where they make their own pills. They could even start an export trade to island 'B.'

Our contemporary people, who are strong believers in the total freedom ethic with no concern for community values, can go and live on Island B if they choose. I know where I would rather live. It is a strange paradox that the only way the B islanders can survive into the future is to rely heavily on a high infant mortality and on lots of young people killing themselves in car crashes, extreme sports and as members of criminal gangs. The odd plague might not go amiss. These are all misfortunes that in real life we try desperately to avoid.

On Island A, where two children are born per couple, the initial 2000 people become 8000, a number that will remain stable into the future.

On Island B, on which 6 children are born per couple, the initial 2000 people become, by the tenth generation, 55,862,000 people. It would be an even greater catastrophe if they kept up the same level of expansion into the future.

Of course at any point before reaching 54 million the population of island B could come to their senses and reduce their birthrate. This is in fact currently happening in the real world, noticeably in Europe and East Asia where the fertility rates are now below 2.0. By 2013, after recent contractions of the birth rate, many governments, including those of Japan and Canada, were speaking of the need to increase the population in order to cover pensions and the economics of providing for a huge cohort of people of pensionable age. Human bubbles were passing through society. These were bubbles of old folk who were likely to live for thirty, or even forty, years after retiring.

So, the governments ask: who is going to provide for these aging population bubbles when they come to retire? One answer it seems will be to increase the population again through immigration. The next question that might be asked is: who will provide for this new immigrant bubble when they reach retirement age?

It is very clear that we must promote fertility rates that are stable in the long term without the cycles of high and low birth numbers.

The above Island B story is the kind of vision for the future that the English Anglican clergyman, Thomas Malthus warned against in the essays he published between 1798 and 1826. He imagined a future where the population increases would outstrip the people's ability to produce food because he could only imagine and foresee an agrarian economy. He thought it would all end in disease and collapse. He wrote at the very beginning of the Industrial Revolution, probably before anyone even realized they were living in a revolution. He was contemporary with the development of the first steam engines and quilled his essay before the first steam railway engine moved along the first rails. He certainly had no foreknowledge of the twentieth century Green Revolution in agriculture. It is likely that he would be amazed that the UK population is now what it is. He had assumed we would have all starved to death years ago.

The Oxford English Dictionary gives a generation as about 30 years. That would place us at about six generations since Malthus's time. During those six generations, the global population has multiplied more than seven times, from less than one billion to seven billion, an increased ratio of about 7.5:1, the same as England's ratio.

In my Island B scenario, the original family group of two becomes 700 by the sixth generation, a multiplication of 350:1. Therefore, it seems that the threats I left out of the island life: wars, disease, infant mortality, early death, non-fertile women, and choice to have small families, have had a really big influence on keeping our numbers down from my worst-case fiction.

The Indonesian Island of Bali is a place where the population has expanded beyond its carrying capacity. Before the 20th century, the Balinese lived well-ordered lives within the Hindu faith. The family property, of a walled compound, living accommodation, temples, and outlying rice paddies, served the population well. The family land was always left to the youngest son.

I have been unable to find a consensus on the historic population figures. However, as the 1950 population was still less than 1 million, I assume the population in 1900 was less than half a million. In 2012, the population was 4.22 million. This followed a few generations of couples typically having 6 children or more, most of whom survived, thanks to modern medicine. So if we assume a population of 500,000 in 1900, that suggests an eight-fold increase in three and a half generations.

Now too many people are reduced to making a living by selling $1 T-shirts to tourists. The Balinese agrarian system, of each family living off their land and passing that land down to the youngest son, has long since fallen apart due to the gross population explosion. The individual farms could not support the large numbers that each family grew to. If we consider it desirable that many people in a given population have had to leave the family land and try to feed themselves by selling cheap T-shirts to tourists - to tourists who may, or may not, come depending on the economy - then that's fine. I personally don't believe such a situation is an improvement nor demonstrates we humans at our best. The Bali government is now trying to encourage a lower birth rate with the slogan 'Two are enough.' There now remains neither much forest, nor much of the wildlife that once lived in it.

The Island is only 90 miles (140kms) by 55 miles (90kms) and has an area of 2,174 sq. miles (5,632 km2). All of the large wildlife are gone including their elephants and the islands own subspecies of tiger, the Bali Tiger, which became extinct in 1937. The Balinese Starling may or may not still survive on the main island.

Indonesia, which had an estimated population of 42 million in 1900, supported a population of 245.9 million by December 2012. Java, the most populous island and the island to which the other islands are more or less colonies, had 25 million in 1900 which had grown to 135 million by 2010.[8]

Peninsular Malaya, which Robert Maxwell described in 1900 as having a population 'of some hundreds of thousands', and where I spent my happy army service, had, in 2010, a population of 22 million. That is in the region of a 30:1 increase in three or four generations. The true population of Malaysia, which includes the Borneo states of Saba and Sarawak, was 28,600,000 in 2010. That's a big increase from about a million a hundred years earlier. In 1900 Sarawak was estimated to have had a population of 320,000, but in 2012 had 2.2 million. Saba, which used to be British North Borneo, contained only an estimated 175,000 in 1900 but by 2012 was 2.8 million.[9] These figures are close to the Island B scenario.

According to the Department of Statistics Malaysia, it is estimated that the Malaysian population in 2040 will be 38.6 million. That is a 35 per cent increase in 27 years. The reason for this increase is not a sustained high fertility rate, which in 2013 was 2.7, but, rather, the very large proportion of young people who are entering the child-bearing years. I was told, in 1974, that the typical Malay family had six children in the desire to outstrip the Chinese half of the country's people. The Chinese seemed disinclined to join in with that particular race and continued to have smaller families.

Since 1900, wherever the human population multiplied at the very high rates, the wild animal population shrank radically. In many places it may be down to only one or two percent of what it was in 1900. So now, with Malaysia's forests already massively reduced, and the population set to increase by another 10 million in the next 27 years, the question is whether any forest will survive over that time. And what of all the other remaining South East Asian forests? One of the big questions is: as the human population continues to increase to 9 or 10 billion in the next forty years, will there be any of nature's natural systems, flora and fauna and checks and balances left? And what will there be to give future generations enjoyment, and protection from ecological catastrophe?

I suspect that over-population does not lead to happy societies. I left England in 1969, when I was thirty, and came to British Columbia on the West Coast of Canada. British Columbia, or BC as it is called, has a land area of 364,764 sq. miles (944,735 km2) and, when I arrived, a population of 2 million. England has a land area of 50,346 sq. miles (130,395 km2) and, when I left, a population of about 44 million. All of Canada, which is the second largest country in the world, had, in 2011, a total population of 34.5 million. The US by comparison has a smaller landmass than Canada but a population nearly 10 times the size, at 312 million in 2011.

So, BC is seven times the size of England, or five times the size of Britain, but in 1969 had a population numbering about 4 per cent of England's.

I was living in London before I left and was lucky to have a desirable job teaching at an art college. Yet life seemed fraught, difficult and demoralizing. Of course I accept that my own particular failings, sensitivities and psychological hang-ups may have been a part of my problem, but I am sure that conditions of life on that overcrowded island were difficult. I loved England, but life seemed harder than I wanted life to be.

When I arrived in BC, I found living wonderfully easy in comparison. I found vast areas of true wilderness in sight, and easy reach, of the small city of Vancouver. A brand new beachside apartment was easy to find and relatively inexpensive. Pay at that time seemed better than in England. The land was vast and filled with resources, which gave wealth to the small population. The traffic on the roads was light in comparison, while the roads were wide. Out of town, or in the interior of the province, a driver could think he was the only one on the road. Towns were maybe a hundred miles distant, instead of ten miles apart. Every town was under-populated and slow compared with the British equivalent. People were supportive of, rather than competitive with, each other. I easily, and quite informally, met people of some note. Had I wanted to, I could have got an appointment with a major architect, a CEO of some large company or a member of the government with little difficulty. In England, most people would never have dreamed of making such contacts with any ease, and probably have had to wait a month to eventually have a meeting. Every aspect of life seemed easy in comparison with the old country. I started a studio, and before long was buying lumber by the thousand board feet. I built large sculptures 8 feet high, instead of making ceramic pieces 8 inches tall. I began to feel confident again.

There are obviously many reasons for these differences between living in England and living in BC, but I felt, and still do, that population size was the main one. The newness of the province was the cause of that happy state. Europeans had only been living there for about 110 years, and the development of infrastructure, and of resource extraction, was relatively new. Everywhere were plentiful, large tracts of forests, mountains and lakes that seemed unexplored. In contrast, by 1970 most resources in Europe had long since been used up, most countries were overpopulated, and much employment was dependent on dying manufacturing industries. There is a lot of tension that evolves amongst people living too close together, and in tight competition for good jobs and good housing.

Now the populations of Britain and the European Union continue to rise due mainly to immigration rather than the birthrate. The average fertility rate for Europe is now well below 1.8. As stated, a fertility rate of 2.1 babies per female is the replacement rate of births considered necessary to maintain a stable population. In a 2008 survey, Slovakia was shown to have the lowest rate of 1.32. In that survey, eighteen European countries had fertility rates below 1.5 and seventeen had rates above 1.5. The only 2 countries above 2.0 were Ireland and Turkey, both coming in at fertility rates of 2.1.[10] Europe is the only continent with a fertility rate below the replacement rate. This low reproduction rate is not yet resulting in a dropping population due in part to the increasing longevity of the senior citizens who are currently in the majority overall.

Why is the European fertility rate dropping? Is it an economic factor? Does it result from a population that is better educated, but which sees hard times ahead? Do people feel pessimistic for the future, or do they feel free of the constraints of religion? Do more young women have career prospects that encourage them to choose to have fewer, or no babies? Does the social safety net, under which so many Europeans live, get rid of that old imperative of needing offspring to provide security in our advanced years? Do they feel more crowded? Is it a matter of choice or is fertility being damaged? Could the fertility be influenced by such environmental factors as pesticides, hormones in food, chemicals in the water, pollutants in the air, or other delights of living in modern industrial societies? Or is it simply an intellectual decision on the part of the majority of the concerned citizens? I don't know the answer, but if it is the last reason, then there is indeed hope for mankind and for our planet, as other continents are sure to follow.

As Europe's population decreases, will the people accept more and more immigration from the other swelling continents? Will other countries wish to use Europe as a population dump, just as Europeans used other continents before? Time will tell, I suppose.

While the European Union in 2011 had a fertility rate of 1.5, Canada's was 1.63, and the rate for the USA was 1.89. According to *The World Bank Development Indicators*, some of the most developed nations in Asia now have very low fertility rates. Hong Kong's, which was above 5 in 1960, was 1.0 in 2009. The following list shows the rates for some other East Asian countries: North Korea 1.1, Singapore 1.2, Japan 1.4, China 1.6, South Korea 2.0, Indonesia 2.1, Malaysia 2.7 and the Philippines 3.2. Only Islamic Malaysia and the Catholic Philippines, come in at above the replacement level. Many West Asian countries, such as Afghanistan and Yemen, continue to show high fertility rates of 5 to 6.[11]

Worldwide, the 1950s fertility index of 5 babies per woman is falling, and is now low in Europe and East Asia. In Africa, it is falling in some countries but is still above 5 in others. It is at 6 to 8 in such countries as

Angola, Malawi, Niger and Uganda. The North African Mediterranean countries and South Africa on the southern tip are expected to have fertility rates of 2.5 in 2012.

The United Nations Department of Economic and Social Affairs report, *2012 Revision of the World Population Prospects*, suggests that, by 2050, all countries will experience a fertility decline, but with a final rise in the fertility in Europe, resulting in a worldwide convergence, in 2050, of a fertility rate of 1.85. With this projection, the world's population in 2050 is expected to be 9.2 billion, or 10.6 billion or 7.4 billion depending on whether the calculations are out by 0.3 above or 0.2 children below replacement level. However, projections of future trends seem to change annually. A May 2011 United Nations report stated the belief that growth could continue to a 15 billion total in the year 2100. It is possible that the African population, which was 133 million in the year 1900, will indeed grow to 2 billion by 2050, but will then continue growing to 3.5 billion by 2100.*

The 2012 UN estimates for the present, historic and future population projections for the different continents are (in millions):

	1800	1900	2000	2050
Africa	107	133	811	2,191
Asia	635	947	3,720	5,142
Europe	203	408	726	719
North America	7	82	313	446
Latin America	24	74	521	750
(Latin America includes Mexico and the Caribbean)				
Oceana	2	6	31	55
Total	978	1,650	6,122	9,303[12]

* One thing worth noting is that a billion is a heck of a lot more than a million. Millions and billions all sound rather similar and a billion or two doesn't make a whole lot of difference. One way to describe that difference, though, is visually with a stack of money. So if we imagine that a million notes of a country's money, when bundled together, measures 1 foot (30 cm) in height. We can now imagine what a stack of a billion notes, or a thousand of those bundles piled on top of each other will look like. That stack will be far higher than the tallest skyscrapers most of us have ever seen. A thirty-story skyscraper is probably about 300 feet high, but we are looking at a thousand feet or 305 meters. It will be a tiny bit lower than the Empire State building. While we might trip over a 30 cm stack of a million notes, we could never miss a billion.

In 2004, the UN Department of Economic and Social Affairs reported on populations to 2300. Apparently, life expectancy and mortality will play a more dominant part in population projections into the future. In recent years, life expectancy has increased quite dramatically on all continents, except Africa. The great baby boom of the 1960s, 70s and 80s will, in time, produce a very large proportion of old folk over much of the world. That, and the fact that fertility is dropping everywhere, is expected to produce a fairly stable world population after 2050. However, the authors of the report spoke of three possible scenarios that are dependent on how much above or below the anticipated fertility rate the actual rate will be. In that case the rates for 2100 are projected at 15 billion or 9 billion or 6 billion.

One older UN report from the 1990s, projected a population of 240 billion, if the 1996 fertility rate continued unchecked, which it hasn't. That would be another Island B scenario.

In 2011, about 42 per cent of the world had a fertility rate below replacement levels. Countries in this group include: Europe, USA, Russia, China, Japan, Canada and Brazil. Another 40 per cent has a medium fertility rate of between 2.1 and 3.0. These countries include: India, Latin America, South Africa and the North African countries along the Mediterranean coast. The high fertility countries, which are 18 per cent of the world's population, include most of Africa, Pakistan, Afghanistan, Yemen, four small countries in Latin America and others.

Between 2011 and 2100 the high fertility countries are likely to triple their populations from 1.2 billion to 4.2 billion. The intermediate countries can expect a 26 per cent population boost from 2.8 to 3.5 billion. The low fertility countries should see a 20 per cent decrease from 2.9 billion to 2.4 billion.[13]

Africa's historic population interests me. Genetic research supports the theory that modern man first emerged in Africa over 200,000 years ago. Some of those moved into Asia about 110,000 years ago. Presumably, only a few migrated while the majority remained in Africa. One might therefore assume that by the turn of the 18th century there would be more people in Africa than in Asia or Europe. However Africa's population was 107 million in 1800, while the population of Asia was 635 million and that of Europe was 203 million. This seems strange, as modern humans are thought to have only entered Europe about 43,000 years ago, or at the beginning of the last Ice Age, when much of Europe was uninhabitable. The ice was only gone some 12,000 years ago. So why did we enjoy this rampant population explosion in Europe and Asia but not in Africa? Surely the majority of Africans stayed home when the first migrants left, so the Africans had a many thousand-years head start on both the Asians and the Europeans. Speaking personally, I would rather make babies in the warmth of the tropics than in the cold of Europe. So what kept the African population in check? Was it the African diseases, or the predatory lions, that kept the population down? Or was it something to do with the hardships of the north having hardened and strengthened the Asians and Europeans? Europe also had diseases and lions, so I have no idea what the answer is. Whatever the answer, something kept the ecosystems of that continent in balance for hundreds of thousands of years. Neither the carnivores, herbivores, nor humans became dominant until industrial man appeared.

What is certain is that the huge continent of Africa in 1800 still held a great number of wild animals, when the human population was just over one hundred million. Now, 210 years later, the population of Africa is ten times larger at one billion and set to rise to 2.2 billion by 2050. Meanwhile the animal numbers are reduced to a few percent of what they were.

During the past era of population explosions, we have spread industry and the agricultural Green Revolution to many emerging countries. This is increasing the prosperity of some, but it has also resulted in increased energy consumption, resource over-use and a polluted Earth. At the same time that many people have, thankfully, moved from poverty to an emerging lower-middle class, the truly impoverished at the bottom of the economic structure, have multiplied. The issues of poverty would be difficult enough within a stable population, but with the poorest populations growing fastest, on an earth that doesn't get any bigger, it is a game of constant catch-up.

I understand the theory that we need large populations to provide the wealth and the human resources necessary for the development of services and infrastructure. I understand how much more practical it is to build an expensive transport system to serve ten million taxpayers, instead of ten thousand. However, against that, a large population uses up the renewable, and the non-renewable, resources more quickly than a small one and in so doing accelerates the destructive forces of mankind.

In 1950, when I was young, the populations of Africa, Asia and South America were tiny compared with today. Since then, many countries have seen up to twenty-fold increases. When I was young, the forests of Africa, Malaysia, Borneo, the Amazon, British Columbia and most other forested lands were still reasonably intact. They were mostly pristine, and places of mystery and high adventure. During my life, huge areas of forest have been destroyed along with the trees, plants, animals and insects that had thrived there. When I was young, the cultures of most parts of the world, along with the ecosystems in which they had developed, were still strong and distinguishable by their customs, languages, clothes, unique housing styles and individual ways of living within the environment. During my life, nearly all have been swept away in a rush toward a mono-cultural conformity. The tribal and indigenous peoples have no chance and are given few rights to remain. The ecosystems are given even less of a chance.

Possibly I shouldn't be so concerned about the population explosion. After all, many of us seem to be living very comfortably thank you very much. And economists, those doubly wise folk who know how we can all become really, really rich, seem to think a big population is great. Trouble is I can't help but observe that we seem to be destroying the planet. We are using up irreplaceable resources at an alarming rate as if our great-grandchildren won't need any. We continue to play fast and loose with the integrity of the environment. We are willing to risk any natural area of grassland, forest, pristine watershed or ocean, by harvesting, mining, drilling or otherwise destroying it. We have reduced the wildlife numbers, and wild places, to a tiny fraction of what they were when I was young. And now we seem happy to kill all the insects with pesticides, log the last wild forests, fish the last fish from the sea and generally treat our earth as if our descendants will need nothing, and as if there is no tomorrow.

10 Unsustainable Energy Use 101

While watching the *BBC World News* early in August 2013, an interesting fact was mentioned. A reporter in China was speaking on a story about Chinese consumers purchasing European commodities, and he said that there were then 400 million highly paid workers in China. That would still leave many million poorly paid workers in China, but that is not the point. 400 million in China, when added to the millions in North America, Europe and the rest of the world, is a massive increase in well-paid workers worldwide. I don't know how 'highly paid' is defined, nor what he meant by it, but I assume he meant an economic group who could afford an automobile or something similar.

There were no automobiles 300 years ago, and probably in the year 1713 the number of well-paid, or well-off, people worldwide could be numbered in the tens of thousands. In those days the vast majority of people, who were mostly the equivalent of peasants, consumed very little beyond what they ate and wore. In any case, there were only about 700 million of us, so the effect of our numbers was quite small. We had killed off the European lions, Auroch, Dodo, most Moa birds in New Zealand, and a few others, but not a lot else. Now though, with seven billion of us, and a large percentage being well-paid consumers with high demands, our industrial economy has grown to consume huge quantities of the Earth's resources.

At the time of Shakespeare's Romeo and Juliet, the rich merchant traders of the city-states of Italy were probably Europe's most wealthy, though the mandarins of China, and some of the maharajahs of India may well have eclipsed them. Next, the Spaniards and Portuguese saw gold flowing in from their newfound American colonies. The Dutch became rich from eastern spices. Then the British did well, gaining wealth from industry, shipping and trade. Finally the Americans eclipsed everyone.

Each of these nations had its turn at having the wealthiest citizens at one time or another.

In March 2012, Citigroup Inc. reported on the number of centa-millionaires, also known as C-millionaires. These are individuals with fortunes in excess of one hundred million dollars. It was announced that in East Asia, which includes China, Southeast Asia and Japan, the number of C-millionaires now exceeds that of North America.[1]

150 years ago, the biggest concentration of truly wealthy people was in Britain and Europe. By early twentieth century, the wealth centre had shifted and included the United States. Now it is shifting again, but this time, all the way back to Asia, where it had probably been half a millennium ago. There were, in 2011, 18,000 C-millionaires in East Asia, 17,000 in America and 14,000 in Europe. These numbers are anticipated to rise by 2016, to 26,000 in Asia, 21,000 in North America and 15,000 in Western Europe. In 1980 a US citizen was 20 times richer than a Chinese citizen. In 2010, an American's household income was 5-8 times as large as those in China, depending on whether we compare median or average incomes.[2][3] So, the income inequality between the USA and China is shrinking. China is expected to have the world's biggest economy by the year 2020.

As a short aside, it is worth mentioning that income inequality has risen over the past 33 years in most western countries including the USA, Canada and Britain. Britain, for example, seems to be heading back to Victorian standards of income distribution. Of all the developed countries, the inequality in the UK is rising faster than anywhere else. According to Britain's Office for National Statistics, the average UK salary was £26,200 in 2011, while the average CEO salary was £112,157. That is a ratio of a little over 4:1, which seems about right.

However the ratio of the top CEOs to average incomes definitely is not right. In the UK, the FTSE is a listing of the one hundred firms on the London Stock Exchange with the highest capitalization. They are used to signal the ups and down of the market. 2010 was a year when the economic crisis and recession were deepening and millions were facing the loss of jobs and income. At that time of presumed restraint, the executives of those 100 companies enjoyed 55 per cent increases to their total earnings, which averaged £4,900,000 for the year. I calculate that as a ratio of 188:1 to the average UK income. This is nearly double what the ratio was in 2002. Those figures are scary enough, but what are truly appalling are the earnings of the most avaricious CEOs. One took home £92.5 million, a second £38.4

and a third £27 million. If we take the average of those 3 incomes to be £52.3 million we arrive at a ratio of 2000:1 to the average worker's income. Meanwhile the UK workers were seeing their incomes drop once more, when compared with inflation.[4]

Assuming these figures to be correct we seem to have exceeded the awful disparity of the times of Jane Austen's novel *Pride and Prejudice*. Her Mr. Darcy was considered very wealthy indeed, with an income, from his fortune, of £10,000 a year. If the average Englishman in 1805 earned £20 a year, Darcy enjoyed only a 500:1 advantage, not a 2000:1 advantage. So now, in some ways, the wage distribution disparity may be even worse than it was before the Victorian era.

I did some calculations and concluded that most doctors, surgeons, lawyers and university professors earn from about three to six times the average salary for their countries. When his business was most successful, my father probably earned about six times the average. To earn two thousand times the average, a person should be extraordinarily worthy. He, or she, must be inordinately more intelligent, ethical, responsible, beneficial, or whatever else it takes to deserve so high an income. The high earners must be at least 500 times as valuable as a surgeon. So nowadays, with some people earning these hugely disproportionate incomes, one may be forgiven for concluding that a fundamental social flaw is developing. It seems possible that the people who are racing to gain great wealth are, at the same time, feeling no compunction in destroying our globe's natural riches.

I think it is worth remembering that some of the results of unethical early industrial business practices and uneven wealth distribution were the rise, over much of industrializing Europe, of revolution, Socialism, Unionism, Communism and Nazism. Some bankers and industrialists seem intent on creating conditions that will encourage extremism and revolution to reoccur. However, some might argue that such social concerns, are rather less important than the overarching matter of our industrial footprint. All of this wonderful wealth building that is taking place in countries all over the world, pays no heed to our Earth's ability to provide the necessary materials or to stay healthy through the process. If the whole world of nine or ten billion people is to become industrialized, where will we find the materials?

I could go on at length on the subject of our evolved, and ever-growing economy, which is fundamental to the quagmire in which we find ourselves, but I won't, as that would require a whole other book.

Just as the human population slowly increased over millennia, until its final acceleration 100 years ago, so it was with our industry. Going from papyrus sheets to paper and the printing press, was a journey of many thousand years. The time it took from harnessing fire or developing the wheel to putting the two together to make the steam engine was glacial. But going from the steam engine to the moon, matches the final meteoric rise of our population. Now the whole world is waiting to become industrialized. By the early part of the 21st century, the industrialization of East Asia and South America has resulted in over half of the globe's population, or 3.5 billion people, now being considered middle class. This is a great success for global economics and industrialization, and it is hoped that in the future all 9 or 10 billion of us will be as fortunate.

One hundred years ago, the great majority of we humans were lucky to own three chickens and a pig. Then, only America and the few industrialized countries in Europe burned oil and coal in power plants and factories. Even so, that small percentage of the globe's population was enough to begin the global warming that we know today. Now, all the emerging economies, and the multiplying middle class are requiring many, many more power plants and factories. This great increase in the number of oil-fed and coal-fed furnaces is accelerating global warming catastrophically. We now also consume very large amounts of materials that are used to make the things we think we need. Being consumers, we now anticipate owning great riches. Three chickens and a pig will not do at all.

The trouble is that all this industrialization and consumerism uses up resources, and while some are renewable, such as agricultural produce, others are not. Many of the resources we use are non-renewable, though we are using them with abandon, and all will run out one day. These resources took millions or billions of years to be made by the Earth's natural cycles. It will take the Earth a similar amount of time to reproduce what we now use in a single year. The non-renewable resources include such plentiful materials as limestone, from which we make cement, iron ore from which we forge steel, and clay with which we fire bricks and pottery. They also include the rare earths such as Rhodium, Rhenium and Ruthenium, which are used in automobile catalytic converters, jet engines, electronics, and other products that we have come to depend on. Also, and probably most important, are the fossil fuels: the oil, coal, natural gas, and methane which resource companies are now trying to develop and sell as fast as possible. Nations, all over the globe, that find themselves rich with coal, oil, or gas, are competitively intent on developing those resources, and cornering the export markets. The resource companies are in such a panic to extract and use them that they pay no heed to the resulting global warming. And again, we wonder what future generations will do when those hydrocarbons are all used up.

British Columbia is on the wet side of the Rocky Mountains, and most of the huge land area is mountainous. From the Pacific coastal mountains, all the way to the Rockies in the east, it is one mountain range after another. There are some rolling hills, but only about 3 per cent of the province is suitable for agriculture. Many of the high mountains still support glaciers and, with its northwesterly position on the continent, BC receives abundant rains - rains that, at higher elevations, fall as snow. Depending upon the amount of heat during the spring and summer, the snow melts slowly or rapidly. It melts to pure clear water that tinkles down the mountain streams and thunders along the rivers. British Columbia has lots and lots of good fresh water. All this fresh water, possibly more than anywhere else in the world, is something for which we give thanks. Ours is a perfect land for developing hydropower. Few other places in the world are so fortunate.

We should not disparage the amount of water that falls in the form of snow. Our Monashee Mountain Range, which is close to mid-province near the US border, but close to the Rockies a little further north, has plenty. I researched the annual snow pack for the highest elevations of that mountain range and came up with all sorts of conflicting numbers. The greatest estimate I found was 60 feet, or about 20 meters, of snow. If there is indeed that much snow, it gives a good idea just how much water is held in reserve high on the mountains till it melts and is able to flow along the rivers to the sea.

As a consequence of our precipitation, British Columbia has been able to generate all the electricity it needs by hydropower. It can't be denied that we have built huge hydroelectric dams - dams that have created large lakes where once mountain rivers tumbled, and that have compromised plenty of once-healthy salmon rivers. But at least our power generation does not contribute to global warming. Once built, our dams hum along adding no $CO2$ to the atmosphere. So BC is green, wet and non-polluting. There is a certain satisfaction for British Columbians in knowing that we are among the good guys in the global-warming battles. We don't pollute the air with dirty coal or oil-fired power plants. Nor do we add $CO2$ gas. At least that is what we like to believe.

British Columbia got a head start when gold was discovered at the tail end of the nineteenth century, and mineral wealth has remained one of the engines of BC's economy. Amongst many other minerals we have huge deposits of coal, natural gas and methane. The government has been encouraging the sale of coal to Japan since 1981. By selling our coal to others we remain pure and pollution free. The Japanese can pollute in our stead. Now with this, many of us have difficulty. We know perfectly well that coal is a dirty fuel, and that the coal we sell will pollute the atmosphere with CO2 that, in turn, will cause global warming. It is therefore stupid to knowingly pollute by using such fuels as coal. However, I think it is unforgivable to profit by selling dirty fuel to other countries that do the polluting for us.

The business all began in 1981, with an agreement to sell coal to a group of Japanese steel mills. In 2011, BC sold coal to the tune of 7.1 billion dollars worth.[5] Research by the Canadian Pembina Institute indicates that in 2006 the coal BC exported accounted for CO2 emissions of 59 million tons.

In 2013, the Canadian provinces of British Columbia and Alberta were intent on a huge growth in the production and export of coal, oil and natural gas.

BC has an estimated 20 billion tons of coal in reserve, and BC is the second largest exporter of seaborne coal in the world. Following talks between the coal mining companies and the government, BC is now set to increase coal exports to Asia to a total of 82 million tons annually.[6]

According to a 2012 study by Dogwood Initiative of Victoria entitled, *B.C.'s Dirty Secret: Big Coal and the Export of Global Warming Pollution,* BC's coal exports will be major contributors to global warming. If all the reserves are exported and burned the total heat-trapping pollutants generated will be nearly 15 billion tons.

The report says:

> This would amount to an unbelievable 6.35 per cent of the total heat-trapping pollution scientists believe humanity can emit globally between now and 2100. Put another way, it is equivalent to adding almost 2.8 billion additional passenger cars to the road. That many vehicles is almost 3.5 times the total number of cars on the road worldwide today.

As well as increasing its coal exports to Asia, British Columbia planned, in 2013, to begin liquefied natural gas (LNG) exports to the same market. In that year, BC had close to a dozen new gas export projects on the go, including one in partnership with China and one with Malaysia. Exporting BC's northeastern gas will mean: constructing miles of roads, drilling a great many wells, fracturing the shale rock deep underground to get at the gas, building many pipelines to the west coast, navigating supertankers filled with LNG along pristine and narrow channels and generally destroying the integrity of the wild land across the north of the province. Roads into wilderness areas invite vehicular traffic and hunters where previously none had been, and that means the destruction of the local wildlife.

One aspect to the BC rush to export our fractured shale gas for monetary gain is that the globe is already awash in gas. According to Dr. Andrew Weaver of BC's Green Party, Russia already has twenty times more known gas than BC, while China has five times more. So, what's the hurry? Why don't we just leave it in the ground for our descendants to develop if they need to? They will be able do it after all the other countries have used up their own. With all the extra pollutants that we are hoping to add to the atmosphere, British Columbians are clearly not the clean innocents that we like to think we are. It will be even worse if we do increase our coal exports to the amounts planned.

Alberta, British Columbia's neighboring province on the eastern side of the Rocky Mountains, is intent on quadrupling the sales of oil from their bituminous tar sands, which are thought to contain between 178 billion and 2 trillion barrels of oil. This places Alberta just behind Saudi Arabia in oil reserves.[7] At the projected future extraction rate of 5 million barrels a day, it is believed the oil will last 170 years. Alberta and the Canadian government were, in 2013, planning on increasing the exports of oil to the USA, and beginning a big export industry to Asia.[8]

The Athabasca Tar Sands as they used to be known, have been lying on the surface of Northern Alberta for hundreds of millions of years. They stretch approximately 300 miles (500km) north to south, and 250 miles (400km) east to west. That is an area of 54,000 sq. miles (141,000km2), which is close to 3000 square miles larger than England. The tar sands consist of thick bituminous oil mixed with sand and clay. They lie on top of a flat limestone rock surface. The thickness of the tar sands varies, but is typically 40-60 meters thick. Above the surface there may be varying thicknesses of clean clay and sand to a maximum of 75 meters. This overburden is finally topped by 1 to 3 meters of waterlogged muskeg or boreal forest. In some places the tar cuts through to the surface of the land.

To transport this oil, four new pipelines are planned. Three pipelines have been designed to transport future oil production out of Canada.[9] The first is the 1,660-mile, 36-inch Keystone XL, which will double the amount of oil going to the US, and will terminate at the Port Arthur refinery in Texas. Proponents have said Keystone will produce 13,000 direct, 7,000 manufacturing and 118,000 spin-off jobs.

The second is Enbridge's Northern Gateway to Kitimat on the north coast of British Columbia. From this terminal the oil will be transported by supertankers to China and Asia. A third pipeline that is proposed is not a new one. It will be an expansion of the present Kinder Morgan Line, which terminates near Vancouver.

The Canadian government under Prime Minister Stephen Harper is totally in favour of these projects and frequently emphasizes the number of jobs lost if they don't go ahead. However, the majority of Canadians seem to be opposed. They are opposed, I believe, in part, out of deep shame of producing such heavily polluting oil at a time of global warming. They are also opposed out of a fear of oil spills. There was also a significant outcry in the US against the Keystone proposal.

The fourth proposed pipeline is to transport the oil to eastern Canada where it can be refined for domestic use. It is incredible that, despite sitting on all this oil, Canada imports the oil it uses from Saudi Arabia, Africa and Venezuela. Although it makes perfect sense for Canadians to stop all that tanker traffic by using our own oil, we have to assume that this isn't done because it is more profitable for the oil companies to transport oil all over the globe.

The Alberta Tar Sands are truly filthy. At least the BC coal mostly pollutes only when it is burned. The tar sands project produces huge amounts of pollution in just wresting the oil out of the tar. In order that the oil can be separated from the sand and clay, natural gas is used to heat water to up to 80 degrees Celsius. To retrieve one barrel of oil, 1900 cubic ft ($54m^3$) of natural gas, and 2 – 4.5 barrels of water, are used. A barrel of oil releases the energy equivalent to 6,000 cubic feet of natural gas. So, it appears that they use one unit of energy to obtain three units of energy, which is an incredibly wasteful way of doing things. A more recent method of extraction has been developed whereby steam is pumped underground, thus turning the bitumen into slurry liquid enough to allow the oil to be pumped to the surface. In the future, once they have used up all the available natural gas on this production, they will harness the bituminous oil itself to heat the water. In 2011 the total daily production was about 1.3 million barrels of oil being mined by more than twenty international oil companies. Nearly a million of these barrels went straight to the United States along a pipeline to the Midwest. The oil industry hopes to increase this production to 5 million barrels per day by 2030.

When it is eventually refined to gasoline, the tar sands petroleum is undoubtedly the filthiest and most polluting in the world. It produces three times the amount of CO_2 of conventional oil. It is believed that the CO_2 emissions will multiply, by 2020, to an annual production of between 108 and 140 million tons of greenhouse gasses.[10] A number of that magnitude exceeds that produced by all the automobiles and SUVs on the roads in 2010. Already the 3.5 million residents of Alberta produce 40 per cent of Canada's CO_2 emissions, and that is just from getting the crude oil out of the ground. It has yet to be refined and then burned in power generators and automobiles. The development and expansion of the tar sands oil makes it totally impossible for Canada to meet Prime Minister Harper's 2007 assertion that he will, by 2050, reduce Canada's Greenhouse gas emissions by 65 per cent. The tar sands industry is condemned by many jurisdictions all over the world for the extremely high level of pollution it generates.

Business reporters are great at quoting the economic advantages of developing the oil, but they never mention the ecological damage. In November 2012, information was leaking to the media that the snow and rain in the area of the tar sands was laced with contaminants. Research by University of Alberta scientist, David Schindler, was discovering Whitefish, from the Athabasca river watershed, suffering large tumors. This may be one of the side effects of the tar sands pollution.[11]

I won't go into all the environmental problems and potential for accidents and damage that the pipelines and tanker traffic present, as the list is very long. However, in 2010 in Michigan, another Enbridge pipeline spilled 3,800,000 litres of oil into the clean Kalamazoo River. On that one, in July 2012, the US National Transportation Safety Board likened the Enbridge officials to the Keystone Kops. Apparently, it took those officials seventeen hours to decide whether or not to turn off the oil pumps after they were informed of the leak. Also, many of us remember what happened when the Exxon Valdez struck the Bligh Reef in Prince William Sound, Alaska in 1989. It spilled 40 million litres, or close to 750,000 barrels, of crude oil into a pristine, crystal-clear environment. That oil spread over some 11,000 square miles (28000 km2) of ocean, and polluted 1,300 miles (2,100 km) of Alaska's coastline killing many thousands of birds, fish and mammals.

Many people in Canada feel ashamed that the Canadian government, along with some provincial governments, is working so hard to sell coal to Asia, and bituminous oil to Asia and the USA, especially at a time when all nations should be cutting their CO2 emissions in the face of global warming. They do not want this expansion in the production of dirty oil. Nor do they want the environmentally damaging pipelines built, as they understand the great damage it will do to the health of our earth. However, the Canadian Prime Minister, Stephen Harper, will brook no interference from the people. In 2013 the government was intent on preventing anyone but the energy and pipeline companies from presenting arguments regarding the plans for expanded dirty energy exports. The environmental groups and dissenting citizens, who were against these energy developments, became a type of state enemy, and great efforts went into muzzling all but the supporters of big oil.

There is indeed an ugly side to enterprise. I do not believe that the developed nations take sufficient responsibility for the actions of their entrepreneurs, nor do they think of their actions in a global context. We have become reckless, wastrel squanderers of our globe's fortune. It is clear we will leave our Earth impoverished. A wise man endeavors to leave his descendants material foundations that are enriched. Our descendants will inherit only the shattered remnants of our profligate indulgence.

It wouldn't be so bad if we directed the profits from dirty resources into green energy research, or used the money to build green power plants. That way some good would come from the bad. Alternatively, the great amounts of money being made could be used for green causes worldwide. We could, for instance, direct the profits to poor countries to enable them to keep their forests intact. Countries such as New Guinea or the Congo need all the help they can get to stop the logging. It could be a sort of pollution trade. But we don't invest those profits in worthy causes. Instead we are using the globe's capital, the hydrocarbons, the way drunkards squander their family inheritances.

I mentioned some of the gas extraction projects underway in Canada in the second decade of the 21st century. More LNG projects are also planned for the USA, Australia, Indonesia, South America, Africa, and anywhere that has any gas waiting to be developed. But that's only gas. On top of all the numerous gas, coal and pipeline projects that northern British Columbia had in development in 2013, were at least 2 copper-gold mines, a hydro electric power dam and a number of run-of-the-river hydro electric projects. All we hear about from government, industry and the media are the potential hundreds of billions of dollars that the province will earn. In all this, there is no heed paid to the resource needs of future generations, to the matter of global warming, nor to the environmental damage we do to ecosystems. If these projects do go ahead we can be sure that the wild and undeveloped north of BC, with its vast spaces and wild animals, will be wild no more.

A mine sounds relatively benign. Most of us, when thinking of mines, imagine a hole in the ground, down which men descend to extract minerals that are useful to us. Not all mines are like that though. Many are surface mines from which all organic materials are scraped for scores of miles around. Mines frequently mean that the local ecosystem is laid waste in all directions and as far as the eye can see. There is nothing benign about most modern industrial mining projects.

As mentioned there is also absolutely no thought given to the needs of our descendants after we have used up all the non-renewable resources. Our politicians, and the voters who support them, can only believe in accelerating our extraction of those useful materials. This growth must continue, regardless of our Earth's long-term inability to provide for our growing economy. Just as those battleship-enthused British politicians forged ahead with building useless capital ships, so, one hundred years later, many politicians have stars in their eyes over economic growth through hydrocarbons. They have no thought of the damage they are doing to the prospects for future generations, nor of our massive footprint that is destroying our Earth.

The issue of our footprint is important. One scary set of figures is the comparison between the human ecological footprint and the earth's capacity to sustain that footprint, known as bio-capacity. The Global Footprint Network describes bio-capacity as: 'The capacity of ecosystems to produce useful biological materials and to absorb waste materials generated by humans . . .' The GFN describes the ecological footprint as: '. . . the world's premier measure of humanity's demand on nature. It measures how much land and water area a human population requires to produce the resource it consumes and to absorb its carbon dioxide emissions, using prevailing technology.'

According to GNF, in 1960, the earth is reckoned to have had a bio-capacity of 10 billion units. In 1970 it was still 10 billion, but was gradually increasing till it reached 12 billion in 2008, where it has remained. However, the total population in 1960 had an ecological footprint of 7.5 billion units or 75 per cent of the capacity. That was healthy and sustainable. But our footprint increased till, by 1970, it balanced the capacity, and, by 2008, our footprint was valued at 18 billion units. That was 50 per cent more than the capacity of 12 billion units. This increasing trend of our ecological footprint over the biological capacity continues on two ever-diverging lines. If we continue using resources at this increasing rate we will quite simply need ever more planets. Nevertheless, by 2025 we won't have two earths to sustain us, any more than we will have the required three or more by 2050.

If we continue as we are, we really will need more planets to support the nine or ten billion people living in the year 2050. By then, my grandchildren will be in their late thirties and turning forty. So this future is not so far away.

I know that some people believe we are not over-using resources. And that the globe isn't warming, that we should do nothing and carry on as usual. But what will those people say to their grandkids after the economy fails, the sea has risen and the kids ask, "What did you do to save our civilization, Granddad?"

Well, the naysayers and despoilers will have died in comfort and over-indulgence by then. They won't have to answer for anything. But the question remains: can the future nine or ten billion of us live with a smaller footprint? Or does that number of humans preclude the possibility of a healthy and sustainable environment? Is it our numbers, or the human character, that spells defeat for the natural world, and ultimately for humanity? I wish the answer was not both, but I fear it is.

The long-term viability of our civilization appears to lie in how we choose to live into the immediate future. It may depend on whether we are capable of giving up on certain learned ideas. Those theories have undeniably earned us great riches and amazing technological developments, but can they continue to serve in a time of unsustainable resource depletion?

Should we continue with the belief in capitalism and growth at all cost? Or should we transit to a belief in no growth, and equality of opportunity for all humans. Such a shift would result in the lowering of expectations for the most prosperous. It's worth remembering that the North Americans are the wealthiest of all, and are incredibly well served. They also have a lifestyle to which all are encouraged to aspire.

When it comes to a North American's footprint, it is by far the largest. The population of the US and Canada is only about 5 per cent of the globe's total. Yet North Americans consume more than 25 per cent of resources. The footprint of a typical US, or Canadian, citizen is about 300 times as big as an individual's in Central Africa.[12] I assume most of us in North America believe in social justice. I further assume we would like all good people to live as we do. The trouble is, for a future 9 billion people to consume at the rate of North Americans we will need many more than just 2 or 3 extra earths.

The people of such northern European countries as the UK, Germany, Switzerland and Norway have very high standards of living, yet their individual ecological footprints are half of that of the citizens of the United States of America, which has a similar standard of living. If we could all be satisfied to live as the Chileans and Argentineans live, the European footprint would be halved and the US footprint reduced to 25 per cent of the present.[13] Yet those South American people live healthy and sustaining lives. The Bhutanese, near the bottom of the GDP list have footprints of about 7 per cent of the USA or Canada, yet those people are deemed very high on their Gross National Happiness index. Many people leave the USA, Canada, the UK, and other advanced countries, for the simpler life styles of countries with lesser economies. They do it by choice and are happy with their simpler lives. So, reasonable reductions in the expectations of the richest societies need not be too onerous. To live lightly on the world, however, is not the ideal for which we tend to strive, though it should be.

Regarding CO2 emissions, as against the total ecological footprint, the USA is again way ahead of the rest with total emissions of 5,762,050 metric tons of carbon dioxide and a per capita rate of 20 tons. That compares with a UK per capita rate of 9 tons, and a Swiss, Swedish or French rate of 6 tons each per person.[14] Well, the people of those three countries probably lead contented lives with little desire to trade them for the American way of life. Yet they are individually creating 60 per cent less carbon than the people of the USA, and are arguably just as happy and proud of the nations in which they live. The per capita production of Canadians is about equal to their southern neighbours. I think it is clear that some easy CO2 reductions can be made without an excess of suffering by the most extravagant of people.

I do understand that people want a rich life and are self-serving, but, and this is where a hint of negativity and pessimism might creep in, I don't believe 9 or 10 billion of us can live this way, based on competition and the economic principle of unending growth. This is especially true when we are relying on empty consumerism to keep industry and trade humming. I certainly don't believe we do our descendants a favour by accelerating the harvesting of fossil fuels and the production of greenhouse gas emissions. To do so is truly, truly stupid as it will hasten, and deepen, very unfortunate environmental results that will be most horribly felt two or three generations into the future. If we try to keep up the present follies, we will have no nature left to work its magic upon us. This will be unfortunate, as nature and the earth's natural cycles keep our globe healthy. So, in the future, unless we change our ways, we may also have no fresh water to drink, nor air fresh enough to breath. It might be argued that our descendants, rather than inheriting an improved and enriched world, will actually inherit a corrupted void.

The fact is, there are not enough resources to continue our profligate ways. There may be enough land to provide food, but only at the expense of wilderness and other species. It is doubtful that there will be enough fish in the sea to feed us at 2012 rates of consumption. It is also unlikely there will be enough potable fresh water, in the regions where the big populations will be, or sufficient water to supply our needs for both agriculture and drinking. Now, we have to ask about all the other materials we use with such abandon, from iron ore to rare earths. When we look at the past two centuries of material over-use and project that into the future, even with new innovations, we have to ask how this can continue.

When we look into the future, not just 50 years, not just 150 but let's say 300 years we have to wonder what our descendants will do for materials. 300 years isn't long in the overall scheme of things, but it should be long enough for us to finally use up all the sequestered oil, coal and gas, and to be done with the last decorative marble to boot. The marble may be frivolous, but in the future, without hydrocarbons, where will our descendants obtain many of their basics necessities?

In our rush to industrialize we were able to use untapped mineral deposits that were building for billions of years. We were able to use thousand-year-old forest trees and untold millions of animals. With all that wealth gone, what will be left for our descendants? What will they use for their economic basics and industrial production? There should still be plenty of granite, which constitutes 75 per cent of the globes' surface, but will that suffice?

It is worth considering which of the nations are bio-capacity creditors and which are bio-capacity debtors. A bio-capacity creditor is a country with more renewable resources than the population uses. The healthiest, in terms of bio-capacity credits, is Brazil at over 150 per cent on the positive side. Canada, Australia and Argentine are also on the plus side, at 100-150 per cent.[15]

A bio-capacity debtor might be a desert country, with a large population but little food-growing potential, and no other resources. Some Saharan African countries and many in the Middle East fall under that category. They are described as being more than 150 per cent on the negative side of sustainability. The UK, Germany, China, Mexico and South Africa all fall on the 100-150 per cent negative. Much of Western Europe, India and the USA, of all places, fall on the 50-100 per cent negative.[16]

By far the greatest amount of our population falls on the debtor side, and many are in parts of the world where we cannot upgrade the productivity. So it is clear that we can't continue over-using resources as we are. We must break our habits and move to a better life while we still have the chance. What this move means is that we must reduce our expectations from unreasonable to sustainable. We must all understand that the Earth cannot expand like a balloon being pumped with more air. The Earth's ecological limits are finite and, no matter how much we might wish otherwise, we are obliged to live within those restraints.

Politicians, economists and others tell us that the only way forward is to follow the path of free enterprise capitalism. They tell us that there is, in fact, no other way to go. But supposing there are other routes to take – routes that we might find if only we were willing to explore alternatives with energy and enterprise. In the last chapter of this book I list a number of suggestions that might take us along an alternative path to long-term sustainability.

11 The Land and Wild Places

As I have no doubt said before: I do realize that we have amongst us multitudinous people who really don't give a hoot about our declining mineral wealth, diminishing wildlife or the loss of species. I hope they are concerned for the quality of our air and water though, as we definitely depend on those two. Another important element worth making a few comments about is soil.

Soil is important because we grow our food in, and on, it. It is made of a number of components. It often contains sand, which is usually ground up rock or seashells. Or it may be heavy with clay, which is decomposed rock from eons gone by. Soil may contain the dust from volcanic eruptions, or the chalk from the Purley Hills. Whatever the character, quality, or the quantity, of the desirable minerals in soil the most important material is humus. Humus is mainly rotted leaves, with a seasoning of dead animals and their excrement. Humus is lovely piquant stuff on which we depend for our vegetables and our meat.

Humus is fundamental, and its health is vital to our survival. It is a home to living soil organisms and a reservoir of nutrients. It is dead animal and vegetable matter digested by larva, worms, grubs and beetles, which are then digested again by microbes and bacteria. It is the 30 plus pounds of grass that has passed through the four stomachs of cows and oxen and lain spattered on the land. It is the corrupted bodies of birds; devoured by the maggots of blowflies, consumed by slime moulds and eaten by viruses. Bacteria and fungi all make the soil delicious to the plants that we love to eat. In an acre of soil may live millions of minute animals, all eating and being eaten. In a handful of soil may live a similar number of microbes.[1] It is lucky those microbes are so small. If they were large we would run shrieking from their horrible ugliness. Soil is life made of death, as the phoenix is reborn of fire. The death in soil feeds us anew. It is truly one of the wonders of the natural world.

We find that plants are fed by whatever constitutes the soil, including the essential minerals, and that the ingredients of the soil enrich and flavor those plants. The soil produces more plentiful and tasty turnips in one area but better Butter Lettuce in another. The cattle do best on this piece of land, sheep on that and grapes on another. Why do the grapes from one hillside make superior wine to the grapes from another? It is, to a large part, because of the earth on which they grow. As a famous fictitious farmer on a hilarious BBC radio comedy used to say in response to any question, "The anzzwer", he would say, "loizz in the zzoil". Well I don't know if it is quite true that every answer lies in the soil, but it is true that our survival relies upon healthy and productive soil.

In the early days of agriculture, we had found it necessary to adapt what we planted to the soil and climate of the land. We then bred animals and vegetables to the specifics of different agricultural regions. Now we try to adapt the land to our desired and standardized crops. One problem is that farmers now give a good part of their time to poisoning the soil with pesticides, herbicides and excessive fertilization.

Seventy years ago, farming and our handling of the soil, on which we all depend, relied upon natural cycles. In one such cycle, we planted different crops on a three-year rotation; thereby some of the crops or animals fed back to the soil some of the nutrients taken by other crops.

One year in three the land would be sown with grass, clover or root crops, on which sheep or cattle would feed. The animals would fertilize the soil with their excrement to bring it to good health. The next year wheat or other high value grains could be sown. The following year such legumes as peas or beans might be sown, as they fix nitrogen from the air in the soil. Pests, that were specific to one crop, found it difficult to get established since they would have to wait two years before the crop was re-planted. In some places a four-year crop rotation was used. The soil, when well treated, improved and supplied the nutrients the crops needed. We ate the crops, and the grass or root crops fed the cattle or sheep that then re-fertilized the land.

Once every aspect of the cycle was natural, and when the farmers returned the cow manure to the land, the land was enriched, in part, by the same nutrients and healthy bacteria that were there in the first place in the feed. Now little of this holds true. Now we grow millions of acres of the same monoculture plants year after year. Not only does this starve the land of nutrients and nitrogen, it also opens the plants to long-established and new pests, pests that evolve to thrive on whatever the single plant is. As the pests multiply, we have to introduce pesticides that are more virulent, till the pests evolve to withstand the poisons. The increasingly effective pesticides kill off every passing insect whether targeted or not, whether benevolent or not. These monoculture crops, and the developing pests, create huge requirements for more nitrogen fertilizer, and more noxious poisons, with which to soak the soil.

Now, much of the land is not enriched by manure expelled from cattle, sheep or chickens. It is instead enriched by nitrogen fertilizers made synthetically from chemicals. Initially these chemical fertilizers created far more productive soil resulting in large increases in agricultural production.[2] The Green Revolution of the post WW2 years has fed the huge increase in population over that same time span. Many believe this is bad for the long-term health of the soil, but feed us it has.

Some of the problems that result from the excessive use of nitrogen fertilizers include the strengthening of such pests as aphids and increased emissions of nitrous oxide (N_2O)–a greenhouse gas. More concerning problems are accumulations of such heavy metals as mercury, lead, arsenic, nickel, chromium and cadmium. A build-up of persistent organic pollutants also results.

Another great problem is the run-off of excessive nitrogen-rich compounds into the waterways. This creates eutrophication, which depletes the oxygen in the water, and in turn results in a serious die-off of the oceans' fauna. When the nitrate ions leach into groundwater that is then used by humans, they can cause what is known as 'Blue Baby Syndrome' in bottle-fed infants.[3] which can lead to hypoxia and eventually an infant's death.

It is a vast understatement to say we should care for the soil. Along with water and air, it is one of the three pillars on which all land-dwelling life depends. But what do we do to it? Amongst other things we practice agricultural and industrial practices that:

- Poison the soil with herbicides and pesticides.
- Saturate the soil with nitrogen.

- Allow the natural nutrients to be depleted.
- Make the soil sick by unsustainable practices.
- Encourage soil erosion.
- Allow the wind to blow it away.
- Allow the rain to wash it away.
- Bury the soil below concrete and asphalt.
- Bury it through blasting and mining.

It's worth remembering the 1930s dust bowls of the American southern prairies. Starting in 1932, 60 mph winds lifted the wonderful rich soil high into the air and carried it thousands of miles away to the Atlantic and Gulf of Mexico. In some areas up to 75 per cent of the valuable topsoil was blown away. Such natural calamities didn't happen when prairie grasses with roots twelve or more feet into the ground bound the soil. Then the grasslands could survive drought and wind storms. However the destruction of all things natural on the Great Plains soon put paid to that. The land affected was over 100,000,000 acres and by the time the drought ended, in 1940, 25 per cent of the farmers had left the land.[4]

If we want an example of the damage humans can do, this might be considered a good one. The prairies in 1850 were a perfect ecosystem of plants and animals living in harmony and even beauty. Then humans removed nearly all the wildlife and, at the turn of the 20th century, deep-ploughed the land. For twenty years they grew monocultured, yet bountiful, wheat crops, but by so doing they made the land untenable. Then sun, wind and a ten-year drought finished the job and eventually the people fled. They were lucky not to have turned the land into a desert. It was a clear example of our potency through ignorance. The story tells of a great and wonderful ecosystem that, since the last ice age, took millennia to perfect. We humans then required a mere eighty years to lay it waste. After ten years the rains did return, and productivity also returned, but another dustbowl could happen at any time.

A new dustbowl seems to be in the offing in California and Arizona. Large areas of Southern California and some cities in Arizona are wonderfully verdant and garden-like. However, the water comes from elsewhere and before the water was imported, much of that land was desert. One result of this diverted water has been the creation of incredibly fertile agricultural land in California. According to California's Agricultural Production Statistic for 2011, the farms and ranches of that state earned

$43.5 billion from their production. That was 15 per cent of the total US agricultural production. Agriculture is a huge part of California's wealth.

The trouble is that California and Arizona are fast running out of water. They have been spraying so much water onto the land (and people have been enjoying such long showers) that the aquifers are now polluted and running dry, and many of the rivers are little more than trickles by the time they reach the sea. One reason is that global warming is causing greatly reduced snow packs to feed both the rivers and the reservoirs, which are all down from the levels of twenty years ago. Situations of polluted aquifers and looming water shortages are presenting themselves in many parts of the globe. Some are similar to those developing in Southern California. A number of people are hoping that desalination of seawater will be the solution. However that may not be viable as the current technology is a heavy creator of greenhouse gases. It also increases the amount of salt in the local body of water. That isn't such a problem in the open sea, but it is a tremendous problem in such enclosed waters as the Persian Gulf. Soil is wonderful stuff for producing the food that all of humanity needs. However to enjoy that benefit we also need very large amounts of safe and unpoisoned fresh water.

Unfortunately North America is not alone in damaging its ecosystems. In China, overgrazing and deforestation has degraded the soils at a rate 30 times faster than nature can replenish them. The speed of soil loss to water and wind can be very rapid once fertile soil is ploughed. Apparently it takes nature about 500 years to produce just one inch of soil in arable areas. In our post-war drive to increase food production, we have succeeded in degrading more than 25 per cent of the Earth's farmland.[5] On top of that, when we now look at the planet's ice-free land, 75 per cent of what we see has been shaped by us. Our influence has been so huge that the latest geological epoch has been named the Anthropocene, or the human Epoch.[6]

Honeybees and bumblebees are in trouble in most of their range worldwide. They are dying in extraordinary numbers all over our Earth and we can't be too sure why. Bees, and other insects, are pollinators, and it is thanks to them that the flowers bear fruit, and that we enjoy much of the wonderful food that is available to us. The pollinators are absolutely fundamental to the health of both the natural world and to most agriculture. Orchards resplendent in fruit-tree blossoms but silent of bees are love unfulfilled. Few apples or pears will swell and ripen to sweet lusciousness without pollinators. By 2013, many orchardists in Canada were having to hand-pollinate, with little brushes, the blossoms on their fruit trees. That is an unbelievable amount of work for a human, though it's all in a day's work for a few hundred bees.

Scientific research is pointing the finger at a family of pesticides named neonicotinoids, which had been in use over the previous 10 years. One would think that even the slightest suggestion of the cause would be reason enough ban the use of that poison, but not a bit of it. The European Union placed a two-year ban on the pesticides, but the North American countries didn't - at least, not at the time of writing.

Will we never learn? We used liberal amount of DDT till it was found to be killing the young of raptors and causing bird numbers to plummet. The Argentinean farmers sprayed monocrotophos on their crops till it was found to be killing not just the grasshoppers, but the Swainson's Hawks as well. Now we insist on using the neonicotinoids that are apparently killing the bees.

For 200,000 years we managed very well without environmental poisons in our lives. Now, after 10 years of using neoncotinoids, we refuse to do without them, regardless of the potential harm. One of the most fundamental acts of nature, the pollination of plants, is threatened by our profligate use of a certain poison, yet we won't stop the poisoning because the proof is not yet positive. This is total madness. Are the farmers and government officials insane? I fear they are and, if we don't protest, I fear we are as well.

The insecticides that are liberally distributed all over the agricultural land don't just affect the targeted specific bug or grub. What is poisonous to one species will also be poisonous to others, though maybe less potently so. The disappearance of birds and butterflies from the countryside isn't just an unrelated coincidence that happened at the same time as the distribution of pesticides. Just as the bugs are poisoned, so are the birds that eat the poisoned insects, and so are the animals that graze the sprayed grasses. And just as all those animals take in the poisons, so do we humans. It is assumed that the amount we ingest won't be enough to kill us, but who knows how our bodily functions, or reproductive processes, may be affected in the long term by small doses? It is now believed that in Canada 46 per cent of men and 41 per cent of women will develop cancer in their lifetimes.[7] 25 per cent of Canadians and 13 per cent worldwide will die of cancer. There has to be a reason for this. It does seem reasonable to assume that the poisons in the environment could damage our health.* They seem to be damaging the health of bumblebees.

Although we use some chemicals with little apparent effect, we should not assume that chemicals that some animals can absorb are not poisonous to other species, or those that do no harm to some animals are not poisonous to us. Certain birdwing butterflies depend on eating the toxic *Aristolacia* vines to make themselves poisonous to potential predators, and Koala bears eat only food that is poisonous to most other animals. The dreaded Poison Ivy *(Toxicodendron radicans)*,[8] of the North American forests, has a dreadful effect on humans, yet is browsed by some animals with no problem. We really don't know what the chemicals we produce are actually doing out there.

I believe the environmental and green NGOs are now vital to our wellbeing. It is the scientists and concerned citizens who, being aware of problems, raise them with governments and industry. They do so in attempts to save us from so many excesses and dangerous activities. They do crucial work. They draw attention to chemical pollution and to health questions regarding our fish, meat and vegetable foods. They lobby corporations and industries that pollute or work unsustainably, and they advise governments, if those bodies will listen. To a world dominated by industrial and business ethics, environmentalists have become increasingly vital both as watchdogs and whistle-blowers. Yet, many governments view environmentalists as the enemy of the status quo, rather than the friend of the people that they truly are.

There are many wise and decent agronomists who use organic methods to grow the foods that we consume. It is assumed that organic crop production, though good for our health, won't feed the billions of us that need feeding, but new experiences show that not to be true. In a 2012 Canadian Broadcasting Corporation documentary entitled, *The New Green Giants*, Saskatchewan farmer Garth Glass, who grows grains for the Nature's Path Company, described his findings over an eight-year period of farming organically. He stated that there was first a flush of weeds till the soil became healthier. "Slowly but surely as we work with the soil it becomes better. As we work with the soil it comes in balance, then we have less of a weed problem."

---

* It is worth remembering here, that we humans and insects are made of the same stuff, proteins and chemicals, of which all animal species are made. The poisons that kill the insects have the potential to kill us too. We just need to ingest enough of them. One problem is that we have no idea how much of any poison we are absorbing over time.

California farmer Dick Peixoto, who produces celery and other salad crops for Earthbound Farms, is able to compare the results of 15 years of conventional growing with his more recent ten-year experience of organic farming. Before going organic he would spray his celery 15 -20 times just to get rid of leaf miners, and over the years the yields would go down, as the ground grew tired. Now, working organically, he says, "The ground has got better over the years." He went on to say, "Organic production is as good or better than it was in the conventional years, in every crop we grow."

Such food companies as Earthbound Farms are by no means small players in food production. Their 150 independent growers have converted 37,000 acres to organic practices, which has meant avoiding the use of eleven million pounds of synthetic chemicals on the soil. It seems that, as organic agriculture becomes more mainstream instead of a fringe activity, the seventy-year old experiment with chemical farming is being shown to be an undesirable practice foisted on us by the chemical companies and the irresponsible mega agri-businesses.

Since my childhood, vast new areas of wild land have been cleared for agriculture and plantations, most of it at the expense of forests and grasslands. I very clearly remember, in the mid-1950s, when I was about fifteen, reading of Brazil's plans to clear part of the rainforest and to build a new capital city. It would be away from coastal Rio de Janeiro, and nearer the geographical centre of the country. In those days, the planned Brasilia was deep in the rainforest, and the world was in a great fuss about it. I remember the concern was that it would be the thin end of the wedge in terms of exploitation of the vast unexplored Amazon. Well that was certainly one prediction that came true. Brasilia is now surrounded by agriculture and a good many miles south and east of where the forest now begins.

Early in 2012, a bill went before Brazil's President, Dilma Vana Rousseff for ratification that would have been a huge step backwards in the protection of the remaining Amazon rainforest. The country's agri-business lobby backed the bill. They wanted free rein to turn the Amazon into agricultural land. The bill, if passed, would have opened more areas of uncut rainforest to deforestation. It would also have made law enforcement in the Amazon more difficult, and have provided amnesty to the criminals who have been caught destroying the protected forest.[9] It is clear that the agri-business people–and we can be sure all resource extraction types are behind this–want a sort of Wild West to be the model in the Amazon. It is also clear that the businessmen and despoilers are also often the members of government who make the laws regarding the forests.

Whether or not the President signs this bill into law we can be sure that more disaster in the Amazon will follow. Apparently 80 per cent of Brazilians want the rainforest protected, and on the earlier election campaign trail Dilma promised to protect the forest. But then most politicians make many promises before elections. The very fact that such a question is even an issue in this day and age, when we all know the consequences of such proposals, is truly disconcerting. It just proves that the destroyers are out there at all times, greedily lurking . . . and waiting to pounce. Still, Dilma was a left-wing radical guerrilla and freedom fighter in her youth,[10] so let's hope she sticks to her guns on this one. However, even if she does prevent the destruction, she won't be president forever, and eventually more sympathetic governments will be elected that will bend to the plans of the developers, loggers and politicians.

With the massive population explosion and the search for more agricultural land, the pressure on the Amazon and all other forests is terrible. So what are the prospects for future wilderness? Will our descendants wonder at miraculous verdant nature, or will they have nothing but agricultural land and smart phones to fire their imaginations? Already the oak forests of old England are known only as history. The eastern hardwood forests of the United States are as diminished as are those of eastern Brazil. The Ganges watershed forests are gone with little trace, while those of the Mekong and Southeast Asia are reduced to small remnants. The forests of the Pacific Northwest still cover most of the original landmass, but as plantation instead of ancient forest. Only parts of the Amazon and African rainforests remain in any great mass. Those two places, parts of New Guinea, and Antarctica are the only areas that might now be described as wilderness.

I wrote earlier that I believed the destruction of the North American prairies the greatest crime till that time. Well, I believe it has now been eclipsed. Now the most wicked and unpardonable crime is the destruction of the earth's great forests in search of more agricultural and plantation land. In the 20th century, we caused the destruction of huge swaths of natural forest worldwide, as well as nearly all the wild animals that those areas supported. That rate of destruction continues into the 21st century with the inevitable consequences for the few animals surviving.

12 Feline Predators and Others

If North Americans won't protect their wolves, how can we expect the Africans and Asians to protect their lions and tigers?

The African wildlife, and most of the rest of the world's wildlife, is going the same way as that of North America and Asia. It had been an unhurried decline compared with that of the large mammals between 1850-1880 in the United States. My guess is that it won't take the majority of African governments long to conveniently designate as vermin the remaining predators once they decide to convert the open rangeland to agriculture and grazing. It certainly won't take long if they use the US and Canadian governments as role models.

In 2011, the British Columbia government lifted restrictions on the hunting of wolves. This was at the insistence of ranchers and hunters who want the wilderness reserved for their own ends. In the United States five or six state governments were also moving to allow the shooting and poisoning of wolves. These wolves were the offspring of recent reintroductions, from British Columbia and Mexico, to some of the states that historically supported large wolf populations. Two steps forward and two steps backwards.

Even in the government of an advanced country such as the USA there are politicians who believe they are entitled to set bad policy examples for the rest of the world. The mindset of the American holocaust, that all but eliminated that country's wildlife and wild places during the 19th and 20th centuries, seems to dominate, though held in check at the moment. If it is given the chance to re-emerge as a force of government policy, as seems likely, it will set an example that could well be emulated in Africa and all over the world. If North Americans cannot protect their wolves, how can we expect the Africans and Asians to protect their lions and tigers?

The hostility by some humans against predators is incredible. It appears that the prime top predator does not want any other to succeed. They are so greedy, these predators!

The world's non-human predators are an integral and necessary part of a healthy ecosystem, yet they are persecuted mercilessly. Lions and tigers may seem tough but they are in trouble all over the world.

In Africa, the lion population has decreased, from about 1.2 million in 1850, to 20,000 in 2010.[1] That is more than a 99 per cent decrease in the past 150 years. Many fear that, as with the cheetah and other predators, the lion will soon be on track for extinction. When this happens the cause will unquestionably be human agricultural and hunting pressures. We may not even have to wait to see what industrial and agricultural policies the African governments come up with to witness the African lion brought to extinction.

Historically, lions thrived from India across west Asia into Europe. There are believed to have been at least three Asiatic subspecies, but since none of the European lions have been seen since the first century CE, little is known of them. It is not known whether they were the Persian Lion *(Panthera leo persica)*, a remnant population of the Cave Lion *(panthera leo spelaea)* or a subspecies of their own. Whatever they were, Greece is believed to have been their last hunting ground. They were considered common in 498 BCE when Xerxes' baggage train suffered frequent lion attacks during his advance into Greece. The Arabian Lions are considered to have been plentiful in southwest Asia into the 19th century. The Persian Lion still hangs on in the Gir forest in eastern India in numbers of about 400 in the 2010 census. There may also have been a Bengal lion. Asian animals must once have been as plentiful as were those of Africa and

North America, though we don't now think of the non-tropical parts of that continent, as being rich in wildlife.

The first known depiction in art of a king hunting the Asiatic lion is from 3000BC. That symbol of the brave king fighting with the king of the beasts has been used extensively since.

One wonderful series of lion images is in the British Museum. They are on the Assyrian slabs from the palace of Ashurbanipal (668-627 BCE) at Nineveh, (across the Tigris River from Mosul in present day Iraq). The slabs, which lined the palace rooms, are of gypsum with some very detailed and sensitively carved images. The carvings are superb records of wars and kingly feats but also, because of the attention to detail, of the fashions, clothing and fabrics of the time. They depict the styles worn, not only by the Assyrians, but also by other peoples of the Fertile Crescent area. The details of chariot construction and decoration are clear and easily read, as are the harnesses of the horses. The hunting scenes illustrate the local flora and fauna of the time such as wild cattle, asses and gazelles fleeing over the forested land.

The lion hunts were often staged affairs with the animals being freed from cages into an area where the indomitable king could demonstrate his bravery, prowess and skill. The scene from one set of panels depicts 18 lions variously, from attacking King Ashurbanipal, to going after his spare horse, to lying dead and injured. Two of the injured, a lion and a lioness are rendered with great sensitivity. The lioness, pierced by three arrows, drags her hind limbs and roars defiantly while a lion, with the wounds from four very large arrows, appears to be staggering, or attempting to flee while coughing up blood. One unintended side effect of the carvings is that the well-armed king appears to be an even greater savage than the lions.

In Julian Reade's book, *Assyrian Sculpture*, he tells of Ashurnasirpal II, a predecessor by some two hundred years to Ashurbanipal. His scribes wrote the record of Ashurnasirpal's achievements, which include the following statement: "the Gods Ninurta and Nergal, who love my priesthood, gave me the wild animals of the plains, commanding me to hunt. Thirty elephants I trapped and killed, 257 wild oxen I brought down with my weapons, attacking from my chariot; 370 great lions I killed with hunting spears." Considering there were thirty-one kings of Assyria from 1132 – 609 BC,[2] one might be forgiven for suspecting they had quite an effect on the local wildlife numbers.

There were, at the time, plenty of large herbivores to support large numbers of lions, cheetahs and leopards. The prey included Wisent (the European species of bison, which was very similar to the American buffalo), wild cattle, Tarpen, Elk, deer, gazelle, sheep, goats and, according to Ashurnasirpal II, elephants. Now you will find few wild animals of any kind anywhere in the Middle East. As mentioned in chapter 5, the Arabian Oryx was one of the most recent to go, finished off by machine guns in the 1970s.

That Ashurnasirpal killed all those wild animals in some form of single combat, says something both wonderful and terrible about humans. It is wonderful that we can be courageous enough to face huge wild elephants with little more than a spear. Our courage has enabled us to undertake magnificent ventures in the realms of exploration, engineering and the rest. But we are terrible in the disregard and utter cruelty that we show to other species. This disrespect has cleared nearly all of Asia of the huge numbers of animals that once thrived there. The terrible disdain still felt by so many humans, is now ridding the rest of our world of its wildlife.

Other lions that have become extinct include the Cape Lion *(Panthera leo melanochaitus)*, the last of which was hunted in Natal by one General Bissett in 1865. Those lions were among the largest, with long and full black manes, tail and stomach tufts. The Barbary Lion *(Panthera leo leo)* was the archetypal lion, and the lion of Coliseum, gladiatorial and Christian-eating fame. It was about the same size as the Cape Lion with a weight of up to 500lbs (230kg) and, again, with a huge mane but of a dull yellow-ochre colour. In Roman times, it hunted across the breadth of North Africa, which was heavily forested at the time, but with Roman collecting, the felling of forests and the desertification of formerly fertile lands, its territory shrank till, in recent times, it was found only to the west of Libya. The killing continued, with the widespread use of firearms. The last Barbary Lion was found trying to avoid humans in the Atlas Mountains in 1922, and was, of course, shot.[3]

There were two contiguous historic ranges for the tiger in Asia, The first is believed to have covered an area south of the Himalayas, from India in the west, to Java in the southeast, and up through China to Manchuria in the northeast. The second area started on the east coast of the Caspian Sea and ranged through northern Iraq, east to the western border of Mongolia. It is hard to work out the total area in which tigers lived, but it must have been somewhere close to 7.75 million sq miles, or 20 million km2. I arrived at that number simply by totaling the land areas of India, China, South East Asia, and of Kazakhstan to cover the northern population. The areas may have been considerably larger, or somewhat smaller if we take into account the land within that mass that had habitat unsuitable for tigers.

Depending on the density of prey animals, a single female is thought to need anywhere from 4 sq miles (10km2) to 156 sq miles (400km2). So, assuming plenty of prey in the old days, and using the first set of figures, we arrive at a one-time potential population of 2 million female tigers. Going on the conservative number we arrive at 50,000 female tigers.

Males are thought to need about double the land of a female, so that suggests a number from 25,000 to 1 million males. Together those numbers give totals of something between 75,000 and 3 million tigers a few hundred years ago. The mid mark might be something close to 1.5 million.

In 2008, the International Union for Conservation of Nature and Natural Resources (IUCN) gave wild tiger numbers as 3,400-5,100 worldwide. The IUCN said that in 2008 they lived in 6 per cent of their former range. It is believed there were at least 100,000 at the turn of the 20th century. Of the nine subspecies three are now extinct. The Bali Tiger (*Panthera tigris balica*) became extinct circa 1937, the Caspian Tiger (*P. t. urgata*) in the 1970s and the Javan Tiger (*P. t. sondaica*) in the 1980s.

The South China Tiger, or Amoy Tiger (*Panthera tigris amoyensis*), is thought by some to live in the area where the original tiger developed. Therefore, it could be a relic of the stem animal from which all others evolved. In the 1950s, the population numbered about 4000 individuals, but by 1987, they numbered about 30 or 40. By 2012, none of these tigers had been seen for twenty years. It is believed that the numbers are too small and inbred for future breeding successes. If they still exist, they do so in such small and separated patches of habitat that the long-term prospects of healthy breeding are poor. The separation of viable numbers of animals from each other is a big problem. It is a problem for many species. One estimate is that no reserve has more than 250 tigers, with many having very few.[4][5]

We hear a great deal in the news about tigers, yet we hear little about the poor old leopards (*Panthera pardus*), which are also diminishing in numbers. Leopards are very adaptable animals and will frequent nearly any type of habitat to which prey animals are attracted. So their range, which covered all of Africa, across southern Asia to a little north of Korea, included nearly all terrains except the Sahara and Arabian deserts. They have now been extirpated from about a quarter of their former range, are greatly fragmented in the majority of their habitats, and only continue in good numbers in sub-Saharan Africa. In 2012 they were considered not threatened.

A total of nine leopard subspecies exist, such as the Sri Lankan, Anatolian and Southeast Asian leopards, so we must assume that some have more secure numbers than others. The Arabian leopard, of which 100-200 survive, is considered critically endangered. The animal used to be widespread across the Middle East, but is now found only in Yemen, southern Oman and the Negev Desert. The human population expansion, and spread of goat-herders into ever more remote regions, pretty well guarantees these animals will not grace our Earth for much longer.[6] The Amur Leopard is the most threatened with an estimated 30-50 animals in the wild. Those few live in Russia, just north of the Chinese border.

The lovely Clouded Leopard of Southeast Asia is in very serious trouble, with habitat loss and poaching being the greatest threats. According to Liz Mellem of ForceChange.com, Clouded Leopards have been losing 10 per cent of their habitat per year since 1997. If that is so, it does give an idea of the amount of habitat lost. And we have to remember that, when it is lost to one species, it is lost to all the species of that biosphere.

Cheetahs *(Acinonyx jubatus)*, 100,000 of which once hunted over most of Africa, and from the Middle East to the Indian border with Burma, now number about 10,000 in twenty-five southern African countries. Possibly 50-100 survive in Iran.[7] They are listed as vulnerable. Cheetahs are of particular concern because they are both poor breeders and not adaptable to new environments. Consequently, they do not survive habitat destruction or change.

The American Jaguar *(Panthera onca)*, though very similar in appearance to the leopard, has a range from the southern United States, to northern Argentina. It is not considered threatened at the moment but it is in a steep decline, due mostly to habitat loss and fragmentation. It is also a prime target of gun toting ranchers and farmers. Following a great decline in numbers due to hunting, they are now protected in nearly all countries. They used to range over much of the southern United States, but have been hunted out of most of that traditional range. It is believed that a few still survive in the US, in southern Arizona. However, there are plans to build a fence across the border with Mexico to keep illegal immigrants from entering the USA. That barricade will make it impossible for animals to move from the south. This in turn will deny the possibility of any new animals entering the southern states to provide genetic variation to the few animals already there.[8 9]

The Mountain Lion *(Puma concolor)*, or cougar, had an historic range in both American continents south of the Arctic. It was hunted out of most of North America, save for a population in the Pacific Northwest and another in Florida. Since protections were put into place, the western cat has built its numbers well. The eastern animal is also returning to a few states in the South. Unfortunately though, the Florida Panther *(Puma concolor coryi)* was thought to number fewer than 100 animals in the year 2012.[10 11]

There are, of course, a great many other species of feline predators not mentioned here. They include: the Golden Cats of Africa and Asia, and the Bay Cat, Snow Leopard, Caracal, Ocelot and so many more. They are all in decline, though there is one feline predator whose numbers we can be sure are not diminishing. The one feline that is increasing in numbers is the domestic cat.

With all the destruction of lions and tigers, it is worth mentioning the return of just one herbivore to Asia that will now be able to live with little fear of predators. The Eurasian Bison or Wisent *(Bison bonasus)*, all of which are descended from 12 zoo animals following the shooting of the last wild animals in 1927, was reintroduced to Kyrgyzstan in 2005. They must be almost the only large animals remaining in Western Asia south of the Arctic Circle.

The small number of wild animals surviving in Europe, the lower 45 States of the US, most of eastern Canada and nearly all of the vast continent of Asia is a terrible testament to the destructive ways of the world's most successful predator and most advanced life form. It is difficult to estimate what the number of large mammals on those three continents would have been, say three thousand years ago but, extrapolating from the numbers in Africa and North America at the time of European contact, it must have been many thousand times more than it is now. Someone has figured that just a few thousand years ago lions outnumbered humans as the topmost predator. Still, we developed firearms and they didn't, so we don't have to worry about the potential for our extinction being caused by lions.

Could today's Asian, European and North American animal numbers be, say, 40 per cent of their historic high number and still allow the human population to be the 5.5 billion that it is today on those three continents? I don't see why we shouldn't have our agriculture and the animals their land too. I do realize that wild lions, wandering hungrily amongst excitable city-goers, might have unhappy outcomes, but I'm sure we could plan around such difficulties. The main change we would have to make is to stop being so greedy and so vicious. I do realize that most people couldn't care less, but I think the wildlife destruction is disgraceful and a horrible indictment of the human stewardship of this Earth.

13 North America & Africa

The impetus toward a more sustainable future got an initial boost with the 1992 Rio Summit, or to give it its full title *The United Nations Conference on Environment and Development*. The intent of the conference was to place the environment and sustainability at the forefront of government policy. It had to do with the things touched on in this book but at a time when it may not have seemed too late. The Rio Summit and the resulting document titled *Agenda 21* dealt with many of the problems that environmentalists, industrialists and economists were concerned about.

108 heads of state attended from the 172 countries that took part, and NGOs sent 2400 representatives. It was a worldwide big deal with good short-term results. At heart, *Agenda 21* went to some lengths to suggest how we might live on this planet without destroying it. The document even provided estimates of the annual implementation costs, to developing nations, of US $600 billion (about 1 trillion in 2012 money). 25 per cent of those moneys would be provided by the developed nations.

It is mostly forgotten now, but it did focus many governments on what needed to be done, even if there were few long-term benefits. The European nations seem to be the jurisdictions keenest to act on the summit's findings, and the North American governments appear to be the least keen to take note. Canada then was a keen participant. In fact Canada was seen as one of the good guys and a jurisdiction in which hope lay. In 2012, under Stephen Harper, Canada was quite shameful in its disregard of good and sustainable stewardship. I am picking on Canada here for two reasons. The first is that Canadians used to feel pride in the nation's role of peacekeeper and good world citizen. Previous Canadian governments were keen signatories to the World Court, the banning of land mines, the Kyoto Protocol and a great many more treaties and agreements, many of which the United States refused to sign. Secondly because, when the Canadian government follows bad practices, we can be sure many less-developed countries will follow such a lead with enthusiasm. They can point the finger at Canada as an example that should be emulated. In June 2012, the Canadian government spoke out forcefully against a UN proposal to control and track the global trade in firearms. On Monday 2 July, 2012, the foreign ministers of the UK, Germany, France and Sweden wrote an editorial for the Guardian newspaper in which they said, "The overwhelming majority of UN member states have shown a true desire to address the problems posed by unregulated trade in conventional arms." They described that trade as "a growing threat to humanity." Yet the Canadian government was against such controls.[1] It is unbelievable how far Canada sank with the result of just one election.

As already mentioned, the Canadian Prime Minister was truly miffed that his country's citizens would denounce his jolly rollicking idea to expand Canada's economy and to jack up Canada's CO_2 emissions to astronomical heights by expanding the tar sands. So he tried to stifle dissent. He and his minister of resources particularly disliked environmental groups putting their oars in, especially if they received any money from outside the country - the theme being that only those directly involved should have any say on Canada's energy proposals. This is rather like saying that we in Canada can have no say on what happens abroad. We can't send money or letters in support of the Penan of Borneo when trying to prevent their homeland forests from being felled. We shouldn't be allowed to offer help in stopping the slaughter of Orangutans in Borneo and Sumatra nor rhinos in Africa or Asia. Nor should we have any say on what happens to the Amazon. Only the Brazilians can speak about the Amazon – and, for that matter, only those actually living in it.

This is total nonsense. Every part of our planet is interconnected and we are all responsible for the whole global community. After all, the poisoned air that emanates from any one country does not recognize national borders, nor do migrating species. Soon we will see plans to develop agricultural, industrial and urban projects in every flora-rich and fauna-rich area, be it in northern Canada, Amazonia or on the African veldt, and, according to Mr. Harper, no one outside of the country in question should have the right to say anything. If we all follow the wise Stephen Harper we will all ignore the destruction and allow the industrialists, the energy companies and the governments to do as they choose. And if any of those industrialists, energy companies or governments happens to be corrupt or careless of the future, well good luck to them. The rest of us must keep quiet and keep shopping.

I don't a double standard think is acceptable; that those of us fortunate enough to live in Canada, or the United States, should be able to criticize the policies of other jurisdictions, if we won't allow outsiders to criticize ours. I believe that when the citizens of the world see injustices or harmful and destructive policies in other parts of the world, they should be free to express their views. We must realize that every flawed argument used by Canada to justify its development proposals can be used by others to justify their own. When the African governments really get steam up on their own 'development at all costs and to hell with the wildlife' strategies, I assume Mr. Harper and his Conservative MPs will be standing on the sidelines cheering them on while saying, "It is their country not ours. Canadians must mind their own business."

One of my personal creeds is that the earth's natural heritage belongs to all of us. It is neither for some local developer with dollar signs in his eyes, nor for the local government of the day, to determine the annihilation of a species or of an ecosystem. They do not have the right. And it's not just for a nation of people to decide either. We are all custodians of our earth. An individual, who might own a piece of land, has the privilege of caring for and protecting that land. He should not have the right to destroy all that lives on it. Nor should he have the right to shoot a threatened species that happens to visit. The same ethics should apply within a nation's borders. Our Earth belongs to future generations and we should all be protecting it for each other and for the future.

A person doesn't have to visit Borneo to want the Orangutans, Proboscis Monkeys and hornbill birds safe from extinction. I have visited Borneo and I have seen rare species, but others may never see them and still wish for, and expect, their survival into the future. I don't have to visit Brazil to know that the Amazon must be protected from destruction. It is just plain common sense.

The majority of us may never see the Cerulean Paradise Flycatcher of Sangihe Island. However, whether or not it becomes extinct is still important to the worldwide community. The people of Sangihe Island, and those of the rest of Indonesia, should not be the only ones allowed a say. We must all have the opportunity, and the right, of involvement.

It is such an interesting double standard. The Canadian Government tells us that only those most closely affected should be involved in the decision-making. Yet the indigenous people in Canada, and first peoples from all over the world, are usually given the least say when it comes to chopping down their forests or developing a mine on their homeland. At the same time the industrialists are given full rights and protections including the benefits of foreign investment.

The Canadian Government wants to preclude everyone from the discussions regarding the proposed oil pipelines across Canada except, of all people, the oil and pipeline companies. It is all so horrible it reminds me of the English expression 'He's dafter than a soft brush'. How much more insane can things get than having those companies police themselves? On top of all this, the government, in April 2012, introduced a bill entitled C-38. This bill was to speed up the implementation of the Federal Budget that had been tabled in Parliament on March 29, 2012.[2] The bill was an easy way to vote a group of acts through parliament without voting on every individual act. The problem was that the budget bill also included lots of issues beyond those of the budget. It included a new environment act which would, amongst other things, abolish the Kyoto Protocol Implementation Act (Canada's way of dealing with climate change), shorten the list of protected species and give the cabinet more powers to ignore the decisions of Canada's National Energy Board. At the time, the Conservative government had a majority in parliament so, without raising the question in the House, they set themselves to gut the country's environmental protections. And this happened in a western industrialized democracy. Imagine the chance the environment has in those less developed and less democratic nations too numerous to name here.

Such appalling attitudes bode very ill for the future of humans and our planet. This is the time when we should be most emphatic in our defense of our globe's integrity, and of the great and fundamental systems that enable life to exist. However, in 2012, the governments of Canada and the USA seem intent on being the leaders of those who act as if we have learned nothing over the past one hundred years.

There are those, the Canadian Prime Minister seems to be one, who deny the human ability to seriously affect our environment. Or if they recognize the fact, believe it to be less important than keeping the economy humming till it crashes. I suppose the most ardent hope for most politicians and industrialists is that, when the Earth does crash, it won't be when they are in office. Do they really believe that once they are out of office the long term effects of their policies won't matter? Speaking just for myself, if I had the authority and power I would want my name remembered with affection for the good I had done. The thought of being dammed by future generations, because of my policies has no appeal to me whatsoever.

Joe Oliver, Canada's Minister for Natural Resources, stated on January 25, 2012, that environmental reviews of proposed industrial projects must be restricted in time. No matter how complex and potentially damaging to the environment, the time spent studying the impacts of such projects must be shortened, otherwise foreign investment dollars will leave the country. "Where will that money go?" you might ask. To poor or corrupt countries where the environmental reviews are non-existent, of course. I believe the Canadian government should be playing the good citizen role and lead by example. Good policies will encourage other countries to introduce more stringent environmental reviews. Mr. Oliver spoke of environmental NGOs as being radical and using abusive methods to delay such projects as the Enbridge Northern Gateway Pipeline. The gulfs between those who wish to protect the Earth, and its future, and those intent on destruction for profit seems to be growing, at least with regard to Canada's right wing politicians and polluters.

This is what is so truly discouraging regarding our future prospects. It seems that the more the planet's health is compromised, and the more critical environmental protections become, the more ruthless and careless become the politicians who are trying to sustain business as usual.

In the Vancouver Sun dated March 17, 2012 Peter O'Neil reported that the Harper government was intent on watering down the Federal Fisheries Act. A previous Conservative government introduced that act in 1986. So presumably it wasn't some dumb foolishness enacted by a radical leftist party that the Conservatives would despise. The government desired to remove any mention of fish habitat. This is in response to pressure from mining groups who find their plans delayed by Fisheries Act decisions. It is absolutely clear, that no matter how carefully a jurisdiction may try to protect the natural environment under its care, there will always be a later legislative body waiting to turn back the clock if they can get away with it.

2012 seemed to have been a remarkably bad year for the Canadian environment. In the spring of that year, British Columbia's provincial government started maneuvering to have BC's protected forests taken out of protection. This was because the Pine Beetle *(Dendroctonus ponderosae)* had killed huge swaths of pine forest. The amount affected was 70,000 square miles, or 18.1 million hectares. So then, the forest industry wanted the protected forests made available to keep the loggers working. It took years of struggle to get those few forests areas protected because of their extraordinary environmental value and because other forests were falling so fast. Now, at the first economic problem, the government was willing to sacrifice them. If BC couldn't save its tiny percent of protected forest at the first sign of trouble, what hope is there for the rest of the world's protected places?

It is worth mentioning here, that British Columbia's interior used to have very cold winters. That cold killed off the Pine Beetle and another tree-killing bug known as the Spruce Budworm *(Choristoneura occidentallis)* that attacks the native Douglas Fir and other species. Now, thanks to man-made global warming, those cold winter temperatures of minus 35 Celsius no longer happen and the destructive bugs are left to proliferate. So our industrial ways created this warming problem, but we now want to use the result as an excuse to destroy even more of the struggling natural world.

In 1995, 15 Canadian wolves, from the province of Alberta, were reintroduced to a Rocky Mountain wilderness area in the US state of Idaho. Idaho is just south of the Canadian border. Canadian wolves, of which there are plenty, were also reintroduced to Yellowstone National Park at the same time. Before the reintroductions, at least 45 public hearings were held in Idaho, Montana and Wyoming. In 1996, a further 20 wolves were released into the Idaho wilderness. These reintroductions were the result of wolves having been extirpated from most of the USA. Some of the introduced wolves were killed by cougars, one was killed by an elk, a septuagenarian rancher shot one while it was eating a stillborn calf, and some of the animals traveled beyond Idaho. By 1999 Idaho was thought to hold 176-180 wolves, by 2004 that number was about 454 wolves and by 2012 the number was close to a thousand.

While this was going on, to the south plans were underway to reintroduce the Mexican Grey Wolf. This animal had been reduced to a total of 5 animals worldwide. These were all captured in 1980 and used in a breeding program, to save the subspecies from total extinction. The program was successful, despite the potential for inbreeding problems due to a lack of genetic diversity. By 1998 the captive population had increased to 300 and releases began in both Arizona and New Mexico.

Now, some 15 or so years after those good news stories, calm and rational discourse has given way to battles of words and the mass killings of wolves. The environmentalists defend the right of wolves to live and breed, while the ranchers and hunting groups apparently want to kill the lot. Congress took the Grey Wolf from under the protection of the Endangered Species Act, allowing wolves to now be treated as vermin. By 2013, about 400 wolves have been killed in Idaho alone, where the state government now wants to limit the total number to 150. This is after previously committing to maintain a population of 518-732 animals. All this in a state that is as close to uninhabited wilderness as you can get.[3]

The wolves are being shot in Idaho, Wyoming, Montana and Oregon in the north and in New Mexico and Arizona in the south. So much for saving those last five Mexican Grey Wolves. The animals are shot from planes and helicopters, poisoned and caught in leg-hold traps. The cruel hunting fraternity in the US is lobbying very hard to be able to kill as many wolves as those semi-humans choose. I am getting the picture that there are people who do not see the value of retaining the natural prey/predator relationship in the wild. In fact, one has to wonder how we can possibly afford the high costs of reintroductions when a minority of a given population will go to such lengths to defeat the undertakings.

So while a great many intelligent and concerned North American scientists and citizens are pumping their time and money into saving such predators as the tigers of Asia and the lions and cheetahs of Africa, another group of less caring US citizens is intent on wiping out the reintroduced carnivores in their own land. How is it possible that, while people over the whole planet are concerned about species extinctions the US state governments name their few wolves 'vermin', and pass laws to encourage their extermination?[4] Now that is a double standard if ever there was one.

In February 2012, the Governor of Louisiana, Bobby Jindel, vetoed a bill that would have helped prevent sea turtles from being caught and drowned in shrimp nets. It is estimated that thousands are thus caught and drowned each year by the fleet fishing in the Gulf of Mexico. Apparently the State has a law that actually bars the enforcement of shrimp fishers using turtle exclusion devices.[5] Is that a cruel and outdated law or what?

The Sea Turtle Restoration project is a non-profit organization that, as its name suggests, is focused on turtle protection and population reestablishment. Responding to the cowardly veto, that group led 26 other environmental conservation organizations to pressure the Governor to repeal the laws. It is impossible to imagine what, apart from nasty underhand nefarious dealings, could have induced the Governor to support such an antiquated and outrageous law.

I am pleased to say that one final piece of news concerning North American wildlife has a happy outcome. What a relief?

In July 2012, a battle between the Canadian province of New Brunswick and the American state of Maine, was finally resolved. It had to do with the River Herring mentioned in an earlier chapter. In 1995, in response to demands from Smallmouth Bass fishermen, the state of Maine erected barriers to deny herring access to an 85-kilometer stretch of the St. Croix River. The complaints of the fishermen were that the herring, or Alewives, were eating too many bass larvae. By preventing the Alewives from getting to 98 percent of their traditional habitat in the lakes and streams of the river's upper reaches, that fish was being destroyed. From two million fish before 1995, the Alewives population quickly crashed to a few hundred. The Canadian Fisheries Department then began trucking the fish a short distance past the barrier, which restored the numbers to about ten thousand.

The US Environmental Protection Agency finally ordered the Maine government to allow the fish free passage. In the letter to Maine's Attorney General, the EPA stated, "The Alewives have co-evolved and co-existed with other native fish and wildlife in Maine's streams, rivers, ponds and lakes for thousands of years."[6]

In a Vancouver Sun article on 14 July 2012, Randy Boswell reported on the EPA's own research, which states:

> It is important to understand that Alewives tie our oceans, rivers and lakes together, providing vital nutrients and forage needed to make healthy water-sheds. Between and within those various habitats, everything eats Alewives: striped bass, bluefish, tuna, cod, haddock, halibut, American eel, brook trout, rainbow trout, brown trout, land-locked salmon, smallmouth bass, pickerel, pike, white and yellow perch, seabirds, bald eagle, osprey, great blue heron, gulls, terns, cormorants, seals, whales, otter, mink, fox, raccoon, skunk, weasel, fisher and turtles.

That is a pretty exhaustive list. A list such as that could be used as a universal template of what happens when we humans, in our stupidity, decide to meddle in nature's millennia-old bio-systems. To every one of the extinctions and wildlife reductions that we are causing, we can apply a list of truths similar to that above. We should also remember here, that when we remove one predator, lets use the Eskimo Curlew as an example, we make it possible for its prey, the grasshoppers, to multiply with nothing to keep them in check. In other words we destroy the balance of nature.

Animals in all areas of our planet are suffering great reductions, but I believe those in Africa will soon be the focus of our greatest concern. Up until now, we have been inclined to assume things aren't too bad on that continent. It may be true that the numbers have been reduced by more than 90 per cent, but some animals still survive in relatively large numbers. The wildebeest are thought to number two million and the African Buffalo nine hundred thousand. There seem to be lots of zebras and gazelles of one sort or another so why worry? Overall though, the iconic animals, those that once roamed the continent, from North Africa to Cape Town, are now confined to fragmentary areas south of the Sahara. Many species are now extinct in many sub-Saharan countries, and prospects for greatly expanded agriculture, to over 60 per cent of the land, make the future look grim. Further fragmentation of the herds from the great abundance of a hundred years ago, is expected to accelerate.

According to Nature Conservancy, elephant numbers had fallen from 12 million a hundred years ago to 5 million by 1950, and to 450,000 by 1989. Following an international effort, the numbers climbed by 100,000; however most countries now number their elephants in tens or hundreds with only southern Africa supporting numbers of about 300,000. Poaching for ivory is becoming more aggressive and better organized. The charity Tusk Trust estimates, based on the amount of illegal ivory seized, that 35,000 elephants were slaughtered for their ivory in 2011. The tusks were all headed for China and one or two other South East Asian countries. According to WWF UK's Wildlife Extra, only 350,000 elephants now live in Africa.

A thoroughly disheartening tale emerged in October 2013. According to Brianna Bridges of ForceChange.com, a gang of eight ivory poachers placed cyanide-laced salts around watering holes in Zimbabwe's Hwange National Park. At the time of the report one hundred dead elephants had been found, many with their tusks hacked off. It was not clear whether the tusks were removed after the animals had died or whilst they lay dying. How many other animals and birds have died and will die from the poison, is not known. We can all imagine the results of such stupid cruelty, especially if it is to be repeated. If elephants are to survive in the wild the wealthy nations must find a way to use aid money to negate the imperative, or the opportunity, of poor Africans to poach wildlife.

The Wildlife Conservation Society reports that in a 10,400 sq mile (27000sq km) area of Central African forest surveyed, Forest Elephant numbers were halved between 2006 and 2011. The numbers fell from 13,000 to 6,300.

On January 28, 2012, the UK's World Wildlife Fund announced that during the year 2011, 448 rhinos, including 19 of the critically endangered Black Rhinos, were poached in South Africa alone. It is difficult to get figures for other African countries but apparently, as more than 90 per cent of all Black and White Rhinos are now reduced to living in South Africa, that is the country to watch. By 1970, following a period of senseless slaughter by white settlers, the Black Rhinos had fallen to about 70,000 individuals. By 1993 they were reduced to 2,473, mostly under heavy anti-poaching guards.

Since the ban on trading in rhino horn came into effect in 1976, over 65,000 rhinos have been killed for their horns. Around 20,000 animals survive. The street value of the horn in 2011 was about $65,000 a kilogram. Again, it is Chinese and South East Asians who pay those prices believing the horn has medicinal advantages.

It is thought that in the 19th century 1.2 million lions roamed widely across Africa and southern Asia. By 1900 the number is believed to have been 664,000, and by 1960, 450,000. Of the areas where they used to hunt, they have been extirpated from 80 per cent of the land. Now they are extinct in 26 countries and are only found in substantial numbers in seven. Some give the remaining numbers as 23,000-40,000.[7] The National Geographic suggests 20,000 lions remain, which is about 0.6 per cent of the 19th century number.[8]

Lions in Kenya could very soon become extinct due to rampant poisonings. Eight were found dead in a few weeks in February 2012. Almost every week, one or two lions are killed following attacks on goats. In June 2012, six lions were speared in one incident involving eight goats. Kenya had been losing one hundred lions per year since the end of the nineties. In 2009 about 2000 still lived in Kenya but it is doubtful any will survive past 2030. According to the Kenyan Wildlife Service, this is due to human settlement, farming, disease and climate change. Apparently the formerly wildlife rich Nairobi National Park is now so surrounded by human settlements that the city can be described as surrounding the park. The result: most of the wildlife corridors, the millennia-old routes the animals take on their seasonal migrations, are now blocked by towns, villages and fences. It is illegal to kill lions in Kenya but, when humans settle on their territory and run tasty goats all over the place, the goatherds are going to retaliate against the predators.

In the May 5th 2012 edition of the *Zimbabwean* newspaper, the Deputy President of the Indigenous Empowerment Board, Sakhile Masuku was quoted as saying, "Lions are being exported to Kenya, . . The responsible individuals claim that there is no land for lions in Zimbabwe and they are crowding out human beings in the areas where they are located." That lions are crowding out humans from land on which the lions lived for millennia is very rich indeed. As already stated the numbers of African lions living on the continent has dropped to about 20,000 from the half million of fifty years ago. Those figures show a clear trend - a trend that can probably be applied to most African wild animals. It is worth remembering that the human population of Africa is set to explode from 133 million in 1900 to two billion by the year 2050. That is a multiplication of 15.[9]

Hippopotami *(Hippopotamus amphibious)* are also greatly reduced. A hundred years ago they were found along the length of the Nile, and over all of Africa south of the Sahara. Now they are found in a few scattered fragments of watery habitat. In 1980 there were 28,000 of them, a typical reduction of over 95 per cent in a hundred years. An example of this decline can be found in Virunga National Park, in the Republic of the Congo. In the 1970's the number of hippos was 29,000. That has dropped to about 800 in 2012.[10]

The Pygmy Hippo *(Coeropsis beriensis)*, which is about 15 per cent the weight of the common species, is believed to number fewer than 3000.[11]

There are two different species of gorilla each having two subspecies. The Western Gorillas *(Gorilla gorilla)* survive in numbers of about 100,000, but Eastern Gorillas *(Gorilla beringei)* are down to fewer than 3,500. The numbers of the Eastern Lowland subspecies have dropped from some 17,000 in 1995 to fewer than 3,000 by 2012. Because most are in the Congo basin, where China has begun logging, and the people are starving and at war, the numbers may well be reduced by a further 95 per cent in the next twenty years. So we can anticipate the numbers of that animal to be somewhere in the 250 range by the year 2030.[12]

On the border between Nigeria and Cameroon, only 300 of the

Cross-river Western Gorillas survive. They live in an area of high human density and natural resource exploitation.

The Eastern Mountain Gorillas total about 800 animals. The animals on Virunga Mountain, where Dian Fossey established the research station, have increased from 250 in 1950 to 380 today. But that is the only area where protections are in place.[13]

The Christian Bible tells us that God gave man dominion over the creatures of this world - a belief that has served the animals, and us, very ill indeed. Over the years such teachings have given us license to shape nature to our needs alone. It has also reinforced our tendencies to callous cruelty. I think it is now time we take more note of the potential for animals to be sentient, sensitive and intelligent beings. We all see TV programs that show studies being undertaken into the intelligence of dogs and chimps and such.

Well, here follows an example of a gorilla with both the ability to learn and teach, and also the authority to direct others. In the mountains of Rwanda live Highland Gorillas, some of which were the subject of Dian Fossey's long study. In the first six months of 2012, two gorillas were killed by human-set snares. These snares are usually attached to overhead branches, or saplings, held by the looped wire under considerable tension. However we now know of an amazing cognitive skill demonstrated in July 2012 by the gorillas. The UK branch of the World Wildlife Fund reported an incident that happened on the mountain. John Ndayambajea, a coordinator with the Dian Fossey Fund, came upon a snare that had been set in the path of the gorilla family known as Kuryama's group. When he went forward to remove the snare, the group's silverback 'Vuba" warned him away. Then two juveniles and a black-backed male ran to the branch and pulled at it till the snare was de-activated. They then saw another snare that they released in the same way.[14] It has been known that silverbacks remove snares, but this is the first time a lead gorilla has warned a human away to enable others under his charge to demonstrate their own proficiency and learned skills. The DNA of gorillas is 98.4 per cent identical to humans.

Another iconic species, the giraffe, is also now only found in small scattered pockets. The numbers have dropped from about 140,000 in 1999 to about 80,000 in 2012. However, of the nine subspecies, three are in dire straights: in 2012 the West African Giraffe was down to 220 animals, the

Nubian down to 250 and the Rothschild's down to 450 animals. Those are all figures that are close to being non-viable for future survival.[15]

In 2010 the President of Tanzania announced three projects that would have devastating results for the wildlife of that country. One was a highway through the centre of the Serengeti Park; the second was the development of a soda ash mine in Lake Natron, the only nesting site for the world's Lesser Flamingos; and the third was the removal of Tanzania's Eastern Arc Mountains from Unesco Heritage status and protection.

The Eastern Arc Mountains is a forested area full of species that are endemic (found nowhere else). It is one of the most bio-diverse places in the world. There are 100 mammal species of which 12 are endemic to the region. There are 120 bird species with 21 endemic, 70 amphibians with 50 endemic, and 50 reptiles with 30 endemic. In those forests are 3500 plant species with 450 species and 40 genera endemic. One doesn't need to visit such a wonderland to know that it should be saved from all interference. Conservation International has named the Eastern Arc Mountains as "one of the world's Top Ten Most Threatened Forest Hotspots." And it is truly threatened as only 11 per cent of Africa's eastern mountain forests survive.

The President of Tanzania, Jakaya Kikwete cancelled an application to have parts of the forest declared a UNESCO World Heritage Site. It appears he wants to open it up to the poor for farming, slash and burn agriculture, logging and other resource development. He says he has to " try to provide for the poor while pursuing western style industrial development."[16][17]

The planned Serengeti Park highway would run east to west, right across the line of migration of the Serengeti's two million wildebeest, zebra and other ungulates, and of the predators – the lions, hyenas etc, that accompany them. The animals make this 250 km annual migration from the overgrazed southern grasslands to the edge of Kenya's Masai Mara in search of water. Such a move back and forth each year across a highway, which would become busier and busier as the years pass, would cause massive numbers of animal and human deaths as a result of collisions. Animals would wander, would be chased when fleeing predators or would surge across the highway during their annual migration. The highway was planned to be a 2-lane road. But we all know what happens to 2-lane roads that are the main route across a country. They soon become 4-lane high-speed corridors and too important to allow wild animals to slow down the traffic. A fence was sure to have been built eventually which would have stopped the annual migration.

In the Canadian Rockies, is the Banff-Jasper Highway that runs north/south, and is four lanes for most of its length. The accidental killing of wildlife along that road has been so great that the highway is now being fenced. There are an infinitesimal number of large animals living in proximity to that highway compared to the number on the grassland of the Serengeti.

There was so much concern and developing outrage at the prospect of the Serengeti road that the World Bank and the German government had both offered to pay to build the road along a different and non-destructive route. However, the Tanzanian government rejected all calls for assistance and seemed to be sticking to their game plan until, in July 2011, they finally cancelled the road. We have all noticed how developers, with good ideas to make money, usually keep re-presenting their proposals till they get their own way, no matter how bad the proposals are for the environment. The Serengeti road, and many others, will probably be in the news again in a year or two.

Lake Natron is the only place in the world where the two and a half million Lesser Flamingos *(Phoenicopterus minor)* breed. One reason the flamingos breed there seems to be the few predators in the vicinity. The birds have been able to nest in peace and until now their refuge has been secure.

It is also a place rich in soda ash. In 2008 the Tanzania Environmental Management Council advised against mining the lake because of the damage it would do to the nesting flamingos. The government however has decided to open a giant mine on the lake and to pipe the soda ash to a nearby town. From there it will be trucked along the new road to a coastal port for shipment to China.[18] A pattern of choosing industrialization above wildlife seems to be emerging.

A horrible tale, relevant to this question of African wildlife, unfolded early in April, 2013. Then President Kikwete of Tanzania – he of the road through the Serengeti renown - announced that the many thousand of Maasai families of Ngorongoro District must leave their ancestral land. The plan is to make the land available to a hunting company named Ortello Business Corporation (OBC). This hunting conglomerate is closely associated to the United Arab Emirates royal family and the military leaders of that country. Ian Michler who reported this for the African Geographic magazine says that 1500 km2 of the Maasai's Loliondo concession, which just happens to be adjacent to Serengeti National Park, will be turned over to the OBC[19][20][21]

The goal is clear. The hunters will shoot the wildlife. The government will make lots of money from the process. The wild animals will diminish in numbers and in no time the government will declare there are too few animals remaining, so the land can be used for other purposes.

If we look at the history of the independent African nations and their wildlife, it is clear that, when independence was first gained, many nations had little to offer but their nature and the animals found there. Most of the great parks – the Kruger in South Africa, the Okavango in Botswana and the Serengeti, amongst many others – were already established. The population of Africa was only 240 million at the time, and it must have seemed a good idea to develop tourism around that bounteous wildlife. But since the 1950s the population has more than quadrupled and is due to be over 2 billion by 2050. It is worth remembering at this point that at the beginning of the great 1850 shoot-up of all living animals on the American grasslands, the human population was only 23.2 million, of whom 3.2 million were slaves.

What is clear is that now in Africa tourism dollars will generate less wealth than can be made from farming or mining the land. The African politicians might make arguments that America has become mighty wealthy since its animals were removed. And America is a country that all should emulate. We like to assume it won't happen. However, who is to say that the countries holding uncultivated land should not turn it to agriculture when so many Africans live in poverty and so many more humans will need feeding? Few governments in the developed world would have any moral authority to argue against it, certainly not when their own past behavior is taken into account.

The great animal slaughters of the 19th and 20th centuries were many years ago, and we have surely learned since then. It seems not. North American governments are still willing to sacrifice, or take great risks with, the integrity of the natural world and wildlife. They legislate for the killing of the few remaining wolves. They encourage drilling for oil in the Gulf of Mexico and Arctic Sea and put oilrigs in oceans where giant icebergs cruise.

They build pipelines across important aquifers and endangered caribou migration routes. They build oil ports on the most pristine and wildlife-important coasts, they allow mining in national parks, and encourage the logging of the last old growth trees. We in the West have no legs on which to stand when it comes to moral authority.

The Canadian government allows, and invigorates, the mining and export of coal and the incredibly dirty and inefficient tar sands oil to other countries, regardless of the effects on human health or on global warming. Along with the government of its southerly neighbour it disregards scientific and environmental studies and gives any sort of agricultural, industrial or resource extraction proposals priority over the security and integrity of the natural world and our future. The sole considerations seem to be profits and employment. Beyond those two, little else matters.

The USA does have the Endangered Species Act. This is intended to protect species at risk from extinction. However the proponents of such activities as logging, mining and development will go to great ends to ensure their projects are not foiled by some critically endangered critter. In July 2011, as part of "The Home Interior Appropriations Bill" – a money bill – conservative right-wing politicians wrote into that bill an 'Extinction Rider'. The rider would have done away with protections for endangered species if those protections imperiled any planned mining, logging, development or industrial projects. Fortunately in November 2011, the House of Representatives voted, by 224-202 votes, to support an amendment to the bill that would continue the protections of species at risk. Some 53 per cent chose to support protecting species from extinction while 47 per cent apparently didn't care.

To my mind, the destruction of the North American grasslands wildlife is one of the worst crimes of all time. We have to remember that it went along with the extinction, in the US, of the Passenger Pigeon, Carolina Parakeet and Eskimo Curlew as well as the earlier near-destruction of the beaver and the later near annihilation of, of all things, the oysters.

The Americans colonized a paradise of natural riches but through greed, stupidity and industrial power destroyed most of it in a surprisingly few years. In the 1970s America and Canada began on paths of conservation with laws to protect their remaining wildlife. But in the early years of the 21st century both governments have fallen back and have shown a worrying lack of leadership. The only governments that are showing any real leadership in matters of wildlife protection are those of Western Europe.

Now, as populations continue to rise worldwide and as we add another two or three billion more, with a similar number already poor, extra land will be needed for food crops. As all those people will also have high expectations for energy in the form of biofuels, more and more pressure will be placed on governments to put all available land under agriculture. As impoverished nations across the globe industrialize, people's expectations will also rise. Rice and vegetables will no longer be good enough. They will want meat, and this means even more land will be needed for raising livestock. In the near future, in the agricultural regions of the globe, it will be important that no land goes to waste. With this in mind, it is clear that the last stands of grassland, forest and woods, and all the small areas of unused marginal land, hedgerows, and road verges, will be cleared for agriculture. It seems very likely that those few remaining areas of marginal land, on which migrating birds and small mammals have found sanctuary and nest sites, will soon all be lost. Forest destruction is likely to accelerate, and those countries with no land to spare will be looking overseas. China is already buying up millions of hectares in Africa, Central Asia, the Americas, and Oceana.

So the question is: What of the future of Africa's 1100 mammal species?

In 1950 the human population of Africa was 221 million, a total that quadrupled in 50 years and reached 1 billion by 2010. During that time wildlife numbers tumbled over a cliff.

We now know there is a potential for Africa's human population to double to more than 2 billion by 2050, and possibly to 4 billion by 2100. According to the McKinsey Global Institute, Africa holds 60 per cent of the earth's uncultivated arable land.[22] Will we protect that land as wildlife habitat, or turn it to agriculture? I think we can all guess the answer to that question. So, will the wildlife decline continue at the same pace as the past forty years, or accelerate? Is it possible that by 2050 very few animals will be found on the continent? I think it is reasonable to assume so. In the USA the 60 million Prairie Bison were brought to 50 animals in the fifty years following 1850. The European Wisent Bison was reduced to 6 animals by 1923, but that was over a very long period of time. Lions have been extirpated from half of Africa and all of Asia except the tiny Gir forest. Why shouldn't the vast number and diversity of African species go the same way? If the agricultural policies of North America can be used as a guide, African wildlife won't stand a chance.

Imagine a report in a fictional newspaper article in the year 2050. That will be the year when any children born in 2013 will be about 37 years old.

> Of the onetime 2 million wildebeests, we report only 258 remaining in the small compound that used to be the Serengeti. The last great migration was in the year 2020 just before that part of the African plains was planted with corn. There are known to be 15 lions, 28 giraffes, 45 Gemsbok, 210 zebra and 17 buffalo. No cheetah, elephant or rhino have been seen since the great fire of 2030. Thompson's Gazelle and Impalas are still found in good numbers. With the felling of the final stands of Congo basin forest the Okapi, the Lowland Gorilla, and the Forest Elephant are now assumed extinct."

On 25th of November 2013, the World Wildlife Fund in London reported that the government of the Democratic Republic of the Congo (DRC) was preparing legislation aimed at speeding up oil exploration projects.[23] One of the developments was an oil law that would recognize no need to safeguard protected areas and national parks. Without the protections, this surely means we will soon be saying goodbye to the last of the Mountain Gorillas and many other rare species that have until now enjoyed some protection. Maybe my worst fears will be realized sooner than I had feared. Certainly some African governments are now beginning to emulate, very closely, the energy and environmental policies of Steven Harper's Canadian government.

14 More on Invasive Species

Mention was made earlier of invasive species, but I think it is worth revisiting that issue.

Not only tropical islands have been affected by introduced species. The islands of Britain have seen the introduction of many exotics over the years. One was at the end of the nineteenth century, when the Eastern Grey Squirrel *(Sciurus Carolinensis)* was brought from North America. This animal has rendered the local, and smaller, European Red Squirrel extinct over much of England, save a few isolated pockets such as the Isle of Wight and parts of East Anglia and Lancashire. The Red Squirrel *(Sciurus vulgaris leucourus)* is the Squirrel Nutkin of writer Beatrix Potter fame. It is a little cuter than the introduced squirrel and, is still plentiful across the channel. But in England, where the grey is now ever-present, most people have adopted the interloper as their new cute animal, and it seems few mourn the native's disappearance.

It is easy to understand why the grey has forced the red out of much of its original mixed woods habitat. Anyone with a garden, and a bird table, will note with pleasure, or with chagrin, how fearlessly those cheeky grey squirrels force themselves onto the bird feeder, and face-off any intruder including, sometimes, irate bird lovers. A mature male weighs nearly double a male red squirrel so, although there is no verified and documented evidence of the greys beating up on the reds, it seems quite likely that the reds are uncomfortable and avoid being around their more aggressive North American cousins. It is also suspected that the introduced species has led to the demise of many of England's songbirds. While the reds live at the rate of one animal per hectare, the intruders are happy to occupy woodland at the rate of 8 animals per hectare. When we consider that they nest in tree cavities it's easy to see how they can reduce the nesting opportunities for cavity-nesting birds. In Nottinghamshire they are known to have caused 27 per cent of nest-box nesting failures in one year. In another study, after the greys were removed from an area, the nesting box failures dropped from 85 per cent to fewer than 10 per cent. Red squirrels are truer vegetarians than greys and seldom feed on eggs. The greys spend up to 80 per cent of their time foraging on the ground, which is between three times and twice the time spent by the native animal. This gives them an advantage, when it comes to searching for new woodland to expropriate, after their own patch has become over populated.

The only advantage reds seem to have is that they do better in the canopies and in the coniferous forests that the exotics are less keen on. As a consequence, they are holding out longer in Scotland and Wales where the forests are mostly evergreens. I became aware of their canopy dwelling propensity in my parent's garden on the Isle of Wight. We had many high elms and Scots pines in the six acres and over the ten year period we lived there I saw families of red squirrels maybe three or four times. They were always high in the treetops, and each time they were a family with four or five kits.

It does seem, though, that the greatest threat the greys present to the reds is the fact that they carry the Squirrel Pox, to which the red squirrels have little immunity.

The population figures are given as 15,000 reds in England, 3,000 in Wales, and 120,000 in Scotland. They now compete with a total of 2.5 million grey squirrels in Britain.[1][2]

British Columbia, the Western-most province in Canada, which, because of the extreme mountainous terrain, one might describe as a relatively intact wilderness, also suffers, introduced species. Not only have many birds and animals been set free there but also at least 500 species of plants grow wild in the most unexpected places. Exotics now make up 20 per cent of the total plant species in the province, which is extraordinary when we consider that few Europeans had even entered the area 200 years ago. Unfortunately, few of these flora species are benign. For an example of the damage they can do, we need look no further than the very attractive Purple Loosestrife, which now crowds out every other plant along the watercourses where it has become established.[3]

The grey squirrel from Eastern North America has also been introduced to B.C. where, for many years, it was confined to Stanley Park. However, it has of course expanded beyond that peninsula. When I first moved to B.C.

in 1969, I had a stream-side home in a wooded part of North Vancouver. It was only a short distance from Stanley Park but was separated from it by Burrard Inlet. There we saw many of the indigenous Douglas Squirrels but never any of the eastern immigrants.

Then in 1983 we moved to Langley, about 20 miles (30km) south east of Vancouver. A remnant patch of forest, which contained cedar, Douglas fir, numerous alder and a few maple trees, surrounded our house. Again the only squirrels that lived there were the Douglas Squirrels. By size, these little squirrels might be likened to Britain's red squirrel except that the colouring is quite different. We lived at that house for 19 years until 2002. It was during the summer of 1999 that I first saw a grey squirrel bouncing down the roadside verge, some ten miles north of our property and heading south. It had the determined look of an explorer, or maybe of a desperate immigrant. The next summer I saw a couple flirting with each other some six miles closer and, in 2001, I saw the first on our land. During the summer of 2002 I saw, in our garden, nearly as many grey squirrels as I did the Douglas. In their natural habitat, in Eastern North America, the greys prefer deciduous trees on fairly open land, so I hope that they won't invade the coniferous forests that cover most of British Columbia. Maybe the dark green forests will protect the little Douglas Squirrel.

Back in the UK, there are tales of Humphrey Bogart and Jimi Hendrix, which fit with the theme of introduced species. Not that Humphrey and Jimi were of concern, as they were just visitors. They were involved with an introduction though. The Bogart tale is that in 1951, when making the movie *African Queen*, with Kathleen Hepburn, at Shepperton Studios, the local English birds were thought not to lend the movie the authenticity of tropical Africa. So birds were brought in from North India - very authentic indeed. Some of those parakeets, which had been employed as bit players, escaped into the wilds of West London.

"Go out and multiply," said the Lord - or Humphrey Bogart - and the birds acted with enthusiasm on both those suggestions.

It is said that, in the spirit of universal love and genuine compassion, Jimi Hendrix released a pair of parakeets from his girlfriend's flat, and they also went out and multiplied. There were probably other releases of these noisy birds by owners who simply wanted a little peace and quiet. In all cases the birds in question were Indian Ring-necked Parakeets (*Psittacula krameri*). Now we think of parakeets as being tropical birds, but these do very well in the Himalayas so are probably well adapted to the cold winters there and, unlike the rest of us, find the weather in England quite acceptable. They are first known to have bred in the wild in 1969. Presumably they spent some time exploring England's fair and pleasant land and reviewing the possibilities before squawking, "Let's multiply." In 2010 there were reckoned to be 50,000 of them screeching fearlessly in the gardens, woods and orchards of Surrey, Sussex and Kent. They have adapted very well to Britain, where they suffer no predators, and eat fruits, nuts, berries and seeds. They also ate half the grapes from at least one vintner's vines, costing him a minimum of £20,000 a year.

They begin nesting very early in the year and well before the British birds. In some years they start in January and, as they nest in cavities, their propensity for early nesting means that the British woodpeckers, owls and starlings are often out of luck in their own searches for nesting holes. The old axiom 'The early bird catches the worm' applies equally well to 'The early bird gets ownership of the nest holes.' The Lesser-spotted Woodpecker's numbers have decreased by 75 per cent since 1970. The parakeets are attractive exotics so most people like them but there is serious talk of a cull being needed soon.

My brother lives in an area of West London where the parakeets are now the most common bird. When I used to visit him in the 1970s, I would delight in going onto nearby Ham Common to listen to the glorious dawn chorus. Now when I go there I hear few songbirds, and I see even fewer. I see no red-breasted robins, nor cute little blue tits. I see no green finches, nor shy yellow hammers. In all my recent visits, though I see lots of parakeets, I have seen hardly any other small birds at all. This, however, may have less to do with the parakeets, which are berry and seedeaters, but more to do with two other birds, jays and magpies. They are both very attractive birds but are known to take eggs and nestlings as a big part of their diet. They used to be kept in check by gamekeepers, who shot them on sight to keep the young pheasant and grouse chicks safe. This was to ensure that the landowners, and their friends, could shoot the game birds when they were adult. Some might argue that being shot in a panicked flight over the heather is no better than being ripped to pieces by a hungry jay. Whatever one's views on predator control, there is now less of it and the two birds are flourishing. When I lived in England, I seldom ever saw any, but now when I go I see plenty but far fewer songbirds. The UK number given for magpies *(Pica pica)* is 590,000 breeding pairs. The number given for jay

(Garrulus Glandorius) couples is 160,000 or 320,000 individual birds. As a comparison the numbers given for the Nightingale and Bullfinch are 5,500 and 190,000. Both numbers show continuing declines from fifty years ago and are nowhere near the magpie's increasing numbers[45].

One other tale of introduced species in the UK concerns a small island off the North coast of Devon, known as Lundy Island or Puffin Island. It is only 3 miles long and ½ mile wide. It was little known beyond being a misty shape off the coast that was known to have puffins breeding there. It apparently has quite an interesting history. The Vikings named it in Old Norse Lundi (puffin) and ey (island), hence Lundiey (Lundy) or Puffin Island. There are 5th and 6th century gravestones, with carved names still just legible. In the 13th century, one William de Marisco murdered the king's messenger, and then tried to murder Henry III himself. The villain fled to Lundy, where he built some battlements. Following a siege and battle he was taken prisoner and carried off to London, where he no doubt paid horribly for his sins. The island has long held a semi autonomous relationship with England, and over the years a couple of eccentrics have named themselves 'King of Lundy'. The island is allowed to print its own stamps and at least one recent owner minted his own coins.

I used to see the island from a distance during our late 1940s summer holidays in Woolacombe, Devon. Then it was always thought of as the island with the puffins, and it seemed few people ever visited it. Somehow, since then, both brown and black rats have reached the island. By the year 2005, there were only two pairs of puffins surviving. Puffins are only 12 inches (30cm) long, and therefore quite small birds. They nest in burrows in the soft soil on cliff-tops, so rats easily reach the nests and attack both the eggs and the nestlings. The rats have now – hopefully - been exterminated, and once more the puffins are breeding safely and their numbers are slowly increasing. After a colony has been reduced to four birds, one can only hope they soon invite some immigrant puffins to move onto the island, and add to the gene pool.[67]

Rats, though disgusting to most people, in some ways seem too small and innocuous to be the major killers that they are.

Maybe, to be the worst kind of threat, small and nearly invisible is the way to be. In 2006 North American bats were dying in increasing numbers. Whether dead or alive, they were often found with white fluff on their noses. Now, six years later, university research has identified the culprit as a fungus named *Geomyces destructans*. This fungus is an import from Europe, which may have been brought to North America on someone's shoes. It is endemic to Europe where the bats are assumed to carry some immunity. The fungus apparently attacks the nose and wings, essentially eating the fine wing membrane. The disease disturbs the animals' hibernation thereby depleting the fat reserves and causing them to fly and hunt too early in the year. The lack of available insects, and the cold, starves and kills them. By 2012 the disease had reduced the bat numbers in eastern North America to below 10 per cent of their earlier numbers. The White-nose-syndrome, as it is called, was first noticed in 2006, so it had presumably been gathering strength for some years before that date. It has to be a truly virulent and fast-moving plague to kill about 5.7 million bats, or over 90 per cent, in such a short period.

Bats are very beneficial little animals as they consume great quantities of flying insects including mosquitoes. Researchers in the US estimate the die-off will result in an annual cost of US$3.7 billion to agriculture.[8]

15 A Little Good News, But Is There Hope?

I remember a day, now so long ago. I was helping Uncle F. take a flock of sheep from the farm down to a meadow some miles away. It must have been 1950 or 51 and an Easter holiday. We started the flock from a field fairly close to the farmyard and, with old Shep the sheep dog, led them the mile or so across the land and then three miles along a country lane to their new pasture. I went on ahead, from up-sloping field to down-sloping field, opening the gates before the sheep arrived. We left the farmland at the main road, and then followed a lane past a nearby village, and finally, a mile further on, we reached the meadow.

The road in those days, though a somewhat major route, saw very little traffic. Just as well it did, as I allowed the sheep to try all three routes at those crossroads. Some thought the coast held a certain attraction, a few chose to go to town, while a very few headed in the right direction down the lane. I seem to recall that Shep was little more use than I was, but then he had the excuse of being rather older than me - older whether you are counting in dog years or in human years. The land where the sheep were going to browse for the summer was a reclaimed river flood plain named Steart Point. It was very flat with a high dyke bordering the muddy river Parrett. I thought nothing of the history of that land at the time. However, before following that train of thought, I first want to mention a family connection that is pertinent at this point.

On our sheep drive past the village we must have passed the vicarage, though I doubt I would have noticed at the time. Had I, I would have seen a large old place that was looking somewhat run-down. As in so many other country parishes, the vicar, and his big house, would have been struggling at that time. Since the early 20th century collapse of British agriculture, village congregations had begun their slow decline until, eventually, the people stopped attending church services. Those large vicarages, second only to the manor in size and importance, were closed one after the other.

It was a very large house with wonderfully extensive gardens, and it says quite a good deal about how times had changed. The time for vicars living in grandeur amongst their flock of village and farm folk had gone the way of so many other English country traditions. The building was sold, and eventually converted into an old folks' home.

It was to that place, in the early 1990s, that my parents moved. They spent their last days there in pretty good health. My father died in 1996 at 92 years and mother died in 2001, aged 97. They were both bright and happy to the end. Dad's passing was as good as such an event can be. He dozed off while watching TV with my mother. He didn't wake up. The last time I visited the village, for my mother's funeral, a vicar was scheduled to visit the church and hold a service on every fourth Sunday.

Uncle F. and Auntie J., who I used to think of as my surrogate parents, both passed away before my father and mother but I still receive Christmas letters each year from their children, Michael and Ann. And very interesting they are too. In the 2011 letter, Michael spoke of his having to sell the acreage beside the river - the very land where we took the sheep. The Department for Environment proposed in 2010, and the government has accepted, that the land be returned to its original state of flood plain and saltwater marshland. Other nearby farms will also have their lands flooded for the sake of bird habitat. Apparently about 2,000 acres of farmland will be affected. This plan is, in part, because the dykes are becoming in need of a general overhaul, and also to replace land in the Severn estuary that is required for conversion to a deepwater port for large ships. The farmers will get compensation but, as in so many cases of forced eviction, it will not be enough to purchase replacement land of a similar value. Michael is a socially responsible, community-minded man of high principles, but even so, he does regret the negative affect this will have on the long-term viability of the farm. In effect it means that he will have nearly 200 fewer acres on which to grow feed for the milking cows.

I have been unable to discover when the dykes were first built on Steart Point. It may have been in the 1600s when a lot of wetlands were drained, or possibly during the Victorian age when we became so good at changing the landscape for commercial purposes. With the high dykes along its banks, the River Parrett is a muddy and unattractive river. It was once, fifteen hundred years ago, the marshy border between the Saxons and the Ancient Britons to the west. Hence the name Parrett, which may be derived from the Welsh 'parwydydd' or 'pared' both of which mean 'partition'. It could also be derived from the Welsh word 'peraidd', which means 'sweet river'. Whatever the derivation, the border fell in the middle of the 8th century, when the Ancient Britons were squeezed further west to a line approximate to the present Devon/Cornwall border.[1] Since those far off days, the river has seen a fair bit of engineering, so dykes may have been re-built many times, over the past millennia. Whatever the history, the earthen dykes will soon be gone, and Steart Point will be the largest wildlife rehabilitation scheme in England. Probably, for the first time ever, the land will be assessed on its wildlife values instead of for its Ancient Brit defensive possibilities or more recent agricultural potential.

I sympathize with Michael's difficulties, but I also applaud the government for accepting the responsibility of returning land to the wildlife that really needs a break after millennia of losing out to human interests.

Unlike most of the continents, where wildlife and nature are daily driven from pristine habitats at the command of mining, agricultural or pipeline interests, Europe has recently been playing something of a leading role in reestablishing and protecting habitat, and in reintroducing species to areas from which they have been lost for many, many years. This is in accord with the *Convention on Biological Diversity*, which was signed by the leaders of 150 governments at the 1992 Rio Earth Summit in Brazil. The government responses also stem from two other European agreements. These are the *Habitats Directive* and the *Birds Directive*, which were both signed in the year 2000. The conventions legally oblige signing governments to the reintroduction of species, to both the country from which they had been lost, and to areas within that country where the wild species are no longer found.[2] This endeavour in England is being overseen by Natural England, which describes itself as: 'an executive non-departmental public body responsible to the Secretary of State for Environment, Food and Rural Affairs. Our purpose is to improve England's natural environment.'

In Britain the reintroductions began before the Rio Summit, and by 2010 Natural England had overseen the return of 25 locally extinct species. They included such animals as the Black Grouse, the Cirl Bunting, the Harvest Mouse, the Dormouse, and the Wart-biting Cricket. The last one sounds like something straight out of a Middle Ages handbook for the practice of witchcraft. The work of moving English species into areas from which they had been extirpated will be ongoing till a healthy rebalancing is achieved.[3] Some of the recently re-established species have not been seen on the British Isles for hundreds of years. By the end of 2011, 18 species had been reintroduced including: 8 species of birds, 5 of animals, 4 of butterflies and one spider.

For information regarding the following reintroductions I have looked at such sites as, Natural England, BirdLife International, the Royal Society for the Protection of Birds (RSPB) and other sites that hold information about these species and their reintroductions.

The first bird of note, though it returned unaided by man, is the Osprey *(Pandion haliaetus haliaetu),* also known as the fish hawk. Ospreys had been extinct in England since 1840, and had not nested on the British Isles since 1916. Then in 1954, a Scandinavian pair began nesting on Speyside, Scotland. Initially, it required heroic efforts to protect the birds from egg thieves. It also took many years for the birds to be free of the contamination of organochlorine pesticides. Nevertheless, despite all the setbacks, the birds did eventually raise chicks, which, in turn, went out and multiplied. By 2011 it was estimated that between 250 and 300 pairs were nesting in Scotland, England and Wales.

The English Ospreys were first introduced to the Midlands as chicks, from Scotland, in 1996. These birds underwent their annual migrations to Africa and back, and in 2001 the first pairs finally bred. In that same year, a pair from Scotland found their own way to the English Lake District, where they also bred. These two breeding successes were the first in England for 160 years. In 2004 two pairs also established nests in Wales.[4]

The first successful bird reintroduction was the White-tailed or Sea Eagle *(Haliaeetus albicilla).*[5] The last of these birds were shot from the Scottish islands at the time of the First World War. The first reintroduced birds were released in Scotland in 1975. The sea eagle is very similar to the North American Bald Eagle, though it has a white tail without the white head.

Another long absent bird that has been reintroduced is the Red Kite *(Milvus milvus).*[6] They may have been Britain's most widespread bird in the old days. Being birds of prey and scavengers, they played useful roles in getting rid of waste. In medieval times they were apparently really useful in pre-flush-toilet London. One can imagine what service they provided. However, once Britain's anti-wildlife campaign was in full swing a couple of hundred years ago, their numbers dropped drastically. By the turn of the twentieth century the last few, hanging on in Wales, had probably all gone. They were reintroduced to England starting in 1989. Red Kites are quite beautiful russet-coloured raptors with black-tipped white primary flight feathers, and forked swallow-like tails. I naturally never saw one when I lived there, but during all of my most recent visits it is the one bird I always do see. It is so strange to see them, but thrilling, as one often appears when least expected. They are apparently now well established.

The Great Bustard *(Otis tarda)* is another recent reintroduction, though it isn't yet known how successful the venture will be. It is a sturdy, nearly four-foot-tall bird, which, at up to 46 lbs (21kg), may be the heaviest flying bird in the world. It has a wingspan of 7-8.9 feet (2.1-2.7 m) and is currently a threatened bird in all of the original range from Europe across Asia to western China. There are thought to be about 40-50,000 breeding birds in about 19 countries, though the numbers vary a great deal. They are most successful in Spain, which has about 3,000, but in the Czech Republic there are maybe 6, and only 4 in Romania. The bird has been in a steep decline for the past 150 years. They are birds of the open grassland and steppe, so they were hard hit when so much of that land was ploughed for agriculture. They were hunted from the UK by 1832.

A number of Great Bustards have been reintroduced to England each year since 2004.[7] They were young birds that had been hatched in Saratov, Russia, and hand reared with no opportunity to identify with humans. They are released into a fox-safe but roofless enclosure on Salisbury Plain in early fall and are free to decide for themselves when to fly the coop. They are released on land specially sown with grasses and plants known to attract them. Two pairs successfully raised chicks in the UK in 2009, and four pairs had success in 2010. At the end of 2011, there were thought to be about 17 birds that had escaped predation in England. Some birds have found their way to Dorset and Devon. It is too early to say whether or not the reintroduction will be a long-term success.

The Northern Harrier *(Circus cyaneus),* or Hen Harrier, is a species of raptor that encircles the northern hemisphere approximately above the 45th parallel. They are beautiful birds that course low over the land with wings held high in a V shape. The males are pale grey, with white below and black wingtips. The females are brown and buff with some white. Its British name derives from the habit of taking the chicks of hens, when such birds used to forage freely in the farmyards or home fields. They were shot out of England in the 19th century, although a few hung on in the more remote areas of the Isles. The bird was first reintroduced in the 1960s, but is still struggling in much of Britain where it is heavily persecuted by landowners with shooting properties. They are doing well in the Orkney Isles off Scotland. However, in England in 2010 only four couples managed to breed, although it is believed there is a potential for 300 breeding pairs in the country.[8] This persecution by gamekeepers is so typical. They know it is illegal, but also know the chance of a successful prosecution is very slim. The shooting is worse on grouse moors, where owners encourage Red Grouse to breed so that they can shoot them themselves. This sense of ownership of wildlife, and the resulting right to shoot every predatory creature that might threaten the person's chosen chicks, is a long-established problem. The landowners say they ensure the survival of the grouse – or partridge or pheasants – by protecting them from predators. If they could speak, the harriers might well reply that there could be plenty to go around if only the humans wouldn't be so greedy. Research carried out between 1992 and 1997 indicates that the harriers do not adversely affect healthy grouse numbers, but do have an influence only after the numbers have dropped to unsustainable numbers. Research at Langholm Moor in Scotland continues. It is to find out whether the two species can live harmoniously over the long term. I speak of grouse and harriers, not harriers and humans.

There is little difference really between the British landowners who kill the harriers because they hunt their grouse chicks, and the Indonesians who kill Orangutans because they eat young palms. They are both people who believe that possessing a piece land, and a piece of paper, gives them custody and full rights to kill every living thing that visits that land.

The Common Crane *(Grus grus)*, with an 8-foot wingspan, became extinct on the British Isles in the 17th century. This followed years of draining fenland for agriculture in the 1600s. However in 2007 they found their own way back and now breed in the Norfolk Broads, on England's east coast. The birds first flew into an area named Lakenheath Fen Reserve, which had been carrot fields until they were returned to fenland, some 11 years earlier. That 500-acre (200h) piece of agricultural land is now wet meadow and reed bed. The fen had been re-established with the intent of attracting bitterns back. The bitterns returned. Reed Buntings and Reed Warblers are no doubt also happy. The cranes' arrival was a surprising bonus, 20 birds being observed there in 2011.[9]

Cranes were reintroduced to the wetlands of Somerset in 2010, so one day soon they may be seen again on the Steart marshes. In the first month of 2012 cranes were sighted six times in England: in Somerset, Cambridgeshire and Suffolk. Hopes are high that they will once more become established after a 400-year absence.

Another bird that left England's shores but has now returned of its own volition is the Chough *(Pyrrhocorax pyrrhocorax)*. This is a bird of the crow family and thought most closely related to the Jackdaw. The Chough is three inches smaller than a crow, is all black but with a bright red beak, legs and feet. The birds inhabit rocky cliff faces and mountains and are found from Morocco and Spain through southern Eurasia. So those that nest on Britain's cliffs are close to the northern limit of their range.

In Britain they were originally called Cornish Choughs before being named Chough (pronounced chuff) – possibly because they were fast disappearing from that county. The last was seen in the 1950s though a few of these birds remained on far-flung cliffs of Wales and the Isle of Man. Some also live on the coast of southern Ireland. A pair returned to the Cornish coast in 2002 and began to build a new colony.[10] A round-the-clock citizen watch was organized, to protect the birds from egg collectors and other beings of selfish intent. What I find interesting about this story is why the birds left in the first place, and then why they returned.

It turns out that Choughs enjoy eating insects, with a particular liking for ants. In the old days lots of sheep grazed on the cliffs, and those animals kept the grass nice and short. This enabled the birds to forage easily for ants. It was then decided that the sheep would do better inland where the grass was richer. Well we can imagine what happened. The sheep left the land, the grass grew long, and the birds, no matter how hard they searched, couldn't get their fill of ants. So each Chough in a huff flew off to ant-rich pastures unknown.

Then in more recent years it was decided to run Highland Cattle over the cliffs where the Choughs used to fly. The cattle shortened the grass, the ants became visible, a passing bird discovered the good eating, put out the word and lo, the Choughs returned. This return was accomplished to the great flapping excitement amongst the English bird watchers. Many tea parties were hosted for those intent on protecting the Choughs. Now the good people sit on the cliffs, through cold and drizzly wet days and nights, drinking nice cups of tea, while watching for the heathen egg stealers and collectors.

I find it so interesting that such simple decisions as moving sheep, can result in a bird species vacating nest sites they have frequented for hundreds of years. One has to wonder what other effects our simple and seemingly innocuous actions, in all parts of the world, have had on wildlife numbers. I am sure that my moving the flock of sheep to the Steart meadows, in the early 1950s, had little effect to the ecology of the land at the time. But then, the changes had happened many years before when the original estuarine marshes were first diked and drained, and turned to agricultural land.

A recent extinction in Britain also has to do with ants and short grass. But in this case it concerns a butterfly. The butterfly is the *Maculinea arion* or what is known locally as the Large Blue. We shouldn't be fooled by the name, as it is only marginally larger than most of the other blue butterflies, all of which are quite small. The young caterpillars feed on wild thyme, but before they pupate they seek out wood ants, to which they feed a sweet sugary fluid from a gland on their backs. The ants like this fluid so much that they carry the caterpillars back to their nests where they feed them their own larvae until the fat caterpillars pupate in the spring. The butterflies hatch in June or July, and when they do they have to make a mad dash for the open air before the ants clue into just how thoroughly they have been duped.

It seems that one reason for the Large Blue's 1970s English extinction, was the disease myxomatosis. Beginning in 1954 and with a lot of help from farmers and others in its introduction and spread, that disease killed off most of the UK's rabbits.* Without the millions of rabbits to keep the wild grasses short, the adult butterflies couldn't locate the wild thyme on

---

* I have a clear memory of when myxomatosis struck our area of the Isle of Wight. I think it was in1955. At that time I was spending hours everyday with my dog rambling over the forested cliffs near our home. One afternoon we were returning along the lane from the shore, when we came upon dozens of rabbits just sitting in the lane and seemingly unwell. I then noticed scores more stumbling about in the surrounding undergrowth. Many appeared to be blind with swollen eyes and sores. By the next day I saw few live rabbits, and after a few days I saw none, nor did I see any carcasses either. Myxomatosis, I believe, killed off nearly every single rabbit on the Island, and it did so very quickly indeed.

which to lay their eggs, nor could the ants and caterpillars get together, so eventually the Large Blue died out. The complexities of the natural world are truly amazing. I wonder if these butterflies were found in England before rabbits were introduced from France in the 12th century. Now this butterfly has recently been reintroduced, with some success.

The European Beaver (*Castor fiber*) was hunted out of Britain in the 16th century and out of most of Europe by the end of the 19th century. It was then, in the years following the 1920s, reintroduced to thirteen European countries, and is now thought to number about 250,000. It was officially returned to Scotland in 2008. In February 2014, the WWF's wildlife extra. com reported that 3 beavers had been observed in the River Otter in East Devon. Those animals must either be unofficial reintroductions or escapes from captivity.

The Pine Marten, which has been gone from England for about a century, found its own way back to Northumberland's Cheviot Hills. Whether it came from Wales or from Scotland we may never know.

Insects that have been reintroduced to the UK in recent years include: the Silver-washed, the Glanville and the Heath Fritillary butterflies, and the Short-haired Bumblebee. In order that insect reintroduction can be successful, it is necessary to re-establish a clean pesticide-free and herbicide-free habitat of native plants and wildflowers. By so doing, it is hoped that other insects, as well as songbirds and small mammals will also benefit.[11]

The UK must have one of the largest and most dedicated bands of nature-concerned volunteers anywhere in the world. They have replanted large tracts of woodland, and have reintroduced species that have not been seen in the British Isles for centuries. One would expect that if wildlife could flourish anywhere it would do so in Britain. It appears not. In May 2013, Sir David Attenborough reported on an extensive study of British Nature entitled the *State of Nature Report*. Of the 3,148 UK species studied, it was found that over the past 50 years 60 per cent have declined, 31 per cent show a strong decline, and 10 per cent are likely to become lost to those islands. Those percentages seem to hold true over most ecosystems from farmland to woodland and moorland to coastal waters. If this can be happening in the UK, where wild animals are protected, imagine what is happening in all those other countries where most people view their wildlife either with indifference or as an inexpensive meal. This suggests to me that, though habitat loss is the most serious problem in all countries, and non-caring citizens a problem in some, it is what is happening beyond the borders that is also important. Migrating species have to run the gauntlet of a host of factors during their travels, but habitat loss and the use of pesticides, herbicides and chemicals in general seem to be the final destructive elements that will do in most species.

Some wildlife are persecuted, poisoned, trapped or shot from their chosen habitat, usually because they are seen as undesirable, or are in competition with human values. Examples of these species would, of course, be mosquitoes, but could also be wolves, raptors or rabbits. Bringing those species back, if thought desirable, can be as simple as educating the persecutors and putting an end to poisoning, trapping and shooting thus allowing the remaining population to rebound naturally. In the case of species dying out as a result of general environmental degradation, the return is much more complex but also very valuable. When the local extinctions resulted from the planting of exotic crops or woodlands, the importation of exotic predators such as cats or snakes, or the use of pesticides, insecticides or herbicides, it becomes necessary to re-establish the foundations of the original ecosystem. When this is done - when the soil, water and air are purified and the original flora is replanted - then the land will welcome both reintroduced species and those previous residents that find their own way back.

Reintroductions are more complicated than just bringing species from abroad and releasing them. Public acceptance is required, habitats must be returned to what they once were, and the original grasses and herbs must be sown to replace the exotics introduced through agriculture. Furthermore, protections against animal predators, and human malcontents, must be put in place. Once the habitats are returned, all manner of native flora and fauna are the happy beneficiaries, and so are we humans. The same process applies anywhere in the world where the original ecosystem has been compromised in the name of agriculture, plantations or mines. For migrating species, however, all the goodwill in the world won't help if the migration routes over other countries are radically compromised or poisoned with pesticides.

Now consideration is being given to reintroducing wolves and Brown Bears to Scotland.

In early summer 2012 the World Wildlife Funds of Austria, Germany,

Switzerland and France published a Brown Bear conservation strategy. The European Brown Bear *(Ursus arctos)*, though considerably smaller, is what in Canada we call the Grizzly or *(Ursus arctos horribilus)*, the most feared large animal in North America. Brown bears are found from Western Canada and Alaska, across Siberia and parts of Central Asia, through the Balkans and up through Bulgaria and Slovenia to Sweden and Finland in the North, and to Spain in the west. In Europe, where there are thought to be 14,000, the bears still survive in ten fragmented populations such as in the Pyrenees, in North East Spain, in Italy and in the Balkans.

The few bears in the triangle encompassing Austria, Northern Italy and Slovenia are often poached by hunters, stockbreeders and beekeepers - another typical example of humans invading an animal's kingdom and then not appreciating them being there. Once not so long ago there would have been a more healthy population of wild honeybees. Now though, most are kept in hives busily producing honey. The honey gives the hive owners their livelihoods, but is also the bears' favorite treat. Surely a way can be found to protect the bees from the bears without killing all the bears. Those bears in the triangle are part of a larger, fairly stable, contiguous population of 3000 that stretches down to Greece.[12]

Naturally some people in Britain, which has a large, closely packed population, are uneasy at the thought of having major predators reintroduced into their local countryside. When people have been free to ramble at will over the wildest parts of their land with no fear of animals, the thought of reintroduced wolves and bears can be daunting to even the most stalwart. Wolves are generally considered threatening, and hikers may well feel very uncomfortable when alone and unarmed in wolf territory. Still, according to National Geographic, wolves almost never attack humans. The preferred food for wolves are deer, and now that those animals are becoming something of a pest in many areas, reintroduced wolves should address the balance. But where, one might ask, is the predator to keep the wolf numbers down when they become threateningly too numerous?

Europe now seems to be one of the most hopeful places in a world of diminishing wildlife. Much of Western Europe, with Germany being one of the leaders, is being very progressive in their wildlife policies. It is ironic that the descendants and compatriots of those British and European colonizers of southern Africa, known as 'Great White Hunters', now seem to be among the keenest people to reintroduce the wildlife species back to their original habitat. They are also enthusiastic to reclaim land and return it to its previous natural state. North America has a huge number of concerned citizens pushing for habitat protections, and wildlife reintroductions, but they have to contend with the lobbying activities of the gun owners, hunters, ranchers and resource extraction companies who are very powerful on that continent. Wolves have been reintroduced from Canada to a number of Western US states but the pressure to shoot the lot is ongoing in that hunting and gun-happy country. We applaud the extinction of few subspecies. However when the last of the regressive human hunting subspecies, *Homo sapiens grande blanchi hunterissi*, (or *Valde niveus venator* to be a little less fanciful) is finally gone, most will not mourn his passing.

North America is truly fortunate to have the wonderful universities and postsecondary educational systems that educate people so well. Generally well-educated citizens seem to be the most concerned about their own nation's environmental degradation. The truly ignorant and uneducated people are the biggest problem.

I don't know when the desire to protect animals began. It may have been when a human first looked at an animal as something of delight instead of a meal. Francis of Assisi may have been an early naturalist. Lady Eleanor Glanville, who lived between 1654 and 1709, certainly seemed to have loved butterflies, though she pinned a great many over her lifetime. King George IV, a bird lover, was another. Johnathan Elphick, in his book *Birds. The art of ornithology*, tells how Thomas Berwick (1753-1828), the wildlife illustrator who published his *British Birds* over the period 1797-1804 apparently cared greatly for birds as a young boy. Berwick's book was only one of many illustrated scientific natural history books published during the 18th and 19th centuries, which may have encouraged people to take an interest in nature.

In Britain, where more or less all the land was developed, owned or lived on, the desire to save the natural seems to have found its voice in the first part of the 19th century. Such romantic poets as William Wordsworth and Samuel Taylor Coleridge expressed this as a desire to save scenic places. The government had begun passing legislation in the 18th century with such bills as the *1772 Game (Scotland) Act*, the *1822 Animal Protection Act* and the *1828 Night Poaching Act*, but they were more to do with protecting the game birds of landowners from poachers and the like. Another 11 wildlife/game acts were passed before the first true act to protect wildlife was established with the *Wild Birds Protection Act* of 1872. That was followed, in 1889, with the Royal Society for the Protection of Birds (RSPB). In 1900, the RSPB had a membership of 25,000 mostly middle class suburbanites. This is a very similar situation to that of North America in the early 21st century, where the main impetus for habitat and wildlife protections comes from the people living in the cities, rather than from the loggers, hunters and ranchers who profit from shaping the land to their own requirements.

So, while the bison and Passenger Pigeon slaughter was at its worst in the US, the first steps to protect nature were being laid in Britain despite the ongoing slaughter of its raptors and large birds. However this was understandable, considering western North America was virgin land at the time, while Britain's development of the land, and persecution of its wildlife had been ongoing for millennia.

The British *1882 Ancient Monuments Act*, protecting significant landscapes and historic monuments, had its genesis in, amongst other things, a privately funded Lake District Defense Society of 1876. That society, like so many environmental foundations of today, was fighting a rearguard action against resource development and industrial degradation in areas of outstandingly beautiful wildness. In that case it was Britain's Lake District. On its heels, came the establishment of Britain's National Trust in 1895 and the *National Trust Act* of 1907. The aims as stated at the time were "to promote the permanent preservation, for the benefit of the nation, of lands and tenements (including buildings) of beauty or historical interest; and, as regards land, to preserve (so far as practicable) their natural aspect."[13]

Beatrix Potter, from the proceeds of *Peter Rabbit* and other children's stories, bought and preserved many Lake District hill farms, which she left to the National trust as a major part of the Lake District National Park.

The National Trust was expanded in 1912 with the Society for the Promotion of Nature Reserves.

On the other side of the Atlantic, English-born Mark Catesby (1683-1749) and John Abbott (1751-1840), American-born William Bartram (1699-1777) and the Scot, Alexander Wilson (1766-1813) amongst others, traveled over large areas of the continent searching for, studying and painting North American birds. It was Alexander Wilson who published the first coloured bird book in North America and who produced eight of the nine books of his *American Ornithology* before his death in 1813.

John James Audubon, the most famous of them, published his books, *Birds of America,* between 1827 and 1838. I don't get the sense that any of these early ornithologists were particularly strong conservationists. Nor were any of the others who were studying flora and fauna in India, Australia, Africa, and anywhere else that Europeans were visiting and colonizing. But then wildlife was still plentiful in those days, and the search for knowledge was the main impetus behind their work. In order to get a close-up understanding of the birds, many of which were fast-moving, secretive or high in the trees, those men first had to shoot them to get them to stay still.[14]

During the settling of America's West, while the great majority of the newcomers saw the land only as somewhere to plough, pillage, fell, or mine, one or two saw it differently. Among the most influential of that group were John Muir, who recognized the sanctity of many areas, including what, in 1890, became California's Yosemite National Park, and President Theodore Roosevelt. Roosevelt was the first president to be proactive in matters of conservation. Following his inauguration in 1901, he added protections to many ecologically and scenically important lands and forests. The Sierra Club was formed in 1892. And Congress created the National Parks Service in August 1916.[15]

Two others, who had a real impact on the preservation of wild places and birds in their habitat, were a German immigrant to the USA, named Kroegel, and his son Sebastian. In 1881 they settled in Florida, on a piece of land opposite a six-acre Island on which pelicans bred. To defend those birds against feather collectors – who I guess had moved on after wiping out the Great Auks – they managed to have the land designated for conservation in 1903. That island became the first property to be named as a US National Wildlife Refuge.[16]

Another tale of conservation is of Boston's Harriet Hemenway who, among others, in 1896 became so upset by the destruction of egrets to supply feathers for the fashionable hat trade, was able to start a boycott of hats with feathers. That boycott resulted in the foundation of the National Audubon Society, and eventually the USA's Migratory Bird Act in 1913.[17]

Probably there were people in every generation, and all over the planet, who railed against the destruction of nature and who wished things could have been different. Nevertheless it does seem to me that the Second World War was a kind of watershed. Not only did that war see the introduction of new industries and agricultural practices, using chemicals and pesticides, and more destructive ways of controlling nature, but it also resulted, in

Europe, in social and economic expectations and revolutions that flowered with the coming of peace. This, in turn, brought new thinking to our relationships with nature's animals. Thinking back, I remember that adults, well beyond our immediate families, were encouraging my friends and I to study nature, to chase butterflies or seek out bird nests if we chose, but not to harm the insects we caught, or to rob the nests we found. A benign interest in the nature around us was fundamental to us all.

Possibly the first person in Britain to use the media to educate children about nature, was a man named Rev. George Bramwell Evans.[18] His mother had been born in a Gypsy (Romani) caravan. He was born in 1884. He became a Methodist minister, and then a writer and broadcaster with the pseudonym of Romany. His first of eleven books, *A Romany in the Fields* was published in 1929. Then, starting in 1933, he broadcast a program called *Out with Romany* on BBC Children's Hour. Whether in a book or a broadcast, he would play the role of a man on a walk in the countryside. He discussed the nature he came upon with two children named Muriel and Doris. In my mind, I still carry his written description of how Peregrine Falcons hunted Wood Pigeons. I must have been about eight when I read that book – whichever one it was. He died in 1943 before I would have been conscious of hearing any of his broadcasts – still his books lived on. His intention was transparent I think. It was to encourage, in small children, the affection and understanding that he felt for the natural world.

In the late 40s, I remember the introduction of the I-Spy club,[19] to which I became an enthusiastic member for a short time. One would receive small booklets on different subjects with such titles as *In the Country, On the Farm* and *Horses and Ponies*. They all sold for sixpence each. For a shilling one could buy *Birds* or *Wildflowers*. They could be purchased direct from the News Chronicle newspaper, or from any newsagent. With these little booklets in hand we were encouraged to seek out and identify the items illustrated and, when the book was full with ticks, to return it to Big Chief I-Spy for a feather as a reward. My favorite booklet was *In the Country*. It listed, amongst other things, traditional gates and other means of allowing humans access through fences and hedges, while keeping farm animals either in or out. Included were cattle grids, stiles of various styles, kissing-gates, whych-gates, five-bar gates and others I have forgotten. Big Chief was actually Charles Warrell, a headmaster, who died in 1995 at the age of 106. I was surprised to find that I-Spy booklets were still being published, though in an updated form, in 2012.

Charles Warrell first published in 1948, but eleven years earlier another series of books that interested both adults and children were published. These were the pocket-sized Observer's Books. The first of them: *The Observer's Book of British Birds* and *The Observer's Book of Wild Flowers*, were both published in 1937. They were followed in 1938 by books on butterflies, trees, shrubs and animals. In 1942 the *Observer's Book of British Grasses, Sedges and Rushes* was published.[20] Although as a boy I used to think that one rather boring, I now find interest in the context of when it was published. 1942 was one of the worst years of the war for Britain, yet they went ahead with publishing a book of such arcane subject matter.

I imagine an old buffer holding the fort while all the young editors were off at war, and saying to another creaking editor,

"Damn it all Basil, we must let Hitler know we will not be deterred. If we quake at publishing 'Sedges and Rushes' he might think he's got us on the run."

In 1942 they departed from nature and also published the first *Observer's Book of Airplanes*. They went on to publish one hundred titles, on topics such as sewing, cricket and tanks and armoured vehicles in 1981.

I don't know if the I-Spy and Observer's books were produced to educate people about nature, or to satisfy a clear demand for books on nature. Whatever the impetus, the books became very popular in Britain and helped foster an interest in the natural world. In those days there were no such beings as environmentalists, but there were certainly a great many citizens, in some countries, who had an interest in nature, and I believe a general revulsion against killing was developing. The time of the scientific explorers and specimen collectors was pretty well over by then, as was the time of the Great White Hunter. His heyday had been during the earliest decades of the century. Possibly, as with my family, people in general were noticing fewer fish in the rivers, the vanishing butterflies, and the numbers of species that were once seen locally, but for some reason were no more. Whatever the reasons, we cannot doubt that attitudes toward wildlife had been changing in Europe for many years.

When, in March 1912, Scott of Antarctica lay dying in his freezing tent he wrote his last letter to his wife, the sculptor Kathleen Bruce. He asked her to ensure their 2 year old son grew up with a love of nature, He wrote "make the boy interested in natural history if you can; it is better than games." He had no idea how influential his request would be. In postwar

Britain, his son Peter Scott was a well-known painter who produced images of waterfowl taking off from, flying above, and landing on bodies of wild water. He also founded a number of wetland sanctuaries for birds in Britain. The bit about games – Britain's word for sport – was unnecessary as Peter Scott went on to win a bronze medal in sailing in the 1936 Berlin Olympic Games. He also won a Distinguished Service Cross for bravery as a Royal Navy Captain in the Second World War.

It was his postwar work for which he is remembered though. In 1948 he founded the Wildfowl and Wetlands Trust. He led numerous ornithological expeditions to different parts of the world, and hosted a BBC TV wildlife program titled, *Look*, which aired from 1955 till 1981. That program was a forerunner to David Attenborough's wonderful series of BBC nature shows, and David Suzuki's series, *The Nature of Things*.

Peter Scott was a co-founder of the World Wildlife Fund and designed the well-known Panda logo. He was also an influential contributor to the International Whaling Commission that halted the commercial killing of whales. The above lists just a few of his accomplishments. When the world lost him in 1989, he died as Sir Peter Markham Scott, CH, CBE, DSC and Bar, MID, FRS, FZS. Clearly some influential people cared about the good works he performed for our Earth's environment.[21]

One Victor Stolan, in a letter to Julian Huxley, first proposed the idea behind the founding of the World Wildlife Fund. The letter was in response to three articles Huxley had written for the Observer newspaper in 1960, regarding the diminishing numbers of African wildlife. Following Stolan's suggestions, Huxley contacted Max Nicholson who, in turn, contacted Guy Montfort, the head of a London advertising agency and co-author of *A Field Guide to the Birds of Britain and Europe* (1954). The first meeting of the fund took place in London in May 1961 with Peter Scott as chair. For such a fund to work as envisaged it needed money and lots of it.[22]

The eventual founders of the World Wildlife Fund were: Julian Huxley, Max Nicholson, Peter Scott, Guy Montfort, Godfrey A. Rockefeller and Prince Bernhard of Lippe-Biesterfeld. It was decided to establish the head office in Switzerland.

The WWF's original mission was "to halt and reverse the destruction of our environment." In the 1990s the mission statement was revised to "stop the degradation of the planet's natural environment and to build a future in which humans live in harmony with nature, by: conserving the world's biological diversity, ensuring that the use of renewable natural resources is sustainable, promoting the reduction of pollution and wasteful consumption." At one point, Peter Scott said, "We shan't save all we should like to, but we shall save a great deal more than if we had never tried."

In 1972, Guy Montfort went on to lead a campaign to create nine tiger reserves in India, and a further eight in Nepal and Bangladesh. In that campaign he was able to get the Indian Prime Minister Indira Gandhi on side.

As well as the World Wildlife Fund for Nature, as it is now known, or the World Wildlife Fund, as it is known in Canada and America, there are now thousands of groups dedicated to saving the environment including such groups as:

- Birdlife International
- The Sierra Club
- The David Suzuki Foundation
- Greenpeace
- Conservation International
- Rainforest Alliance
- Nature Canada
- The International Rhino Fund
- Sea Turtle Restoration Project
- Project Seahorse
- Living Oceans Society

and many, many more.

16 More Good News

It is such a problem, that while so many thousands of decent and concerned citizens see the need to support non-government environmental organizations that work toward saving our home planet from abuse and degradation, some elected governments see those selfsame concerned citizens as something akin to enemies of the state. Why do officials, like the Canadian and Malaysian Prime Ministers, live in such a totally different world than the environmentalists in Vancouver, or the Penan in Borneo? It is the economic argument of course. They believe that anything suggesting a curtailment of the full-speed-ahead economic growth model is wrong-headed and a socialist plot. But surely they can't believe the rest of us are evil for wanting to save the forests or the planet's ecosystems. And, conversely, they assuredly don't choose to be evil by so wantonly encouraging the destruction. It is as if the governments cannot conceive the possibility that environmental sustainability and economic responsibility can go hand in hand. I believe it is in the people who support the environmental groups that hope resides.

The environmental battle is hot and ongoing in British Columbia. The majority of people in that province live in Vancouver, and it is in that city where most people support environmentalism. Beyond the city, where the resource-extraction industries thrive, where the loggers log, the miners mine, and the hunters hunt, there is less support for environmentalism. In Britain on the other hand, the environmental battle appears to have been won, but of course Britain doesn't have any resources left to extract. There are few people's livelihoods at stake when saving the natural world, and the focus is more on repairing the damage done over previous generations.

All the environmental groups formed, led and supported by concerned citizens across the globe are winning a few small victories. It is hard though, as they are always so impoverished when compared with the rich landowners, giant international companies, and money-taking politicians that they are up against. And then, even when they do defeat some awful development or mine proposal, a revised version will be presented time and time again, till it is bulldozed through all resistance. Still there are occasional good news stories. One such was the passing of the 1973 *Endangered Species Act* in the USA, from which came protection for, amongst others, Bald Eagles.

Bald Eagles *(Haliaeetus leucocephalus)* are not actually bald at all. They are in fact very handsome birds with dark umber brown bodies, pure white heads and tails, and magnificent deep chrome yellow beaks. They are the American national bird, chosen as a symbol of the bravery and freedom of the American people. We see lots of them around Vancouver with some actually nesting in trees in the city. Another name is the White-headed Sea Eagle. They gather in great numbers when the salmon return along the rivers and streams, as they are greatly attracted to the smell of rotting fish. It is thought that, a couple of hundred years ago, there were probably over two hundred thousand nesting pairs overall, with a hundred thousand pairs south of the Canadian border. The numbers were drastically reduced in the lower 48 states as a result of pesticides, lead shot, habitat destruction, and over-fished and destroyed salmon runs. In 1940 the bird received some US protection under the *Bald Eagle Protection Act*. Even so, by 1963 there were just 400 pairs south of the Canadian border.

In 1962, Rachel Carson published *Silent Spring*. In that book, she publicized the impoverishment of the ecological systems of the United States. She listed, amongst other problems, the damage the insecticide DDT was doing to America's birds of prey. It was shown that DDT worked its way up the food chain to the raptors, which suffered thin shells to their eggs and failure to produce viable young. This same problem applied to nearly all the birds of prey everywhere that DDT was being used. The numbers of most species were crashing. The Peregrine Falcon became the poster icon for the cause. In 1972, a ban on DDT use in the USA was put in effect, with the result that raptor numbers began to increase. In 1973 the *Endangered Species Act* became law, and recovery plans were established.[1]

Slowly the Bald Eagle numbers climbed again, until there are now thought to be over 10,000 pairs in the lower 48 states, and about 60,000 pairs across all of North America – that is some 30 per cent of the original numbers. They have done so well that they were removed from the federal list of threatened and endangered species in 2007.[2] They are still protected, from wanton shooting and nest destruction, under *the Bald and Golden Eagle Protection Act*. It is one of the most successful recoveries of all, and bodes well for the future. The Bald Eagle recovery illustrates just what can be possible when we are really determined to improve on dire situations.

I remember 1970 as a watershed year for nature. I was new to Vancouver, and in the workshop where I had my first job our conversation seemed full of talk of the natural world and of the horrors that we humans had wrought on it. Attention was drawn to the environment at that time, thanks to some pretty awful ecological catastrophes that had recently taken place. Rachel Carson's book had certainly raised awareness, but so did reports of the 1969 oil-drilling blowout off the Californian coast and the fire on the Cuyahoga River. That the Great Lakes were dying didn't do much to allay peoples' fears. In any group the air was abuzz with matters of the environment. The United Nations was introducing environmental committees about then, and citizens were making the environment as much an issue as banning the bomb. Greenpeace formed in Vancouver, first as the 'Don't Make a Wave Committee' in 1971, and as Greenpeace in 1972. In those years, of the 1970s and early 80s, a number of environmental protections were enacted, with the 1982 legislated international ban on whaling being a high point. The ban took effect from late 1985. That was not before time as the killing had, by the 1930s, become totally unsustainable with over 50,000 whales being killed annually.

In the early 1970s, a number of International incentives were underway toward ameliorating environmental concerns, so I know our discussions were in no way unique. But for Vancouver they may have been particularly appropriate. BC, and most of the West Coast, had been pristine such a very short while before. Few white men lived in the Pacific North West before 1850, and when I arrived I came upon few people who had been born there. Those that had been, had many anecdotes to tell.

"My Dad remembers when thousands and thousands of salmon returned to the Capilano River each year. Now they're bred in a hatchery, thanks to the dam."

"That's nothing. Granddad used to have to fight the eagles for the fish, but I haven't seen many eagles, or many fish for that matter, for years."

"My grandma says, that for the first few years of marriage they never went to a store. They lived off the salmon and their vegetable garden."

Well those days are gone now, but reports are that the seas around

British Columbia are slowly returning to greater health, thanks to legislation, fisheries management and controls on pollution. The marine mammals are returning, some slowly and cautiously, and some at a watery gallop. From Sea Otters to whales there is reason for hope. All along the coast, from Alaska and Haida Gwaii in the north to Washington's Olympic Peninsula and on down to Southern California in the south, mammals are returning. Some seem to be returning in good numbers, but it is difficult to get precise counts on such ocean traversing animals as whales.

It is one thing to get reliable numbers of the whales killed during the years of whaling, but it is more difficult to find reliable estimates of their present numbers. Generally though, according to the International Union for Conservation of Nature *Red List of Threatened Species* most whales are recovering. In the Eastern North Pacific, both Grey and Humpback Whales, of which there were considered to be no more than 1,500 in the 1960s, now number close to 20,000. Apparently about 1,300 humpbacks are feeding in BC waters.[34] Here are a few other tales of whale numbers:

- Five of the very rare Blue Whales - the largest animal to have lived on earth - were identified off Haida Gwaii, British Columbia in 2007.[5]
- The whale research group, Cascadia, had, in 2011, photo-records of 400 individual Fin Whales off North America's Pacific Coast.[6] Fins are renowned for their fast speed of travel.
- In 2013, a very rare Right Whale was seen off BC's coast for the first time in 60 years.[7]
- It is not known whether Sei Whales are recovering in the North Pacific.[8]
- Transient Killer Whales, or Orcas seem to be thriving in BC waters, while the resident Orcas continue to survive. There must be plenty of seals, which the transient whales favour, but down in the depths, there may be too few salmon, the main diet of the resident whales, to satisfy the their huge appetites.

With regard to the seals and sea lions; their numbers are even more encouraging. Harbour Seals, which numbered 15,000 in 1960, now number 105,000. The number of Steller Sea Lions that winter on the BC coast is estimated at 48,000, which is a great improvement over the 3,400 before they finally won protection in 1970. These animals received their name from our Georg Wilhelm Steller, who recorded the Sea Cows' plight in the Bering Sea. California Sea Lions are doing so well they are beginning to be judged a bit of a problem, and the Elephant Seals have increased to 200,000 from their one-time number of fewer than one hundred. The number given for them covers the population all the way from Alaska to Mexico.[9]

The mammal population numbers are very encouraging. However, while they are improving, the number of threatened and endangered fish and bird species off BC's coast has doubled in the two years to 2012, from 64 to 113. Nothing, it seems, is simple.

Overall though, in southwestern British Columbia, including the sea, rivers and land areas, selfless private citizens and NGOs are going to great efforts to improve the environment, with the goal of returning local ecosystems, as close as possible, to the original pristine conditions of not so very long ago.

Possibly one of the most encouraging international tales is that of Kenya's Green Belt Movement. The Movement, or GBM, was formed at a time when many parts of Africa were suffering from deforestation, serious soil erosion and threats of desertification. Deforestation is caused by too many people cutting excessive amounts of wood for cooking.

The GBM had its genesis at the 1972 United Nations Environment Program (UNEP), which was established in Nairobi, and was one result of the earlier Stockholm Conference on Human Environment. In 1976 Dr. Wangari Maathai proposed the idea, with the official movement being founded a year later. She was a member of the National Council of Women of Kenya, and had earlier become the first female in Central and East Africa to earn a PhD.

Her big idea was to plant trees to prevent the continuing land degradation. Kenya's GBM soon developed into a broadly supported grassroots movement led by women who planted more than 20 million trees on church, school and private farm properties. It then evolved with the discovery that trees planted in long rows grew to be very beneficial belts of woodland. The trees gave shelter, and shade, and breaks to the wind. The new woodland also created habitat that invited back the birds and the animals.[10]

Despite great opposition from Kenya's President Daniel Moi and other political difficulties, including Dr. Maathai being beaten and jailed, the Green Belt Movement was a success. In the more than 40 years since it was founded, over 40 million trees have been planted, and 30,000 women have been trained in a great many trades. The skills and the small business practices they now have help them to earn money, while they also protect the environment and integrity of the land. The resulting improvements also strengthen their cultures and economies.[11]

Since the 80s the movement has been adopted in many other countries including Zimbabwe and Tanzania. I can't help wondering what the madman President of Zimbabwe, and the development-road-through-the-Serengeti enthusiastic President of Tanzania, think of such initiatives. They are initiatives that give democratic power to the people, while taking authority from the presidents.

Although despised by most Kenyan governments of the past 40 years, Wangari Maathai received the most wonderful international endorsement when she was given the 2004 Nobel Peace Prize. She unfortunately died in October 2011, but her work, and her big idea 'to plant trees', is growing to be an arboreal giant with propitious fruits. In Kenya's 2010 National Climate Response Strategy, the government proposes to grow 7.6 billion trees over the next 20 years. This proposal is within the *Forestry Development Plan*. To quote the Kenyan Government's paper:

This will be done by the growing of trees by 35,000 schools; 4300 women groups; 16,350 youth groups, and the six regional Development Authorities. Each school will be supplied with a 10,000 litre water tank to support harvesting of water for the establishment and management of tree nurseries as well as watering of planted out seedlings. In addition, large scale land owners with at least 50 acres of land will be encouraged to construct dams for water harvesting and storage in order to support establishment of irrigated private forests. (sic)[12]

The government is now responding in a rational way to the terrible recent catastrophe of deforestation. Why, though, had it taken 40 years to come to such a policy when ordinary citizens started taking action all those years ago? And why did the concerned and intelligent citizens have to be persecuted by the government for being progressive? Because it went against the opportunities for the leaders to profit from the development of industry, unfettered by freethinking citizens. The people put into practice policies that the government itself is now adopting and promoting. Illogical animosities, like that of Kenya's government to the Green Belt Movement, can probably been found in many countries all over the world.

We know that in the democratic West, the citizens could usually have their say, but in other places, stepping out of line and recommending good policy can sometimes bring severe repercussions. Political dissent is not often a life and death issue in Europe or North America, but in some countries it takes true courage to argue with the government.

Kenya's population has multiplied 5 times in the past 50 years. It has grown from 8.1 million, in 1960, to 42 million in 2012, with 50 per cent of Kenyans under 19 years of age. The population explosion, which first led to deforestation and to desertification, will inevitably explode even more when those 21 million children and teens have multiple babies.

Similar questions to those regarding the Kenyan president's animosity can be asked in Canada and the USA where significant numbers of good citizens understand the environmental problems, but where the governments apparently don't. In Canada the government won't even listen when their own scientists provide facts it finds unpalatable. Always the environmentalists are treated as the bad guys. Why should environmentalists be vilified, in a developed western democracy, when all they try to do is save the country they love from pillage? I guess the answer is that the governments see profit in pillage.

It is indeed good that citizens are finding the courage to face off against their governments, and the big business that supports the status quo. Whether the government leader wants to build a self-aggrandizing statue to himself and a high-rise office tower that will destroy a city park, to fell a 130 million year old forest in Borneo to plant oil palms, or to build a pipeline for dirty oil across pristine northern forests, those in power say it is the only way to proceed. Be it in Kenya, Borneo or Canada, the government will always state the project is in the national interests or is an economic imperative. To argue against that is to be named anti-development, a fool and even a foreigner.

The protestors are always portrayed as troublemakers, naïfs, economically ignorant, foreigners, fools, criminals or whatever else the government spokespeople can come up with. They are therefore arrested, fined, beaten, prosecuted, jailed or murdered, or whatever else is acceptable to the particular jurisdiction where the protest is taking place. Yet across the planet more and more people are protesting the destruction of their natural places.

In 2006, the British Columbia government finally announced that some protections would be put into place to save the Great Bear Rainforest. This is one of the last pieces of the Northern Pacific temperate rainforest left un-logged, and it was a mighty battle to finally save even this. The battle had been ongoing for years. It started in the early years of the twentieth century when a few lone voices suggested that parts of this unique forest should be saved. When I arrived in BC in July 1969 I didn't know much about BC's forests and logging at first, but I soon heard about it. Possibly the first time I knew something was up was when a recent acquaintance spoke of a flight to the west coast of Vancouver Island. He returned totally appalled by what he had seen. He said that below the plane every valley was shorn of trees. Not just the valleys but the mountains too, all scraped of every tree and sign of life. He said it was pure desolation in every direction. The type of trees taken would have been evergreens: Douglas Fir, Western Red Cedar, Sitka Spruce and others.

When Captains Cook and Vancouver visited the coast, of what we now know as the Pacific Northwest, but what they thought of as the bleak and desolate end of the world, they found dense coast-embracing forests towering to the sky. It was not a place of meadows or open deciduous parkland like in Europe. Few apple-green leaves welcomed those far-traveled sailors. The woods were dark green, soaring, dense, lichen-covered, rain-soaked and dripping. Behind them, walls of immense grey mountains offered little enticement to inland exploration. That forest stretched from the drier Northern California to the sub-polar rainforest of Alaska – over 1,500 miles. Along that length, a number of different climatic zones exist, which support varying tree types and ecologies. In California the giants of the forest were the Sequoia Redwoods. In Southern British Columbia Douglas Fir and Red Cedar were the main trees, while on Vancouver Island and the North Coast the Douglas Fir gave way to cedar, spruce and hemlock. In Alaska Sitka Spruce and Western Hemlocks predominate. The true giants were the Sequoia and Douglas fir.

BC's forests have seen full-scale scale logging since 1869, but following the Second World War, the force of logging became ruthless and relentless in its industrial authority. Now 95 per cent of the forest is gone.[13][14] California has 4 per cent of the redwood forests protected; Washington and Oregon have 10 per cent between them. One needs to be clear of just what we are talking about here. In BC after the forest is felled new seedling trees are planted. So after some years the land returns to being forest. What is in question is the virgin or old growth forest. A forest of mixed age trees of 500 to two thousand years old is not the same as a plantation of 20 to 60 year-old mono-cultured trees. The ancient forest habitat, and the breadth of species it contained, is very different than that of the plantation. And plantation forest now covers nearly all the land that had been old growth but has now been logged.

BC is 60 per cent forested but 75 per cent mountainous, and the forest on the west and wet side of the Coastal Mountains is quite different than that on the east and drier side and in the province's interior. Because of the difference, in both rainfall and temperature, the narrow coastal strip of Pacific Coast Rainforest is where the trees grow to immense sizes, if given time. For instance coastal Douglas Firs typically grow to 280 ft (85m) tall while in the interior they grow to half that size or 140 ft (42m). Furthermore trees don't grow as well on thin-soiled, and steep-sided, granite mountain slopes, as they do along rich and moist valley bottoms. In the fight to save the old growth trees, the government was often willing to compromise and set aside forests in the areas of stunted trees, but required a real battle before it would save the valley bottoms where the largest trees grew. The tallest recorded tree in BC was the 'Cary Fir' of North Vancouver. It was 417 ft (127m) tall, 25 ft (8m) in diameter and 77 ft (23m) in circumference. It was felled in North Vancouver in 1895.[15] When it was lying on its side the base of the trunk must have been nearly as high as a three-story building.

Old residents can remember groves of firs, nearly as large, that stood in the Fraser Valley to the east of Vancouver into the 1940s. Improved logging technologies did for those after the Second World War. By 2011, just .05 percent of these forests of giant trees still stand in British Columbia. One tree that does, is a cedar named Cheewat Cedar. It is 60 ft in circumference and 182 ft tall. It is thought to be about 2000 years old.[16] The height is truncated as a result of breaks near the top. It may have been a small sapling at the time of Jesus' birth, or maybe a 100 ft tree by then.

We must remember that a tree in a 100-year-old wood is very different to a mature forest of two thousand year old trees. The mature trees become a habitat themselves and will support a huge number of plants, animals, insects and birds. Huckleberry bushes may grow from a cleft fifty feet up. Mistletoe and other parasites, epiphytes, mosses and lichen will smother much of the bulk while cracks and hollows will provide bird and animal sanctuaries and nests. Such birds as the Marbled Murrelet, and the Northern Spotted Owl require these old trees for their nesting survival, and any one of those ancient trees may have supported hundreds or even thousands of animals and plants of one sort or another. The hundred-year-old tree, in contrast, is rather a lifeless thing. It is as an isolated rock jutting from the sea. Some crustaceans will cling at the water line and some seabirds will settle, but it cannot compare with a long established island clad in dense jungle and alive with shrubs songbirds and multitudinous insects.

A mere handful of isolated big trees do still survive, but humanity will have to wait another 2000 years, or until 4000CE before forests of such huge trees can possibly be seen again. Even then they will only grow to their full potential if we stop all logging in their rich valleys and give them the chance to grow unmolested. For that matter, we will never again see the great forests of New England, certainly not for many centuries, nor will we again see the great oak forests of Old England.

In British Columbia, the real fight to save old growth coastal forests has been ongoing since the early nineteen-seventies, but neither the logging companies nor the government would give an inch. The battles had been valley by valley. A few victories have been won: an island saved here, parts of a valley saved there. But throughout the past 40 years it has been upsetting knowing that thousand year old trees were falling daily. The government's argument was always that the loggers needed the jobs and the province needed the income. What would they have done had there been no trees in the first place?

There is one place named Cathedral Grove where tall trees still stand. It is a rather small tourist spot on Vancouver Island where trees of up to 800 years old stand miraculously protected since 1911.

Environmentalists have gradually convinced the provincial government to save areas from logging, till now a total of 12.5 per cent of the province is protected. However very little of that is old growth forest, with most being view properties of lakes and high mountain alpine meadows, which is good for tourism, but not good for old growth pacific rain forest. The first true breakthrough came in the early 1990s when Clayoquot Sound on Vancouver Island was saved from clear-cutting.

Then in 2006 a breakthrough was announced and celebrated. Following a huge effort by a consortium of environmental groups, the government was finally shamed into protecting about 33 per cent of the coastal forest between the north end of Vancouver Island and the southern tip of the

Alaska panhandle. This stretch has been named the Great Bear Rainforest and covers about 27,000 sq miles (70,000 km2) of which 7,700 sq miles is protected. A further 1,200 sq miles has been designated as 'biodiversity, mining and tourism areas, where commercial logging will be prohibited.' A victory for common sense, but still not as good as it might have been had the government had any sense of history. It is interesting that the trees that fall on the West Coast don't offer much employment to British Columbians beyond that of loggers. They don't go off to sawmills where the people enjoy the value-added advantages of producing lumber from the trees. Instead the logs are taken out to sea where they are loaded on ships bound for Asia. The Asian people enjoy the employment obtained from turning raw logs into building materials.

The Western Canadian province of Saskatchewan contains the northern-most area of the Great American Prairie. Like the vast stretch to the south, it also lost the bison, wolves and other North American animals that were extirpated by the beginning of the twentieth century. Now a few bison can be seen on the land, mostly brought in by ranchers with an eye to raising them for meat.

The province is another huge landmass at 227,100 sq miles (588,276 km2), not as big as BC but then, in 2011, it only had a human population of 1,053,960, and most of the residents are happy with that much land to share. Early in the twentieth century, there were so few people that the government encouraged settlers to farm the land by offering it free, if they would plough and plant crops on 10-acre blocks. Many tried and, in certain areas close to the Montana border, many failed. Most of those stopped trying by the beginning of the First World War and after it was over, those who came home, went into ranching.

In 1956 the Saskatchewan Natural History Society began lobbying the federal and provincial governments to establish a prairie grasslands park to preserve some remnants of the prairie. This, the governments finally agreed to do in 1981. As of 2012 the park consisted of two separate blocks of prairie along the north side of the Saskatchewan/Montana border. The habitat is known as 'undisturbed dry mixed-grass/short-grass prairie grassland'. The name 'grasslands' suggests soft rolling land, but that land is further north and well exploited for wheat. The park's land is quite rugged in parts with plenty of coulees, buttes, badlands and cliffs. Some of the flatter patches were ploughed and planted long ago, but much is still true prairie.

Now efforts are being made to remove the exotics from the ploughed areas and to re-establish only the plants of the true prairie. When all the land is assembled, and the 350 sq miles (900 km2) of the final park is finished, the completed grassland should be as close to the original as it's possible to make it. Already there are known to be 40 grasses, 36 rare plants and a great many flowering plants on the undisturbed areas. One of the established sections, the West Block, holds the only colonies of Black-tailed Prairie Dogs in Canada while the park protects rare Burrowing Owls, Long-billed Curlew, Greater Sage Grouse, Loggerhead Shrike and other species in steep decline. Reintroductions of bison, the once believed extinct Black-tailed Ferret and the Swift Fox are ongoing, and apparently successful so far.[17] Pronghorn Antelope are increasing, and presumably White-tailed and Mule Deer will find their way back in greater numbers. It may be too much of a miracle for the declining Greater Prairie Chicken to return. We can never hope to see the Plains Grizzly or Plains Wolf, which are both extinct.

Any block of prairie, even just 350sq miles, will surely help the struggling prairie birds. These include Chestnut-collared and McCowan's Longspurs, Horned Larks, Sprague's Pipits, Baird's Sparrows and so very many more. Let's hope they can at least hang on for a while longer before descending into extinction.

An interesting historical fact about the east block of the new park is that in 1876 Chief Sitting Bull, and his Sioux followers, found refuge there after the Battle of Little Bighorn. The Great White Mother – Queen Victoria - and her brave few North West Mounted Police made sure the vengeful American Cavalry stayed on their side of the border and therefore saved the Sioux for a while from guaranteed extinction.[18]

Not only are the people of Saskatchewan working to save and reestablish areas of grassland prairie, some good souls south of the border are working to the same goal. There the Prairie Preservation Alliance, amongst others, is working to save some short-grass prairie, while the Grassland Heritage Foundation is saving tall grassland, of which only 1 per cent of the original tall-grass prairie remains. The tall grass is even more problematic than the short grass as it is the land of the true Wheat Belt with rich soil up to 15 ft deep.

It is wonderful that these people are attempting to save examples of our impoverished prairie ecosystems, but I fear these are just the first steps. Establishing isolated patches of prairie with few other refueling stops on the migrating birds' flight paths may not be enough to save the birds, which are declining fast. Isolated pristine locations, which require migrating birds to fly over thousands of miles of agricultural monoculture, laced with insecticides and herbicides, won't necessarily halt the decline in bird numbers. The diets for most of these birds are plant seeds and insects. The prairies were once rich with both, but now millions of acres of wheat fields, poisoned by years of insecticide and herbicide application, give little food to the original inhabitants when they stop off for refueling. The only places now remaining, where the birds might find a meal, are on the road margins and on the rangeland given over to cattle. It is truly tough for the few remaining prairie wild birds.

Trevor Herriot, in his book *Grass, Sky, Song. Promise and Peril in the World of Grassland Birds,* recounts how, between 1996 and 2001, 15 per cent of Saskatchewan farmers left their land, and how, in the drier grassland areas where growing crops has always been a marginal enterprise, some of the farmers who remain are returning the land to grass for cattle. He also observes that "there are more bison on the prairie right now than there have been for 130 years." That is encouraging news for the ecology, though maybe not for the struggling farmers.

It would be great to believe that the grass-seed the ranchers are using, is of a type native to the land, though that might be too much to expect. Still, a return to grass has to be good news for all those struggling prairie animals, birds and insects. We should remember, though, that these pieces of land are miniscule when considered against the original prairie acreage. For instance the 350 square miles of the new Saskatchewan Grasslands National Park is only 0.000004 per cent of the original 1.4 million sq miles of untouched North American prairie.

According to Nature Conservancy only 5 per cent of grassland is protected worldwide.

Once, long ago, in the mid nineteen seventies, I went to the Singapore Zoo. There, immediately after entering was a restricted open area and garden where families could gather, get their bearings, and decide what to explore. It was an enchanting place, because it was alive with the most appealing small longhaired golden monkeys. They sat on fences, ran amongst people's feet and generally captivated everyone. They were beautiful in their red golden silkiness. Then we read about them on the information boards, and found that they only numbered about two hundred animals worldwide, and that their forest in Brazil was all but gone. They were Golden Lion Tamarins (*Leontopithecus rosalia*). They are small, 10 inch (26cm), monkeys with long golden-russet silky hair overall and hairless faces surrounded by a fuller mane. They have attractive personalities. In the wild they live in family groups of about ten animals, which defend a home territory of about 100 acres (40 hct). They typically live 15 years, though one has been recorded at 30 years of age. Between 1960 and 1965, it has been estimated that, 200 to 300 Golden Lion Tamarins were caught and exported per month for the overseas pet trade. At the same time, the destruction of their forests accelerated mightily.

Brazil, like Canada, renowned across the world for its inherited riches and wanton destruction of the forests, has now taken a small step in the right direction. Brazil has established two reserves on the Eastern Atlantic coast where the tamarins lived, and where the first captive bred animals were returned to the wild in 1984. They are now expanding in numbers. In 1996 they were listed as critically endangered, even though by then the numbers had risen to about 400 in the wild. That categorization was then downgraded, in 2003, to endangered. In 2010, it was believed the numbers had continued their rise to 1000 in the wild, with 500 others in captive breeding programs.

When looking at a map of Brazil to find their distribution, one will find a tiny dot smaller than a pinhead on the East coast. This represents their range fairly well. They now exist on only 59 square miles (154km2) of remnant forest, which is split into 14 fragments, none of which is old growth. Of those fragments two areas have been set aside as national protected territory. They are the Poco das Antas Biological reserve at 24 square miles extent, established 1974, and the Uniao Biological Reserve at 12.4 square miles. Neither reserve is fully forested with Uniao having one of the largest forested areas at 9.27 square miles. In 2010 Poco das Antas was thought to hold 230 tamarins while Uniao held 120. Of the original 500,000 square miles of Atlantic forest a little more than 7 per cent still remains. The Atlantic Forest is described as "the most devastated and highly threatened ecosystem on Earth." According to the National Primate Research Centre at the University of Wisconsin, Madison, it is subject to "fuelwood harvesting, illegal logging, plant and animal poaching, mining, urbanization and infrastructure development, and the introduction of alien species."[19] Prohibitions on cutting vegetation in the region were proposed in 1990, but were still being discussed by Congress in 2010. An awful lot of forest can be destroyed, while the politicians discuss the matter for twenty years.

By re-establishing the Brazilian Atlantic Coast Forest, Brazil could so easily secure the future for the Golden Lion Tamarins and all the other species that are part of that forested ecosystem. Kathryn and I visited the small Tres Picos State Park in 2011. This park is an old banana plantation that has been allowed to return to forest, so it was very definitely young secondary trees at the time, but we were stunned by the wonderful array of colourful avian fauna we saw in the three days we were there. The birds included seven species of multi-coloured tanagers, three of brilliant euphonia, a dacnis, parrotlets and parakeets and many more. Tamarins have returned to the park.

It seems just a little protection is all it takes, so why is the government so loath, or slow, to add the final protections?

One strategy to protect the ecology that has met with some success, has been an effort to educate the locals about the need to preserve the unique ecosystem and wildlife that exists in their forests. One result of this has been the return of 20 pet tamarins. They are very cute, so caring humans are concerned about the wellbeing of such animals. There must be a great many non-cute species in the forest that no one either cares about, or even notices whether their numbers are up or down, yet they are deserving of protection too. With luck, once adequate forest has been protected for one iconic species, many of the other endangered species will also see their numbers increase and a healthy balanced ecosystem will be recreated.

Thanks to tireless people with good hearts, there are other good news stories.

In 2012 a new 1,977-acre (3.08 sq. miles) Peruvian cloud forest park named Monte Potre Municipal Conservation Area opened. It is an area of steep cloud-forest mountains where can be found Andean Cats and a number of endemic birds, most with very descriptive names. These include the following notable ones: the Fire-throated Metaltail, White-chinned Thistletail, White-browed Spinetail, White-browed Conebill, Tschudi's Tapaculo and the White-browed Memispingus. Two birds that are both rated vulnerable are the Bay-vented Cotinga and Rufous-browed Himispingus. It seems to me that someone has given the Peruvian birds some mighty weird names.

The park was established, thanks to the efforts of the American

Bird Conservancy's Peruvian partner Asociacion Ecosistemas Andinos (ECOAN), and local communities. Again it is great news that some land is being set aside for protection, but when I think of how vast the Andes are I can't help but wonder why only such a tiny piece of land is being preserved.[20]

In March 2012 the Wildlife Conservation Society announced that an agreement had been signed to protect 80,000 acres (125 sq. miles) of Guatemalan forest within the Maya Biosphere Reserve. The MB Reserve covers nearly 5,000,000 acres of species-rich forest that, although supposedly protected, suffers ongoing debasement through illegal logging, illegal hunting, slash-and-burn agriculture, ranching and mining from, amongst others, mighty Canadian mining companies. It is an area containing some of the most famous Mayan archeological sites, so it is also an area of artifact looting and drug trafficking. The new agreement is with the community of Carmelita and follows two previous ones with the communities of Uaxactun, and with Paso Caballos in Laguna del Tigre National Park.

Director of WCS's Latin America and Caribbean Program, Julie Kunen said, "Conservation agreements are a win-win for both the people and wildlife of the Maya Biosphere Reserve. The agreements address pressing development needs and provide real incentives for the people living in and around the reserve to protect its animals and conserve its forests." The list of animals that this agreement should help to protect include: Jaguar, Ocelot, Tapir, Harpy Eagle, Ocellated Turkey, Scarlet Macaw and the native monkeys, all of which will now come under an enforced hunting ban in the area. The agreement will also provide education and health services while reducing deforestation.

The agencies involved include the Guatemalan government's Protected Areas Council, the UK's Department of International Development, the Prospect Hill Foundation and the community of Carmelita. Nature Conservancy and all who work for, and subscribe to, that foundation should be congratulated for the great work they do.[21]

The one negative to all this is the memory of all the pieces of land set aside as protected nature reserves that hold good till precious metals are discovered in the reserve. Then the unscrupulous mining companies offer money, jobs and bribes and all the protections are cancelled. By that time, the people and NGOs who worked to establish the reserve have moved on or have passed on, and the battle begins anew. In the world of capitalist business, environmental protections put in place to last for all time usually last till the first business opportunity presents itself.

In March 2012, Wildlife Extra reported that Niger has announced the formation of the Termite and Tin Toumma Nature and Culture Reserve. This protected park is on 38,610 sq miles (100,000km2) of Sahara Desert sand seas, mountains and dry grass plain. African national parks are thought of as being large, but this will be one of the biggest.

The Tuareg and the Woodaabe peoples live there, as do Addax, Scimitar-horned Oryx, Dama Gazelle, Barbary Sheep, Cheetah and other rare desert species. We can only hope it will be successful at protecting both the rare animals and the culture of the people there.

One aspect to this story that is remarkable is the number of enterprises and individuals that contributed to bringing this conservation effort to fruition. The Sahara Conservation Fund was the driving force, but other such major donors supporting it were the European Union, Fonds Francais pour l'Environnement Mondial, the Convention on Migratory Species and especially the Niger Ministry of Environment's Wildlife Service. On top of that were at least seventeen zoos, a dozen conservation organizations, foundations, funds and untold numbers of individuals.[22] A tremendous amount of effort and wealth is put into an accomplishment such as this, but unlike the developers, big businessmen and bankers, the effort is not expended for monetary profit, but for the health of our Earth.

As mentioned in an earlier chapter, the last free Spix's Macaw died in the wild in the year 2000. Efforts to secure a future for the bird are ongoing under a committee named The Working Group for the Recovery of the Spix's Macaw. This committee involves many organizations including the 1990 established Brazilian Institute of Environment and Renewable Natural Resources, the Loro Parque of Spain and Al Wabra Wildlife Preservation, Qatar. Now the captive-bred bird numbers are increasing in the different breeding facilities to a total of 36 young. This brings the full number of birds to 73, with another 12 in captivity but not participating in the breeding program. However, having cage-bred birds with nowhere to live in the wild is not going to satisfy the long-term aims of this effort. So now two other important steps are necessary. The first is the re-establishment of suitable habitat in the state of Bahia where the birds used to live. The second will be finding ways to release these tame birds that have no knowledge of predators or how to live in the wild.

The Brazilian government is committed to a ten-year program of restoring habitat, building reintroduction facilities and developing breeding facilities.[23] Those are long term plans, but the most practical immediate step has been taken by the Al Wabra group who, in 2009, purchased the 5,500 acre (2,200 hectare) Concordia Farm, where the last Spix's Macaw was seen in 2000.[24] This farm is the immediate neighbour of Gangorra Farm, a smaller piece of land purchased earlier by a different group. The two farms, in the arid centre of North-east Brazil, have a total area of 6,500 acres (2600 hectares). It is hoped that the land will, in time, be returned to a natural habitat of the birds' required nesting and food plants. It has been concluded that the Spix's Macaws nest in Caraiba gallery woodland trees, and feed on two species of the *Euphorbiaceae* plants. The Caraiba tree is just one species in the *Tabebuia* genus, which is renown for the clusters of bright yellow flowers that adorn all 100 species. The trees in question grow along seasonal creeks but have been largely felled over the past few hundred years. They seem not to regenerate easily.[25]

Researching the habitat necessary to the reintroduction of Spix's Macaw was apparently no easy task. With only a handful of birds in the wild, in the twenty years before the last wild male disappeared, the researchers had to rely to a large extent on the observations of hunters and trappers for the pet trade. Without the birds to observe, how else can one guess at their preferred habitat? It had been assumed that they liked Buriti Palm, but the last wild bird seemed to like Caraiba trees and that is the species finally assumed desirable. A study written by A. T. Juniper and C. Yamashita, and published in Bird Conservation International in 1991, gave credence to the Caraiba open woodland being the birds' preferred habitat. The trouble is those trees require moisture or flooding from seasonal streams. That is also the preferred land for the farmers who grow maize, or range cattle, on those few fertile areas in otherwise arid land. The cattle naturally enjoy chewing on young shoots and saplings which is why the only trees still standing are very old. To encourage the trees to regenerate, the cattle and any other browsers have been removed from the Concordia and Gangorra farms. The shoots will now be able to grow into saplings, but it will still be a long process before sufficient habitat will be available for reintroducing the birds, no matter how many are bred in captivity.

The two species of *Euphorgiaceae*, required for the birds, are natural to the caatinga habitat of northern Bahia where the birds once flew. Presumably the two are deemed a requirement because of their fruit. *Euphorgiaceae* are part of the spurge family, which has about 7500 species within 300 genera. Within that great number of flowering plants are herbs, succulents, shrubs and trees. We can only hope the people involved have chosen the correct trees and plants to satisfy the needs and tastes of that little blue macaw.[26]

The other difficulty, once the habitat is reestablished and there are sufficient birds, will be finding a way of releasing them with a reasonable chance of survival. I don't know how long it will take for the plants and trees to be established well enough to suit the birds, but I guess it will be after quite a few more years of safely living in cages. Releasing naive birds into the natural habitat of hungry hawks, and aggressive snakes, won't be too smart. Releasing each bird as Noah did with the dove and uttering the words "Be free. Live wild." might be a romantic gesture but it would be a sentence of quick death for the birds.

I assume the birds chosen for release will need long training periods when fear of raptors and snakes will be inculcated into their consciences. If that can't be done I imagine the caged birds will be kept as egg-layers and never be set free. The eggs would probably have to be put in the nests of similar, but different, species of wild blue macaws that will be able to train the young birds. The problem there is that most other macaws, such as the Illiger's Macaw, favour different nesting trees and habitat. At least that's what I understand. It would be such a huge disappointment, after all the efforts to breed the birds and reestablish the habitat, if no safe way could be found to bring the two together. For a lasting reintroduction of these renowned birds many obstacles still remain. If all the conjecture is correct, and the birds did in fact nest in the yellow flowering Caraiba trees that only grew along the banks of the seasonal streams, their distribution before the advent of the Europeans must have been along narrow strips of habitat that covered some considerable length, but never much depth, across the arid Caatinga. We can only hope that the areas of re-established open gallery woodland will be sufficient to host a viable population of the birds. It will be lovely to again see the blue-grey birds perched amongst the big yellow flowers, which is about as good a colour combination as we can get in nature.

One question that I am sure many are asking is whether it would not be better to pour all our few resources into saving threatened species, instead spending so much money on bringing back species that may, or may not, be viable in the wild. Maybe the answer is that most of the threats to the endangered species are controlled by individuals and corporations who will lose too much profit if they curtail their activities in any way.

One final piece of good news concerns small songbirds that were mentioned earlier. These birds are called the Cerulean Paradise-flycatcher *(utrichomyias rowleyi)*. They are vivid cerulean blue over the whole body except the breast and belly, which is paler blue. The underside of the tail is of a pale grey. The birds, which are 7 inches (18cm) in length, lived on the Indonesian island of Sangihe where they had been assumed extinct for nearly 100 years. That has turned out to be incorrect. In 1998 the bird was rediscovered in five patches of woodland on the base of the Gunung Sahendaruman Mountain. The small patches of forest total less than 5 square miles (8 km2). Presumably, when the rest of the island was cleared for agriculture these few steep gullies were of no agricultural use, so were left alone. That fortunate omission seems to have saved the bird. There are believed to be from 19 to 135 birds living. Now BirdLife International, the Wildlife Conservation Society and others are working with the villagers of the island to establish measures to protect the bird, expand its habitat, educate the people, and develop bird tourism as a means of bringing money to the islanders.[27]

17 A Finite Earth

> The Earth's ecological limits are finite and, no matter how much we might
> wish otherwise, we are obliged to live within those restraints.

I set off with this writing to explore the relationship between human overpopulation and environmental degradation leading to species extinctions, and I'm surprised with what I have discovered. I find that a few well-known extinctions happened before the great population explosion. The depletion of Europe and West Asia's large animals - the Auroch cattle and Wisent bison, the lions, tigers and the rest - happened over millennia of hunting, though most of the final extinctions happened in the 19th and 20th centuries.

The most famous extinctions, those of the Dodo and Great Auk, resulted from, in the first case, cowardly human cruelty – thought of as sport – and, in the second, from commercial necessity. The first happened long before our population began its great climb, and probably only involved a few score individuals. The killing of the great Sea Cows resulted from a few totally ruthless men, with limited economic options, encountering very gentle mammals with little inbred sense of fear and flight. Any creatures of gentle and ruminative temperament, such as the Sea Cows, Dodos or giant tortoises, had no defenses against exploitation and destruction. Introduce a handful of poor and desperate men, those who arrived in new lands long before the setting up of government or the rule of law, and the results were inevitable.

One little-known extinction, that of the hundred-million-year evolving great Moa birds of New Zealand, happened after the Maoris landed on those islands ten centuries ago. It was, as with the Dodo, a typical case of humans arriving and immediately becoming the top predators. They were the top predators in a land of unafraid sitting ducks – or in the case of

Moas, towering 13 ft (3 m) two-legged birds with no wings. So those early extinctions resulted from many different causes.

Then again, the accidental introduction of alien species to island communities of fearless birds and ground-dwelling amphibians, was a quite unforeseen cause of a host of extinctions. The destruction began as soon as Europeans discovered those unknown lands - at least unknown to them - and enabled rats and cats to get ashore. It was on those islands that the alien animals became the top predators and multiplied at the expense of their prey.

The rush of local extinctions from the British Isles coincided with the rapid population expansion following millennia of wildlife killings. In general, nature was deemed to be in competition for food with humans; therefore, animals, if delicious, were for eating. If not edible, they were probably in competition, so were killed anyway. The perception of competition applied to the likes of eagles eating small lambs or otters consuming fish. So while the Brits ate the birds and fish they really did a number on the raptors and predators. They shot them out of the sky with glee, and they trapped the animal carnivores mercilessly. This dynamic still applies in much of the Third World as well as in some European nations today. In many countries, the population will eat any wild thing that moves. The Chinese, apparently, eat absolutely every living thing, and in Africa the hunger for bush meat, including the likes of gorilla, chimpanzee and Okapi is driving some recently secure animal populations toward oblivion.

Turning grassland or forest to agricultural land, as on the Great Plains, the Argentine Pampas, the Amazon Basin, South East Asia, in fact on every continent except Antarctica, has also had the result of destroying habitat, and crowding untold numbers of original wildlife inhabitants off the land.

The worst single slaughter till 1900, the buffalo, wolf and animal slaughter on the Great Plains, began when the United States had a relatively small population of 23 million, with very few living on the prairie itself. That carnage was caused by the officially sanctioned policy of eradication, with the eventual goal of getting rid of the First Nations people and opening the land to settlers. That calamity coincided with another nearly as bad. That was the British felling of the great Indian forest of the Ganges plain, and the shooting of the wild animals living there. That was a result of the desire to develop railway infrastructure, the need for railway ties, and the need for more agricultural land. It was also the consequence of the British determination that lions, tigers, cheetahs and other Asian predators were vermin and, as such, should be removed.

The annihilation, before 1980, of nine large African animals including the Atlas Bear, two subspecies of lion and five herbivores was bad enough, but that was the total for all of Continental Africa.[1] Continental North America, on the other hand, suffered a total of forty identified animal extinctions including, the Arizona Jaguar, the Mexican Silver Grizzly, eight wolf subspecies, six large grazers, seven bird species and a bunch of fish.[2] The majority of the large animal and many of the bird slaughters were intentional, ruthless and unforgivable.

The unfortunate results that came from rats heading for shore, or men ploughing land, can be forgiven. Those results were either accidental or unintentional. But to forgive the wholesale slaughter of the large carnivores and herbivores, by men with guns, requires the judge to be blessed with the holiness of a saint.

So it seems that, although most of the extinctions were the result of the age of exploration and many can be blamed on callous intent, some were the outcome of accident or ignorance. Now though, all the escalating and concluding assaults on species, both flora and fauna, are a result of our own great population explosion coupled with our incredibly shortsighted selfishness. During the four hundred years before the middle of the 20th century our numbers seemed to have been less a problem than our aggressive, careless and cruel character. One result of this huge overpopulation of humans is that it produces so many poor, desperate and disenfranchised individuals - individuals who will do anything for food and some money. Those things include turning every last piece of original habitat into cropland, slashing and burning for agriculture, eating any living thing that presents itself, illegally logging the last stands of forest, fishing the last fish from the sea and poaching the last ivory and rhino horn. Aside from being unable to prevent poverty, we have seldom educated anyone to care for the land. We denigrated the search for spiritual wisdom, and instead encouraged everyone towards materialism, to be adventurers and to be risk takers. We encouraged an ethic of make-your-own-way exploitation. It is an ethic that adds wealth for a few in the undeveloped areas, but also destroys the environment. So the population explosion is resulting in the destruction of the natural world as an unavoidable consequence of two destructive characteristics: mere survival on the one hand, and our search for wealth on the other.

Now we are losing vast expanses of the natural world, and multitudinous numbers of animals each year, simply as a result of trying to provide for the exploding human numbers. If the richest billion or two of us were only expecting the bare essentials, the results might not be such a disaster. The trouble is, we now hope, in the future, to have every one of us living, if not as rich as Croesus, at least as rich as an average westerner, and we are unwilling to question the results of such expectations. One result is the unsustainably huge amount of resources we now harvest and use up in our attempts to provide for the great number of expectant humans now living on this planet.

Someone once described humanity as a plague, a harsh assessment to be sure, and certainly not a view to which most people would adhere. We speak of plagues of locusts. We fear plagues of sickness but surely we can't be described as such. So I checked the definition in the dictionary.

Under 'Plague' *The Oxford English Dictionary* says:

'Plague
Noun 1/ a contagious disease spread by bacteria and causing fever and delirium.
Noun 2/ an unusually large quantity of destructive insects or animals.
Verb 1/ cause continual trouble to: he grew up on an estate plagued by crime.
Verb 2/ pester someone continually.'

Humans are animals, we are destructive and there is an unusually large quantity of us, so maybe we do fall under 'Noun 2'. The non-tribal, modern and industrial humans, have certainly destroyed, and have killed mightily – though not always with intent. We have also destroyed nature almost everywhere we have settled. So, according to the dictionary, I suppose the term plague can be applied to us – at least the modern us. This does give one cause to pause, as I'm sure most of us would rather not be thought of in that way.

To argue against us being a plague, as described in the dictionary, we have to believe we are not part of the animal world. In fact, we have to believe that we are separate from nature. This is hard to do when we review the findings of the past hundred and more years in such areas as evolutionary biology and physical anthropology. *Homo habilis, Homo erectus* and the rest, along with our genetic closeness to the great apes, seems to disprove the 'not part of nature' theory.

The most recent catastrophic destruction of wildlife can be traced to the explosion of our population. In such places as Asia and Africa humans multiplied enormously over the past hundred years and all those people needed land and needed feeding. Nature simply had to go. Some of the extinctions mentioned, and other near misses such as the decimation of the whales, had roots deep in our need for materials. The historic reality is that only flora, fauna and minerals provided us the materials for most of our everyday needs. That was until the development of plastics, made from hydrocarbons.

Traditionally, our clothes came from animals in the forms of leather, wool and silk, and from plants such as hemp, flax, and cotton. Cotton now provides 50 per cent of our clothing, which means a lot of land given over to growing cotton. Our warmth in cold climates came from furs and feathers and our oils were mostly from animals and fish, with a little from plants. Clay bricks, stone and slate gave us much of our basic housing, while the wood from trees provided the rest. Wood also provided nearly all of our furniture and transportation needs. The farm carts I knew in the 1940s, were nearly a hundred percent made of wood, as were the ones I saw in Nicaragua in the year 2010. The rubber of the inflatable tires, of course, came from the rubber tree. The metallic earths provided our metal tools. At the other end of the scale, I can think of no children's toys that were not of natural cloth, metal, lead or wood. Dolls' heads were ceramic.

Fortunately, during the most explosive increase in our population, that which occurred post 1945, we invented some alternative materials to supply our needs. Had we not, the recent depletion of nature would have been even more rapid and very much more complete. Imagine all of us still lubricating our automobiles with whale oil. Now, in 2013, we can't buy many wheeled transportation devices that are made with anything other than steel, aluminum or plastic. Most pneumatic tires are of synthetic rubber. Few toys are made of anything but plastic.

Think of how many fewer animals there would be if, instead of polyester and micro-fibers, we were still clothed in wool, feathers and furs.

Consider the ski business without the new lightweight and warm fibers we now have. The ski slopes could be alive with athletes wearing sheepskin and woolen knitted knickers.

"My word Priscilla! I do like your new ski pants."

"Yes! They're mink you know. I found the chinchilla became a trifle froid when the wind-chill became a factor. Also I didn't like the way the hairs fluffed up around my hips at unexpected times. One tries to keep one's figure, but such subterfuge from dead animals was truly unacceptable."

"Oh look Leticia, here comes Brent. He's wearing his new polar bear."

"Why, Priscilla dear, he is almost invisible against the snow."

"He is, isn't he . . . but I think you have to agree that the polar is better than that old grizzly he was so proud of. He is quite a slim man you know, but the grizzly made him look three hundred pounds. I've not met anyone who could wear grizzly fur without appearing obese."

"Still, dear, what is one to do? Finding a fur that stays warm when wet is so difficult, and they are all becoming so dreadfully expensive."

"Oh! You are so right. Do you know? I think I spend more money on ski-wear than I do on gas for the SUV."

The new alternate materials are petrochemical-derived, and come in the form of polypropylene, polystyrene, polyurethane, nylon and the rest. Adding those to the dominant mineral materials of steel, aluminum, sand-based glass, ceramic clays and cements derived from limestone, took the pressure off many animal and plant-derived materials. I never thought I would be apologizing for, nor praising, plastics but without them our huge population would have required a great many more millions of square miles of natural habitat planted to cotton, given over to sheep for wool or needed to grow all the other materials that plastics replaced. We would have also logged more trees, and mined more mineral and natural resources, had most of what we use not been made of plastics. Now nearly everything is of that material, from clothes, carpets and computers to patio tables, TVs and automobile interiors; however, the hydrocarbons, from which we make the plastics, are finite and will one day be all used up.

Hydrocarbons are repositories of truly useful chemicals from which we can build so many materials. The trouble is, though, that the main thing we do is burn them to provide us with unsustainable energy. Without the hydrocarbons, from oil and natural gas, the ecological footprint of our huge population could be very much larger than it already is. Not only would the world of nature be greatly reduced, our economic model and our politics may well have taken a different turn.

Possibly, without plastics but with only flora and fauna to supply our needs, we would have developed a less wasteful and more circumspect society. A community of small-footprint, non-consuming individuals educated to understand the need for both smaller expectations and small families. Maybe we would have developed a society less obsessed with consumerism.

On the other hand, with fewer consumer products to produce wealth and comfort, a less well-off population may have grown even faster. After all, in the post war baby boom, the greatest numbers of children were produced in the poorest regions, such as Africa and Asia. That suggests that without plastics we might today have an even larger population.

Whatever might have been the population outcome, had the past 60 years been plastics-free, I think there is no doubt that we would be mourning a great many more species extinctions than we do today.

Energy and green power
It means recognizing that unending economic growth on a finite planet is an impossible dream.

While our goal of taking all people from poverty to the living standards of the developed world is laudable, it seems it is not practical. Consumer capitalism has, until now, worked to create wealth for many people. But as it requires far more resources than our earth can provide, we have to assume that that system is another cul de sac. The Earth's bio-capacity cannot sustain the huge ecological footprint needed to give all nine or ten billion future citizens consumer lifestyles equivalent to those of the wealthy west.

Noting that, but focusing on global warming, one might anticipate that we would all be bending over backwards to cut our expectations, to reduce growth, and thus cut our CO_2 emissions. Oh how naïve that thought is. Not only is Canada intent on selling coal to Asia, developing the dirty tar sands and fracking for rock-sequestered natural gas to export, now the USA is planning to develop its coal beds for export to China. Excuse me for stating the obvious, but it was only a few years back that all the developed nations, except the USA, signed the Kyoto Protocol with the intent of slowing down global warming. Now, though, the US is intending to join Canada in exporting global-warming coal to Asia. Doing this will have a number of results.

- First, it will make the developers of the coal very rich, which is the point I suppose.

- Second, it will discourage and delay the industrializing nations of Asia from developing green energy technologies, since it is easier to burn coal.
- Third, it will rapidly exacerbate global warming.
- Fourth, it will set a terrible example to the rest of the world when the globe's richest countries develop and export the dirtiest resources for profit. If we can do it, everyone should be encouraged to do it.
- And finally, it causes some of us to tear our hair out, go into mental depressions, succumb to deep despair, and write books like this.

We have to ask the question whether or not we should be developing our natural resources with such gusto. By 'we' I mean we in Canada and we all over the world. We should think of the oil, coal and natural gas as capital that is banked within the earth's crust for the use of future generations. It is energy that we can tap into over thousands of years, or use as quickly as possible. Once it is gone the potential energy will be gone too. Surely economists would suggest we invest capital for the future. We are not supposed to spend it on one big party. When the oil, coal and natural gas are all used up, as they will be one day soon, what will our descendants use to replace them?

Imagine no oil or natural gas from which to make plastics, nor oil to power our electricity grid or our cars, nor any oil to lubricate our machinery. Europe is already left with few resources. Most had been used up over the past couple of millennia, so resource exhaustion does happen. We could turn the land to growing crops for biofuels, but that will both cut into our food supply and destroy the last few stands of nature. That is neither an intelligent, nor practical, approach.

By spending our capital as we are, I am reminded of the fairy tale in which the nincompoop killed the goose that laid the golden egg. He did that, as he was dissatisfied with the idea of the long-term security of only one egg a day. Instead he opted for a boost to his short-term wealth. Another apt comparison might be that of some fictional castaways wishing to celebrate their landfall on a small island. Being unable to reach the only food supply – out-of-reach coconuts – the castaways chop down all the palms and have a joyous feast, but in the process leave the island denuded of any more food in the future.

I would like to believe that, if we have to use the hydrocarbons now, we are at least investing the profits in a future of green energy. However,

Canada's government, for one, shows little interest in encouraging green energy research.

Maybe one day we will truly be able to power all we use from the sun, gravity or the attraction of the moon. Maybe Fusion Power or thermal exchange from sea water will do it. Possibly we will find that hydrogen holds the answer, or maybe it will be synthetic, carbon-free fuel. Maybe we will find the secret to perpetual motion. Through innovation we may invent any number of wonderful new energy systems. We may even invent ways of using oil and gas at a thousand times the efficiency of today. If so, it would be a pity if we have none left by then. It would be an even greater pity if we were unable to find a more viable energy system than that of hydrocarbons.

If our intention is to have green power in the future, why isn't Canada doing something to develop it now instead of rushing to sell off all our hydrocarbons cheaply, and in such an irresponsible way? Sure, building a solar plant costs about double a coal-fired plant. But once its built the energy that powers it is free. Many countries in Europe are building them and achieving success with them.

Why is it that the governments of the US and Canada take so little interest in alternative green energy sources? The answer to that question, no doubt, has a great deal to do with the powerful oil and coal lobbies. The people in those industries are enthusiastic to keep their extractors, pipelines, refineries and supertankers working at full output. They wish to continue along the path that is tried and true and has given them all great wealth. None seem to consider the possibility of slowing down production with an aim to making the oil and gas last far into the future.

There is a frightening division building in many western countries between the people who want to exploit everything now at whatever the environmental cost, even if it means destroying the natural world in the process, and those who want to slow down and protect the remaining areas of wild nature. It is a division that can only get worse and will take us to civil strife if some sort of compromise is not found.

No doubt it is hard to believe that solar energy, for instance, is powerful enough and reliable enough to replace oil. But refusing to even explore the potential of green energy is despicable. These actions, or inactions, are what give us so little hope for the future.

Europe, though, is apparently well on the way to disproving the naysayers. At the end of May 2012, the Director of the Institute of the Renewable Energy Industry in Muenster, Germany, spoke on some recent solar power generation milestones in that country. He said that on Saturday, May 26, 2012, 22 gigawatts of solar power fed into the national grid, which was very nearly 50 per cent of Germany's weekend midday power needs. On the previous Friday, photovoltaic electricity satisfied a third of the country's workday needs. 22 gigawatts are apparently the equivalent of the power output of 20 nuclear power stations. Granted, this was during a very sunny period, but it does prove that solar energy is viable.

Despite all the critics who doubt the reliability of renewable energy, the German government aims to prove them wrong. In 2012 it was getting 20 per cent of its energy requirements from renewable power sources and is aiming to continue building and increasing production. By 2020 Germany hopes to decrease its greenhouse gas emissions by 40 per cent from the 1990 levels.[3] If Germany can do it, so too can the US and Canada. It just requires the will. Following the 2011 Japanese earthquake, tsunami and Fukushima nuclear disaster, Germany intends to close all its nuclear power plants by 2022 and replace them with solar, wind and biomass power plants.

I realize that green energy, despite the recent German successes, is not yet well enough developed to power the whole world at our present rate of consumption. New systems using the sun, wind, tides, hydrogen, artificial photosynthesis, or human waste, are still in the early stages of development. Some systems are still theoretical gleams in some dreamer's eye, but the richest nations should be supporting the designers and developers of these systems - not ignoring them.

Many of us believe it to be imperative that we invest much more heavily in the research and development of new green systems. We should be investing as we would in a time of war – as if our very lives depend on it. We should also be reducing our power use as much as possible. To be burning energy in order that some dumb concept, such as Las Vegas, can continue powering billions of lights throughout the night is criminal.

The sun is an obvious potential source of power. It heats the planet for goodness sake, and makes such places as the Sahara desert unbearably hot. So surely we can find a way to harvest that potential. I suspect that photovoltaic cells are just the first of a long line of developments before we find the one system that will ultimately win the challenge and bring us reliable inexpensive power.

The Earth's tides show incredibly unrelenting power. The moon moves the water of the oceans from east to west and back from west to east, and raises tides to great heights in places. That constant and predictable raising and lowering of tides, along thousand mile seaboards, must have the potential to provide a huge amount of energy. King Canute, that redoubtable eleventh century Norse king of England, Denmark and Norway, was unable to defeat the tide's purpose and I don't see anyone else being able to either. So maybe instead of foolishly telling the tide what to do, as did Canute, we should start harvesting its power for our good.

Every part of the world is blessed with some natural potential. Britain isn't well endowed with perpetual sunlight but it does have powerful tides, while the equatorial countries enjoy plentiful sun though not much in the way of tidal power. Others have great potential in hydrothermal or wind power. Places such as the Sahara have potential for vast solar farms if only we can develop good ways to transport that power to where it's needed. Maybe large banks of batteries, the size of shipping containers, would do the trick. They could be powered up in North Africa, trucked to the coast, then towed on barges to the coasts of Europe and the countries in need of clean power. Maybe nuclear fusion will soon become a reality, or maybe Ocean thermal energy conversion (OTEC) will be the system to free us of oil.

Naturally, the development of all this would cost money, but then so does building pipelines across Canada's wilderness. Personally, I would be far more sympathetic to these pollution-creating oil and coal projects if the Canadian government was talking about them as a means to a clean end. My attitude would be different if I believed the profits from dirty oil were going to fund the research and development of a green energy infrastructure. In that I could believe, if it truly was the only way to build a clean system.

However, over all the questions of new and unknown sources of green-energy systems, hangs the question, "What if they don't work?" What if there is no designed system that will enable the planet to provide enough energy to satisfy the needs of 9 or 10 billion people living as we in North America live now. If that comes to pass, what will our future descendants do when all the hydrocarbons have been used up? I don't know the answer to that, though I fear what it might be. So I believe that truly wise people should try to make their energy consumption last until they know for sure that an alternative is workable.

When we review these questions against a backdrop of the wonderful new world we have created, against the towering cities with their gleaming public buildings, clean streets, green flower-filled parks and confident, optimistic citizens, the answer seems to be that everything is great and there is no problem. But when we review them against the daily reports of pollution, of destruction, of diminishing this and now-used-up that, and particularly in terms of the end of cheap oil, we have to conclude that all is, in fact, not well.

Earlier I tried to indicate that I grew up in a family that was well off. For the time of the 1940s and 50s, we lived very comfortably and were considered affluent. However I don't believe we ever lived with the incredibly wasteful spending of the typical middle-class North American family in the years before the 2008 crash. It seems to me that those families consumed many times more resources than my family did. And yet we lived really, really well. I suppose the sky is the limit when it comes to expectations.

I have been unable to find figures that compare our total resource extraction in, say, 1950 with those for the year 2009. However, I believe the increase has been massive, especially when we take into account the great increase in the number of consumers between 1950 and now. But can such an increase continue growing indefinitely into the future? If we use logic, it is clear that we cannot continue into the future as we have been for the past sixty years. And we have to remember that we have not been enjoying a worldwide civilization of equality for all. We have been living lives of incredible inequality with at least 2 billion of the current 7 billion people living close to starvation.

To build a world based on social justice and equality, we, the rich, must consider living at a lower level of consumption. But would the wealthy westerners go for that? Are we willing to adapt to such a notion? Are we capable of seriously reviewing the assumption that progress means growing as we have been since the dawn of our industrial and modern economic systems? To succeed, it will definitely mean recognizing that we cannot all live as we in the West have been for the past sixty years. It means recognizing that unending economic growth on a finite planet is an experiment that is an impossible dream.

If, on the other hand, we in the West wish to retain the advantage of more wealth than most, it will mean having to forgo our desire for a worldwide society of equal opportunity and fairness.

I suppose ultimately the question comes down to whether or not our present capitalist-based economy of unending growth is the system that will ensure our ability to live on the planet in an economically and environmentally sustainable way. Or conversely, whether, following our present path, we will ultimately destroy the potential for a long-term systemic survival. I believe we can only survive within a healthy global environment. And we can only do that if we anticipate lifestyles that are far less profligate than the current western ideal.

One long-term solution might be to encourage a smaller population.

A smaller population

With fewer of us humans I believe we could indeed allow our earth to heal. We might even rebuild that Garden of Eden that we once held as the ideal of life, but which we have worked so hard to destroy.

I don't, for a moment, believe there is any way to reduce our human population to smaller numbers by any means that would be acceptable, but I do think the question is worth looking at.

Even if such an idea were given a chance, because the majority voted for it, a small minority would soon put paid to that little experiment. We would never encourage a smaller population for economic reasons alone. There would be too few young people to earn the money to keep the old folks' pension money flowing. A smaller population would mean fewer employees for the big companies, which would have to shrink instead of expand. And it would play havoc with real estate prices and with our pension funds. It would be very difficult to return to smaller numbers by popular choice. But regardless of all that, even by any type of planned and acceptable process, it would take centuries to achieve.

The process of multiplying from one to seven billion took two centuries and it took seventy years to add the last five billion. To go back to two billion using some form of birth control would take centuries by any humane and reasonable process. Family-planning education would certainly help. Promising citizens money or pensions for having no children might work, but which governments could afford that?

To significantly reduce the population we would have to enjoy generations of one-child families. Two-child families would simply sustain the numbers at the current highest level.

A horrible pestilence could do it, but that is something we all want to avoid like . . . well, like the plague. While we are on such an awful subject it is believed that the Black Death of the 14th century killed up to two thirds of Europe's population and one-in-four worldwide. So, to introduce a little black irony to the Black Death story, that plague would not reduce our projected 2050 nine billion population to any number much smaller than about six billion. The diseases introduced to the Americas by the conquering Europeans are believed to have killed ninety percent of the American natives. So a similar new disease has the potential to bring our numbers to about a billion. However no one is waiting for that plague with anything other than fear and trepidation. I don't think that's the way we would choose to reduce our numbers.

It is interesting that, to my knowledge, the United Nations community has never discussed the matter of population reduction beyond encouraging birth control education. This is surely because such a discussion would reek of Nazism. There is no acceptable way to bring the human numbers down other than by education or by financial rewards for having fewer than two babies. I can think of no acceptable ways to encourage small families on an international basis. Individual nations may try to bring in one-baby policies, but while they do that, others would be encouraging their citizens to have more. Even today, many people equate large families with future security, though well educated women, with prospects of meaningful jobs, seem to have led the way in limiting family size.

In 2012, the Canadian government was looking for ways to increase the population over the following twenty or thirty years. This was because the baby boom generation was preparing to retire. That huge cohort would need pensions at a time when there would be too few workers to generate the required wealth. I understand the concern, but surely increasing the population will simply perpetuate the problem into the future when the next bulge comes to retire. It is putting off the inevitable for our grandchildren to deal with.

The thought of the international rumpus that would accompany positive population control suggestions, is indeed daunting. That is, if such a thing could even be discussed. But if it were, one question might be on what would we base the future human distribution? The obvious answer would be an across the board percentage cut of current numbers. Assuming a population of two billion was considered a desirable goal for a date some one hundred years into the future, it would mean reducing the population to about 28 per cent of the 2013 numbers. That would reduce Britain from 60 million to approximately 17 million, which is what it actually was in 1851. If the USA were reduced to 28 per cent of today's 313 million, it would host a population of about 90 million, or about the population in 1909.

Malaysia, with possibly less than a million spread over the three territories in 1900, and 28 million in 2012, would come out at 8 million. Canada, the second largest country by area, would finish up at about 10 million.

On the other hand, a desirable future population could be based on relative size of landmass, on bio-capacity, or on the agricultural potential of each nation to feed a given number of people. Whatever the suggestions, attempts to manipulate populations by anything other than free consent would never be acceptable. Even suggesting the idea would result in unholy wars of words. Trying to enforce a population reduction through birth control or other means would result in wars far worse than those of words. As it won't happen, I should leave the subject at that; however, it is worth considering how a world of two billion could potentially be different.

For those who find it abhorrent to even contemplate the human community trying to influence how we should live, or how quickly we should be allowed to multiply, I can't help mentioning that we have, in the past hundred years reshaped over 75 per cent of the inhabitable natural world. If we can reform so much of nature, why, one might ask, can we not attempt to reform the humans that are also a part of the natural world? We are apparently willing to control everything on earth but ourselves. That being said, I do think it worth exploring how we might live if there were just 2 billion of us.

Projections of renewable resource use indicate that, each year, we are using one and a half times what the earth can supply. That suggests that our one earth can just support 66 per cent of the current population or around 5.6 billion humans. However, in 2012, a minority of the people was using a majority of the resources. Since the poor and emerging people from all over the world like the look of the western lifestyle and want to live it, we should assume that we must make a world of equally prosperous citizens. If that level of prosperity is close to the present most well off, North Americans, our globe could possibly support about two billion of us. That number would also allow space for healthy natural ecosystems.

A population of two billion is about where it was when I was born, but still double the one billion when my grandfather's grandfather was born. In his day the number of people living to our contemporary standards of consumer comfort was infinitesimal. At that time, most of the population trod very lightly on the land, some also living lives of awful grimness, though not as many as do so today.

By using our most advanced low-energy technologies we could, in the future, live with a lighter impact on the earth than at any time since the dawn of science and industry. Then, they burned coal and over-built their steam engines to huge sizes. I am sure that, with the green energy, the internet, smartphone and nano-technologies, a population of two billion could live touching the earth quite lightly. We could have all the advantages of modern industry but without the desperation, destruction and desolation of so many of today's people. If we could plan it and were wise, the wonderful conveniences of this future life could be available to help us live fulfilling lives of gentleness, community values and, maybe even, greater spirituality. I envisage a future world where we would no longer be seduced by consumerism and the lies of future promise. Nor would we listen to those that cloak selfish intent in the seductive rhetoric of everlasting growth and perpetually increasing living standards. The many industries that we now use with such wasteful abandon, could be used more sparingly than they are at present. Whoever the fortunate ones to live in this imagined nirvana might be, they would have the knowledge of all our mistakes, greed and shortsighted follies to guide them along more enlightened paths. With wisdom, restraint and an eagerness to learn from the mess we made, our descendants could remake and repair nature's paradise - the one we lost while trying to refashion it into an unsustainable ideal of everlasting growth.

The lucky ones in my unlikely paradise might enjoy living in a world of pleasant cities, small passive-low-energy homes, efficient appliances and clean, efficient transit systems. They could have small personal moving devices available to them to drive on less congested and smaller highways. They would consume organic food that neither sickens the consumer, nor the soil in which it is grown. Possibly a large percentage of our agricultural land could then be returned to its original habitat. The cities could be within reach of healing woodlands and forests, or of grasslands, downland, desert or veldt, and of estuaries and marshes. Animal and bird numbers might recover. Rare species might breed again on recovering habitat, and the seeds patiently waiting their chance to sprout might bring rare trees and flowering shrubs back to the sunlight. Even some plant species, we assume gone forever, may be found in some seldom-visited place. Given time a balance of agricultural land and wildlife habitat could be re-established. There would still be mines, resource extraction sites and industrial complexes, but fewer of them and much less polluting ones.

With fewer of us humans I believe we could indeed allow our earth to heal. We might even rebuild that Garden of Eden that we once held as the ideal of life, but which we have worked so hard to destroy.

Nature in crisis
We must find a way to live within nature not at war with it.

I believe it is due to environmentalism, and concerned individuals, that we have seen fewer known recent extinctions than might be expected with such a burgeoning population. Nonetheless, the situation for many species is becoming truly dire. Now all over the world creatures hang on in the final few acres of their once extensive habitat, as illustrated by the maps of historic and current Asian Rhino populations. Whether they are large or small, brilliant or plain, beautiful or ugly, scientists say that thirty percent of our earth's species are on the brink and will likely be gone within the next few years. This is despite the number of caring people worldwide who are dedicated to protecting our wildlife at almost any cost.

Now, more than at any time in history, with wild nature so dreadfully reduced, more and more ordinary people, in nearly every nation, are standing up to the despoilers in attempts to stop the destruction. In some places they are lonely voices speaking out against huge conglomerates. But in other places such people are becoming the majority.

In the UK, with an educated population, but one that is growing less rapidly than it once was, competition with nature is no longer such a concern. In fact the citizens are generally exceptionally sympathetic toward nature. There are still a few dinosaur farmers who plough up old grassland meadows, and landowners and gamekeepers who poison badgers and shoot raptors, but penalties for such behavior are having an effect, and reintroduced raptor numbers are rising as on a good thermal. In most countries now, as a result of international communications and hard working environmentalists, there are some government rules that protect the most endangered species.

Nonetheless, still the destruction continues and still the habitat falls. In the Congo, warlords exchange forest trees for armaments, and the people kill the gorillas, chimpanzees and bonobos for bush meat. In Burma and Indochina logging, both legal and illegal, continues apace to keep the Chinese furniture factories producing. In Borneo and Sumatra, forest is felled for a thousand acre palm oil plantation here, or for an unemployed Javanese's five-acre homestead, there. According to the BBC, in Borneo in 2011, more than 1800 Orangutans were killed as a result of forest clearing for palm oil plantations. In the Amazon rapacious ranchers, avaricious agriculturalists and poor peasants continue to clear the forests despite government protections. And everywhere the paper conglomerates continue felling the trees for pulp to make paper and toilet tissue.

When we see TV news items about the people in a town somewhere in the tropical forest belt, we seldom see any trees. What we usually see is that all the surrounding land, whether flat, hilly, or mountainous, is naked of trees and usually holds but a few remnant shrubs. The poor in these towns simply cut wood for their survival, and when the close-by vegetation has all gone, they travel further afield, till the surrounding land is all but barren.

This ongoing destruction of the Earth's woodlands cannot be forgiven. The forest destruction of 100-200 years ago took place in a different age. That was an age of pride, but also of incredible ignorance of the effects of our actions. We now know how very wrong forest destruction is, in terms of both the species that are eradicated and the increase in CO_2 production. Yet in Borneo, New Guinea, the Amazon, Central Africa, and Canada the poor and the loggers blithely continue their destruction. They continue with devastating results for the plants, birds, animals and insects; in fact for all living things that rely on the forests to survive. This deforestation also causes changed weather patterns and reduced rainfall in some areas, desertification in others, landslides and flooding off mountainsides, and a general global warming.

I suspect that some people assume that when a forest is felled, all we lose are trees. It is true that we lose untold numbers of trees but, as mentioned earlier, we also lose a great deal more. A five-hundred-year-old forest tree may have growing in its canopy untold numbers of orchids, parasitic plants, epiphytes, mistletoes, vines and the Lord knows what else. Each of those plant species may feed a particular bird, bat, frog, caterpillar or other insect, all of which may have very limited ranges. The canopy may be home to scores of animal species, or offer food to dozens of visiting mammals and birds that cruise through the forest feeding here and feeding there. The ancient forests are said to support millions of species. So, when we clear a forest, we destroy millions of plants and animals that have evolved to live in only that forest. We speak of the web of life and, as with all places in nature, the web of life of the forest is totally destroyed when we fell the trees.

Yes, the wildlife numbers are in a steep decline. And agricultural interests and industry are happy to see that decline continue. But opposing the corporations are an increasing number of concerned citizens, people who are willing to stand up and fight to halt the destruction. Of course, half a dozen individuals stand little chance against a multi-national company with untold millions of dollars, invincible bulldozers at their disposal, and the glint of profits in their eyes. Nor is it easy to stand against national governments such as Canada's, which seem to always take the side of the industrialists.

It is disappointing that often the more developed and wealthy a country is, the less willing it becomes to enact environmental protections. In some cases, it is a result of industrialists and landowners with vested interests employing lobbyists to argue against the protections. In others, it is the general public, you and I, who have become so comfortable with our conveniences that we can't imagine a future without them. In North America we have become so extravagant in our basic expectations that we now treat luxury conveniences as bare necessities. I must say, I am often quite sickened by the sense of entitlement that I see displayed daily by people in my Vancouver neighbourhood.

The trouble is, we really do need environmental protections, and here follow some of the issues we should be concerned about:

- Following the 1992 Rio framework for Climate Change, and the Kyoto call for us all to cut our CO_2 emissions from the 1990 amount, our abject failure in that regard is proven by the fact that we are now pumping 45 per cent more CO_2 into the atmosphere, than we were in 1990.[4]
- Global warming is melting Canada's and Siberia's tundra. The result of this will be the release of millions of tons of previously frozen methane gas into the atmosphere.
- As heating continues, the ice on Greenland and the Antarctic continent may melt and raise sea levels by 15 ft (5 m) or more during the 21st century. Such rises will put many coastal cities in a fight to stay above water.

The global warming and rising sea level may have all sorts of unexpected results that we can't yet know. For instance, will Britain become warmer or colder as a result of icy water sweeping down from the melting glacier that is Greenland? What effect will that cold outflow have on such warming ocean currents as the Gulf Stream? Will the UK be warmer in winter, or will it be a lot colder?

As we know, these aren't the only long-term problems arising from our industry-based economy. Along with the planet heating up, we can state:

- Every one of the Earth's natural systems is failing.
- Glaciers that feed river systems are melting into oblivion.
- Fresh water aqueducts are running dry due to over-use.
- 60 per cent of the Earth's rivers are under stress, and are polluted.
- The poisoning of the earth, as a result of the production of designed and accidental toxic chemical compounds, continues apace.
- Ocean acidification also continues.
- The resulting destruction of the oceans' foundation feed stocks – of the plankton, corals, mollusks and small sea creatures – continues and accelerates, as does the destruction of the top predators.
- Over-fishing is leading to the inevitable collapse of fish stocks.
- Many of the Earth's non-renewable mineral resources are getting close to the point of exhaustion.
- We are using the Earth's renewable resources 50 per cent faster than they can be replenished. I cannot imagine a more clear indication that we are on the wrong track than that.
- The abundant numbers of insects, which used to help keep the earth healthy and feed the birds and river fish, have suffered great diminishment.
- Finally, although unimportant to many, but of great importance to our Earth's health, it is worth repeating that 30 per cent of species are expected to be extinct by 2050, and 50 per cent by the year 2100. The total numbers of birds are tumbling fast, as are the numbers of fish. In fact, nearly all animals, whether vertebrates or invertebrates, are losing numbers with bone-crushing certainty. Jellyfish, humans, and a few others, however, continue to increase.

And finally some news that truly speaks to how global corporations now believe they can behave. According to the website, SumOfUs.org on September 22nd 2013:

Tobacco giant Philip Morris was suing the Australian government to overturn public health laws aimed at reducing teenage smoking. Chevron had hired 2,000 lawyers to avoid paying Ecuador $19 billion in damages due for the horrific oil spills they inflicted. And Bayer was suing Europe to overturn the ban on bee-killing pesticides – all while investing millions with Monsanto to defeat an effort to label GM foods in the US. All those lawsuits are attempts to undermine the people's rights to defend themselves against corporate injury, and to hold corporations to account for the damage they do. Some corporations can be anti-democratic in the extreme.

The above are just a few of the continuing and growing problems that we are leaving our grandchildren to deal with. The over-riding solution, in my opinion, is for us to redefine our relationship with Earth's natural order. We must give the natural world a chance to redevelop strong roots, strengthen, and become re-established as a healthy fundamental pillar of our planet. It is crucial that we find a way to live within nature, not at war with it. Allied to that, we might consider the 2008 near-collapse of the world's economy. Apparently we were within days of a total meltdown. We were saved at the eleventh hour when the US Congress allocated $700 billion as bailout money for US banks. If that near-disintegration of our underlying economic system didn't prove something fundamentally wrong, nothing will.

Unlikely paradise – The Better Life

If it is reality to state that the natural systems are failing, why, I wonder, can't it be reality to state that our economic system is part of the cause and needs to change?

The difficulty is that, even if some thought it desirable, changing our expectations and the system that sustains them, would be about as easy as changing the direction of a small pony in the centre of a charging herd of buffalo. We seem to be riding an economic system that is either gallop ahead as fast as possible, or falter, dare to turn aside, and be flattened by competing business interests. Whenever a country tries an idea that curtails the interests of business, the corporations simply up stakes and move to a part of the globe where they can profit without interference. So, it seems to me that, to make a change from our present system to a more earth-friendly and future-responsible economic system we need to do it together.

I want to make it clear; I am not arguing against the present system of free enterprise and innovation. I enjoy the wonderful improvements we have seen over the recent past. I'm not against well-paid jobs, universal education, health care, nice houses, holidays in the sun, or comfortable retirements. These are all the advantages of the present system that a few of us enjoy, and those who don't, crave. If I wasn't blighted by a sense of guilt and concern for future generations I could be as big a consumer as the worst of us. Notwithstanding my liking for the simple life of open air and nature, I enjoy comfort and security. However, I also recognize that the present rate of resource consumption cannot continue for much longer without big problems cropping up for the following generations. This, as far as I can see, isn't fair; in fact it is downright immoral.

I accept that many readers, noting my suggestion that we should consider a different way of living on this earth, will say I am somewhat detached from reality and that I am not being realistic. However this book is heavily based in awful reality.

- That we use non-renewable mineral resources millions of times more quickly than the Earth's natural cycles can replace them, is a reality.
- That we are using more renewable resources than the Earth can supply, is a reality.
- That the natural systems are all under attack and failing, is a reality.
- That the globe is warming despite the wishful thinking of the deniers, is a reality.
- That the acidity of the seas is increasing, which in turn is killing off the foundation Crustaceans, is a reality.
- That the seas are being over fished, that fish numbers are collapsing and corals are dying, are all realities.
- That the oceans are now filled with millions of tons of plastic waste, is a reality.
- That 60% of rivers worldwide are in trouble, that glaciers are melting and groundwater levels are dropping and becoming polluted, are all realities.
- That the soils and seas are polluted with pesticides and poisons, are realities.
- That precious little wild grassland remains, and that forests are being massively depleted, are realities.
- That the insects at the bottom of the food chain are being exterminated, is a reality.
- That bird numbers are being drastically reduced worldwide, and that the lions, tigers, elephants, rhinos, and just about every other large animal species are heading toward extinction, are all realities.

If it is a reality to state that the planet's natural systems, on which all life depends, are failing, why can't it be a reality to admit that our economic system is the root cause and must be changed?

One problem with the world in the early part of the third millennium is that while we read such newspaper headlines as, 'Earth near point of no return, scientists warn,' every other headline is telling us we need more growth in energy and, in fact, more of absolutely everything. The first article, the doomsday one, appears as a short two-column piece. The rah-rah articles cover pages galore. So, even if the reader takes note of the dire warning, he or she is soon engulfed in a tide of glowing proclamations of the need for more and more energy or business investment.

I do realize that the more cheap resources we develop, the better become some of our lives. I also recognize that, as our living standards rise and we become more comfortable, the less willing we will be to anticipate an end to those good times. The economic system has improved many peoples' lives, but our over-use of the earth's carrying capabilities, and the declining energy supplies, are both leading to a future world of impoverishment. The modern capitalist/industrial, forward-surging behemoth is rapidly heading toward a wall as unforgiving as a granite mountain. When we finally hit it, it will cause a cataclysmic collapse that none of us will enjoy. Our huge population, and near total reliance on international trading systems and food supplies, will make local survival really, really difficult. We could find ourselves back to conditions far worse than any we have seen for centuries. Yet all this could possibly be avoided if we just showed a little wisdom and a lot of restraint.

Alternative futures
What it comes down to is either fewer footprints, or smaller footprints.

So just to recap: in this time of burgeoning population, overcrowded cities and failing ecosystems, it seems we may be limited to a few future routes, none of which involves planned population reductions.

1. The most obvious and the most likely alternative, is that we continue as we are. We embrace the idea of winner-take-all competition and we hope for the best. We put our trust in freedom of choice and whatever beliefs we individually hold dear to our hearts. We take a chance that everything will work out in the end and assume that

collapse and chaos will not occur. In this, we probably include the belief that unbridled capitalism is the best route forward. We assume our descendants will 'sort it'.

If we assume that the wealthy west is the way we must go then we continue the economy of growth. We do so with the intent of raising all 9 or 10 billion people of the future to the living standard of the wealthiest developed economies. We do this on the understanding that in the future we will develop technologies to replace our exhausted resources. We ignore the doomsday prophets who say we need many other planets to support such a wealthy population. We keep going until . . . until who knows what? We will cross whatever unpleasant bridge presents itself, when we are on it.

Furthermore, we assume that Venus and Mars hold harvestable mineral wealth to cover the Earth's shortfall. We also assume that we will develop spaceships capable of bringing back to Earth the billions of tons of minerals that we will need. We trust that this enterprise can be undertaken without depleting our own energy supplies even further.

2. An undesirable alternative is that we continue the consumption habits of the established wealthy nations, but assume, by necessity, reduced consumption and fewer opportunities for the rest of the globe's population. This will still keep us using more resources than the Earth can support.

3. The third alternative is that we choose to live in a world of social and economic equality and long-term sustainability. To attain this, with a population that is too large for the resources available to us, we accept the need to adopt a benign and reduced lifestyle for the wealthy nations. At the same time we assist the undeveloped nations in increasing their wealth to the new medium level. Let's call it *The Better Life*.

4. We wait for a very nasty plague or cataclysm to take the decision out of our hands.

Failing these four suggestions, I see no other way to stop and reverse the systems destruction than by cutting our resource use, or by reducing the number of resource users. What it comes down to is either smaller footprints, or fewer footprints.

Personally, I believe the third suggestion, *The Better Life*, is the best: to gradually move the globe's economy to one of sustainability. No growth is more likely to achieve long-term success and social adhesion, than the other three options. The question is whether humanity would accept the suggestion of lowering our individual expectations to the sustainable level. Frankly, I fear such a far-sighted suggestion would never fly – at least not before humans wear angel wings. Am I being negative? Am I viewing my fellow humans through sandblasted glasses? It would be nice if I was but I don't think I am. The USA can't even reduce gun use. Nor can the rest reduce the use of plastic bags. We only have to remember what happened to the Rio Summit and the Kyoto Accord, to assess what chance the most well-intentioned plans have. They both promoted relatively small amendments to our national and personal aspirations, yet seem to have failed in most countries.

For myself, I believe I could accept *The Better Life* readily. The act of producing worthwhile projects has, for me, always been far more important than some monetary reward that I may or may not receive at the end. I never wanted to be poor, but neither did I need much more than enough. With enough, I can live reasonably well, creatively and happily.

Unfortunately, whenever I suspect that I must be wrong in my doomsday projections, I only have to read the words of the United Nations Secretary General, Ban Ki-moon, given in a 2011 speech in Davos, Switzerland, to become encouraged in my beliefs:

For most of the last century, economic growth was fuelled by what seemed to be a certain truth: the abundance of natural resources. We mined our way to growth. We burned our way to prosperity. We believed in consumption without consequences. Those days are gone.

In the 21st century, supplies are running short and the global thermostat is running high. Climate change is also showing us that the old model is more than obsolete. It has rendered it extremely dangerous. Over time, that model is a recipe for national (sic) disaster. It is a global suicide pact. . . We need a revolution. Revolutionary thinking. Revolutionary action. A free-market revolution for global sustainability. It is easy to mouth the words "Sustainable Development", but to make it happen we have to be prepared to make major changes – in our lifestyles, our economic models, our social organization, and our political life. . .[5]

18 A Better Life

I am not arguing against our modern way of life, which I enjoy. I am arguing for a sustainable way of life that our descendants will enjoy.

Earlier I referred to the empire building belief in a mission to bring the 'backward' peoples to the advantages of enlightenment, science and the rule of law. In Victorian times, it was thought the 'Noble Savages' required the advantages of European knowledge and advancements. They needed to move out of subsistence living and such pastimes as blood-sacrifice, tribal warfare and the taking of slaves, if any of those applied.

In this civilizing zeal, Europeans went to great lengths to destroy the rich and, in some cases, highly developed cultures of the natives nearly everywhere they lived. As an example, in 1885 in Western Canada, the government passed a law to ban the coastal tribes' potlatch*, which was really the foundation of their cultural and economic system. The government later forced all native children to attend residential schools in an attempt to 'take the Indian out of the Indian'[1] - a precursor of the Malaysian government's removal of the Orang Asli from their forests.

The reason I mention all this is to note that a great many of the tribal people in those empire-building days had very small environmental footprints. They also had the disadvantages of no western medicine, no knowledge of modern technologies and, usually, no democracy. What they did have though, was a minimal effect on the earth and a low population growth. Their cultures could probably have continued for another few

---

* The potlatch was an important tribal ceremony in which the host gave away his riches to his guests. For this he would gain great honour and respect within the tribe. A balance of wealth was retained as others in the tribe did the same. As each member became wealthy he would hold a potlatch and redistribute his wealth. Honour and respect passed to many this way, and the social advantage of equality within the group was retained.

thousand years into the future, with very few negative effects on the environment. The people of those cultures would possibly also be living in more happiness and contentment than they are now.

Had the Europeans not come to their lands, the aboriginal peoples of British Columbia would probably still be living their traditional lives. They would be living culturally rich and spiritually wholesome lives within the context of their many-thousand-year-old beliefs. The forests would today be as intact as they were two hundred years ago. The waters would be as clear. The sea otters would be as plentiful, the migrating salmon as bountiful, and all the natural world as healthy as it was before the white man came. The same applies to many cultures everywhere. The Europeans, on the other hand, had all the advantages of scientific, technical and economic progress, of improving medical care, and the ability to govern vast areas of the globe. But with that came uncontrolled and unsustainable growth, and the possibility of exhausting the Earth's carrying capacity within a few generations.

In a nutshell: the indigenous peoples of the world lived subsistence based lifestyles, adapted to the environment. In so doing they developed unique cultures that were perfectly attuned to where they lived, and that had the potential to continue forever. On the other hand, we in the industrial world became adversaries to the environment. We thought we were apart from nature. We attempted to adapt the environment to our needs. We built a monolithic culture, but created an unsustainable economy and a dire future.

The Industrial Revolution gave us the underpinnings of industry. It gave us some of the energy sources: coal, steam, gas and electricity. It gave us the materials and tools: the steel, the lathes and boring machines. It gave us the firm roads and rail lines. It gave us the steam ships and the steel ships. It gave us the telegraph, telephone and radio, but also the factories and the horrors of early industrialization. The Americans followed this up with the development and mass production of household conveniences: the vacuums and fridges, the freezers, the nylon and the consumer goods. They also gave us the new high-tech computer industry. That industry has the potential to be the rescuer and liberator that we will need in the future.

In hindsight, it is easy to compare the long-term viability of the two alternatives. First, we had the native cultures, enduring and spiritual, though sometimes cruel, but also with the possibility of short lives lived with some contentment. They had lasted thousands of years and could have continued for thousands more. Secondly, we have the advanced industrial system with all its economic advantages, sometimes democratic and sometimes not, sometimes cruel and sometimes socially just. The industrial system is barely two hundred years old, but hell bent on a charge toward exhaustion of the earth's resources and a suicidal cul-de-sac.

We can't go back, and we certainly would not want to revisit the conditions of early industrialization. But, as we go forward, it might be worth learning something from those traditional, and contented, cultures that the new industrial economy has tried so hard to destroy.

Now, in 2013, the emerging countries are continuing to industrialize by producing, for the mass market, consumer goods made to high standards and for low cost. This development is good in the way it enriches the lives of many people and gives them hope. The emerging economies of China and Brazil, of India and Malaysia, and of so many more, accounted, in 2012, for 66 per cent of global growth. The majority of people in those economies were still earning under $10 a day, but the middle class was growing by 70 million each year. The total population of this new block is nearly 2.5 billion.[2] However, the materials required to feed these new industries are fast depleting the resource base. Also, the people in the countries of the first waves of industrialization are now finding their economies failing as the manufacturing employment leaves their shores.

When the people of the emerging economies are added to those of the old economies, we are closer to having four billion reaching toward, or indulging in, the living standards of the wealthy West. Assuming we achieve the outcome of that many people living with US-sized footprints, we will be far further over the carrying capacity of the earth than we were in 2012. On top of that we will have to raise the other three billion, most of whom are living in poverty, and the two billion unborn, but expected by 2050. Nine billion US-sized footprints will take us far beyond today's problems of unsustainability.

Surely we now have to find a different path. A system that takes advantage of the technological advances, and the knowledge gained over the past two centuries, but that frames it in a construct of minimal resource use, long-term viability and the advantages of the democratic rule of law. What must be avoided would be attempts to step backwards. We must step forward to a post-consumer economy. We need to believe in a new way that melds supply longevity with the opportunities of the modern western society.

A new way is emerging. It is a way of worldwide industrialization and possibly democratization, but it also includes forever-expanding raw material use, so it is not the sustainable one we need.

The revolution, of which Ban Ki-moon spoke so earnestly, should have taken place years ago and certainly needs to be undertaken soon. We can't keep putting it off to be dealt with by future generations. Like a house with dangerous wiring, it is better to re-wire, though the cost be great, than wait till the house catches fire, putting the children and residents at risk of awful deaths. So it is with our need to revolutionize our economic underpinnings. The political gyrations will be daunting, and the initial economic effects will be great. Nevertheless, for the sake of future security, we have to use our imaginations and build a different economy. We have to imagine a life using fewer resources. We have to imagine ways of sharing, of realizing that being born in an agriculturally and industrially rich country endows us with responsibilities to share with, not the right to pillage, those born to poverty. We must imagine a world where all can live well, but without the nature-crushing consumer habits of today. We must imagine richer lives lived with true riches, not gross consumerism. We have to imagine a better way of taking care of our Earth.

We must begin to live within the Earth's carrying capacity. Within a finite planet it is ridiculous to expect infinite growth. We must think of ways to leave more for future generations. We must dream of an economy we never before envisioned. We must conceive a way of living that probably few humans have lived before. We must imagine a way of living whereby every generation leaves the Earth more richly endowed, not more impoverished. We must replace the extravagant life, and the selfish life, with a wholesome life – with a life close in character to my *Better Life*.

The following are a few suggestions of the kinds of things we might consider to get us living within the carrying capacity of this planet. Whether they are desirable, practical or plausible, we will each have to decide. Some suggestions may be outlandish, and some may be found to be undesirable. We may only need to embrace a few to make the difference needed – or we may have to adopt many others. Still my list is just a start and we have to start somewhere. So, maybe everyone should write his or her own individual list of the ways we can live more sustainable lives.

- First, although we need a revolution in our thinking, we should avoid dangerous revolutionary economic changes. We need evolutionary changes. Our democratic governments and politicians must speak the truth to their people, not say only what they believe will get them re-elected.
- We need a very serious and informed discussion about what kind of society we want to build, and what kind of earth we want to nurture.
- Collectively we must determine how many future generations we should plan for - for five, for ten, or for twenty generations. At the same time we need to determine for how many generations we divide, apportion and allocate our non-renewable resources.
- Based on that decision, we must use science to determine what percentage of the known non-renewable resources we can afford to extract each year.
- We then determine to restructure the global economy accordingly.

- We wrest influence and decision-making from the industrialists, wealthy elite, and bankers and return that function to the elected representatives of the people.
- We review, and redevelop, the concept of both public and private debt.
- We determine the quantity of renewable resources that can be used each year without going into resource deficit. The goal should be the sustainable use of materials only.
- We determine a way to gradually slow down the economy, and we plan for reduced consumption in the wealthy west.
- We adopt a healthy mix of free enterprise, non-government organization, and publicly owned enterprise.
- We continue to encourage innovation and free enterprise, but on the understanding that the entrepreneurs' monetary rewards will be moderate multiplications of the average person's salary, and not the gross multiplications we have seen of late. We develop policies to reward altruism, not greed.

- We imagine a new economy whereby manufacturers take back their products for recycling. We must show zero tolerance for manufactured products entering the biosphere as waste.

- We ensure that all packaging worldwide is, at the very least, recyclable.
- We stop producing the billions of non-recyclable plastic cups, packaging and other conveniences that are presently used.
- We strive for a zero-waste society
- Environmental sustainability must be the benchmark against which all energy and business decisions are made.
- We encourage the belief that corporate responsibility in regard to social and ethical values becomes balanced against the responsibility to shareholder profits.

- We strive for an economy where housing, food, healthcare, education, a secure retirement, and democracy, are considered privileges that all should be enabled to enjoy; however, we dispense with the idea of a social hammock for the lazy, in favour of a safety net for deserving citizens.
- We discourage the impossible idea that all seven, eight, or nine billion of us are each deserving of untold wealth and riches, beyond those needed to allow us to enjoy life comfortably and securely.
- We re-direct our advertising industry away from brainwashing people into buying consumer items. Instead, we direct it to stimulate people to desire sustainable lives, lives that are lived more simply and with more profound significance.
- We educate all to understand the negative results of unsustainable material use.
- We encourage the idea that we are on this earth to help our fellows, and to create and maintain a sustainable world for all. To that end we encourage all to compete to be the most altruistic and unselfish.
- We educate to anticipate lives of security, serenity, wisdom and creativity.
- We promote disdain for aggression, plunder, excess and outlandish wealth.

- Wealthy nations stop funding the fossil fuel industry to the many billions of dollars that they funded it in 2012.
- All nations must stop funding unsustainable and damaging agricultural and fishing industries.

- We support, with money and research, green methods of manufacture, whereby we remove, where possible, the negative and poisonous byproducts of the manufacturing processes.
- We make it an international challenge to invent new green energy systems that will power global humanity into the future.
- We accelerate the building of green energy technologies for installation wherever locally sensible. Large deserts seem perfect places to establish huge solar farms. Areas of high tides may be places for tidal power. Because these places may be far from large populations, we prioritize research into efficient energy-carrying systems and transportable large batteries.
- If science proves green energy to be viable worldwide, we proceed with that development as rapidly as possible.
- We only use fossil fuels in the most limited ways. We use them only as transition fuels to sustain us till the green technologies are well enough established.
- We aim for a low carbon society. We think of fossil fuels as second line support fuels, and use them only when absolutely necessary.
- We conserve as much fossil fuel as possible, on the understanding that later generations might need some. In other words, we stop stealing from our grandchildren and from their grandchildren. They too will need resources.
- Should we conclude that green systems will not answer our energy needs, we still reduce our hydrocarbon use to the minimum possible, again on the understanding that following generations, for hundreds of years into the future, may also need hydrocarbons.
- We support new research into the possibility of developing nuclear power plants that are safe and have greatly reduced spent-fuel problems.
- Using current green technologies we first work toward equality of opportunity between the cities and rural areas. In some parts of the developed world it is considered highly desirable, when one is connected electronically, to live and work in country villages where life is tranquil.
- We make it a priority to get the rural areas in the Third World powered up using appropriate and available green technologies. We ensure that rural village schools, at the very least, are connected electronically.

- We encourage interactive online businesses to be established in rural areas so that the young will not have to go to the city for work. With innovative online businesses employing rural and village workers with well-paid jobs, it should be possible to establish more balanced city/rural population densities.
- We encourage homeowners, singly and in groups, to adopt green energy systems in order that they can draw less from the grid.
- In warm sunny climates all air conditioners, refrigerators and computers, for instance, should be solar powered.
- At the same time, we wean the cities off hydrocarbon-burning power stations as more efficient green technologies are developed.

- We expand the building of, and the use of, public transit systems. The European, American and Indian railway systems moved people all over their continents quickly and efficiently before the era of mass personal autos. The British railways moved people from small town to small town, and from village to village. Public transit may be a little less convenient, but it is a whole lot more efficient and sensible than private cars. A single bus can, depending on size, carry the same number of people as sixty or seventy cars. It can do so more quickly when most cars are taken off the road.
- We imagine the automobile anew. A typical 4,000 lb car carrying a 150-200 lb single driver is using about 98 per cent of the fuel to move the vehicle from place to place and about 2 per cent to move the person. This is ridiculous. We must design small efficient transportation devices that use less fuel, are less polluting, travel within the speed limits, and are less lethal to humans when they collide. Think rubber ball rather than a lump of steel.
- We take advantage of new media for communicating instead of physically moving ourselves vast distances.
- We reduce all frivolous and flippant air and sea travel. We even consider enjoying fulfilling lives lived more locally. Personally, for instance, I would rather know that certain wildlife species live securely in Madagascar, than fly there myself to see them, and by so doing hasten their demise.

- We truly reduce the amount of paper we use. We recycle and reduce wood-pulp consumption, thereby reducing the amount of forest felled.
- We make throw-away paper items, such as toilet tissue, from recycled pulp.
- We legislate a worldwide halt to primary forest destruction.
- We find sustainable ways to harness the resources of the sea.
- We determine the worldwide production of food according to the biological capacity to grow it. If this means reducing the number of cattle we rear and increasing the production of vegetables, so be it.
- We ease away from pesticide and herbicide production and use.
- The industrial nations quit promoting agricultural poisons to poor nations.
- We consider the protection and survival of insect species as an important aspect of caring for our planet. We recognize that bugs and insects are vital parts of healthy environments. They should not all be poisoned willy-nilly.
- We stop ploughing wild grasslands.
- We return as many ecosystems to health as possible.
- We replant forests.
- We halt wasteful building practices. In Europe, people live in buildings hundreds of years old. In Vancouver buildings are often knocked down and rebuilt after 60 years - this despite the emissions from concrete manufacture that are 5 per cent of the global carbon footprint. We recognize that concrete use, and every new concrete building, adds to global warming.
- We find ways to adapt to our Earth's environment, instead of working so hard to convert the environment to our needs.
- We create, and believe in, ways of living on this Earth that use the political and economic system to ensure the long-term survivability of all species, whether animal, plant, or human.
- We encourage every nation to reward its citizens for having fewer than two children, and we look for other ways to encourage a smaller human population.

The above are my suggestions, though I am sure that a working list could be quite different once, and if ever, we begin serious discussions on the need for change. I don't know how to encourage the people on this planet to adopt this new economic and political better life, though I can imagine how desirable that adoption could be. I am fully aware that every one of my suggestions will have some downsides and many detractors. None will be without controversy, and the opposition from those holding contrary views would be stiff. Certainly vested interests will fight, with large pots of money, to retain the status quo. Still, that being understood, for the sake of future generations we should at least explore the possibilities of change.

Assuming it is unacceptable and impossible to legislate a reduction in the number of human footprints, The Better Life would mean that those 4.5 billion who are now considered to have middle-class lifestyles, should expect lower rates of consumption. At least the people at the top of that group will have to reduce their expectations. Those who have recently entered at the lower level of the middle-class lifestyle may still have scope for enrichment. The poorest two or three billion should enjoy significant improvements in their expectations.

I understand that most people will find the thought of lowering their expectations intolerable and unacceptable. That view is understandable. But against that are the many people who fear that there is no future for their children, and that the long-term future for humans on our globe is extremely bleak. To continue wringing hands, but to put forward no suggestions to improve the situation, does nothing to alleviate it.

I don't know how we will arrive at any kind of consensus, or the mechanism by which we will begin to live sustainably. I can't envisage what forms the politics and economics will take to start us living within the planet's means. But then, can the naysayers tell me what forms they will take after the coal, oil and gas have run out and voluntary change is no longer an option?

One would be a fool to suggest that developing a better life will be easy. So my suggestions are tendered because I believe it is vital that, to future generations, we leave an earth they can live in. I am not arguing against our modern way of life, which I enjoy. I am arguing for a sustainable way of life that our descendants will enjoy.

I totally understand that redirecting the current economic systems, curtailing the way many of us live and establishing new goals in life will be a mighty tall order. The faint of heart, which probably includes most of us, might say it will be impossible. It certainly won't be easy, nor will it happen overnight. But if we don't begin the process who will? Do we hand the task onto our children? Do we pass it to our grandchildren? As things progress, the decision to turn will be harder, so I believe we should be brave and strong. This is no time to be timorous.

I am not pragmatic enough to suggest how all 7 or 9 billion of us will adapt to this new way of living. However, remembering the pony in the charging herd of bison, a change to our economic direction will be very perilous indeed unless coordinated. Any economy that tried to go it alone, and is seen as a threat by a majority of less progressive economies, would see all capitalist enterprise flee and its economy flattened in no time. There would be a great many people dead-set against it. Probably the most powerful, certain banks with vested interests and a desire to dominate the economy, for instance, will be the most reactionary and vitriolic. But still, if enough of a mass worldwide, under the leadership of the United Nations, could get behind the need for change, the reactionary voices could be quieted.

For those of you who are now convinced that I should be thrown onto the compost pile, I again refer to the UN's final statement from the 1992 Rio Summit: "... that nothing less than the transformation of our attitudes and behaviour would bring about the necessary changes ..."

Or, to repeat the words of Ban Ki-moon the Secretary General of the United Nations,

> For most of the last century, economic growth was fueled by what seemed to be a certain truth: the abundance of natural resources. We mined our way to growth. We burned our way to prosperity. We believed in consumption without consequences . . . . . It is a recipe for national disaster. It is a global suicide pact. We need a revolution. Revolutionary thinking. Revolutionary action. A free-market revolution for global sustainability.

So, to recap why it seems necessary to develop a new way of living on our planet:

In 2012, seven billion humans are, each year, using 50 per cent more of the Earth's renewable resources than the planet can provide; however, only one or two billion of us are the heavy users. Yet a just society suggests that we should bring the other five billion to an equal level of consumption.

On top of that, our population is projected to rise to nine or ten billion in the next 40 years. That population increase will accelerate all the other negative conditions.

If we achieve the American dream for all, we will be using 300 to 400 per cent more resources than the planet can provide.

We are also exploiting the non-renewable resources to a point where their end is in sight. We will leave no resources for our descendants to use. Yet we have to assume that their expanded population will need even more than we need.

Our industrial ways are causing unstoppable climate change, and our greed nearly plunged the globe's economic system into a bottomless abyss in the year 2008. The economic structure, upon which we base everything, is clearly an extremely fragile structure that could apparently collapse at the slightest nudge.

Every one of the Earth's natural systems is near collapse. We are destroying the ecosystems and biosphere on which all life depends, including fresh water aquifers. We are on track to reduce the wild animal numbers to less than 0.1 per cent of what they were in the year 1900, and to cause a 30 per cent species extinction rate over the next few years. Again, is this any way to run a planet?

It is worth remembering, at this point, that nature's abundant wild species are not just items that the planet can do without. The natural world is a huge and vastly complex machine where each animal and vegetable species, each bacteria and each microbe works with, and balances, other species. Every living thing is interconnected and necessary to the smooth and successful running of our biosphere. When we make 30 per cent of the species extinct, we dreadfully compromise the long-term viability of the whole. The whole is the earth on which we live. Think of it as a good quality Swiss watch. Can we really remove some of the cogs and mechanisms in the watch and expect it to keep accurate time? I don't think so.

On top of all that, many of the species we wipe from the surface of our earth could, in the future, have been found to be essential for humans, providing a gene pool for better crops or new medicines.

Upon reviewing my list of suggested changes, changes that might enable us to live within the carrying capacity of our planet, I realize I am implying changes that will create lives that are more than just free of consumerism. It seems to me that I am recommending, not just an end to the hunt for more wealth and more possessions, but also a quest for wisdom and lives lived more spiritually.* This was not intentional. I am not religious, though I do recognize the need for fulfillment beyond the material and superficial. I notice that underlying those 60 suggestions is a current taking us toward greater spiritual health instead of accumulated wealth. The Better Life seems to suggest a world of humans seeking profound values to replace the hollow consumerism and excess energy use from which I believe we must free ourselves.

One thing we humans are good at is denial. Many will choose not to acknowledge that we are living unsustainably, or that the present good times could end. For those who don't believe in inevitable things happening it is worth remembering the experiences of a few cultures both long ago and recently.

The Prairie Indians of North America lived for millennia in partnership with their grassland homes. Every year the vast herds of bison, pronghorn and elk took their seasonal migrations, the birds winged in from the south and the multitudinous flowers carpeted the grasslands with colour. It was paradise, even though the white winters were harsh. Traditions continued with little change and the raids between tribes were ongoing, but the cultures were strong. Then one day some strangers appeared and were welcomed by most of the tribes. Then more and more strangers arrived whose behaviour was foul and who were not welcome.

In a few short years the paradise was laid waste. The millions of buffalo were gone. The pronghorn and elk were gone, and those prairie tribes, the first people, were not allowed to live on their land. East of the prairies the sky-darkening Passenger Pigeons were gone, as were bright green Carolina Parakeets. Those people didn't know it, but before their calamity, millions of their southern relatives in such places as Mexico and Peru had suffered similar catastrophes. It happened to the Aztecs, it happened to the Inca, it happened to the First Nations of North America. If it could happen to the first people of the Americas, it can happen to anyone.

Another example of the unthinkable happening when we don't believe it can, began in Edwardian England. The Edwardian British lived in an age that might be described as the most wealthy, benign and self-satisfied of

---

* This is an interesting echo of a sculptural interest I had thirty years ago. Then I was producing gallery-sized architectural glass sculptures that I considered metaphors for the human quest for spiritual wisdom. Though I didn't explain my thinking very well at the time, I thought it a desirable quest, but one that was almost unachievable. I had taken my lead, in part, from reading about the Essene sect of pre, and early, Christian times.

any period to that time. The Victorian era ended with the Great Queen's death in 1901. Edward VII ascended the throne when England was the richest country in the world. She was mistress of the greatest empire the world had ever seen. Through the Industrial Revolution the British had invented and developed the underpinnings of the modern world. They were leaders in scientific discovery and industrial innovation. Great Britain was the greatest trading nation, and the Royal Navy kept the peace worldwide. England was the Mother of Parliament. Over centuries she had developed the underpinnings of 20th century democracy and was a leader in social reform. The nation was one of the founders of universal education, and it introduced the concept that all children in school should build physical health and strong characters through sport. The United Kingdom introduced the rest of the world to soccer, rugby, cricket, golf and tennis, which are major international sports today. In many ways, British democracy, despite the many social injustices of the time, was the foundation on which our modern world has been built.

The Edwardian gentlemen had every reason to feel superior and to strut and puff out their chests. The Edwardian ladies, of wealth and means, could look forward to a future of increasing gentility and never-ending tea parties. The future was rose-coloured. The Empire might last long into the future, and they were building Jerusalem in that green and pleasant land. One might observe that Great Britain in 1912 was similar to the USA before 2008.

But then, as a portent, the unsinkable Titanic sank, and two years later the Archduke Ferdinand was shot in some far off town called Sarajevo. The young British men went marching off to the shooting weekend in France and nearly a million of them stayed there–dead. The financial cost of the war crippled the country and four years after its end Britain owed so much money to America that, in 1922, it could no longer deny the US naval parity with the Royal Navy. The order of things was turned all asunder and Britain began its long decline. If it could happen in Britain, it can happen anywhere. If it could happen to the Edwardians it can happen to anyone. If it can happen to anyone, it can happen to everyone.

A more recent example is the Newfoundland fishery. For five hundred years the Northern Cod on the Grand Banks supplied the world's greatest fishery. Fishing towns and villages were built on that fishery. Foreign fishermen sailed from all over the North Atlantic to plunder the plentiful cod. The provincial economy was fish-based and fish-reliant. From the

1850s we were taking about 200,000 tons of fish per year, slowly rising to 300,000. By the late 1960s we were taking 800,000 tons a year till, by the mid 70s, the take crashed to 150,000 tons. But still we kept fishing. Then one day in 1992 the catch crashed again - but to very little this time.[3]

The Northern Cod was gone. The fishery was closed to give the fish a chance to breed and multiply. In Newfoundland, 35,000 fishermen and plant workers became unemployed. 400 coastal communities lost their work and income. Now, 20 years later, the fish have not greatly recovered. They have increased to about 10 per cent of what they were in recent years. Villages have not only emptied of people, but some have gone with barely a trace. Those fish, once so plentiful they impeded the passage of boats, are no more. If it can happen to the Atlantic Cod industry it can happen to any industry. If it can happen on the Grand Banks, it can happen anywhere. If it can happen anywhere, it can happen everywhere.

I believe we have to ask ourselves, whether we are collectively willing and able to create a revolutionary better life for everyone by reducing what we use. If the answer is 'no', and we fail to imagine new ways of living, then we have to ask what our descendants will do. If we say we cannot make changes because today's economy will fail, or because we won't be able to pay for public education, health care or the military, then we have to ask how our grandchildren will pay for those things. The emerging problems won't go away. They will only get worse. If we say we cannot diminish our resource use, and must leave our descendants an unsustainable, depleted earth of starving people, we have to question our own morality. If we can't make the right decisions, we have to ask what will be the options for future generations.

If I am unwilling to make a difficult and hard decision why should I expect my son and daughter to? If they are unwilling, why should they expect their daughters and sons to do it? The trouble is, someone has to make the move soon. The longer the delay, the worse the situation will become. Ours has become a world of consumerism, aggressive winner-takes-all competition, and advertising. We are told that this competition is the only way to manage a successful economy, an economy that relies upon ever-accelerating change driven by new technological developments. We are told to always want more, with little opportunity to resist. However, although I know little, one thing I know for sure: there are, out there, sustainable ways of living that are quite as satisfying, and full of wonder, as our current one.

Can we live with greater simplicity? Yes we can. Many already do. In the year 2012 the Prime Minister of Great Britain still lives in the modest four-bedroom row house known as Number 10, Downing Street, a house built in the 17th century. In 2012, the Lord Mayor of London, Boris Johnson, regularly cycled to his office at City Hall, as did Gregor Robertson, the Mayor of Vancouver.

Some entrepreneurs, of Buddhist, Hindu or Jain faith, while running family businesses, live their lives in a quest for purity, liberation and nirvana. The pursuit of Aston Martins and fat bank accounts hold little appeal for these people. To live at peace, neurosis-free, and striving for wisdom is satisfaction enough.

In Thailand, some men, after having lived lives of endeavour and enterprise, divest themselves of the trappings of success, renounce the world of possessions and move to the monastery. There they revoke ambition and acquisition. Instead, they embrace their inner solitude, and psychological health.

In the few remaining forest patches of Malaysian Sarawak, the last of the Penan live, as did their forebears for many thousands of years. Their culture remains unique, and they are perfectly adapted to tread softly among the trees. They wish to continue their light-touch subsistence ways, but the government, in its ignorance, won't let them. The government, of course, knows better and believes that people should live with greater ambition and more possessions.

The people of Bhutan, who rank high on the Happiness Index, believe that prosperity is incompatible with happy living unless the natural environment is well protected. They live in the mountains and valleys in their little kingdom between India and China taking very little; yet living contented lives of low consumption.

The 20,000 remaining Arajavos still live their traditional lives in the high sierra of Colombia. They wear the white clothes and hats that their forebears did at the time of the Spanish invasion. They believe in the law of Saman Oyac - the Great Mother, a law that protects all of nature. They call themselves the Older Brothers, and dream of the day when we, the Younger Brothers, will develop some wisdom and also learn to live at peace with the Earth and to protect nature.

On Ometepe Island in the great Nicaraguan Lake Cocibolca, the subsistence-farming young boys ride their ponies bareback into the cool waters to become refreshed. They live as their forebears of a hundred years ago lived. To this witness on the beach, they appear far richer than the computer-playing, movie-watching, couch potato children back home in North America.

Up in Jinotega, on the high mountains of Nicaragua, the air is cool and the scenery spectacular. So far, the poor farmers have been unable to afford expensive insecticides, so the lanes and hedgerows are alive with radiant birds and sunshine butterflies, and being there, in that tranquil calm and gentle beauty, is like tasting paradise. I ask the old Englishman why he lives there. He says, "Because it is as I remember England, seventy years ago."

But are most people and politicians interested in reasonable and sustainable expectations? It seems not. A few realize the need, but those on land holding riches and resources wish to continue with obsolete development at any cost. We are not talking of just Tanzania or the Democratic Republic of the Congo, but of the USA, Canada and Australia too. They set back the clock, and now reduce the environmental protections – reduce protections at a time when they should be ever more stringent.

There was a time, not so long ago, when one could read the newspapers for weeks on end with barely a mention of the environment or of looming catastrophes. Problems were there, of course, but were not part of our consciousness and so were not reported. Now, everyday, the media reveals a new or ongoing tragedy in some corner of our earth.

The individual tragedies are bad enough, but it is the aggregate, the combination of catastrophes that together scream of worldwide degradation and ecological collapse.

One wonders how loud the Earth must scream before we will listen, and finally take action.

On December 31st 2013, The Associated Press announced findings by the Chinese Government that large areas of Chinese farmland are too polluted with chemicals and heavy metals to grow food that is safe for human consumption. A deputy minister of the Ministry of Land and Resources, Wang Shiyuan gave the number of hectares contaminated as 3 million, or 2 per cent of China's arable land. Some independent scientists suggest the area is closer to 24.3 million hectares, or 16 per cent of the country's total farmland. The pollutants include cadmium, lead, pesticides and many other toxic chemicals and metals.[4]

For the sake of our earth, do we need to change expectations and our actions?

Yes! I do believe we do.

Meanwhile, at steamy old Tulum, on the Yucatan's Caribbean coast, are lovely creamy beaches and forests still filled with colourful birds and fluttering butterflies. All around the town and on the long road leading to the beach, billboards proclaim that on this particular piece of forest you can build your dream home or, on that, you can develop a new enterprise. And all around in the forest, from sunrise to sunset, the chain-saws buzz and growl, and a nightmare future is clear.

Post Script

To today's young, seventy years ago is ancient history. But to some of us, those times are sublime memories that are still fresh like the recollection of a newly found nest of delicate Mistle Thrush eggs. They were the best of times. Granted, I was only a child, but the late nineteen-forties and early fifties were years when, despite all the post-war difficulties of food rationing and national and personal financial straights, there was high employment and life was reasonably straightforward.

Though the globe was recovering from a terrible ordeal, great improvements seemed to be ahead. What were then new inventions and developments were truly inspiring and seemed even more exciting and forward-looking than the latest technologies of today. We certainly recognized fewer environmental problems in their development, and the future promised more ease, not more complications. We could travel anywhere by train or bus with few traffic jams. Now our Earth is suffering horrible injury with few signs of a bright future. A better life seemed to be achievable then. But in those days we mistakenly thought our Earth was relatively whole, and we believed that we only had to make life better for 2 billion people instead of the great numbers we must help forward now.

In 2011, I visited Purley and the sites of my happy childhood of all those years ago. I would have searched for the Glade where we once searched for Peacock and Red Admiral butterflies had the Woods still been there. But they had long gone. I walked past the place of our remnant downland, of the Sheep's Fescue, Quaking Grass and Horseshoe Vetch, of Hawthorn bushes and bird nests, but I found nothing but houses and large gardens. I visited the wasteland where we could always catch Chalk hill Blues but again saw little other than houses. Very nice houses to be sure, but houses nonetheless. Nothing remained of those places of enchantment and engraved memories, of adventure and of learning. And nothing remained of the Smitham Downs or of their grassland. It is clear that none of the bird species that flew in a hundred years ago will ever visit those lands again.

Surprisingly, the Copse is still standing, though now as a wood of mature trees of considerable size. They are mostly beech, which are the trees of the chalk downs. Those trees now dominate the houses on either side. On the high fence a sign appears, "Copse Hill. Spinney Bird Sanctuary. Keep out." It is good that it is a sanctuary for garden birds, but I wonder where the grassland birds of old now go. I also wonder where today's seven-year old boys play and dream, and whether they are excited to be out in nature as we used to be?

Bibliography

For the information pertaining to the species that were rendered extinct by 1980, my main source was David Day's wonderful book *The Doomsday Book Of Animals* published in 1993. I quote freely from that book when using the words of George Wilhelm Steller, RCL. Perkins and Chief Pokagon of the Pottawottomi Indians.

References:

Allen, Charles editor. *Tales from the South China Seas: . . .* London. BBC, 1983.

Book of the British Countryside. London. Drive publications Limited, 1973.

Chapman, F. Spencer. *The Jungle is Neutral.* Singapore. Times Books Int.

Day, David. *The doomsday Book of Animals.* Weldon Owen Pty, Sydney, Aus, 1993.

Elphick, Jonathan. *Birds, The Art of Ornithology.* Scriptum editions, UK. 2008

Hasting, Max. *Finest Years.* Churchill as Warlord 1940-45, London. Harper Collins, 2009.

Herman, Arthur. *To Rule the Waves.* New York. Harper Collins. 2004.

Herriot, Trevor. *Grass, Sky, Song.* Toronto. Phyllis Bruce. Harper Collins. 2009.

Lambert, Andrew. *Admirals.* London. Faber and Faber. 2008.

Lim, Kean Siew. *The Eye Over Golden Sands.* Selangor. Pelanduk Publications. 1997.

Maxwell, George. *In Malay Forests.* London. William Blackwood and Sons. 1911.

Reade, Julian. *Assyrian Sculpture.* London. British Museum Press. 1983.

Russell, Sharman Apt. *An Obsession with Butterflies*. Cambridge, MA.
    Perseus.2003.
Stutchbury, Bridget. *Silence of the Songbirds*. Toronto. Harper Perennial.
    2008.
Townsend, Peter. *Duel of Eagles*. London. Cassell Publishers. 1970.

When the information came from newspapers and other media, the
articles are entered under Sources and References. However, I have to
mention that, as I didn't begin by noting my sources, I occasionally found
it extremely difficult to re-discover some of those original references.

Sources and References

Introduction

1. Cogswell, Alan and Mickey: *A Search For A Heritage*, Self published. 1982.
2. www.economist.com/global-livestock-counts.

Chapter 1: Invasive species and Historic extinctions

1. wikipedia.org/Burmese_pythons_in_Florida.
2. Fears, Darryl. *In Florida Everglades, pythons and anacondas dominate food chain*, The Washington Post, Jan 30, 2012.
3. wikipedia.org/Brown-tree-snake/Guam.
4. wikipedia.org/Asian_long-horned_beetle.
5. Boswell, Randy, Invasive beetle poses threat to Canada's maple trees, Postmedia News
6. Cameron, Elizabeth, *Cane-toad*. australianmuseum.net.au Nov. 22, 2012.
7. Dell'Amore, Christine, *Wild pig explosion may spread disease to humans*, National Geographic, Daily News. May 2, 2011.
8. wikipedia.org/Wild_boar.
9. Day, David. *The doomsday Book of Animals*. Weldon Owen Pty, Sydney, Aus, 1993.
10. Ibid.
11. Ibid.
12. Ibid.
13. Ibid.
14. Ibid
15. Ibid

Chapter 2: Reminiscences
A: Purley and First Memories

1. www.oldcoulsdon.co.uk/history
2. www.domesdaybook.co.uk
3. www.localhistories.org/population.
4. en.wikipedia.org/ Demography_of_England.
5. en.wikipedia.org/Industrial_Revolution.
6. www. Rail.co.uk/british_railway_history.
7. en.wikipedia.org/Rail *Transport_in_Great_Britain*.
8. en.wikipedia.org/History_of_rail_transport.
9. en.wikipedia.org/Indian_Railways.
10. Kendall, Joshua. *The Man Who Made Lists: love, death, madness and the creation of "Roget's Thesaurus"*. New York: G. P. Putnam's Sons. 2008.
11. en.wikipedia.org/tire/John_Boyd_Dunlop.
12. en.wikipedia.org/tire/Robert_William_Thomson.
13. en.wikipedia.org/London_Underground.
14. en.wikipedia.org/History_of_London.
15. britainnature/extinct_mammals_in_Britain.
16. Encyclopedia Barsa. *Changing demographics of the city of Sao Paulo*.

Chapter 2: Reminiscences
B: Mogdandle, The Farm & War

1. en.wikipedia.org/Harold_Macmillan.
2. Fromkin, David. *A Peace to End All Peace*. New York. Henry Holt & Co. 1989. P.233
3. en.wikipedia.org/maxim_gun.
4. Townsend, Peter. Duel of Eagles. London. Cassell Publishers. 1970.
5. Herman, Arthur. *To Rule the Waves*. New York. HarperCollins, 2004.
6. www.navweaps.com/ WNBG_18-40_mk1.
7. Lambert, Andrew. *Admirals: The Naval commanders who made Britain Great*. London. Faber and Faber. 2008.
8. en.wikipedia.org/V-1_flying_bomb.
9. www.nationalarchives.gov.uk.
10. www.wood-database.com/cubanMahogany
11. w.bluwwemoonexoticwood.com/cuban-mahogany

Chapter 2: Reminiscences
C: The Farm

1. Book of the British Countryside. London. Drive publications Limited, 1973.
2. WWF Global. http//wwf.panda.org.
3. en.wikipedia.org/Borneo.

Chapter 3: Farming and the Natural World

1. Stutchbury, Bridget. *Silence of the Songbirds*. Toronto. Harper Perennial. 2008.
2. Gilbert, Bill. *The Old West:The Trailblazers*. Alexandria Vg. Time-Life Books 1973.
3. en.wikipedia.org/American_Bison.
4. en.wikipedia.org/Prairie.
5. Day, David. *The doomsday Book of Animals*. Weldon Owen Pty, Sydney, Aus, 1993.
6. Herriot, Trevor. *Grass, Sky, Song*. Toronto. Phyllis bruce. Harper Collins. 2009.
7. Day, David. *The doomsday Book of Animals*. Weldon Owen Pty, Sydney, Aus, 1993.
8. Ibid.
9. ukwildlife.wordpress.com/a-history-of-animal-domestication.
10. Ibid.
11. en.wikipedia.org/Intensive_animal_farming.
12. Lymbery, Philip. Farm-agedden: No birds. No Bees.Daily Mail. 25 January 2014

Chapter 4: The Avon and Other Rivers

1. en.wikipedia.org/Pesticide#History.
2. en.Wikipedia.org/Great_Stink.
3. www.choleraandthethames.co.uk.
4. Ibid.
5. Ibid.
6. en.Wikipedia.org/Ganges.
7. Ibid.
8. Ibid.
9. Ibid.
10. Nelson, Dean. *Historic waterway a holy Mess*. Daily telegraph, Oct. 5, 2011.
11. www.india.com/Yumana+pollution.

12. Telegraph.co.uk *Taj Mahal falling victim to chronic Pollution.* Dec 3, 2010.
13. Telegraph.co.uk *Half of India's cities have no piped water or sewer systems* Oct 31, 2011.
14. en.Wikipedia.org/Cuyahoga_River.
15. Ibid.
16. www.pbs.org/return-of-cuyahoga.
17. healthygulf.org/massive-fish-kill-in-pearl-river.
18. Alan Sayre. *Paper maker says its Black liquor spill* . . . August 19, 2011 Global Justice Ecology Project.
19. en.Wikipedia.org/Mississippi_River
20. Gosman, Sara. *The Good,the bad and the ugly: implemation of the Great Lakes Compact.* Nat. Wildlife Fed. Ann Arbor 2011.
21. en.Wikipedia.org/Potomac.
22. HealthyHouseInstitute.com March 11,2012.
23. US environmental Protection Agency *TSCA Chemical Substance Inventory* Feb 25, 2013.
24. Ibid.
25. Ibid.
26. Ibid.
27. PetzScholtus, Tree hugger, Oct 15, 2009.
28. Jonathan Manthorpe, *Canada World*, Van Sun. Sept 26, 2012. Page 108
29. *Position paper on Dams and the Environment,* The international Commission on Large Dams.
30. en.Wikipedia.org/Mekong.
31. Ibid.
32. PetzScholtus, Tree hugger, Oct 15, 2009.

Chapter 5: Malaysia and Borneo

1. Maxwell, George. *In Malay Forests*, William Blackwood and sons,1911.
2. www.rhinos.org?professional-resources/iucn-asian-rhino.
3. International Rhino foundation. Maps.
4. en.Wikipedia.org/tropical_rainforest.
5. Chapman, F. Spencer. *The Jungle is Neutral.* Singapore. Times Books Int.
6. Wikipedia/history of Malaya/Pangkor treaty Page 127.
7. Lim, Kean Siew. *The eye over golden sands.* Selangor. Pelanduk Publications. 1997.
8. Allen, Charles editor. *Tales from the South China Seas:* . . . London. BBC, 1983.
9. www.panthera.org/tiger/subspecies.
10. Demographics of Malaysia Wikipedia.
11. worldpopulationreview.com/Malaysia-population.

12. No citation provided due to conflicting reports.
13. Sophie Yeo. Responding to Climate Change (RTCC.Org) 18 july 2013
14. Jane E. Bryan et al. Extreme Differences in Forest Degredation in Borneo: . . . www.plosone.org
15. Geology.com/usgs/Hawaiian–hot–spot
16. pubs.usgs.gov/gip/dynamic/himalaya
17. Wikipedia.org/Lake_Toba
18. USGS. Ice sheets and Glaciations
19. North American wildlife. Edit. Susan J. Wernert. Readers Digest Ass., Inc 1982
20. wwf. Panda. Org/ Borneo wildlife.
21. Kurokawa, Hiroko et al., *The age of tropical-forest canopy species, Borneo ironwood (..) determined by c dating.* Journal of Tropical Ecology. Vol 19. Jan 2003..
22. en.wikipedia.org/Penan_people.
23. www.culturalsurvival.org/penan.
24. Allen, Charles. Editor. *Tales from the South China Seas:* . . . London. BBC, 1983.
25. Ibid.
26. Ibid.
27. Ibid.
28. www.forestpeoples.org/Human rights
29. National Evangelical Christian Fellowship Malaysia. www.necf.org.my
30. www.rimba.com/spcpenan
31. www.culturalsurvival.org/societies-danger-death-
32. News.Mongabay.com/2005/Malaysia.
33. www.wikipedia.org/Deforestation
34. Nicholas, Colin. *The Orang Asli of Peninsular Malaysia.* Centre of Orang Asli Concerns. Subang Jaya, Malaysia 1997.
35. Ibid

Chapter 6: Art and Extinctions

1. en.wikipedia/ Johann_Baptist_von_Spix.
2. en.wikipedia/Spix_Macaw.
3. BirdLife International/ Spix Macaw.
4. en.wikipedia/Macaw.
5. en.wikipedia/Bali_Mynah.
6. Collier, N. J. (editor in Chief), *Threatened Birds of Asia*: BirdLife International Red Data Book, 2001.
7. Bali Starling. *Conservation Project on Nusa Penida*, Begawan Foundation.

8. Wildlife Extra. *Humans were the cause of more than 1000 bird extinctions.* March 2013. WWF. UK.
9. Day, David. *The doomsday Book of Animals.* Weldon Owen Pty, Sydney, Aus, 1993.
10. www.wildlifeextra.com/Taiwan-leopard2013.
11. www.pbs.org/wnet/nature...lonesome_george.
12. www.wikipedia.Gir_Forest_National_Park.2010.
13. www.wildlife extra/India-lions-Kuno/2013.

Chapter 7: Of Wheatears and Other Birds.

1. Bairlein. F., Norris, D., *Cross-hemisphere Migration of a 25g Songbird*, Biology letters. 2012
2. rsbl.royalsocietypublishing.org/2012/...
3. Jonathan Manthorpe, *New Zealanders urged to save a bird, kill a cat*, Van Sun, 28 Jan, 2013
4. Wildlife extra.com. April 2013
5. Wildlife Extra.com. Dec 2010.
6. www.ploseone.org/ An Estimate of Avian Mortality at Communication Towers ...
7. www.wildlife extra.com/European-widlife-2011
8. migration.wordpress.com/ambelopoulia
9. www.wildlifeextra.com/songbirds-trade-Albania/2012
10. www.wildlifeextra.com/Malta-peregrine/July18/2012

Chapter 8: Oceans

1. en.wikipedia.org/Cod_fisheries.
2. Ibid.
3. en.wikipedia/ Collapse of the Atlantic northwest cod fishery.
4. Ibid.
5. en.wikipedia.org/Tuna.
6. Ibid.
7. Ibid.
8. en.wikipedia.org/Fishing_industry_in_China.
9. en.wikipedia.org/Pacific_herring.
10. www.fishaq.gov.nl.ca?research_development/fdp/herring
11. en.wikipedia.org/Atlantic_herring.
12. en.wikipedia.org/Trawling.
13. www.marine conservation.org
14. en.wikipedia.org/Bottom_trawling.

15. Ibid.
16. en.wikipedia.org/Seine_fishing.
17. en.wikipedia.org/Gill_netting.
18. en.wikipedia.org/Drift_netting.
19. en.wikipedia.org/Longline_fishing.
20. www.livescience.com/27575-100-million-sharks-killed-annually
21. en.wikipedia.org/Longline_fishing..
22. Yale Environment e360 digest. 25 Jan 2012
23. www.eoearth.org/view/article/153602/
24. en.wikipedia.org/Humboldt_current
25. www.wildlifeextra.com/go/news/mauis-2012
26. wwwfishingmuseum.org.uk/cod_war.
27. en.wikipedia.org/Cod_Wars
28. Agence France-Presse,Vancouver Sun, Jan 26, 2012.
29. The Guardian. 12 February 2013.
30. Guynup, Sharon. State of the Wild. 2006. Wildlife conservation Society. Island Press 2005
31. Stewart, Ian, Professor. How the Earth Changed History, BBC Productions
32. Ambergris Caye.com Forum. Garbage on Beach Causing Problems
33. oceanlink.info/ocean_matters/noise.html
34. www.oceanmammalinst.com/underwater noise.html
35. en.wikipedia.org/wiki/Speed_of_sound.
36. www.cnn.com/nature/9906/30/sea.noise.
37. see-the-sea.org/Topics/Pollution/Noise.
38. McAvoy, Audry. Associated Press, Vancouver Sun, May 12, 2012).
39. phys.org/news/2012-02-oil-drilling-arctic-nears-reality.html
40. Perry, Nick. The Associated Press, Vancouver Sun, Sept 15, 12.
41. Pynn, Larry. Vancouver Sun, 20.2.12
42. Ibid
43. Scanlan, Craig. *Update: Philippine and Chinese Vessels continue standoff Over Scarborough Shoal EEZ Rights.* Asia Security Watch. Apr 13, 2012

Chapter 9: Population

1. www.popultionmatters.org/Humanpopulationhistory.
2. en.wikipedia.org/Demographic_history_of_the_United_States.
3. Hasting, Max. *Finest Years.* Churchill as Warlord 1940-45, London. Harper Collins, 2009. pages31,86,138,171-173.
4. www.geography.learnontheinternet.co.uk)geotopict)urbanization.
5. Cogswell, Alan and Mickey: *A Search For A Heritage,* Self published. 1982.
6. Office of National Statistics. *UK. Births and Deaths in England and Wales.*

7. Ibid.
8. (Hirschman, Charles. *Population and Society in twentieth-Century Southeast Asia.* journal of Southeast Asian Studies 25, 2 (September 1994).
9. Dept of Statistics Malaysia. Population.
10. epp.eurostat.ec.europa.eu/fertility statistics.
11. data.worldbank. org/indicator. Fertility rate total (births per woman).
12. The United Nations, Department of Economic and Social Affairs, *2012 Revision of the World Population Prospects.*
13. Ibid.

Chapter 10: Unsustainable Energy Use 101

1. www.bloomberg.com/2012/citigroup-study-shows-asian-rich-toppig . . .
2. Citigroup. Knight Frank Research. The Wealth Report 2012
3. www. theguardian.com/2013/china-us-how-superpowers-compare
4. Stevens, Robert. *UK's top CEOs see 55 percent earnings rise.* 10 Nov 2010. wsws.org).
5. Government of B.C.. Ministry of Energy and Mines. Coal.
6. Ibid.
7. www.oilsands.alberta.ca.
8. en.wikipedia. alberta.oilsands.
9. In 2012 and 2013 such an enormous amount of information was written on the subjects of tar sands oil and pipelines that I have deemed it unnecessary to list my sources, which were multitudinous. They are easily available to us all.
10. insideclimatenews.org/oil-sands-mining-alberta.
11. Mike De Souza. *Ottawa to monitor oil sands' impact on environment.* PostmediaNews, Van Sun, 6 Nov. 2012.
12. mindfully.org/consumption-US.
13. Ibid.
14. Ibid.
15. footprintnetwork.org/Ecological_Wealth_of_Nations.
16. Ibid.

Chapter 11: The Land and Wild Places

1. Agriinfo.in/microbes.
2. soilhealth.com.
3. World Health Organization. Wwwwho.int/water_sanitation_health/methaemoglob/
4. www.pbs.org/kenburns/dustbowl.

5. United Nations Food and Agricultural Organization. *State of the World's Land and Water Resources for Agriculture.* 2011.

6. Prof Iain Stewart, *How the Earth Changed History*, BBC Productions

7. www.cancer.ca

8. Ontario Ministry of Agri. & Food. Gov.on.ca.

9. www.theguardian.com)environment)Amazon rainforest

10. en.wikipedia/dilma_rousseff

Chapter 12: Feline Predators and Others

1. nationalgeographic.com/African lions.

2. Reade, Julian. *Assyrian Sculpture.* British Museum Press, 1983.

3. Day, David. *The doomsday Book of Animals.* Weldon Owen Pty, Sydney, Aus, 1993.

4. www.panthera.org/ node/972

5. www.wikipedia.org/Tiger.

6. International Union for Conservation of Nature.

7. Cheetah Conservation fund. Fact sheet. www.cheetah. Org.

8. nationalgeographic.com/mammals/jaguar.

9. en.wikipedia.org/jaguar.

10. nationalgeographic.com/mammals/puma.

11. en.wikipedia.org/puma.

Chapter 13: North America & Africa.

1. www.theguardian.com/2012/jul/02/arms-trade-treaty-un-tlks-weapons

2. Bill C-38. www. Pariament of Canada. GC.Ca

3. www.defenders.org/.../federal-employees-shoot/wolves-.

4. www.defenders.org/wolf/wolves

5. Allen, Carole. *Conservationists Demand that Louisiana Governor Reverse Obsolete Turtle- Deadly Shrimp Law.* SeaTurtles.org, February 6th, 2012

6. www2.canada.com/vancouversun/news/archives

7. Goldenberg, Suzanne. US enviro. Corresp. Guardian. UK. 1.3.11

8. National geographic webpage

9. Endangered Species International

10. Ibid

11. Ibid

12. Ibid

13. Ibid

14. www.worldwildlife.org/

15. Endangered Species International

16. www.wildlifeextra.com/serengeti-natron.
17. news.mongabay.com/hance_tanzania_gov.
18. www.change.org/halt buiding_of_seren . . .
19. Michler, Ian. *Maasai locked out of Loliodo.* African Geographic Mag. April 3, 2013
20. www.avaaz.org/save_the_maasai
21. Patinkin, Jason. *Maasai fury as plan to lure Arabian Gulf tourists threatens their ancestral land.* The Observer. 30 March 2013
22. Endres, John. *Whose land is it, anyway?* Africa in Fact. Good governance Africa. Nov 2012
23. Field, Anthony. Virunga: *Oil crisis deepens in Africa's oldest National park.* WWF Virunga Campaign

Chapter 14: More on Invasive Species.

1. Book of the British countryside, Drive publications, Automobile Association.
2. http: www.sqirrels.info/uk/Sqirrels in the UK.
3. Invasive Species Council of British Columbia.
4. www.talking-naturally.co.uk/ring-necked-Parakeets-uk
5. www.rspb.org.uk/wildlife/ birdguide
6. www.devonperspectives.co.uk/Lundy.
7. en.wikipedia.org/Lundy.
8. Munroe, Margaret., *Deaths of millions of bats in North America.* Vancouver Sun, 10 April 2012.

Chapter 15: A Little Good News, But Is There Hope?

1. en.wikipedia.org/River_Parrett
2. ec.Europe.eu)Environment)Nature & Biodiversity
3. www.naturalengland.org.uk
4. www.naturalengland.org.uk)Osprey
5. www.naturalengland.org.uk/whitetailedeagle
6. www.rspb.org.uk) Red Kite
7. greatbustard.org/life_project/life
8. en.wikipedia.org/ Hen_Harrier
9. www.naturalengland.org.uk
10. www.naturalengland.org.uk
11. www.naturalengland.org.uk
12. www.euronatur.org
13. Environmental history resources, *Nature conservation in Britain, ca. 1870-1945*
14. Elphick, Jonathan. *Birds, The Art of Ornithology.* Scriptum editions, UK. 2008

15. www.sierraclub.org/john_muir
16. www.fws.gov?pelicanisland/history
17. Souder, William *No Egrets,* Smithsonian, March 2013.
18. www.romanysociety.org.uk
19. en.wikipedia.org/I-Spy
20. www.observersbooksociety.co.uk/
21. en.wikipedia.org/Peter_Scott
22. en.wikipedia.org/World_Wild_Fund_for_Nature

Chapter 16: More Good News.

1. www.fws.gov/Midwest/Eagle/recovery.
2. en.wikipedia.org/Bald_and_Golden_Eagle_Protection_Act.
3. www.canadiangeographic.ca/blog
4. www.livescience
5. wildwhales.org/blue-fin-and-sei-whale
6. www.cascadiaresearch.org/finwhale.
7. www.livescience.com/37686-rare-whale-spotted
8. wildwhales.org/blue-fin and-sei-whale
9. Pynn, Larry, *State of the Salish Sea*, Van Sun, April 14, 2012
10. Wangari Maathai, Nobelprize.org
11. www.greenbeltmovement.org/
12. Government of Kenya, *National Climate Change Response Strategy.*
13. www.worldwildlife.org/ecoregions
14. www.wikipedia.or/Old_Growth
15. www.for.gov.bc.ca/Forest_History_
16. www.Ancientforestalliance.org/news-item =246=247
17. econet.ca/sk_enviro_champions/grassland.
18. Virtual Saskatchewan April 3,2012.
19. Galindo-Leal & Gusmao. *Camara* 2003).
20. Wildlife Extra News, March 9 2012
21. Wildlife Extra News, April 13, 2012
22. Wildlife Extra News, March 9 2012.
23. www.icmbio.gov.br/docs-plano-de-acao/
24. awwp.alwabra/restoring/Spix.
25. www.birdlife.org/datazone/speciesfactsheet
26. en.wikipedia.org/Euphorbiaceae
27. www.birdlife.org/datazone/speciesfactsheet/

Chapter 17: A Finite Earth.

1. Day, David. *The doomsday Book of Animals*. Weldon Owen Pty, Sydney, Aus, 1993.
2. Ibid
3. Kirschbaum, Erik. Reuters, Van Sun, May 29, 2012
4. Munroe, Margaret. Van. Sun 6.16.12
5. www.un.org/sg/statements/index.asp?nid=5056

Chapter 18: A Better Life.

1. www.bcarchives.gov.bc.ca/. . ./potlatch
2. Anderson, Fiona. *Asian and emerging markets: Our Economic Salvation?* Van Sun Aug 25, 2012.
3. www.canadahistory.com/Cod_Collapse
4. *Associated Press, Vancouver Sun. 31 December 2013*

About the Author

A lifelong environmentalist, the author is a professional sculptor and painter. He taught art at the university level in both England and Canada.

He has exhibited internationally, had two one-person exhibitions at the prestigious Vancouver Art Gallery, and been awarded a number of sculpture commissions in Canada

He lives in Vancouver, B.C.

CPSIA information can be obtained at www.ICGtesting.com
Printed in the USA
LVOW05s0118170614

390283LV00006B/26/P